The Fixers

HISTORICAL STUDIES OF URBAN AMERICA

*Edited by Lilia Fernández, Timothy J. Gilfoyle, Becky M. Nicolaides, and
Amanda I. Seligman. James R. Grossman, editor emeritus.*

Also in the series:

Crossing Parish Boundaries: Race, Sports, and Catholic Youth in Chicago, 1914–1954
by Timothy B. Neary

Evangelical Gotham: Religion and the Making of New York City, 1783–1860
by Kyle B. Roberts

Chicago's Book Clubs: How Neighbors Shape the City
by Amanda I. Seligman

The Lofts of SoHo: Gentrification, Art, and Industry in New York, 1950–1980
by Aaron Shkuda

The Newark Frontier: Community Action in the Great Society
by Mark Krasovic

Making the Unequal Metropolis: School Desegregation and Its Limits
by Ansley T. Erickson

Confederate Cities: The Urban South during the Civil War Era
Edited by Andrew L. Slap and Frank Towers

The Cycling City: Bicycles and Urban America in the 1890s
by Evan Friss

Making the Mission: Planning and Ethnicity in San Francisco
by Ocean Howell

*A Nation of Neighborhoods: Imagining Cities, Communities, and Democracy in
Postwar America*
by Benjamin Looker

A World of Homeowners: American Power and the Politics of Housing Aid
by Nancy H. Kwak

Demolition Means Progress: Flint, Michigan, and the Fate of the American Metropolis
by Andrew R. Highsmith

Metropolitan Jews: Politics, Race, and Religion in Postwar Detroit
by Lila Corwin Berman

Blood Runs Green: The Murder that Transfixed Gilded Age Chicago
by Gillian O'Brien

*A City for Children: Women, Architecture, and the Charitable Landscapes of Oakland,
1850–1950*
by Marta Gutman

A World More Concrete: Real Estate and the Remaking of Jim Crow South Florida
by N. D. B. Connolly

Additional series titles follow index

The Fixers

Devolution, Development, and Civil Society in Newark, 1960–1990

JULIA RABIG

The University of Chicago Press   Chicago and London

JULIA RABIG is a lecturer of history at Dartmouth College.

The University of Chicago Press, Chicago 60637
The University of Chicago Press, Ltd., London
© 2016 by Julia Rabig
All rights reserved. Published 2016.
Printed in the United States of America

25 24 23 22 21 20 19 18 17 16   1 2 3 4 5

ISBN-13: 978-0-226-38831-1 (cloth)
ISBN-13: 978-0-226-38845-8 (e-book)
DOI: 10.7208/chicago/9780226388458.001.0001

Portions reprinted from Julia Rabig, "'The Laboratory of Democ-
racy': Construction Industry Racism in Newark and the Limits of
Liberalism," pp. 48–67, from *Black Power at Work: Community Control,
Affirmative Action, and the Construction Industry*, edited by David
Goldberg and Trevor Griffey. Used by permission of the publisher,
Cornell University Press.

Library of Congress Cataloging-in-Publication Data

Names: Rabig, Julia, author.
Title: The fixers : devolution, development, and civil society in
    Newark, 1960–1990 / Julia Rabig.
Other titles: Historical studies of urban America.
Description: Chicago ; London : The University of Chicago Press,
    2016. | Series: Historical studies of urban America
Identifiers: LCCN 2015050879 | ISBN 9780226388311 (cloth : alk.
    paper) | ISBN 9780226388458 (e-book)
Subjects: LCSH: African Americans—New Jersey—Newark. |
    Newark (N.J.)—Social conditions—20th century
Classification: LCC F144.N657 R33 2016 | DDC 306.09749/320904—
    dc23 LC record available at http://lccn.loc.gov/2015050879

Contents

Abbreviations

ACTION Inc.	American Committee to Improve Our Neighborhoods Inc.
AFL-CIO	American Federation of Labor and Congress of Industrial Organizations
BAT	Bureau of Apprenticeship and Training
BICC	Business and Industrial Coordinating Council
BSRC	Bedford-Stuyvesant Restoration Corporation
CAP	Congress of African People
CDC	community development corporation
CFUN	Committee for a Unified Newark
CNC	Citizens Negotiating Committee
CORE	Congress of Racial Equality
CRSS	Community Relations and Social Services
DCA	Department of Community Affairs
EBTC	Essex County Building Trades Council
ERAP	Economic Research Action Project
FHA	Federal Housing Administration
GNUC	Greater Newark Urban Coalition
HARYOU	Harlem Youth Opportunities Unlimited
HARYOU-ACT	Harlem Youth Opportunities Unlimited–Associated Community Teams
HEW	Department of Health, Education, and Welfare
HUD	Department of Housing and Urban Development
ICBO	Interracial Council for Business Opportunity
NAACP	National Association for the Advancement of Colored People
NCC	New Community Corporation
NCG	Newark Collaboration Group
NHA	Newark Housing Authority
NUC	National Urban Coalition
OEO	Office of Economic Opportunity

PDTA	Poor and Dissatisfied Tenants Association
SCLC	Southern Christian Leadership Conference
SDS	Students for a Democratic Society
TELACU	The East Los Angeles Community Union
Tri-City	Tri-City Citizens Union for Progress
UCC	United Community Corporation
UE	United Electrical, Radio, and Machine Workers of America

Introduction

Later, Gustav Heningburg would claim that he "didn't have a plan" when he strode onto the tarmac of the Newark, New Jersey, airport in 1970 to shut the place down.[1] Maybe he would stand in front of a plane. Airport managers would panic; flights would be delayed. Passengers in Terminal B would stare through the glass at him. They'd ask who he was and what this was all about. And somehow—Heningburg hadn't thought this part through either—they would find out: it was about jobs. And jobs were about freedom, about the struggle for civil rights, about the so-called long, hot summers, and about the age of black political power he believed would soon be coming.

Heningburg was just shy of forty, tall and slim with light-brown skin, a dimpled chin, and thick brows that could convey disarming skepticism. Well-trimmed sideburns were his nod to style. He could see idling aircraft, including, he later learned, a private plane belonging to Prudential Insurance, Newark's premier white-collar employer. Prudential was also a major donor to the Greater Newark Urban Coalition, which paid Heningburg to pursue change through compromise—to be a mediator, a benign fixer. He was accustomed more to conference rooms than direct action. But none of his corporate connections had helped him secure a meeting with the officials of the Port Authority of New York and New Jersey who managed the region's airports. He had tried for months with no success to secure construction jobs for the city's black and

Puerto Rican tradesmen on the airport's monumental expansion from regional to international hub.[2]

Evidence of construction under way intensified his sense of urgency. Three years had passed since one of the deadliest urban uprisings of the 1960s had rocked Newark. The national press had seized on New Jersey's largest municipality as the epitome of urban apocalypse. By 1975 *Harper's* magazine would declare it "The Worst City of All."[3] But Heningburg believed Newark could be a model for a more just city—if he could only find the jobs. The airport's expansion was a prize, but like so many publicly funded construction projects in this now majority black city, it threatened to proceed without unemployed black and Puerto Rican workers. Despite passage of antidiscrimination laws, most minority workers remained shut out of the region's white construction unions.[4] Something had to be done.

He opened a door and bolted.

Heningburg's quixotic sprint across the tarmac appeared to be the deed of an activist too marginalized to work through conventional channels. Yet Heningburg was a savvy player in Newark politics. He was the Greater Newark Urban Coalition's executive director and had served as a high-level fundraiser for national organizations such as the National Association for the Advancement of Colored People (NAACP) Legal Fund. He had collaborated with labor unions, churches, tenants, and opponents of urban renewal. He was a proud US Army veteran drawn to Newark's growing black power movement, and he helped elect Newark's first black mayor, Kenneth Gibson, in 1970. Heningburg was not a man anybody expected to make a run for it with airport security in hot pursuit—which is why his run mattered.

"I got nowhere near the planes," he later said. "Almost immediately security tackled me." But nowhere near was close enough.[5]

Once security dragged Heningburg off the tarmac, his networks sprang into action. Soon, Donald MacNaughton, president of Prudential, secured Heningburg's release. Most important, Heningburg got what he wanted: the Port Authority's formidable director, Austin Tobin, agreed to meet with Heningburg's Black and Puerto Rican Construction Coalition.[6] Heningburg had set in motion negotiations that, over two years, secured both construction jobs for minority workers and contracts for minority concessionaires at the airport. Heningburg said that he "didn't have a plan," but he was a consummate strategist.

People like Heningburg and the organizations they created indelibly shaped the trajectory of the black freedom movement in cities such as Newark. Heningburg thrived in the midst of unstable coalitions: blurring the lines between protest and politics, between radical and moderate, between the public realm of legislation and elections and the quasi-private realm of civic associations, unions, businesses, churches, and nonprofits. Heningburg was not alone. Community organizations with similar roles proliferated throughout cities in the 1970s. What, precisely, distinguished such individuals and organizations from likeminded social movement activists? They organized and protested but also built new institutions; they pressed for reforms but also understood the limits of reform and set out to circumvent it. They brokered agreements among activists, government agencies, and the private sector. But they did more than mediate—many sought to do nothing less than "fix" their cities in a literal sense: to create equitable cities. They responded to urgent needs, but they also pursued longer-term visions, remaking institutions or devising alternatives. They pursued these goals even as the force of civil rights victories, antipoverty legislation, and black power waned. In so doing, they functioned as fixers in another sense, one analogous to a chemical fixer used in film development: they ended up fixing enduring patterns of activism and reform.

"Fixers" is a loaded term, and its application to these individuals and organizations requires careful explanation. The term may invoke images of political operatives working behind the scenes or individuals using extralegal means to win influence. It recalls the late nineteenth- and early twentieth-century ward heelers bargaining with party bosses to win favors for immigrant neighborhoods. Jersey City's Frank Hague, arguably one of the state's more influential political bosses, rose to power as a fixer of this sort, jostling between the demands of reformers and the lure and power of existing political machines.[7]

The term "fixer," then, resonates in urban political history. The fixers that emerge in this book also sought to move between worlds. But I adapt the term to a different historical moment in the conjoined trajectories of the black freedom struggle and late twentieth-century urban history. In this moment, "fixers" embody the reformist vision, political savvy, and deliberate "in-betweenness" of people like Heningburg.

Understanding how some individuals and organizations in the complex and vibrant landscape of 1960s activism came to act as fixers illuminates two intertwined developments that shaped twentieth-century US history: the uneven political incorporation of black Americans and the evolution of the urban crisis. By incorporation, I mean black Americans' attempts to transform an economic and political system from which they had been excluded. They did so in the face of the persistent discrimination, private-sector disinvestment, disproportionate poverty, and increasing disparity between suburb and city that constituted the urban crisis.[8] A range of activists in the 1960s and early 1970s who addressed these problems achieved fleeting victories; in the political retrenchment that followed, the fixers among them recalibrated their strategies and institutionalized some gains. But their roles are overlooked in the sweeping narratives of political history. They make only marginal appearances even in the rich, fine-grained recent scholarship on the black power movement and the War on Poverty. Yet their archival shadows span gaps between the passage of liberal reforms and the reality of their stalled implementation from the 1960s to the 1990s.

Fixers are only part of the multifaceted black freedom movement, but their emergence offers distinctive insights into the amplification, institutionalization, and appropriation of social movements. They reveal what was lost and gained as the liberationist politics of the late 1960s and 1970s waned and what changed and what remained the same as the urban crisis settled into the status quo. To understand the circumstances that gave rise to fixers and how they operated, we must first locate Newark at the intersection of black political incorporation and urban crisis, of the freedom movement and the "worst city."

Newark Will Get There First: Urban Crisis and the Black Freedom Movement

The tension between the promise of the black freedom movement and the reality of Newark's decline was starkly drawn by 1970, when thousands gathered to celebrate the June election of Kenneth Gibson. Their joyful chants of "Power to the People!" offered a coda to the Newark uprising three years past.[9] The campaign had made news around the nation, part of the historic wave of black electoral victories in the late 1960s and early 1970s. "Wherever American cities are going," Gibson declared—ominously or optimistically, depending on one's perspective—"Newark will get there first."[10]

But the memory of the uprising was still fresh. On the evening of July 12, 1967, two white police officers beat an unarmed black taxi driver named John Smith after the three argued during a minor traffic stop. They then dragged his seemingly lifeless body across the precinct parking lot. A crowd watched. Rumors spread that police had killed Smith. In fact he was alive, but angry residents gathered at the precinct.[11] Some people threw rocks at the precinct house and clashed with cops surging at them. Several days of fighting and looting followed.

4

The uprising ended with an assault on the city's Central Ward by both National Guard and police, who shot into black-owned stores left untouched by looters.[12] By July 17, nearly one thousand people had been injured; twenty-six were dead. Photographer Bud Lee captured one of the most enduring images of the uprising for *Life* magazine's July 28 cover: twelve-year-old Joe Bass, bleeding and crumpled on the street after police shot him while killing Billy Furr, twenty-four, for stealing a six-pack of beer. All but two of the dead, a police detective and a fire chief, were black. They ranged in age from ten to seventy-eight. Some, like Eloise Spellman, were shot while hiding at home.[13]

In the aftermath, Newark appeared to the rest of the country to be in ruins. Political scientist Paul Friesema notes that by the time black politicians like Gibson came to power a few years later, such cities were "hollow prizes"—no longer the engines of industrial growth and social mobility they had been.[14] "Hollow prize" evoked the diffuse sense of loss underscoring popular depictions of Newark as hopeless and of its struggles as futile.[15] But media depictions, whether earnest chronicles of victimhood or exaggerated profiles of depravity, revealed little about how Newark residents actually shaped their city's history. Newarkers who lived through their city's nadir tell a different story.

In 2004 several dozen local college and high school students, Newark residents, historians, and educators gathered at the New Jersey Historical Society to discuss new research on the uprising and to share recollections of its effects. They paid rapt attention to those who mourned friends or family killed decades before. Murmurs of affirmation, sometimes applause, greeted comments about the inequality with which Newark still struggles.

One man, David Barrett, recalled how quickly the black community mobilized after the uprising. Even as Newark still smoldered, residents helped one another. Newarkers dug deep into their wallets to support their neighbors. People who had left Newark returned home. Experienced leaders and newcomers to the black freedom movement were eager to rebuild. They sought to reverse their political and economic exclusion in the process—an aim that went far beyond electing Gibson.[16]

On the one hand, it seemed unsurprising that black Newarkers would have adapted existing social networks and traditions of self-help to meet a crisis. Many were less than a decade removed from life in the segregated South and still socialized with neighbors and family from their hometowns in Georgia, Virginia, or the Carolinas. Both newcomers and established residents had also confronted New Jersey's own manifestations of Jim Crow.[17] On the other hand, the insights of these conference participants revealed the gulf separating popular and even scholarly accounts of the urban crisis from lived experience. Barrett's assertion that Newark's black power movement grew from established networks dovetails with newer scholarship on the black freedom movement, which locates its roots earlier in the twentieth century. Recent historiography also delineates black power's far-reaching effects on coalition building, cultural politics, and concepts of racial identity beyond the culminating struggles of the late 1960s.[18]

Black power advocates mobilized new voters, won elections, forged black studies programs, and infused public schools with black history. But these gains were curtailed by political backlash, state surveillance and disruption of black organizations, and the stalled implementation of reforms. Also, the movement could not stanch the outflow of jobs and capital from cities like Newark. Such a task required activists to maneuver in a new landscape wrought by the liberating potential of the black freedom movement and by the threatening changes in urban political economy.

In response, many activists sought to institutionalize a holistic approach to the interrelated problems their communities faced; they saw civil rights and economic justice as inextricably linked; they approached the urban crisis by pointing to the underbelly of putatively progressive reforms, indicting the policies that had produced and reinforced inequality. The commitment to blending civil rights and economic justice runs through many threads of the black freedom movement, but it has been obscured by an emphasis on integration and equal opportunity. Martin Luther King Jr.'s concern with economic justice was embodied in the Poor People's Campaign. The Black Panther's "What We Want, What We Believe" lays out the connections between state violence, capitalism, and the economic disadvantage facing black communities and the conditions they share with colonized and formerly colonized peoples.[19] Even some advocates of "black capitalism" emphasized the reformulation of business practices, aiming to address collective economic needs, not just individual advancement. To varying degrees, black power in all its forms demanded a redistribution of state power and private resources.

Organizations throughout the black freedom movement were thus considering similar problems in a holistic way. Fixers were a subset of this contentious range, but their methods and understanding of inequality and self-determination had a distinctive impact on how the movement responded to the limits of reform and the question of institutionalizing its gains. Fixers advanced a holistic understanding of the urban crisis but often worked in a piecemeal fashion. Individual fixers such as Heningburg tried to enforce antidiscrimination laws by bringing together activists and political authorities or corporate leaders who possessed the power to overcome bureaucratic stonewalling. Organizational fixers, such as community economic development corporations, acted as mini–state builders: they literally wanted to fix Newark by building houses, providing health care and childcare, and democratizing the urban-planning process. Fixers negotiated an ever-shifting border between public and private, religious and secular, radicalism and reformism. Fixers pulled together the threads of what Alice O'Connor calls the patchwork welfare state; they also advanced their own vision of economic and political self-determination.[20]

My fixers bear some resemblance to sociologist Mary Pattillo's "middlemen" and "middlewomen," politically astute, community-minded black professionals who mediate between their poor neighbors and white-dominated municipal agencies and corporations.[21] Some fixers indeed saw themselves as mediators or entrepreneurs, but they emerged in an earlier period and differed from Pattillo's middlemen and middlewomen in other respects. As federal civil rights legislation and the War on Poverty unfolded, fixers found they had to tailor poorly defined, unenforced mandates to their cities' circumstances. They gained influence by responding to policy shortcomings, functioning as what political scientists might call "policy entrepreneurs," or by advancing what Thomas J. Sugrue calls "policymaking from below."[22] Fixers wanted to shape housing markets and create neighborhood businesses themselves. They often advocated some kind of market engagement, collective or individual, as a means to the end of economic redistribution and provision of services to neglected communities.

A deep pragmatism characterized fixers as they assessed the forces arrayed against them.[23] Yet visionary and occasionally radical goals motivated fixers, and they frequently deployed militant strategies. They won some victories; they occasionally reinforced the very balance of powers they sought to overturn. Fixers are crucial to understanding the fraught institutionalization of the black freedom movement. They established new patterns of reform and neighborhood institution building that shape the cities we live in today and loom large in urban history.

To understand why fixers emerged in the late 1960s and what distinguishes them, we must first understand the problems they promised to address, problems that Newark shared with many other cities around the country but that were also exacerbated by New Jersey's particular history of localism and suburban expansion.

Newark's Rise and Fall

Newark spreads north, south, and west from an S-shaped bend in the Passaic River. Unless you have a reason to travel Newark's local streets, you are most likely to encounter the city by highway, speeding along I-95 between Liberty Airport and Newark Bay, skirting a lively Portuguese neighborhood called the Ironbound—or perhaps along highways I-280 and I-78. These two products of midcentury urban renewal legislation cut across the Central Ward—heart of Newark-born poet Amiri Baraka's vision for a black nationalist "New Ark."[24] They whisk drivers past the birthplace of singers Sarah Vaughan, Dionne Warwick, and Whitney Houston. To their south lies the once-affluent neighborhood of Weequahic, childhood home of Philip Roth; to the west, verdant suburbia. To the northeast, cars soar over the arc of the Pulaski Skyway. Beneath it, estuaries breaking off from the Passaic and Hackensack Rivers reflect planes crisscrossing the sky, and threads of railway and highway weave through a historic industrial landscape: stacks of shipping containers, oil tanks, barges, the neon eagle of the Anheuser-Busch Brewery. From these transportation corridors extend grids of residential neighborhoods that appear to crest against the skyscrapers of Jersey City and Manhattan.

Founded in 1666, Newark grew from a swampy farm village to become the largest city in a heavily suburban state. It boasts a long manufacturing history, producing carriage parts, leather, and clothing throughout the nineteenth century.[25] Newark's location above the Port of Elizabeth made it an early shipping center and a crossroads for travelers to New York, Philadelphia, and beyond. By 1900 Newark ranked sixteenth among the country's largest cities, with 246,000 residents. In the years before World War I, Newark's native and immigrant workforce built their city into a leading manufacturer of chemical and cutting-edge electrical products.[26] Newark's location made it a nexus of organized crime during Prohibition. By the 1930s "Swing City" hosted the most famous musicians and vocalists of the day.[27] Later, Prudential Insurance Company and Mutual Benefit Life Insurance Company led the expansion of Newark's financial sector and the region's suburbanization.[28] Prudential's headquarters has for generations towered over Newark's downtown, much like the imposing rock of its internationally recognizable logo.[29]

While Newark's financial industry grew, manufacturing began to decline in the 1930s, and the once-collaborative relationship between corporate elites and city officials began to fray. City officials sought more revenue from local industries that had customarily enjoyed low tax rates. One comparison revealed that "the city's nine investment trust companies, with assets of $150 million, paid taxes averaging $120 a year. A homeowner with a $10,000 home would pay about $365."[30] Welcomed by suburban leaders with promises of lower taxes, many of the city's surviving businesses left; officials' lackluster political responses magnified the consequences.[31] But decades before the Great Depression took its toll, harbingers of Newark's grim future appeared.

Newark's decline is often told as a late twentieth-century history, but its roots are found at the turn of the century, amid growth and anticipation of future prosperity. Newark's municipal leaders balked at furnishing the costly infrastructural improvements their growing city required. Faced with the need for a modern sewerage system and waterworks, for example, they responded haphazardly compared with Jersey City or New York. As a consequence, the city later had few options for controlling the costs of infrastructure and little leverage in the form of better services or lower taxes to offer potential targets of annexation. By the time Newark's leaders attempted to annex surrounding towns to secure a stronger tax base, their target suburbs had no need for city services and opposed municipal consolidation.[32] Newark turned inward for revenue and taxes soared.[33]

Newspaper editorials from the early 1930s reflected the city's desperate search for new sources of revenue and alerted readers to the exodus to neighboring counties, "where taxes were low and lot sizes were large."[34] Editors scolded "the good citizen who escapes every night to his suburban home," where he invests the money earned at his downtown job—an image of suburban parasitism that future leaders would revisit. By the 1960s this gap was generations in the making and had been widened by federal, state, and local policies, as well as private-sector restructuring.[35] Midcentury municipal leaders agonized over insufficient tax rates. They bemoaned the large number of tax-exempt institutions that occupied over half of Newark's acreage, fueling hunger for federal urban renewal funding and the massive construction projects it would enable. City leaders could expect little from the state. Reflecting on the factors that contributed to the Newark uprising, the Governor's Select Commission on Civil Disorder noted, "New Jersey traditionally has had the doubtful distinction of spending less per capita in State aid to local governments than any other state in the Union."[36] In the late 1960s New Jersey's government supplied half as much revenue to localities as similar states, and Newark received even less than the state's average. "Newark relies on its property tax to raise $7 out of every $10 of total revenue, while cities in other states of comparable size, in the aggregate, raise $4 out of $10 in this manner."[37]

The longstanding rural and suburban orientation of New Jersey's governing coalitions also squeezed Newark. Where some have found a bland and indistinct commuter state, the political scientists Barbara G. Salmore and Stephen A. Salmore see "one of the strongest bastions of the individualistic political culture among American states."[38] From colonial days onward, New Jersey politics was defined by an "emphasis on keeping state government weak and maximizing local self-government and control."[39] Political alliances were split between the more urban north and the rural south. "More than any other populous American state," write Salmore and Salmore, "New Jersey politics then and now has been dominated by those generally unfriendly to cities—rural interests before 1970 and suburban ones thereafter."[40]

Until the 1960s the steady departure of Newark's chemical companies, small manufacturers, and white-collar employers proceeded at a pace that was more slow asphyxiation than stomach-churning drop. In the 1940s, for instance, Prudential executives opted to displace the centralized structure radiating from Newark with a network of regional offices they believed would bring innovation and efficiency to the insurance behemoth.[41] Still, Newark initially retained this and other prestigious white-collar firms, even as they shifted some operations out of the city.[42] In 1960 Prudential replaced its late nineteenth-century Gothic headquarters with the modern Prudential Plaza.[43]

Newark's department stores, such as Bamberger's, S. Klein, and Kresge's, anchored a vibrant downtown. The expansion of hospitals and educational institutions into downtown Newark in the 1950s bolstered the city's white-collar foundation. But the new jobs went predominantly to skilled and college-educated people who tended to live outside the city, deepening inequality between the residents of Newark and the rest of New Jersey.[44] This pattern mirrored the national economic realignment by which right-to-work states in the Sunbelt lured companies away from their northeast industrial origins with promises of lower taxes and fewer regulations.[45] Similarly, Salmore and Salmore identify an internal "Sunbelt" within New Jersey, as jobs and skilled residents relocated to the state's southern and western suburbs.[46] Between the late 1940s and early 1960s, Newark residents' earning power declined compared with that of their suburban counterparts. Manufacturing shrank from 47 to 33 percent of total employment between 1958 and 1970, a loss of 20,056 jobs.[47] Meanwhile, Newark residents held only about one-third of the 87,400 white-collar jobs in the city by the 1960s.[48]

The regional balance of power that weighed against Newark's economic fortunes both contributed to and reflected race and class segregation. Racial inequality intensified as black southerners moved to the city during the second phase of the Great Migration and whites departed for the suburbs, a migration dialectic abetted by federal incentives for highway and housing construction and discriminatory real estate practices. While Newark's total population began a long slide from its peak of 442,000 in 1930, its black population increased steadily throughout the midcentury, expanding most dramatically following World War II. In 1940, 11 percent (45,760) of the city's population of 429,760 was African American. By 1950 African Americans were 17 percent (74,964) of a population of 438,776. In 1960 the black citizenry made up about 34 percent (138,035) of the city's population of 405,220, and by 1970 they were the city's majority, constituting 54 percent (207,408) of a total population that had dwindled to 382,417. "The change was cataclysmic," notes Robert Curvin, a political scientist and founding member of the Essex County chapter of the Congress of Racial Equality (CORE). "Only two other cities—Washington, D.C. and Gary, Indiana—changed more rapidly."[49] A 1958 survey of Newark neighborhoods confirmed the significance of the Great Migration: 76 percent of black household heads had been born in the South, and only one-third had lived in Newark for more than ten years.[50]

The segregation that came to characterize Newark followed a course parallel to that of many other cities.[51] Prior to the Great Migration, Newark's small black population had been dispersed in enclaves across the city, amid neighborhoods of first- and second-generation Italians, Irish, Germans, and Slavs. But as the pace of migration quickened and the African American population grew, many were confined to older, overcrowded housing in the city's Central Ward.[52] Landlords took advantage of the tight market by subdividing apartments and renting them at a premium.[53] Banks denied credit, in part because of the redlining of neighborhoods with significant black populations, a practice the Federal Housing Administration (FHA) endorsed.[54] In both city and suburb, FHA and Veterans Affairs mortgages went to a minuscule percentage of minority home buyers. Discriminatory practices ensured that, as Lizabeth Cohen writes, "the racial boundaries of New Jersey's postwar suburbia grew even more impermeable than its class ones" and shaped housing markets long after their explicit manifestations were outlawed.[55]

In the face of New Jersey's racialized suburbanization and the formation of Newark's ghetto, black Newarkers created a rich associational life and sustained the civic ties through which to resist discrimination. Although Newark's black population grew most dramatically between 1950 and 1960, Clement Price argues that "the roots of Newark's black ghetto were virtually intact" decades earlier, including the institutions that anchored black neighborhoods for generations.[56] During this time, the city's fourteen oldest African American churches—among them Thirteenth Presbyterian, Saint James African Methodist Episcopal, Saint Phillips Episcopal, and Bethany Baptist—provided "pre-migration race leadership."[57] As in other cities transformed by the Great Migration, Newark witnessed the growth of block associations, fraternal organizations, and informal groups formed by people who hailed from the same southern towns.[58] New storefront churches and religious sects proliferated between 1910 and 1940, including Newark's Moorish Temple, which fused elements of Islam with a doctrine of racial pride and self-help.[59] By the 1940s the ranks of the black middle class had also grown to support a range of secular professional associations, neighborhood groups, youth councils, and settlement houses that occasionally vied with the established churches for leadership and more vigorously challenged northern Jim Crow.[60] Affiliation with black religious organizations, civic organizations, and neighborhood clubs offered entrée into dynamic social scenes. The *New Jersey Afro-American* and *New Jersey Herald* carried news that the mainstream white press neglected, as well as job listings.[61] Yet these institutions lacked the political or economic clout to counter employment and housing discrimination on a sustained, citywide scale.

By the 1960s new coalitions of civil rights and black power activists would call for a transformation of black civic life, prioritizing the expansion of black political leadership and the economic regeneration of Newark over suburban integration. Many would probably have agreed with Malcolm X's "Message to the Grassroots" that political power necessitated the control of land and its resources.[62] They would no doubt have concurred with Martin Luther King Jr. when he said several years later, "Now since they're just going to keep us here [in the ghetto] what we're going to have to do is just control the city. We got to be the mayors of these big cities. And the minute we get elected mayor, we got to begin taxing everybody who works in the city who lives in the suburbs."[63] Newark activists fused the criticism of suburbia that had been simmering from the early twentieth century to fresh calls for black political power.

By 1967 the tax rate in Newark saddled many residents with bills that exceeded the worth of their homes, motivating landlords to abandon upkeep.[64] Photographs of Newark's decrepit private-sector rentals in the late 1960s depict neatly attired tenants attending to battered appliances, woodstoves, and crumbling ceilings. By the time the Governor's Select Commission blamed such inequities for fueling the Newark uprising, black communities in Newark, as in Detroit and Oakland, had been mobilizing to transform housing for decades.[65] In Newark, the movement had arrived at a crossroads in 1963.

Fixers Emerge

The history through which a fixer ethos emerged from the crosswinds of the black freedom movement is traced through the three sections of this book. As discussed in part 1, protests against employment discrimination and the launch of the War on Poverty illustrate the acceleration of the city's black freedom movement. New organizations formed while federal laws and movement gains around the country lent pressure to local demands for housing, jobs, and political power.

But as civil rights victories and antipoverty programs promised a better future, urban renewal policies produced displacement, distrust, and inequality. In the years leading up to the 1967 uprising, officials congratulated themselves on Newark's progress, while black residents confronted perennial impasses: the letter of the law meant little when it came to practices of policing, discriminatory employment, and urban renewal. The conflict over the construction of a massive medical college, a battle that contributed to the uprising, wrested open a space for once-disparate causes to intersect. In public forums, diverse activists exposed the contradictions of midcentury liberalism, successfully challenged officials, and formed new alliances to push with some success past the limitations of reform. Amid the sense of crisis and urgency, new possibilities emerged.

Newark's uprising and the subsequent negotiations over the medical college set in motion a cycle of protest and persuasion that yielded some gains for ordinary residents. But these required vigilance and persistence to maintain, especially in the face of structural pressures weakening the city and slackening federal commitments. Parts 2 and 3 examine the individual fixers and the organizational fixers who devised the strategies to implement and institutionalize these gains. In part 2, I discuss how Gustav Heningburg's bold airport dash to secure construction jobs was founded in his broader social justice vision.

Uneasily shifting between the white corporate elites who courted him and local black power advocates with whom he was allied, Heningburg also sought to elect black and Puerto Rican candidates to office, extend affirmative action beyond the building trades, cultivate black capitalism, and reckon with suburban parasitism. His experience illustrates how individuals with conflicting ideologies briefly mobilized around a multifaceted view of black self-determination. It encompassed black cultural nationalism, petit bourgeois entrepreneurship, and an understanding of the ghetto as an internal colony anchored in Marxist and Pan-African thought. But in managing these many strands, black power advocates could become entangled in the very cul-de-sacs of liberalism they had contested.

Heningburg was the hub of a wheel, and his various campaigns were its spokes, radiating outward. But other Newarkers attempted to fix the city by turning inward. The second chapter of part 2 shifts away from Heningburg's individual role to a case in which he acted as an advocate and mediator. Between 1970 and 1974, Heningburg supported tenants in the enormous Stella Wright Homes, who led what became the longest rent strike in the history of US public housing. After unsuccessfully pressuring local and federal authorities to resolve a longstanding and national decline in public housing, they took matters into their own hands. The Stella Wright tenants' campaign recaptures a missing chapter in the maligned history of public housing and refines the concept of the fixer. Tenants countered depictions of public housing as unmitigated social disorganization while federal and local officials traded accusations of blame. Stella Wright tenants acted as fixers by emphasizing the interconnectedness of reliable housing and employment while cultivating support from an array of allies at the local and federal level. They won several critical legal victories, but ultimately, as public housing programs shifted toward subsidized private rentals, tenants' successes as fixers were contained within a shrinking corner of the city's public housing system. Their experience illustrates the difficulty of advancing expansive reforms or tenant self-determination in the 1970s. Yet the Stella Wright strike identified problems that fixer organizations, the subject of part 3, would attempt to solve.

Institutionalizing the Movements

While three of Newark's most prominent first-generation community development corporations (CDCs) had distinct experiential and ideological roots, they all saw housing as a fulcrum for more radical and enduring transformation. Their strategies would become a mainstay of urban redevelopment policy in subsequent decades—although not necessarily in the ways they envisioned. The term "community development corporation" has been applied to a broad range of organizations that share the goal of building economic and political power in the form of community-run housing, businesses, job training programs, and social services. Though many are nonprofit corporations, they often include profit-making enterprises in their missions and "tend to defy conventional boundaries" separating political advocacy, social service provision, and entrepreneurship.[66]

Newark's early CDCs—the Tri-City Citizens Union for Progress, the Congress of African People/Kawaida Inc., and the New Community Corporation—positioned themselves in a continuum with elements of the black freedom movement: the first organization reflected its founders' years in the labor movement; the second drew immediate inspiration from black power theorists; the third was shaped by the civil rights movement, the fledgling doctrine of liberation theology, and Catholic lay activism. Though these three organizations worked independently, they advanced a shared claim that viable inner-city communities were crucial components of a healthy national economy.

In their founding years, Newark's CDCs saw themselves as working against the thrust of federally supported policies like urban renewal and as supplying a corrective to the once-promising but shortchanged programs of the War on Poverty. All three emphasized property ownership. Early CDCs attempted to re-create a social safety net on the neighborhood level for people who had never even enjoyed the full support of the New Deal state.[67]

Organizational fixers also argued that the revival of their neighborhoods depended upon a cultural revolution. Black cultural nationalists, for example, sought to institute new ethical and civic rituals to reinforce their shared history and make individuals accountable to one another. In less self-conscious but similar ways, both black cultural nationalists and left-leaning Catholics attempted to reinvigorate or preserve historically grounded and more authentic expressions of faith. While early CDCs are not typically considered part of the 1960s counterculture, these three nonetheless shared with it a celebration of communal life, a quest for authenticity, and a critique of bureaucracy that very occasionally challenged bourgeois codes of individuality and privacy. In both their political and their cultural work, these organizational fixers sought to institutionalize a range of social justice agendas in the 1970s and beyond. By the 1980s, as the federal government retreated from cities and devolved spending power to states and localities, these fixers' successes and failures would come to reveal the long-term consequences of racial inequality and urban policy in a neoliberal age.

Newark Neoliberalism

Rivalry and conflict have often characterized the relationship between Newark's fixers and the municipal government since the 1970s. Mayor Gibson, for instance, retreated from the grassroots networks that had enabled his election, calling "citizen participation" a "bugaboo"—a distraction from the demands of municipal governance—and rebuking community activists.[68] Gibson's trajectory may have dismayed reform-minded supporters, but it was hardly surprising or unique, as black-led and interracial reform coalitions around the country gradually lowered their expectations of what conventional party politics could offer them in the 1970s and 1980s.[69] But Newark's experience amounts to more than a cautionary tale of ambitious grassroots reform thwarted by the regeneration of an urban machine.[70] The city's political trajectory was embedded in a broader shift to a neoliberal footing that Newark's fixers both fought and shaped.

Advocates of the deregulation of business and the privatization of government functions seized an opening for neoliberal reform when seemingly irresoluble inflation demolished the expectations of economic growth on which liberalism's ambitions—Kennedy's New Frontier and Johnson's Great Society—had thrived less than a decade before. To be sure, the replacement of urban manufacturing by specialized white-collar industries and low-skilled service work abetted stratification and further splintered liberal governing coalitions already divided over civil rights, feminism, and the antiwar movement. Neoliberalism also had specifically urban cadences. Elites, officials, and voters argued that the lawless poor, indebted public institutions, and demanding workers of crime-ridden cities succored on the vestiges of the War on Poverty needed the strong discipline of a new governing strategy. Funding for infrastructure and public services shrank, while a resignation to the permanency of urban crisis set in as cities such as New York toppled into bankruptcy. Yet in the neoliberal calculus, this crisis was an opportunity. Poverty was no longer a war to be fought but an outcome to be managed and mined, an opening for the privatization of public services and the promotion of piecemeal voluntary and entrepreneurial efforts to replace the frayed social safety net and loss of employment. In Newark, many municipal officials were politically to the left of the Democrats who supported some neoliberal approaches by the 1990s. Yet they governed in a state and federal climate not of their own making.

Urban neoliberalism of this moment had particular purchase in cities like Baltimore, which David Harvey declared "a mess. . . . Not the kind of enchanting mess that makes cities such interesting places to explore, but an awful mess."[71] Neoliberalism gave primacy to downtown speculation and corporate interests; government efforts to address escalating inequality were cut or eliminated in the throes of an incessant budget crisis. Officials exhorted poor, working-class, and middle-class city dwellers to answer scarcity with entrepreneurial self-sufficiency even as private development schemes demanded public financing. Municipal leaders justified loans, infrastructure additions, tax breaks, and bailouts as the price that cities must pay to remain competitive.[72]

Such policies had immediate human costs in terms of services and programs slashed. But they also dampened the spark of political resistance that had animated early fixers, turning any vestiges of collectivism toward the commodification of public space.[73] This is the paradoxical moment the fixers attempted to negotiate by holding on to that visionary impulse even as the demands of survival pushed local efforts at self-determination toward managing the minute crises of a retreating welfare state.

Neoliberal policies not only contributed to rising inequality within black communities but also diminished the potential for vigorous social movements by obfuscating the political roots of inequality. Neoliberal governmentality—the bureaucratic demands, technologies, and often-unspoken commitments that motivate populations to govern themselves—ultimately rationalizes intraracial inequality. In Lester K. Spence's words, "a range of problems within black communities have been taken outside the realm of the political by rendering them technical and actionable."[74]

My study of the winnowing of social movement strategies in the 1970s illuminates the point where the pressures and incentives to promote neoliberal policies meet the traditions of collective self-help on which fixers drew, and their assumption of state-making roles in the absence of government-provided resources and protections. At first glance, fixers, with their urgency and pragmatism, may seem to be "problem solvers" who unwittingly justify a neoliberal gloss on the importance of self-help and the diminished role of government. Indeed, it is difficult to imagine a universe of political mobilization in Newark during the 1960s and 1970s that did not involve some conception of problem solving. But the nuances are crucial. Some fixers sought to problematize conditions that were taken for granted; others, to subvert or upend institutions deemed beyond reform. But their emphasis on pragmatism and immediacy was not meant as an all-hands-on-deck panacea for entrenched political problems, as later neoliberal problem solving seemed to endorse. Instead, they wanted to exploit the sense of urgency created by the black freedom movement and the uprisings to push through—and hopefully beyond—the entrenched barriers to change.

Expertise and the deployment of technology are critical to the neoliberal project. CDCs appear to prefigure the rise of urban neoliberalism in their decentralized, nominally entrepreneurial orientation to the provision of social services, public health, and education. Yet this was not the future many early activists had in mind. Early community economic development called for a collective, critical engagement with expertise. They sought new methods for engaging ordinary residents in issues of planning and municipal politics that were typically reserved for experts and to institutionalize a space for counterexpertise. While only one element of a multifaceted social justice movement, such fixers have much to reveal about the cities we live in today.

If cities are especially useful laboratories for testing neoliberal convictions, Newark shows that its hallmarks existed much earlier than the 1970s for the black Newarkers at the margins of midcentury liberalism's postwar embrace. Even urban renewal—originally touted as a progressive reform—restructured the city's economic base in ways that ultimately followed neoliberal logic: officials sought to solve their revenue problems by remaking central-city Newark for corporate and white-collar interests rather than for the people who already lived there. By the 1980s and 1990s Newark's fixers—its CDCs—exhibited both convergence with and divergence from this neoliberal trajectory.[75] CDCs had played a significant role in institutionalizing vestiges of black power and the War on Poverty. Some continued to build and manage housing, but few sustained businesses on a scale that permitted self-sufficiency and significant local employment. Many abandoned self-determination and instead contracted with government agencies to provide social services. By the 1980s the ascendant Right recast them as centerpieces of a decentralized approach, or what Jack Kemp called "a conservative war on poverty."[76] CDCs faced urgent questions about the extent to which they would preserve their founding visions or adapt to the changing demands of funders and policymakers. Ultimately, the fixers of the 1960s and 1970s ended up straddling a thin line between midcentury liberalism and neoliberalism: individually, they may have embraced a range of political convictions, from the radical Left to the conservative, but they collectively acted as muffled voices of reform, managing a parallel city-state while attempting to secure a social safety net.

For those who live and work in Newark, the persistent image of the city as hopelessly imperiled makes static victims out of people who fiercely, often shrewdly, fought long odds to save their city. Working house by house, job by job, they won real gains. Yet their efforts may have appeared much like those of Gustav Heningburg's on the tarmac that day in 1970—one man confronting a phalanx of machines. Fixers altered the calculus of urban policy. They did not stop the machine in its tracks but instead sought to harness its mechanism toward different ends. The fallout of recent economic crises—rural areas devastated by globalization, suburbs decimated by foreclosures, and cities gentrified beyond the reach of working-class people—reveals the paucity of the concept of urban crisis to describe what has occurred in the United States over the past half a century. Fixers illuminate strategies for addressing the inequality that has been reproduced and also provide insight into the power and limitations of working from the bottom up.

PART ONE

At the Crossroads

ONE

Fighting for Jobs in the "Laboratory of Democracy"

Four summers before the 1967 Newark uprising, two hundred activists who had been rallied by a local civil rights coalition called the Newark Coordinating Committee amassed at a construction site for the new Barringer High School. Nearly all the construction workers—also two hundred in number—were white. Arriving for their jobs on the morning of July 3, 1963, they encountered demonstrators in picket lines at every entrance to the new $6.5 million building. The workers charged toward the picketers, leading with their fists.[1] Mayor Hugh J. Addonizio (a Democrat) and Harold Ashby, the first African American president of the board of education, suspended work on the school until the city's Commission on Human Rights could investigate the Newark Coordinating Committee's claims of discrimination. Lest the protesters interpret his intervention as a victory, Addonizio was dismissive of the committee: they were "not interested in resolving the problem," he complained, "but rather in prolonging and aggravating the differences."[2]

The scolding tone Addonizio took toward the Barringer protest contrasted with the optimism he had expressed at the US Commission on Civil Rights hearings held in Newark the previous fall. Among the many facets of discrimination disclosed at the hearing, the most striking was the near-total absence of skilled black workers in the city's building trades.[3] Union leaders denied responsibility, contending that members of the city's largest minority, soon to become its majority, rarely applied for union apprenticeships.[4] While Mayor Addonizio conceded that much remained to be done to redress racial inequality, he still expressed optimism about the city's future. "Newark is the working laboratory of democracy," he assured the commission, citing the record of support for civil rights legislation he had established during his thirteen years as a congressman. "What we learn and develop here will be used in every major community throughout the world."[5]

The *Newark Evening News* declared the Barringer clash the official beginning of Newark's civil rights movement. That facile designation erased the decades of activism that had often gone unnoticed by the paper, but it did capture the significance of the Barringer protest. The escalation of the city's civil rights movement upended existing patterns of patronage and more widely exposed ineffective federal, state, and local antidiscrimination measures. Employment protests disrupted the fragile strategies with which liberal officials sought to manage yawning racial inequality as their city shifted from a white to a black majority. Black Newarkers expanded the repertoire of strategies they deployed in the interlocked struggles for decent housing, employment, and political power. But progress was slow—if it happened at all—and the obstacles to change required a different approach, one that fixers would hone in the years to come.

In protests over the next several years, activists sought an immediate end to discrimination in the building trades and reached beyond the union hall and the construction site to achieve it. The Barringer High School protest ushered in widespread direct action by newly formed civil rights groups. In conjunction with new policies at the federal level, direct action challenged—but did not completely displace—the gradualism practiced by established civic organizations, corporations, and municipal officials. The second protest campaign, at the construction sites for Rutgers Law School and the Newark College of Engineering, positioned employment discrimination on publicly funded construction as part of African Americans' claims to full access to the goods and services for which they paid taxes. Both protests targeted construction projects because they promised to generate well-paying jobs. They highlighted the exclusion of black residents from the planning and construction of large public institutions, a problem that would also spur opposition to urban renewal later in the decade.

Opportunities Foreclosed: The Roots of the Barringer Protest

In 1963 Newark's population was about 382,000, a decline from its midcentury peak. Its unemployment rate—7 percent—exceeded the national rate of 5–6 percent in the early 1960s.[6] The unemployment rate among African Americans, 34 percent of the city's population by 1960, hovered around 13 percent. The construction industry employed only 4 percent of Newark's workers in 1960, but locally, construction industry wages had nearly doubled between 1949 and 1963, far outpacing the cost of living in the city or its suburbs.[7] The construction trades also stood at the center of the urban renewal building frenzy that was predicted to bring more stable, high-wage employment in the coming decades and "a sound basis for establishing equal job opportunities for all."[8]

The construction industry was also intimately connected to the physical creation of community: schools, hospitals, public housing, and other institutions that had so frequently denied African Americans full access. Barringer High School was especially significant in this respect. Black parents sought to enroll their children in Barringer, one of Newark's best schools, despite threats from the predominantly white student body.[9] By asserting that black workers were as entitled to construction jobs at Barringer as white workers, the Congress of Racial Equality (CORE) also implicitly rejected the idea that black students would be interlopers there or at any of the city's schools. Following on the heels of black-led efforts to desegregate schools in nearby New Jersey suburbs, the Barringer protest underscored wider claims: black workers would help build the city's schools and their children would attend them.[10]

The summer of 1963 seemed an especially auspicious time for the Barringer demonstration. Throughout the northeast—in Philadelphia, Brooklyn, Pittsburg, and neighboring Elizabeth, New Jersey—activists targeted publicly funded construction projects with few or no black workers to demonstrate how little had changed despite increasing federal attention.[11] In 1961 President John F. Kennedy had issued Executive Order 10925, which officially called for employers to take "affirmative action" to prohibit discrimination in hiring.[12] In 1963 Kennedy turned to the construction industry specifically, calling for intensified Labor Department oversight of apprenticeship programs, and in late June, two months after protests in Philadelphia had begun, Kennedy issued

Executive Order 11114 prohibiting discrimination in federally con-tracted construction.[13] These measures lent crucial thrust to the move-ment for equality in the building trades but did not transform them.

Newark leaders were aware of their city's patterns of racial discrimi-nation in the years prior to the Barringer protest, and their responses fit squarely in the vein of postwar liberalism. Throughout the 1950s, they spoke of public tolerance programs and studies of individual prejudice as fundamental to the ongoing struggle for equality, one upon which a US victory in the Cold War depended. To be sure, such efforts sus-tained a small interracial activist community and kept the issue of civil rights alive in a political culture that prized complacency. But the same anticommunist reasoning that made moderate progress on civil rights essential to protecting the nation's image in the Cold War inhibited radical critique of the racial *and* economic dimensions of inequality, while dampening a sense of urgency.[14] The effectiveness of these ac-tivists was often inversely related to the loft of their rhetoric in part because they lacked recourse to meaningful enforcement mechanisms that would have allowed them to move beyond condemnations of per-sonal prejudice to combat structural discrimination.

Nothing captures this dilemma as clearly as the experience of the Mayor's Commission on Group Relations. In 1950 Newark's municipal government created the commission in part to respond to black migra-tion from the South. The mass departure of white residents for class- and race-stratified suburbs was just as transformative for Newark, but that subject received less attention, although some in the commission recognized its significance.[15] Of greater concern to white officials were the political consequences of the city's demographic changes and the demands they would face from increasing numbers of black voters and organizations.

A series of municipal reforms dating back nearly half a century im-pacted African American representation in municipal government. In 1917 Newark had replaced the aldermanic system, in which each ward elected its own representatives, with a city commission, in which citywide elections produced five commissioners to lead municipal de-partments.[16] Newark reformers sought this change to short-circuit the patronage expectations entrenched deeply within each ward, but the commission system merely shifted patronage from the wards to the city departments and agencies under each commissioner's su-pervision. When Irish Americans began to move to the suburbs of sur-rounding Essex County in the 1930s and 1940s, Italian Americans and Jews ascended in city politics. Upstart candidates had to engage seriously with Newark's neglected black voters, who now served as a wedge in close races against the Irish Americans. Yet even though their votes gained value, citywide elections mandated by the commission system undermined the influence black voters could have had by virtue of their concentration in the Central Ward.[17] In 1953 another wave of reform produced the mayor-council system. A blend of aldermanic and commission systems, the mayor-council arrangement featured a council comprising one representative elected by each ward and four additional representatives selected in citywide elections. In 1954 Newark elected an Irish American former labor leader named Leo Carlin as mayor, while the Central Ward (originally called the Third Ward) elected the city's first black councilman, Irvine Turner.[18]

The revival of the ward system did not substantially change the way city politicians operated, but it helped propel Turner into a role that brought some concrete benefits to black residents in the Central Ward. Ten years into Turner's political career a journalist described him as "a traditional ward boss . . . who boasts that he feeds more people than the Newark welfare department."[19] While this was no doubt an exaggeration, Turner did advocate fiercely for Newark's poor and working-class blacks.[20] Yet he lacked independent leverage to translate his militant rhetoric into reality and challenge other councilmen.[21]

The Newark City Council may have proved indifferent to the implementation of its Fair Practice Ordinance. But the Mayor's Commission on Human Relations insisted that the protection of civil rights not only was mandated by the state's constitution and the moral bonds of "brotherhood" but also constituted a bulwark for national security.[22] At a US Senate subcommittee hearing in 1954, the commission's chairman, David M. Litwin, compared prejudice to a "cancerous body" and warned that "the invasion or violation of any one of our civil rights gives the communistic countries an advantage for propaganda purposes in their cold war of attrition."[23] While the commission earnestly accepted its charge, it had no significant power to enforce antidiscrimination measures and had to resort to private negotiations with resistant employers. Litwin and the commission walked a tightrope between emphasizing the need for stricter federal antidiscrimination laws and insisting that such mechanisms would rarely be used—that the mere existence of a federal law would pressure employers into preemptive, voluntary compliance.[24]

The Mayor's Commission emphasized communication and compromise in response to documented allegations of discrimination and offered few details about the resolutions it reached. The tone of the commission's publications—measured and optimistic—seemed intended to ease white residents' anxiety about their future in an increasingly black city while assuring black residents that they, too, had the administration's ear. The organization seemed to serve as a rhetorical panacea rather than a foundation for effective action, although some commission members publicly chafed against these constraints.[25] Absent government power to enforce nondiscrimination law, the Urban League emerged as the most effective—if still quite limited—organization in Newark, assisting individual African American and Puerto Rican job seekers. Thousands of workers registered with the Urban League in the late 1950s and early 1960s, and the group placed about one hundred of them—mostly skilled and professional workers—in positions annually.[26]

By 1963 the Barringer controversy brought together Newark activists frustrated by the narrow scope of established organizations and liberal leadership. They turned to the newly formed Essex County chapter of CORE, which attracted militant working-class activists and college-educated men and women pursuing more direct tactics and immediate solutions.

Robert Curvin, one of CORE's early founders and an organizer of the Barringer protest, had a history of challenging northern New Jersey's racial conventions. While in high school during the 1950s, Curvin and his circle of politically active friends, both black and white, joined the NAACP Youth Council and used its meetings to launch informal direct actions against segregated swimming pools and roller rinks.[27] Curvin served several years in the army and returned to Newark to attend Rutgers in 1957, gravitating to what he perceived as the "more activist" CORE rather than the NAACP. As in many other cities, Newark's CORE boycotted businesses that refused to hire blacks or that relegated their black employees to the worst jobs.[28] Members also regularly protested hiring bias at a local White Castle hamburger stand, holding aloft signs that read "More jobs now" or "We want a Black and White Castle" and informing black customers who bypassed their pickets that they "weren't ready for freedom."[29] Propelled by a heady sense of spontaneity and formidable stamina, CORE staged protests across the city addressing a range of issues from police brutality and calls for citizen review boards to housing discrimination.[30]

The Barringer protest sparked a summer of intermittent picketing and caustic negotiations that forced employment discrimination into the news and called attention to the failure of existing, largely voluntary policies. CORE, a major participant in the Newark Coordinating

Committee, moved from the margins to the center of Newark's civil rights movement. The Newark Coordinating Committee itself provided an alternative to the vague emphasis on tolerance that characterized so much civil rights discourse and the essentially toothless options offered by the Mayor's Commission. To activists seasoned by the Barringer protest, the city's liberal reform efforts not only had failed to address the needs of Newark's black communities but appeared to abide their marginalization. But established black leaders viewed these upstart activists with suspicion.[31] Irvine Turner publicly opposed the pickets and criticized Curvin specifically, while the Newark NAACP initially refused to join the Newark Coordinating Committee–led protest.[32] Although Curvin himself had joined the NAACP Youth Council as an adolescent, he clashed with the Newark branch as an adult. At one "very tense meeting," Curvin was ejected by a prominent NAACP leader and Addonizio appointee, Larrie Stalks, one of the few black women close to municipal power in Newark at the time. She objected when Curvin asked to talk about CORE's plans to bring young activists to the city for a summer organizing project.[33] Curvin called the NAACP leaders of the 1950s and early 1960s "literal token representatives" because Addonizio had appointed them to secure support for him among Newark's black voters and sustain the reputation as a liberal on race relations that he had enjoyed in his previous career as a congressman.[34] Indeed, prominent NAACP members did have municipal sway. Like Stalks, Harry Hazelwood Jr., president of the NAACP in the late 1950s, had numerous ties to city government and served as a city magistrate. The NAACP president at the time of the Barringer protest was Carlton B. Norris, Newark's first black detective, who had investigated nearly "every case of major violence or murder in Newark since the end of WWII."[35] Under Norris, the NAACP had persistently advocated for the integration of Newark-area schools, but the strengthening of the organization's institutional base through highly successful fundraising and membership drives constituted his most significant achievement.[36] Curvin's history with the organization no doubt shaped his subsequent perspective, and other scholarship on the waning years of broker politics echoed his interpretation: many established black leaders were cautious about expending the political capital they had gained through professional accomplishments and measured activism on new strategies.[37]

Like the NAACP leadership, many black clergy initially refused to endorse the Barringer protest.[38] But there were exceptions, including Reverend Dr. Eustace L. Blake, who told his congregants at Saint James

African Methodist Episcopal Church that "the price of freedom is not cheap" and urged them to join the NAACP, the Southern Christian Leadership Conference (SCLC), or even CORE.[39] Reverend John Collier, a young African Methodist Episcopal minister and leader of Ministers' Alliance for Progress, went further, becoming a spokesman for the Newark Coordinating Committee.[40]

Once the pickets were up and construction stalled, negotiations with the mayor, unions, and contractors became more likely. Newark's civil rights movement was shifting: the Newark Coordinating Committee gained clout as former naysayers now supported the protest. The Urban League agreed to compile lists of skilled black tradesmen to apply for jobs, while the NAACP's President Norris said he approved a freeze on the Barringer project until additional black workers were added. Even as Turner continued to dismiss activists as troublemakers, he announced plans for his own investigation of the Barringer matter.[41]

The construction trades responded angrily when school board members, officials, and contractors met to discuss the Newark Coordinating Committee's demands in early July. The Essex County Building Trades Council (EBTC) insisted that the board of education and the project's contractors had excluded labor from the initial decision to stop construction. They argued that the work stoppage was illegal; some members threatened to boycott future school construction.[42] As the Mayor's Commission investigated the committee's claims, Addonizio tried to placate union officials by stacking the commission's board with representatives of local unions.[43] Nonetheless, the commission announced on July 10 that its investigation had, in fact, revealed racial bias in the industry and urged action.[44]

Even as the Newark Coordinating Committee forced employment discrimination on to the municipal agenda and garnered more support, it was still not universally recognized as legitimate. Although Norris of the NAACP, James Pawley of the Urban League, and Reverend Blake of Saint James American Methodist Episcopal Church—all men Addonizio considered "responsible members of the Negro community"—had by now expressed support for the committee, its members were still excluded from meetings with the mayor and slots on the Citizens Negotiating Committee (CNC), the team of civil rights leaders that would negotiate with the trade unions.[45] But as the "responsible" black leadership of Newark increasingly criticized Addonizio, its purportedly "irresponsible" counterpart eventually gained representation. In mid-July, Addonizio invited Reverend Collier, a member of two Newark Coordinating Committee affiliates, the Ministers' Alliance for

Progress and CORE, to join the CNC. Soon after, the Newark Coordinating Committee gained substantial representation, replacing some of Addonizio's handpicked appointments.[46]

In late July, the CNC proposed that African Americans and Puerto Ricans should compose half the workforce on municipal construction jobs in order to correct "an imbalance of decades."[47] The EBTC rejected this proposal as "arbitrary, unrealistic, and unreasonable."[48] The Newark Coordinating Committee vowed to picket Barringer until the unions agreed to eliminate discrimination. Louis Vehling, president of the EBTC, countered with a threat to withdraw from negotiations unless the pickets stopped. The unions, Vehling asserted, would "not lower our standards . . . or grant any group super-seniority."[49] He told the press that "unless more jobs are created, the cost of eliminating discrimination will mean the loss of a job by someone else. We have no intention of permitting civil rights leaders . . . to play musical chairs with the job opportunities or employment status of the members of the union."[50]

Vehling argued that civil rights activists wanted the unions to abandon their objective, meritocratic hiring prerogatives to grant apprenticeships to less qualified workers in the name of rectifying hiring bias. Collier countered that Vehling had misconstrued the Newark Coordinating Committee's proposal as an illegitimate seizure of jobs for unqualified workers. In fact, Collier said, the committee had only asked the unions to consider skilled minority tradesmen or apprentices who had been vetted by the Urban League and met union requirements. But Collier also questioned the objectivity of union membership criteria. In his view, Vehling's defense of union meritocracy obscured the historical weight of racial exclusion and the structure of interpersonal relationships that preserved white workers' advantages. Many white workers, Collier noted, relied on relatives to inform them of job openings and sponsor their apprenticeships or their participation in "unofficial" training programs.[51] Although he disputed Collier on this point, Vehling and other union leaders had acknowledged as much during their testimony before the US Commission on Civil Rights hearing. They admitted that unions' professed commitment to strict meritocracy did not prevent them from bending apprenticeship rules for relatives of current union members.[52] Vehling used the language of meritocratic individualism to defend his unions even though the benefits of union membership accrued precisely because they had more expansive aims: union membership provided job security not just for individuals but for multiple generations. For Collier and the Newark Coordinating

Committee, the protest was not merely about the employment of a few tradesmen but about a recognition that unions could play a significant role in reducing economic inequality and about a definition of what the freedom promised by the civil rights movement would entail.[53] The dispute between the unions and civil rights activists intensified because they shared a conception of what union power could achieve, but disagreed over who should wield it.

For the black civic leaders drawn together during this debate, the Barringer protest opened up new possibilities for unity, but it also highlighted abiding schisms. Councilman Turner, for instance, acknowledged the persistence of discrimination but consistently followed Addonizio's lead in criticizing those who exposed it.[54] Meanwhile, some civil rights activists on the CNC supported the protest but clashed with the Newark Coordinating Committee over strategy, warning that picketing would derail negotiations. Curvin rejected critics who claimed the committee's forcefulness jeopardized white leaders' willingness to pursue reforms or imperiled a unified black movement. Noting that the unions had yet to make any substantive concessions to the protesters, Curvin remarked that "the only thing we're wrecking is 100 years of misery."[55]

Curvin's claim speaks to the long history behind the Barringer protest and its stakes, which rose in light of emerging federal policy on racial exclusion in the construction trades. Much liberal optimism about early-1960s civil rights reform rested on the promise of accommodating demands for greater inclusion of minority workers within a growing economy. But debates within the Department of Labor's Bureau of Apprenticeship and Training (BAT) suggest that for officials the goals of expanding and modernizing apprenticeship training *and* enforcing antidiscrimination measures were often irreconcilable. Both Vehling and Collier suggested that more jobs would open more opportunities for minority workers. But federal policymakers conveyed more pessimism about the promise of economic growth.

As the civil rights movement escalated in the late 1950s, advocacy for racially inclusive apprenticeship programs appeared to dovetail with federal Labor Department officials' concerns about the future of the construction trades. In 1959 BAT predicted that new highway and suburb construction, population growth, and attrition among skilled workers would require an additional 2.3 million workers by 1970. But the current spectrum of union and nonunion apprenticeship programs could accommodate only a small fraction of these prospective workers.[56] While acknowledging that many workers advanced to journeyman status through observation and informal training, Labor Department officials argued that "this haphazard procedure usually takes longer than serving an apprenticeship and seldom results in complete mastery of the trade."[57] Such a system, officials feared, would not produce a workforce capable of meeting future demands and adapting to new technology.[58] As BAT officials considered the extent to which they could use federal contracts as an incentive to shape a future construction workforce, they also determined that stricter antidiscrimination policies could potentially increase the number of apprentices in the trades. But the price of uniting these two goals soon became evident.

BAT officials sought to enhance the capacities of Joint Apprenticeship Councils, the regional organizations of contractors, trade union leaders, and businessmen who developed criteria and procedures for training the building trades' workforce. In 1959 BAT official Millard Cass proposed that the federal government take an unprecedented step: fortifying the country's inconsistent training system by writing universal requirements into its contracts.[59] Though integration of the trades was not foregrounded, Cass's proposal could have provided an opening for more inclusive policies, but it drew impassioned criticism from Labor Department officials. "WOW! This goes against all concepts I thought we were working on," wrote one.[60] Other unsigned comments scrawled across Cass's plan argued that by requiring and underwriting additional training programs, the government would give compliant contractors an advantage over future competitors "at government expense."[61] Another critic was more ambivalent, arguing that Cass's plan was a "necessary step from persuasion to force in an area hitherto largely free of government intervention." Yet he withheld full support because "the reaction would be strenuous from businessmen. It might well inhibit the effectiveness of present programs."[62] Ultimately, BAT officials retreated from more robust oversight of apprenticeship programs with the hope that fewer requirements would encourage experimentation.[63]

BAT officials prioritized cordial relationships with apprenticeship training programs over other goals. This discouraged officials' use of more aggressive methods to impose their vision on Joint Apprenticeship Councils and shift the industry away from the "haphazard" methods Cass described. But it also deflated the possibility of addressing discrimination in the trades. Around the same time that BAT officials debated the efficacy and political wisdom of training requirements in government contracts, a BAT official named Newell Brown circulated an NAACP-authored investigation of the construction trades to his colleagues. Only sixteen states had formal prohibitions on discrimination, and authorities in these states would not exert their full powers to enforce them. The report's conclusion that existing antidiscrimination rules had increased minority workers' participation very little would have been familiar to Newark's civil rights activists and black job seekers in the early 1960s.[64]

Brown praised the investigation to his colleagues, but he also warned, "Where the report in its recommendations goes beyond proposals for expanding and improving Apprenticeships generally, it calls for Federal action which we would have to oppose if we are to retain employer and employee goodwill."[65] Brown ultimately doubted that the BAT would act, for fear of alienating white workers and employers and thereby rendering their office ineffective. Indeed, even after Kennedy established the President's Committee on Equal Opportunity in 1961 and Secretary of Labor Arthur Goldberg instructed the BAT to require all newly registered apprenticeship programs to adhere to nondiscriminatory standards, BAT officials remained reluctant to intervene for fear of antagonizing sponsors and impeding their overriding goals of expanding and modernizing apprenticeship programs around the country.[66] Instead, BAT emphasized the use of civic organizations within the private sector to elicit compliance from unions and employers. Black communities, BAT officials suggested, needed to develop social capital in the form of "circles of gossip," in one official's words.[67] For publicizing construction jobs and for preparing young black men for those jobs, the BAT preferred to focus on community-based channels that replicated those through which white applicants found jobs. From the BAT's perspective, emphasizing recruitment, education, and civic activism within the black community permitted officials to step in as facilitators between activists and hostile unions, an alternative they preferred to enforcing laws against resistant white-led unions.

Even so, Kennedy's executive orders and greater federal scrutiny of apprenticeship programs suggested that more rigorous enforcement might be forthcoming when the Barringer protest drew Department of Labor officials to Newark in August 1963. They urged Addonizio to start a referral system for minority apprentices similar to those instituted in New York City, Cincinnati, Cleveland, and Pittsburgh and reminded the mayor that the Department of Labor could revoke federal certification of union training programs throughout the city if unions failed to comply with E.O. 11114.[68] Meanwhile, the New Jersey Division on Civil Rights insisted that unions supply information on the race and ethnicity of their apprentices under threat of subpoena. Leaders of the New Jersey AFL-CIO sided with the Newark Coordinating Committee in the Barringer dispute, angering Essex County trade unions and highlighting fractures within labor.[69]

A breakthrough finally occurred in mid-August when the building trades agreed to devise a response to the Coordinating Committee proposal if the NCC refrained from picketing.[70] Optimistic about this turn of events, civil rights groups began preparing young men to take advantage of the new opportunities they hoped would open up. While "picket lines, sit-ins, and boycotts had taken center stage in the civil rights drama," the *Newark Evening News* reported, "a great deal of less spectacular action has been going on behind the scenes."[71] The NAACP Youth Council descended upon public housing complexes and encouraged residents to fill out applications for construction jobs, while the Negro American Labor Council sought to link African American and Puerto Rican high school students—mostly men—to opportunities in the building trades.[72]

Persistent agitation had also compelled the city's private sector to respond to movement demands. The Newark Coordinating Committee had threatened to picket downtown businesses and establish a boycott if Newark businessmen refused to use their own power to encourage the construction trades to alter hiring practices. Although department store executives had refused to become publicly involved in the Barringer dispute, they privately consented to speak to union leaders and pressure Addonizio to stall construction until black workers were hired.[73] In exchange for calling off store protests, businessmen also agreed to participate with civil rights activists, such as Curvin, as well as with leaders of the Urban League and other social service agencies, in the Business and Industrial Coordinating Council (BICC) to open up more jobs across the city.[74] The work of CORE and, later, BICC paralleled similar efforts in other cities. In Philadelphia, for example, the 400 Ministers organization combined research and negotiation with direct action by intensively studying the hiring histories of local companies, making hiring demands in a series of meetings with employers, and following up with church-based boycotts if they refused.[75] By the fall of 1963, the BICC had placed a few dozen African Americans in jobs as department store buyers, porters, clerks, kitchen workers, and bank tellers.[76]

Newark's major white-collar businesses had multiple incentives for joining the BICC. First, the BICC conformed to the programmatic and ideological consensus that the federal government advanced to persuade the private sector that workplace integration could happen peacefully and profitably.[77] In this respect, the BICC resembled a more grassroots version of Plans for Progress. A corollary to the President's Committee on Equal Employment Opportunity, Plans for Progress commenced in 1962 by staging annual conferences at which corporations pledged to hire minority workers.[78] Some companies also found modest steps toward integration good for business. Curvin, who worked on over a dozen CORE-led efforts to persuade executives to hire more black workers, recalled that corporations proved more receptive than most unions to CORE's demands that they intensify recruiting in black schools and communities.[79]

Unlike construction unions, which sought to control labor supply, corporations—such as Bell Telephone and General Electric—benefited from relationships with civil rights organizations that would help them to access large pools of entry-level workers or to recruit college-educated math and engineering majors from historically black colleges.[80] Meanwhile, department stores conceded to some hiring demands to avoid embarrassing negative publicity that would turn away customers. But entrenched racial barriers remained: CORE activists found that increasing the numbers of black workers in entry-level positions proved easier than securing promotions for those already employed.[81]

In early September 1963, a few days after the historic March on Washington drew 250,000, the Newark Coordinating Committee reached a tentative—and ultimately fleeting—pact with the EBTC: the unions agreed to consider apprentices screened and referred by the city's Youth Career Development Center as well as skilled minority craftsmen vetted by the State Employment Service. Companies bidding on municipal contracts would now have to prove that all employees were hired through a nondiscriminatory process.[82] State officials promised to monitor the plan's implementation.[83] Measured against the demands issued at the start of the Barringer protest, the agreement lacked immediacy and specificity and resulted in only a few hires.[84] Numerous contingencies remained to prevent applicants from proceeding from the referral and screening stage to acceptance as an apprentice or journeyman, as unions in both cases refused to alter hiring policies to swiftly place African Americans and Puerto Ricans on jobs.[85] Buildings rose while agreements languished—the evolving Newark skyline serving as a symbol of minority workers' exclusion.

During the course of the Barringer protest, the Newark Coordinating Committee had reoriented the city's civil rights leadership and prepared an African American constituency divided by class, status, and ideology to make sustained collective demands on municipal and state officials in the years ahead. Yet the organization's prominence does not bolster a straightforward narrative of increasing radicalization among civil rights leaders. The NAACP's moderate membership continued to grow.[86] Rather than displacing established civil rights leaders, the Barringer protest unfolded in a way that seemed to codify the dynamic of the militant and the moderate: groups like the Newark Coordinating Committee and CORE served as weapons—threatening pickets, boycotts, and, some municipal officials feared, violence—if the demands of their moderate colleagues went unheeded. Their efforts during the Barringer protest resulted in few jobs and more often demonstrated—especially in the case of the construction trade unions—both the unwillingness and the inability of local officials to enforce New Jersey's employment laws. But the protest did shift the tenor of the local freedom movement in the years that followed: it clarified the limitations of the city's civic infrastructure in a way that reoriented some black activists toward black power strategies.

Confronting the "Three-Party Conspiracy"

In 1964 Edward Andrade and Rebecca Doggett, a young couple from neighboring Orange, New Jersey, who were active in civil rights and electoral politics, complained to Ernest "Big Train" Thompson about the limits of the Barringer agreement. A former organizer with the United Electrical, Radio, and Machine Workers of America and a National Negro Labor Council leader, Thompson had survived the McCarthy era to become a mentor to young African American activists, bridging the Old Left and black-power-in-the-making. Thompson urged younger activists to analyze the problem structurally, identifying what he called a "three-party conspiracy" among the contractors, their employers, and the unions that maintained status quo hiring policies.[87] The Newark Coordinating Committee could not win solely by confronting union leaders or the mayor, Thompson warned. It must also target contractors, those that hired them, and authorities at the state and local level that funded and regulated construction. Most importantly, Thompson urged activists to lay the foundations for such confrontations by engaging officials before taking to the streets.[88]

Between 1964 and 1966, the Coordinating Committee entered a new phase in its struggle against discrimination as activists' reach extended to state officials and their tactics grew more sophisticated. Under Thompson's guidance, the committee recast discrimination on the construction sites for Rutgers Law School and the Newark College of Engineering as a problem that concerned not only minority job seekers but also the broader taxpaying public. Edward Andrade wrote in 1964 that construction projects at Rutgers Law School and Newark College of Engineering "hold out for us the prospect of adding a new dimension to our arsenal": "the use of Negro and allied political power to smash job Jim Crow where the taxpayers' money is involved." The committee, Andrade wrote, would pressure the government agencies and university authorities to aggressively enforce antidiscrimination stipulations in their own contracts, "instead of initially attacking the unions and thus pitting white workers against Negro workers."[89] The committee looked beyond workers' competition for union slots and targeted the state's role in prohibiting discriminatory practices. It also began recruiting and preparing African American and Puerto Rican workers for the apprenticeship tests, a role in which state agencies and existing organizations had only dabbled.

Over the next two years, the committee pressured Louis Danzig, the director of the Newark Housing Authority and the city's domineering urban renewal strategist, to insist that contractors abide by antidiscrimination laws. The committee also sought support for the hiring of minority workers from both the Newark College of Engineering and Rutgers Law School. College of Engineering officials agreed only after the committee picketed, but the dean of Rutgers Law School, C. Willard Heckel, was enthusiastic.[90] Heckel called for contractors and unions to submit lists of minority workers before construction on the school began, and when they stalled, Heckel threatened to halt construction. The list they finally submitted to Heckel revealed that the only minority workers were unskilled laborers.[91] The unions and the contractors were attempting to use the mere presence of African Americans on the site to mask the reality of a two-tiered labor system.

Under pressure from Heckel and the Newark Coordinating Committee, several unions agreed to reexamine their apprenticeship criteria and to bring Puerto Rican and African American apprentices into the trades. Others, especially ironworkers and plumbers, resisted. The committee demanded that Heckel file a discrimination complaint with the New Jersey Division on Civil Rights and won a symbolic victory when they persuaded some of their critics, including Councilman Turner and the NAACP's Larrie Stalks, to join picketers at the construction sites on a brutally cold day in January 1965. The presence of Turner and Stalks, who less than two years earlier had denounced the Barringer demonstrators, illustrated how that protest had begun to reorder the city's civil rights leadership, bringing some of the very leaders who had previously criticized the committee into the streets.[92]

By winter 1965, Governor Richard Hughes, in the midst of a re-election campaign, had grown eager to resolve the construction crisis. Hughes had previously proposed that all involved simply air their complaints at a public hearing, but he now reluctantly agreed with Coordinating Committee and Heckel that the Rutgers State University system should file discrimination charges with the state's Division on Civil Rights. The committee deemed Hughes's support a "worthwhile step" and called off protests.[93] The group also attempted to exploit the subtle give-and-take with state officials in the service of more dramatic reform: the immediate hiring of black apprentices; new contract stipulations—enforceable by executive order—to permit parties to stop construction if hiring goals were not met; and a promise by the President's Committee on Equal Opportunity to ensure enforcement.[94]

Even with the threat of a lawsuit and pressure from Governor Hughes, the plumbers and ironworkers unions refused to budge. No black applicants passed their summer apprenticeship tests.[95] Activists responded with demands for standardized tests administered by third parties. They also recognized that given the inequality and de facto segregation of New Jersey's school system, many minority applicants lacked the educational advantages of the white majority.[96] Unions committed to integrating their membership, the Coordinating Committee argued, would have to eliminate questions that were irrelevant to job performance and revise admissions criteria. At the same time, the group called for immediate "training, preparation, and counseling" for minority applicants. Without this kind of support, committee activists wrote, "even where we win we lose." They thus began advocating for state-funded training centers in New Jersey's inner cities and the provision of remedial math courses, a significant departure from the group's prior strategy, which had revolved almost exclusively around direct action protest that called attention to discrimination.[97]

But by the fall of 1965, the Newark Coordinating Committee campaign began to unravel. State officials reneged on their promise to file formal complaints against segregated apprenticeship programs, and Charles Danzig, special counsel for the state, announced that he would no longer resort to an injunction to compel contractors to hire workers from nonunion sources. Instead, he would merely seek a public hearing on the matter.[98] To justify this retreat, Danzig offered evidence of exceedingly modest success—Plumbers Local 24 had at last hired a single African American apprentice, while the sheet metal workers planned to "screen" nonwhite applicants.[99]

The Coordinating Committee acknowledged that the Rutgers Law School and the College of Engineering campaigns had produced procedural improvements and small numerical increases at the bottom tier of the workforce. "Some of the lily-white unions have yielded to placing non-whites on the job and have adopted a fairer standard of test." But the unsatisfying outcome angered and dismayed them. The state's retreat, they argued, meant new buildings would rise while black and Puerto Rican workers waited for yet another airing of well-established injustice.[100]

The Rutgers Law School and College of Engineering campaign demonstrated once again that union leaders' and contractors' thwarting of antidiscrimination policies and commitment to local control over apprenticeship programs, along with state officials' tepid stabs at enforcement, would ensure that change would come slowly, if at all. Substantial transformation of the construction trades necessitated persistent action and political pressure.[101] But it would also require an expansion of the strategies activists had begun to develop: circumventing exclusionary union practices with their own parallel training programs and leveraging the influence held by multiple actors.

As Mayor Addonizio had predicted, Newark would become a laboratory, but not the type he had anticipated. Bayard Rustin's classic essay "From Protest to Politics" identified 1963 as a turning point in the civil rights movement. Images of police unleashing fire hoses and dogs on black youth in Birmingham, Alabama, seared televisions screens while Martin Luther King Jr.'s "Letter from a Birmingham Jail" exhorted moderates to abandon gradualism. Negotiations over jobs from Birmingham, to Philadelphia, to Newark struck at the heart of racial and class inequality and amplified a movement for which the term "civil rights" now seemed inadequate.[102] At stake in 1963 was the movement's transformation: "No longer were Negroes satisfied with integrating lunch counters," Rustin wrote. "They now sought advances in employment, housing, and school integration, police protection, and so on."[103] While many already knew that the struggle did not begin or end with the integration of public space, Rustin's essay posed trenchant questions about how the movement could continue. "I fail to see," he wrote, "how the movement can be victorious in the absence of radical programs for full employment, abolition of the slums, the reconstruction of our educational system, new definitions of work and leisure."[104]

In the mid-1960s the activists discussed in this chapter and the next posed similar questions about what was possible. Protest campaigns and new legislation yielded official acknowledgment of the problems— but to discouragingly little effect. Rustin argued that the aims of many black people "to enjoy the fruits of American society as it now exists . . . cannot *objectively* be satisfied within the framework of existing political and economic relations," therefore giving a revolutionary potential to the movement.[105] Various black organizations and their allies expressed this potential differently, but the individuals and organizations that emerged as fixers perceived less of an evolution from protest to politics than a strategic comingling. Protest combined with political intervention of all types to prime the city for change.

TWO

Restructure or Rebel?
Newark's War on Poverty

The War on Poverty linked unprecedented federal legislation to neighborhood activism in Newark, upending the
status quo but falling far short of its promise. Still, it set
in motion changes that manifested long after officials had
forfeited the war. Antipoverty programs offered a model
from which a range of activists would subsequently draw,
among them the fixers who confronted its contradictions
and unfulfilled potential. The passage of the Economic
Opportunity Act of 1964 ushered in early-education, job-
training, and recreation programs for Newark, but its most
contentious element—community action—promised a realignment of municipal politics to include poor people.[1]
Around the country, antipoverty activists seized upon
community action to expand representation and economic rights. Clashes among residents and officials at all
levels of government defined the programs' first few years,
and yet Newark briefly established one of the more independent experiments in community action. While short-
lived and limited, this accomplishment distinguished
Newark from cities where the War on Poverty was summarily folded into existing social services and political patronage.[2] But officials came to view Newark as a city where
"good things get carried too far." They blamed the antipoverty movement's participatory ethos—"too much poor
domination"—for fomenting the 1967 uprising.[3]

Newark's War on Poverty neither displaced existing institutions nor overran municipal authority, as its critics

feared and some of its supporters no doubt hoped. But it left a complex record worth exploring.[4] One supporter argued that it "energized a group of people who had not been energized before" and "taught people how courts work, how politicians act, how you can act if you stick together."[5] But others contended that the War on Poverty ultimately lacked the funding, longevity, or employment provisions required to succeed. Without a "multiplier effect," argued one administrator, poor people could not expand upon their gains to achieve economic self-sufficiency.[6] Others insisted it bred bureaucracy and dependence; one city official claimed that it "distorted democracy."[7] Anchored in newly formed community action groups, black and Puerto Rican Newarkers amplified political opposition to the white-dominated Democratic Party. They demanded policies authored by the people they would serve, attacked bureaucratic stalling, and rejected philanthropic paternalism. They tried to adapt antipoverty goals to a context in which economic and racial inequality could never be disentangled, and their experience illuminates the bifurcated landscape of activism that fixers encountered in the decades to come.

Federal Context, Local Complications

Lyndon Johnson launched the War on Poverty in 1964, the same year he misled Congress about the Gulf of Tonkin incident to prompt full-scale US intervention in Vietnam. Yet unlike the undeclared war in Vietnam, the War on Poverty, formally known as the Economic Opportunity Act of 1964, was avidly touted. Johnson's Great Society—a vast agenda of antipoverty and civil rights measures, coupled with Medicare and Medicaid, extended funding for public arts, more accessible student loans, and transportation and environmental initiatives— capitalized on early-1960s prosperity to make tangible the promises of John F. Kennedy's New Frontier. Johnson wanted to revive the New Deal ethos that had forged his expectations of what government could achieve and to outdo Franklin D. Roosevelt's legacy by routing poverty from the rural hollows of West Virginia to the cramped streets of Newark's Central Ward.[8] He signed the Equal Opportunity Act and the Civil Rights Act into law the summer before he won a landslide victory over Republican Barry Goldwater, aiming to solidify his Democratic constituency during what appeared to be a "high tide of liberalism." Yet the War on Poverty was subject to a range of objections before it even passed in 1964 and has generated fierce debates among scholars, activists, and policymakers ever since. The only point on which most agree is that the War on Poverty offers a stunning example of unintended consequences.[9]

In 1963 Johnson charged Walter H. Heller, chairman of the Council of Economic Advisers, with translating into a politically feasible agenda the growing public awareness of poverty stoked by exposés such as Michael Harrington's *The Other America* and John F. Kennedy's 1960 campaign tours.[10] Heller gathered policymakers from the Labor Department, the President's Committee on Juvenile Delinquency, and other agencies. Some emphasized employment, citing New Deal policies that served as Johnson's inspiration and Labor's recent emphasis on manpower for a coming decade of fiercer competition and displacement due to automation. Jobs for male breadwinners, argued Labor Department officials such as Secretary Willard Wirtz and Daniel Patrick Moynihan, offered the most effective solution to poverty. Yet leaders of the President's Committee on Juvenile Delinquency and Youth Crime—notably David Hackett and Richard Boone—embraced the novel social theories tested in a series of so-called demonstration projects funded by the federal government and the Ford Foundation. One of these was a Harlem-based youth program, Harlem Youth Opportunities Unlimited (HARYOU), which employed Cyril DeGrasse Tyson, future executive director of Newark's antipoverty agency. Hackett and Boone drew from antipoverty theory that emphasized "indigenous participation" to press for the direct incorporation of the poor into decision making, a policy that became known as *maximum feasible participation*.[11] Both factions knew that without some explicit overture to the poor, the War on Poverty was likely to end up in the hands of existing agencies and, in the South, to bypass African Americans altogether.[12] These convictions found their fullest—and most provocative—expression in the community action component of the War on Poverty.

Johnson appointed Sargent Shriver, the Kennedys' brother-in-law and the former director of the Peace Corps, to extract a cohesive policy out of the plans circulating among officials and to lead the new Office of Economic Opportunity (OEO). Shriver chose to blend jobs and community action. Johnson deemed job training necessary to reach the so-called "hard-core poor," of whom he said, "the sum total of their lives is losing."[13] Johnson also preferred job training to more expensive job creation programs.[14] He was desperate to take advantage of the impetus for reform following Kennedy's death—"always conscious that his days were numbered."[15] And yet Johnson recoiled from a major public works agenda, fearful of both its financial and its political risks.

Johnson's commitment to "guns and butter"—fighting the Cold War in Asia while building his Great Society at home—captured the optimism, even hubris, of midcentury liberalism.[16] But the military metaphor conveyed by the War on Poverty belied the confusion at its heart: it implied a full-scale effort to root out poverty even as prevailing Keynesian assumptions posited unemployment as a by-product of prosperity. Although 20 percent of the US population in 1964 fell below the recently established poverty line, the "equal opportunity" in the bill's title implied that persistent poverty was exceptional and avoidable. Beyond the internal contradictions, compromises among Democrats over the 1964 budget required Johnson to downscale his vision for the program from $11 billion to $1 billion.[17] Earnest calls to "war" could not compensate for the almost-miniature scale of a program he once hoped would rival the New Deal.

The substance and funding of the War on Poverty may not have measured up to its rhetorical promise, but that promise still energized many communities. "I truly believed in my heart and soul that that program was going to solve our problems," recalled social worker and former public housing tenant Mary Smith.[18] Though it did not bring jobs on the scale many residents anticipated, they seized what potential the legislation offered to devise a vigorous antipoverty agenda. Although community action had roots in earlier theories of poverty, it nonetheless emerged as the most novel element of the War on Poverty, one that promised to directly address the political marginalization of the poor.[19] But it was left to agencies and activists on the local level to convert this idea into action. Cyril DeGrasse Tyson, trained in social work and sociology, was one among the many who took up this task in New York City. By the time Newark leaders hired him to direct their own community action agency, Tyson's career had intersected at key moments with the very demonstration projects that became precedents for the War on Poverty and foreshadowed the challenges awaiting Tyson in Newark.

From Harlem to Newark

Tyson had overseen contentious attempts to integrate education and housing while employed by the New York Commission on Human Rights and the City Housing Authority during the 1950s. In 1963 he began working for HARYOU with noted psychologist Kenneth Clark, whose research with Mamie Phipps Clark on the negative impact of segregation on children's self-image in the 1940s and 1950s was incorporated into *Brown v. Board of Education of Topeka*.[20] Clark hired Tyson to coauthor a study commissioned by the President's Committee on Juvenile Delinquency and Youth Crime, *Youth in the Ghetto: A Study of the Consequences of Powerlessness and a Blueprint for Change*.[21] Clark and Tyson, both African American, had grown up in Harlem and shared a commitment to addressing the poverty from which they had escaped.[22] Tyson's experience with HARYOU further embedded him in the milieu of academics, activists, policymakers, and public administrators energized by the civil rights movement and eager to test new theories.

HARYOU's youth-focused agenda reflected the research of Columbia University sociologist Lloyd Ohlin and his student Richard Cloward and the "opportunity theory" of delinquency. Ohlin and Cloward rejected the assumption that delinquency sprang from adolescents' individual psychological pathology. Instead, they posited delinquency as a social and adaptive behavior enacted by adolescents in neighborhoods starved of legitimate employment or political incorporation.[23] Adolescents would eschew delinquent acts, they argued, if provided with better schooling, employment, and self-determination.[24] Back in Washington, President Kennedy's Committee on Juvenile Delinquency and Youth Crime expressed keen interest in such scholarship. The committee collaborated with the Ford Foundation, the Russell Sage Foundation, the Housing, Education, and Welfare Department, and a host of New York City–based agencies to test Ohlin and Cloward's theory by "affiliating the unaffiliated" in a demonstration project.[25] HARYOU, founded in 1962, was among these initiatives, connecting scholarship on juvenile delinquency and poverty with the civil rights movement.[26]

Harlem Youth Report depicted HARYOU's evolution in comic-book form, the intimate urgency of word bubbles and cartoons contrasting with the bureaucratic brainstorming they narrate. The illustrated Tyson is pictured at a conference table, surrounded by HARYOU coworkers and teenagers. Conditions in the ghetto are an affliction, Tyson warns. "We're not talking about treating a few symptoms," he says, "nor about helping people merely to survive in the sickness, but about the creation of health. Our weapon will be Harlem's most valuable resource—its young people. If they succeed, the result will not just be a Negro Revolution, the result will be an American Renaissance."[27] This shift from "revolution" to "renaissance" encapsulated Tyson's perspective on integration as well as his goal of pursuing radical change in the condition of Harlem's poor youth while working largely within reform-minded institutions. To Tyson, the achievement of black economic power was fundamental to this struggle and would require a substantial—even revolutionary—reordering of the status quo. Yet his allusion to a "renaissance" suggested that this struggle was not separate from but integral to the nation's health.

Initially, HARYOU and demonstrations such as the Mobilization for Youth on the Lower East Side of New York elicited cautious admiration from the President's Committee on Juvenile Delinquency and Youth Crime. But they had their detractors.[28] Clark was unable to steer an independent course from the formidable Representative Adam Clayton Powell, who insisted on folding HARYOU into his own youth group—Associated Community Teams (ACT).[29] The short-lived HARYOU-ACT was dogged by patronage accusations. Some claimed it crossed the boundary from youth empowerment to criminality by inadvertently encouraging young men to take part in the 1964 revolt that erupted after police killed an unarmed Harlem teen.[30] Similar claims would shadow the War on Poverty in Newark—and other cities—after the long, hot summer uprisings of the mid-1960s. Clark had resigned before that, in 1963, and Tyson soon followed. When Tyson accepted the job of directing Newark's antipoverty program, he approached his charge with both enthusiasm and trepidation.[31]

Launching Newark's War on Poverty

Newark's War on Poverty originated in the work of neighborhood activists and the political calculations of city leaders responding to New Jersey's entrenched poverty. By the 1960s the Garden State was one of the country's wealthiest, embodying the contradiction of "poverty in the midst of prosperity."[32] Even amid its affluent, sprawling suburbs, one could find the isolated communities of poor people sociologist Michael Harrington famously called the "other America." In 1959 New Jersey's overall poverty rate was around 12 percent, nearly half the US total of 22 percent, but this number did not reflect the state's regional and racial disparities. Black workers' unemployment rates were starkly higher than the national average. The State Division of Welfare in New Jersey found the typical discretionary income earned by African Americans in Newark "one of the lowest outside of the Deep South" and estimated that 45 percent of Newark's black population was poor.[33] Narratives of the War on Poverty frequently speak of policymakers' "rediscovery" of poverty, but poverty had not been forgotten by Newark's poor, its civil rights activists, or the leftists and liberals who had long called for full employment policies.[34] Newark was not a site of the demonstration projects that became models for the War on Poverty, but it already had elements of a vigorous antipoverty movement when the federal decrees came down.

Civic leaders had long pressured Mayor Hugh J. Addonizio to address poverty, but the promise of federal funding galvanized him. In the summer of 1964, Addonizio charged a dozen mostly middle-class and elite Newark civic leaders—the director of the board of education, a vice president of Prudential Insurance Company, officials at the welfare federation, municipal administrators, academics, and members of President Johnson's Anti-Poverty Task Force—with devising a local war on poverty. President Johnson's task force members assured Addonizio that Newark would be eligible for $500,000 of federal antipoverty funds, prompting the mayor and city council president Ralph Villani to launch a new organization, the United Community Corporation (UCC), with $15,000 from the city and matching contributions from the Welfare Federation of Newark and the superintendent of schools. The UCC emerged from these meetings with two provisional leaders selected in part to showcase the administration's support for interracial collaboration: C. Willard Heckel was white, a dean of Rutgers Law School, and an advocate of civil rights; Timothy Still was African American, a lifelong resident of Newark, a Democratic Party activist, and an employee of the Ballantine Brewery. At Still's suggestion the UCC hired Tyson.[35] By offering targeted employment programs and highlighting black leadership, Addonizio hoped to secure reelection support from the near majority black population without alienating white voters.[36] The initial UCC—some sixty people in all—was divided between black and white members, with only three Puerto Ricans.[37] The racial and occupational identity of the UCC's leaders and the pedestrian details of Tyson's employment merit attention because they became points of contention in later battles between the UCC and the city council. Similar disputes simmered across the country as public officials, administrators, and residents questioned who would truly benefit from federal antipoverty funds and who could claim to represent the poor.

On the Frontline of Newark's War on Poverty

Newark's city council initially celebrated the independence of its new antipoverty program, and indeed the UCC did appear to enjoy more autonomy than its peers. Atlanta politicians administered "a top-down antipoverty program that brooked no interference from the poor."[38] Meanwhile, the Chicago Committee on Urban Opportunity ensured that "community action, as OEO envisioned it, was absent in Chicago."[39] Chicago's powerful mayor Richard Daley perceived "loyalty to the Democratic machine, patronage jobs, and eventually political clout" as the proven route to economic and political inclusion of African Americans, as it had been for white immigrants.[40] Daley's Democratic machine absorbed antipoverty programs into an existing calculus of patronage that rewarded white and black power brokers but preserved de facto segregation.[41] In contrast, Newark's program initially seemed more open to influence from below. Yet the city council's professed enthusiasm for UCC independence belied discomfort with community action that soon became clear. Newark's council may have understood that maximum feasible participation required inclusion of marginalized people in the War on Poverty. But as Daniel Patrick Moynihan noted of municipal officials across the country, "it was taken as a matter beneath notice that such programs would be dominated by the local political structure."[42]

Many Newarkers threw themselves into the creation of new programs. The Newark Preschool Council, a group led by poor and working-class parents, mostly women, created the city's Head Start program. The Preschool Council held classes in churches, housing projects, and community centers, a departure from the practice in most cities, in which Head Start operated through public schools or traditional social service agencies.[43] Newark's Head Start also persuaded the OEO to include hundreds of families who lived in impoverished neighborhoods but whose incomes slightly exceeded the federal poverty level on which Head Start was based.[44] Newark's growing Puerto Rican community also took an unprecedented role in crafting War on Poverty policies, particularly the Spanish-language component of the Preschool Council. "[F]or the first time we were significantly consulted and listened to," wrote members of the Council of Puerto Rican Organizations.[45]

While the Preschool Council loomed large among the early successes of Newark's War on Poverty, the UCC also oversaw the development of remedial education and employment programs for hundreds of high school students, some of which placed young African Americans and Puerto Ricans in skilled, semiskilled, and white-collar jobs. In the shadow of such citywide programs were smaller initiatives. One group of women on welfare organized their own grocery cooperative with support from the UCC, pooling their money to buy in bulk.[46]

Yet even as these programs won the admiration of federal officials, Tyson pursued the organization of local area boards in eight neighborhoods across the city. The area board concept required residents to collaborate in proposing and voting on poverty programs in their own neighborhoods and to choose representatives for the UCC board.[47] While Tyson believed this was the surest route to achieving maximum feasible participation, it also proved to be the most contentious phase of community action, one that jeopardized support for the broader War on Poverty.

"Do You Want the Stigma of Being Povertized?": Fighting for Area Boards

The UCC provided each area board with a budget, small staff, and review of its constitution and financial statements. But Tyson and the UCC's trustees encouraged residents to devise their own approach to maximum feasible participation and choose a name that reflected it. "[I]t is bad form to include the word 'poverty' in the title, even with 'anti' before it," administrators were warned. "A more positive word, such as 'opportunity' is less likely to offend the poor."[48] This advice would soon seem dated, as poor people proudly claimed their identity in the wake of Martin Luther King Jr.'s Poor People's Campaign of 1968 and the rejection of poverty's stigma by the welfare rights movement. But in 1964 Newark groups hewed close to these suggestions with names like "People's Action Group," "People in Progress," and "Progress in Action." Such names implied that antipoverty work necessitated both democratic deliberation by the "people" and political empowerment in the form of "action." Names such as "Project: Concern," "Operation We Care," "Operation Ironbound," and "Mutual Concern" depicted organizations steeped in mutual aid and neighborly compassion. And the distinct reactions of residents in the Clinton Hill, Weequahic, and Vailsburg neighborhoods to the area boards reflected the city's spatial inequality. Some harnessed the area board to advance more radical ends, while others resisted the concept altogether, arguing that it threatened the middle-class status of their neighborhoods while failing to help the poor.

Board 3—People's Action Group—was established in Clinton Hill, a neighborhood shifting from majority white to majority black, home to a mix of middle- and working-class homeowners and a growing number of poor renters. People's Action Group encompassed a fractious assortment of civil rights activists, reform-minded residents, and new leftists. Among its members were nationally prominent and locally notorious members of Students for a Democratic Society (SDS), including Tom Hayden, Phil Hutchings, and Carol Glassman.[49] Stanley Winters, a history professor at New Jersey Institute of Technology and dedicated, if acerbic, leader of the Clinton Hill Neighborhood Council, had originally invited the SDS to Newark at the urging of Stanley Aronowitz, a fellow Clinton Hill resident and emerging New Left leader. The SDS accepted the invitation in the hope of making Newark a satellite in the network of Economic Research Action Project (ERAPs).[50]

The ERAPs constituted what the SDS hoped would be its own War on Poverty and a northern variation on the Mississippi Democratic Freedom Party. Many ERAP participants brought to Clinton Hill experience in the southern civil rights movement; they believed its next phase should be an interracial movement for economic justice.[51] The young adults of ERAP committed themselves to living among and organizing the poor.[52] Many in ERAP were skeptical of Johnson's War on Poverty. They preferred the kind of full employment policies advocated by unions, such as the United Auto Workers, which had supported SDS at its founding. Nonetheless, ERAP perceived area boards and neighborhood organizations as tools for unifying the poor and extending its participatory ethos to the people most in need of representation.[53] When Mayor Addonizio began predicting that "divisive elements" could undermine Newark's War on Poverty, he usually meant members of SDS and the Student Nonviolent Coordinating Committee.[54] Although neither group achieved the influence in Newark that its enemies later claimed, Addonizio certainly had reason to be concerned. As activists predicted, community action did become a means of registering new voters to challenge entrenched Democratic machines, much the way the Mississippi Freedom Democratic Party had organized a parallel institution to challenge white rule.[55]

In early 1964 ERAP had barely arrived in Newark before its members alienated some of the Clinton Hill Neighborhood Council leaders who had invited them. Winters and the other neighborhood council members were no civic novices. They had already confronted slumlords and launched a lawsuit to resist city plans to demolish part of their neighborhood for urban renewal.[56] ERAP's commitment to militant direct action and efforts to redirect the Clinton Hill Neighborhood Council's strategies struck some in the council as "dogmatic," arrogant, and counterproductive, according to Winters.[57] But others, including one of the neighborhood council's founding black leaders, Bessie Smith, decided to join with SDS to create a new organization called the Newark Community Union Project. SDS members soon deemphasized their initial focus on full employment in favor of organizing poor tenants around immediate problems: rent gouging, housing-code violations, welfare conflicts, police brutality, and the need for children's recreation programs.

When the newly formed Newark Community Union Project then joined Area Board 3, People's Action Group, "they translated their agenda into a strict interpretation of maximum feasible participation."[58] Early area board planning meetings across the city often concerned income eligibility and whether or not to include homeowners and middle-class residents with an interest in antipoverty programs. Operation We Care (Area Board 2), for example, "mandated that its board include thirty-five residents of housing projects, and that the majority of the board members must identify themselves as poor."[59] In the case of People's Action Group (Area Board 3), Tyson had casually recommended that slightly over half of the group's membership should be tenants earning less than $4,000 annually. When the Newark Community Union Project members advocated for this structure, however, another faction within People's Action Group rejected it on the grounds that representative democracy should trump a strictly income-based interpretation. But the rejection of income requirements disguised an equation of democratic participation with middle-class status. "[P]oor people don't participate much anyway," they predicted, "and middle-class people will be the ones who show up mostly."[60] People's Action Group ultimately defined poverty as "earning $4,000 or less annually for a family of 4, being unskilled, being unemployed, being on welfare or public assistance, living in substandard housing, or living in an area that has been declared blighted."[61] A close vote determined that poor residents would occupy all the positions on the group's governing board.[62]

Residents may have hotly debated membership criteria for People's Action Group and Operation We Care, but they concurred on the value of area boards. But in Vailsburg's Area Board 8 and Weequahic's Area Board 9 (Weequahic Center) the maximum feasible participation of residents who opposed any involvement in the War on Poverty prevailed. Located on the city's periphery, both neighborhoods identified themselves as middle and working class. Residents' wariness about recognizing the poverty in their midst easily merged with city councilmen's open hostility to derail area board formation.

White residents, primarily Italian Americans, maintained a shaky dominance in Vailsburg, a suburban settlement annexed by Newark in 1905. They passed a unanimous resolution in late fall of 1965 rejecting the UCC's advances, insisting that "we are not poverty stricken and do not warrant being so labeled."[63] Councilman Frank Addonizio (distantly related to Mayor Addonizio—I will hereafter refer to each by his title to avoid confusion) took credit for Vailsburg's unified opposition. His constituents had been on the brink of approving an area board before he warned them that participation in antipoverty efforts could drive down property values.[64]

Councilman Lee Bernstein's antipathy to the UCC extended to his neighborhood of Weequahic, where response to the proposed area board—the "Weequahic Center"—was just as contentious as in Vailsburg. Weequahic, the childhood home of novelist Philip Roth, was the center of Newark's still sizable but rapidly shrinking Jewish community and the location of some of the city's most attractive homes and best public schools. Customers of the local Berkeley Savings and Loan branch threatened to close accounts after the bank provided space to the UCC for meetings, prompting the bank to renege on the offer. A meeting that finally occurred at an alternate location entailed "two hours of rough-and-tumble debate" before residents voted in favor of the area board by 56 to 35.[65] Despite this victory, wrangling continued at a raucous meeting the following month: "Do you want the stigma of being povertized?" demanded Councilman Bernstein. He urged the UCC to reallocate resources intended for Area Board 8 to the more impoverished Central Ward. William Payne, a UCC member active in civil rights and one of a small group of black candidates to run for city council in the early 1960s, countered Bernstein. "I can show you poverty less than a block away," he said, probably referring to the several hundred families living in public housing nearby, "and we have a chance to put the best program in the country to work."[66]

Councilmen Addonizio's and Bernstein's actions demonstrate in microcosm how the strategies white municipal officials employed to retain their control over federal antipoverty programs cultivated white urban Democrats' growing disaffection from the War on Poverty. Though resident opposition was expressed in putatively altruistic terms—spend the money on the truly poor, not us—it elicited a churning cocktail of white fears about racially mixed neighborhoods, poverty, and property values. Councilmen rarely spoke in explicitly racialized language, yet they encouraged white constituents to equate area boards with slums, slums with the influx of black residents into formerly white neighborhoods, and all of it with plummeting hous-

ing values. Their claims about area boards portending decline generated fear among middle-class homeowners precisely because of the
city's experience with blockbusting and urban renewal.[67] Residents of
these neighborhoods were no doubt familiar with the recent history
of Clinton Hill, for example, which had seen a deterioration of housing stock and city services after Newark officials declared it blighted.
The composition of Newark's neighborhoods had been shifting for
years as black residents moved out of the Central Ward while white
residents left the city altogether. Meanwhile, displacement caused by
urban renewal had also pushed poor families into neighborhoods that
conceived of themselves as solidly middle class. Bernstein riled such
constituents by depicting community action as a virus that would in-
fect property values.

Given the UCC's limited budget, Weequahic's and Vailsburg's antipathy to area boards, and Councilmen Bernstein's and Addonizio's
attempts to undermine the program, why did the UCC persist in trying to organize in these neighborhoods? In fact, Tyson, Heckel, and
Payne debated this very question at UCC meetings even while they
publicly encouraged the establishment of area boards. Executive board
members remained committed to the universal strategy because they
believed maximum feasible participation demanded representation of
poor people who lived in middle-class neighborhoods. Tyson suspected
that the UCC's opponents would have accused the organization of bias
or political maneuvering if it had not made sincere efforts to establish
area boards in every neighborhood.[68]

Tyson correctly anticipated that the War on Poverty's opponents
would continue to treat the UCC with suspicion. White northern officials may have recognized the electoral value of their black constituents, but they did not want to empower them to run for office or take
over municipal agencies themselves. Officials in both regions "were
uniquely threatened by a seemingly government-sponsored effort to
politicize the black masses of the Northern cities and Southern coun-
tryside," Moynihan observed.[69] Years after these local battles, Bernstein
himself frankly confirmed Moynihan's early assessment: "They were
going around trying to incite the black people to change things, to do
things, to upset the city, and mainly upset me as the South Ward Councilman."[70] Indeed, Bernstein's formulation—the "they" refers to antipoverty officials and activists—resembled southern officials' blindness
to the discord in their own communities and their claims that civil
rights protests were the result of "outside agitators" inciting otherwise-
contented black residents to revolt.[71]

Three-Ring Investigation of the United Community Corporation

Before the UCC's first anniversary, local opposition to community action combined with state and federal apprehension about the implementation of the War on Poverty to produce three investigations of the organization. First, Representative Adam Clayton Powell of New York, chair of the House Education and Labor Committee, called for a reevaluation of the War on Poverty in April 1965, arguing that it failed to cultivate maximum feasible participation of poor people, engaging instead in "giant fiestas of political patronage."[72] Republicans in the New Jersey State Senate launched a second investigation the same month that focused on patronage and complaints that ranged from excessive salaries allegedly paid to antipoverty administrators to the sluggish pace of implementation.[73] In August, Newark councilmen Addonizio, Bernstein, and Michael Bontempo launched a third investigation, by far the most aggressive. They scrutinized not only hiring, accountability, and the efficacy of antipoverty programs but what they deemed the "autocratic" nature of Tyson's leadership and the UCC board's hostility to municipal leaders. They even challenged the very constitutionality of the UCC under New Jersey state law.[74]

The leaders of these three investigations held barely disguised political interests: Powell was a powerful advocate of civil rights, a stalwart representative of his Harlem district, and an early champion of the Equal Opportunity Act. Powell argued that the legislation insufficiently equipped local community action programs to confront municipal machines and genuinely represent the poor. Yet in Harlem, Powell acted like other local officials, staffing agencies with loyalists while strong-arming dissenters. His decision to wrest leadership of HARYOU-ACT from Kenneth Clark derailed the organization. The HARYOU-ACT fracas, combined with allegations of corruption, prompted suspicions that Powell had taken advantage of the House of Representatives' investigative powers before he himself became a target.[75]

The New Jersey investigation, led by state senator Nelson Stamler, a Republican from Union, unfolded alongside the reelection campaign of Democratic governor Richard J. Hughes. OEO employees speculated that Stamler's investigation was designed "to possibly produce . . . ammunition" for the Republican campaign against Hughes. Stamler, a potential gubernatorial candidate, may have sought evidence that Hughes overlooked excessive patronage, exorbitant salaries, and waste in his enthusiasm for the War on Poverty.[76]

While the state investigation trafficked in claims that the War on Poverty was wasteful, its impact on the UCC was fleeting. In contrast, Powell's investigation contributed to the subsequent retreat from community action and reassertion of municipal control. And the attack of city council members Addonizio, Bernstein, and Bontempo proved most immediately damaging to the fledgling UCC, advancing misconceptions about the War on Poverty that would fuel a federal backlash.

The unconventional structure of the War on Poverty invited scrutiny. Maximum feasible participation necessitated critical distance from municipal social service departments and traditional charities, yet community action programs were also expected to work alongside existing agencies. Municipal officials unsurprisingly perceived community action as a disruptive usurpation of their managerial powers, a threatening "new bureaucracy." Community action administrators, they argued, sought "political power financed with federal funds which can stir up house against house and neighbor against neighbor."[77]

Allegations that War on Poverty administrators earned excessive salaries figured into all three investigations. The New Jersey State Senate investigated claims that antipoverty officials were paid more than bureaucrats at similar levels in other branches of the government. Tyson, whose $23,000 salary approached Mayor Addonizio's, was predictably a target of such inquiries. Nick Kostopulos, an OEO administrator, defended these salaries, which he said tended to be slightly lower than those of comparable public employees. Nonetheless, Kostopulos warned that the salaries of OEO employees would continue to be subject to public scrutiny. Early phases of the investigation also revealed councilmen's opposition to the hiring of nonresidents by the UCC and featured the testimony of rejected Newark job seekers.[78] As a New York resident and the public face of the UCC, Tyson served as a target for the complaints on this front. Newark residents justifiably expected that the city's antipoverty program would draw primarily from the city's unemployed workforce.[79] When contrasted to the poverty of community action participants and the high rates of unemployment in Newark, high salaries earned by out-of-town workers could delegitimize the entire program.[80]

Investigators' anxiety about salaries also figured into their apprehension over future municipal obligations to fund the War on Poverty. The Equal Opportunity Act called on the federal government to provide 95 percent of antipoverty agencies' funding for their first two years, after which the federal share would decline to 50 percent and cities would assume greater funding responsibilities. Mayor Addonizio feared the day when Newark would be burdened by half the cost of sprawling antipoverty programs on which its citizens had come to rely and around which the UCC had organized an insistent constituency.[81]

Convinced they would be compelled to fund an unmanageable program indefinitely, the city council's investigative committee questioned the very constitutionality of the UCC. Although Mayor Addonizio himself had overseen the UCC's founding, councilmen claimed that the UCC was a "private entity," ineligible to receive municipal funds under a statute of the New Jersey State Constitution, even if these funds were required by the OEO to release the majority of the UCC's budget.[82] The UCC's lawyer, Norman N. Schiff, refuted the council's argument, citing a 1932 case in which the New Jersey Supreme Court had rejected a similar claim lodged against a municipal redevelopment agency. Since the mayor had incorporated the UCC to coordinate federal antipoverty efforts, Schiff argued, it "made the private organization an instrument of government" and therefore compliant with state law.[83] In this way, the UCC resembled most community action agencies founded with support from city officials and civil rights groups.[84] Although many of the council's claims about the UCC's questionable legal status appeared exaggerated, if not outright manufactured, they did raise questions about the legal and fiscal obligations of municipal governments to nonprofit groups that would become more pressing in the coming decades as social services and governmental functions were subcontracted or privatized.[85]

The report the council released in December 1965 incorporated all the allegations levied against the UCC but considered none of the counterevidence the agency had offered in its defense. The UCC's "luxury loving, gimmick-minded bureaucracy" would bring "house against house," warned the report, blaming the antipoverty agency for much of the controversy city officials themselves had cultivated.[86] Councilmen offered little concrete evidence of their claims against the UCC, focusing instead on how the UCC's understanding of poverty had diverged from what they perceived as the spirit of the Equal Opportunity Act.[87] Drawing on a quotation from show business entrepreneur Mike Todd—"Being broke is a temporary situation. Being poor is a state of mind"—the councilmen argued that "[p]overty, despite its grim reality, in this sense is an abstraction. It is an idea, which must be overcome with a more powerful idea. This is the idea of self—above and beyond poverty. It begins by the restructuring of the self image through education, training, and accomplishment."[88] The report exploited the ambiguity of the language used by federal antipoverty warriors to translate maximum feasible participation into an emphasis on self-esteem. It noted accurately that Newark's antipoverty program was distinguished from others in the country by its independence from city hall. But they exaggerated the UCC's independence by tracing its origins to a "well-intentioned" group of citizens and expunging Mayor Addonizio's decisive role in launching the organization.[89] They argued that neither the mayor nor the city council had retained sufficient oversight of the funding and administration of the agency. As a result, the UCC had focused on "healthy salaries and material goods, organizational procedures, and political action" instead of the plight of the poor.[90] The authors predicted that the UCC would soon compete for resources with the city's other agencies and impede the progress of urban renewal.[91] "The continuation of such a situation is unthinkable," the report's authors asserted, recommending that the city council assume control of Newark's antipoverty program.[92] These recommendations were released amid the UCC's fraught attempts to establish area boards in Vailsburg and Weequahic and around the same time that the *Newark Evening News* published a critical series on the War on Poverty's first year in New Jersey. Public complaints in the newspaper echoed many of the report's conclusions.[93] The report and the series together amplified the council's perspective and lent credence to the sense that the War on Poverty was in headlong crisis less than two years into its existence.

The report also came at a grim moment for advocates of maximum feasible participation. Just that fall, the OEO had praised Tyson's leadership and favorably cited the Newark Preschool Council and Blazer Youth Council for making New Jersey a leader among states in implementing the War on Poverty. Federal officials also singled out for praise the UCC's emphasis on area board creation, calling it "a model of a large city program."[94] Yet there were indications of growing federal ambivalence about community action. In late October, the OEO canceled a press conference to highlight Newark's successes. More significantly, a dispute brewing between the Bureau of the Budget—an office of the White House—and the OEO seemed to boost the position of the UCC's local critics, who believed that maximum feasible participation usurped power rightly belonging to municipal agencies and their professional staffs. The *New York Times* reported on a memo allegedly issued by the Bureau of the Budget insisting that Shriver diminish OEO's mandate for maximum feasible participation, what he had once called "the prime offensive weapon in the war on poverty."[95] Such reports startled antipoverty workers, who had received the opposite message from federal officials.[96] The Regional Office of Economic Opportunity, for example, still appeared to define maximum feasible participation as direct inclusion of the poor in community action agencies. According to advice circulated to area groups: "There is still some controversy about whether this means an actual poor person or a person from an impoverished area. . . . I recommend an actual poor person. . . . [H]e may be shy or he may speak poorly, or he may have off-beat ideas. But he is a true representative and as long as he sits on the board, the problem of poverty will be personal and real to the other members. With him there, it will be impossible to do what well-meaning middle-class people often tend to do—work from their second and third-hand ideas of poverty."[97] But even while such advice circulated, the federal Bureau of the Budget's director, Charles Schultze, insisted that "we ought not be in the business of organizing the poor politically."[98] In the face of mounting discontent from Democratic mayors, Schultze counseled Johnson to retreat from community action.

Although Johnson privately agreed with Schultze, he was angered when the Budget Bureau memo became public, enraging Shriver and prompting unfavorable press. Schultze insisted the memo reflected internal discussion, not official policy, but according to historian Robert Dallak, by 1966 "it was an open secret that the President's commitment to Great Society–War on Poverty programs had waned."[99] Johnson was convinced that community action was endangering broader support for the Great Society and that Shriver had grown too ambitious, transforming the OEO into a launching pad for the presidential aspirations of his brother-in-law, Robert Kennedy. Johnson quietly set in motion plans to devolve OEO functions to other agencies.[100] Meanwhile, Chicago mayor Richard Daley unequivocally denounced maximum feasible participation as divisive.[101] Within a week of the release of the city council investigation of the UCC and a month after the Bureau of the Budget fracas, Shriver spoke at the Conference of Mayors, hosted by Daley. Amid protests by antipoverty groups who called for more representation of the poor, Shriver endorsed Chicago's version of community action, called the Committee for Urban Opportunity and operated under Daley's strict oversight, as a model for the country.[102]

Rabbi Jonathan Prinz, a leader of the UCC, argued in a letter to the *New York Times* that attacks on community action represented a "throwback to a well-meaning but archaic concept of social service," one that "long labored under the idea that intelligence and responsibility are the possessions only of the middle and upper classes."[103] Local antipoverty agencies defended maximum feasible participation more emphatically than the OEO itself. With such inconsistency from federal policymakers, antipoverty workers had no stable mandate upon which to stake their own claims to maximum feasible participation.

In early 1966 Adam Clayton Powell singled out the UCC in his critique of community action. Powell's criticism shocked UCC board members Hilda Hidalgo and George Richardson. Hidalgo, a respected leader of Newark's Puerto Rican community, and Richardson, a civil rights activist and former member of Addonizio's administration, appealed to Powell for support when the city council first launched its investigation. They had hoped that Powell, an outspoken advocate for the poor and a steadfast critic of racism, would see that beyond the objections of the council's white majority to the UCC lay a commitment to torpedoing any program that would empower African Americans and Puerto Ricans. After all, Bernstein himself claimed that "there's a group of—what do you call it—idealists and enemies of the administration that's running the thing now. They're setting up a political party, a party run by the political 'outs.'"[104] But when Powell addressed a session of the House Education and Labor Committee attended by Councilmen Addonizio and Bernstein, he called Newark's antipoverty program "so politically pure that it had antagonized all of the city councilmen and ignored the mayor." Newark and Chicago, Powell said, occupied two ends of the spectrum: "Somewhere between Chicago's maximum participation of the politicians and Newark's maximum feasible participation of the poor," Powell explained, "is an administrative middle ground which should be established."[105] Community action programs amounted to a diversion from the goal of ending poverty, he argued. He called instead for a "reorientation" of the War on Poverty toward job training and integrating the poor into the "current booming economy."[106] Powell was not so different from other officials who consistently diverted residents' claims to power into job training and preparation. When civil rights activists called for construction jobs at Barringer High School, officials demurred by recommending more training and recruitment at the high school level. When antipoverty activists sought—and sometimes wielded—real influence over War on Poverty programs, officials similarly tried to defer political conflict over these gains by emphasizing training over participation. "Training" served as a euphemism for a future when full-time employment and full-fledged citizenship would be achieved without cost.

Shriver's bow to Daley and Powell's retreat dismayed the UCC's leaders, but they received an unexpected show of support from Councilman Irvine Turner. Turner, who had fallen ill during the investigation, questioned the conclusions of the city council investigative committee—of which he was a member—in a surprising "minority report" issued about a week later. Turner claimed to have neither read nor approved Bernstein and Addonizio's report, while Bernstein and Addonizio claimed that Turner was too ill to have authored or even approved his own report. Turner urged other city council members to support the UCC. Mayor Addonizio remained curiously silent; perhaps he feared the council's aggressive campaign to rein in maximum feasible participation would undermine his goal of shoring up votes in the 1966 election.[107]

The strongest defense of the UCC naturally came from the organization itself. The UCC's Dean Heckel rejected the council's report as erroneous and incomplete. He countered the report's suggestion that the War on Poverty was the project of private citizens under no public oversight. "The attempt by the city council Committee to make it appear that some Newark citizens happen to get together," he noted, "belies the fact Mayor Hugh J. Addonizio convened a meeting on August 10, 1964 of both public and private officials and caused the United Community Corporation to be created."[108] Heckel unequivocally rejected the committee's claim that funding UCC programs exposed the city to unprecedented liabilities and violated the state constitution, pointing to the twenty other community action agencies operating in New Jersey without issue. He denied that Tyson exerted "autocratic" control over the UCC, asserting that trustees, task force members, and area board leaders all participated in hiring, policy, and programming decisions. Despite the consistent criticism the council had directed at Tyson, Heckel noted, they had not called him or the UCC staff to testify, only job applicants who had not been hired by the UCC.[109] Nor had council members ever attended UCC meetings, even though they later claimed to have been shut out of decision making.[110]

How were ordinary Newarkers to make sense of the accusations traded between the UCC and its critics? To be sure, the UCC, like many early community action programs, was overambitious in its goals, sometimes haphazard in its administration, and contentious in its deliberations. In some ways, its process echoed the Johnson administration's fevered attempt to secure passage of as much Great Society legislation as possible before Johnson's political capital expired. "Every day that I am in my office I lose part of my power," he warned his aides in 1965. "I want you to sleep with those Congressmen if you have to. I want you to get that legislation through now! While I still have the Power!"[111] Tyson and other administrators urgently sought to establish as many antipoverty programs as possible, knowing that political support and funding for community action were unpredictable. Still, even some supporters of the UCC complained that this strategy left little time to assess programs' viability.[112]

The slow pace of area board creation frustrated Tyson and puzzled some Newarkers, but Tyson's record compared well with those of community action directors in other cities, even as he weathered three investigations that impeded progress.[113] On the urgent question of antipoverty jobs for local residents, the OEO's regular evaluations contradict the council's claim that the UCC systematically overlooked Newark residents or permitted Tyson to seize sole power.[114] Given his occasionally technocratic bent, Tyson had a high tolerance for the tedious nature of local democracy. He was prepared for the competing demands made of the UCC and the sparring over federal resources but was nonplussed when area board members occasionally picketed his office, alleging the UCC had neglected their concerns. Tyson insisted that the UCC's success required harmonious relations with Newark's municipal government, although mounting evidence suggested the opposite would prevail. Tyson proceeded cautiously, yet even if he had rebutted his critics more forcefully, the UCC's initial board—still packed with Addonizio loyalists—would no doubt have constrained him. Tyson held back from more vigorous confrontation with city council opponents because of his conviction that the virtues of community action would be evident to all upon its proper implementation. The poor of Newark's Central Ward, the middle-class residents of Weequahic and Vailsburg, and the Addonizio administration, Tyson insisted, would benefit from the exemplary War on Poverty programs the UCC had established. Recounting one of his arguments with Bessie Smith and Tom Hayden of the Newark Community Union Project over the goals of community action programs, Tyson remembered arguing for "institutional restructuring efforts rather than rebellion as the major focal thrust" of community action.[115] But even as he insisted that community action was consonant with democratic processes and improved access to social services, Tyson occasionally seemed to ignore the truly disruptive political implications perceived by both conservatives and radicals.

Some of these implications played out after the council investigation when the UCC closed ranks against city officials during an election of new members to the board of trustees. The UCC had planned to nearly double the board during its general membership election to bring dozens more people into leadership roles. Mayor Addonizio proposed that the UCC reserve about half of the new positions for municipal officials. Heckel, Tyson, and most of UCC's leadership endorsed Mayor Addonizio's plan, but the membership soundly rejected it. Laura Hayes, a member of Area Board 2 who had moved to Newark from North Carolina with her sharecropping family, denied that the middle-class politicians now vying for board seats understood the poor. "The only thing we need the politicians for is to stand in back of us," she said, "to make sure we got the funds we need."[116] Others appeared to share Hayes's position: at a meeting attended by over five hundred, the UCC membership voted to add more area board representatives to the group's board of trustees but to limit the city council's representation to six slots.[117]

Mayor Addonizio decried the vote but said it should prove "once and for all that City Hall politicians are not controlling the UCC, as so often has been charged." Councilmen Bernstein and Addonizio blamed the defeat on the out-of-town radicals associated with SDS and People's Action Group. Defenders of the UCC, such as Reverend Kim Jefferson, director of the Greater Newark Council of Churches and a UCC board member, attributed the defeat to the city council's own single-minded focus on the investigation of the UCC's accomplishments.[118] Tyson resigned in 1966, but his rigorous analysis of the War on Poverty's failures serves as a blueprint for the kind of work fixers would attempt in the decades that followed. Tyson interpreted the defeat of the mayor's membership proposal as a rejection of the UCC's leadership, not Addonizio. Members questioned why the board did not more vigorously defend the UCC against its council critics, especially when the OEO had publicly praised the UCC as one of the country's most accomplished community action programs. Instead, the leadership appeared to welcome more involvement from the very council critics whose investigation Heckel had called "purely imaginary and without substance."[119] UCC members, he argued, perceived that Tyson, Heckel, Still, and the rest of the organization's executive leadership had betrayed the UCC by compromising with municipal officials.[120]

While the membership momentarily stymied its council opponents, the UCC continued to spar with the city council. By 1968 the council had contributed only $28,000 to the UCC's budget—a fraction of the contributions made by other municipal governments to their community action agencies. This compelled the UCC to make cuts or compensate with private contributions.[121] Meanwhile, criticism of antipoverty programs as wildly radical and unaccountable persisted and justified the turn against maximum feasible participation. By the late 1960s municipal officials and state legislators blamed community action for the "long, hot summers" of civil unrest in US cities, including the uprising in Newark. Congress responded with the 1967 Green Amendment, which, according to Leila Meier Rice, spelled the "beginning of the end for community action."[122] The Green Amendment permitted cities to take control of antipoverty programs, ensuring that community action agencies reserved no more than one-third of their seats for representatives of the poor and divided the rest among municipal officials and representatives of business and civic groups.

Community action was barely established before the tide of federal policy turned decisively against it, but even so, the UCC persevered. The state's report on the causes of the 1967 Newark uprising prepared by the Governor's Select Commission on Civil Disorder (Lilley Commission) perceived the UCC as a stabilizing force in the city. The authors acknowledged the organization's "mixed record." They deemed the UCC's early emphasis on community action rather than housing and employment as misguided, and they found the organization's structure to be chaotic. But they also saw value in the UCC's early work and argued that it constituted an important phase of the organization's growth. "[I]t would be a mistake to over-react in favor of administrative efficiency at the cost of community involvement," the commission warned, exhorting federal, state, and local officials to rally behind the embattled UCC.[123]

The Lilley Commission also noted the UCC's overlooked accomplishment: jobs. By 1968 UCC-affiliated programs employed about one thousand people and provided job training for around a third of the city's unemployed.[124] The Legal Services program funded through the War on Poverty had helped devise new rent control policies, while the Preschool Council was led largely by parents from the surrounding communities and employed residents as aides in the district.[125] Edna R. Thompson worked her way up from an entry-level position at the UCC, eventually attending New York University. "I didn't know what I could do," she recalled, "until I went to that school and came back prepared." Another worker recalled with great pride having his name removed from the welfare rolls when he was hired by the UCC. Such accounts suggest their life-changing significance for those who were hired.[126]

Even so, the War on Poverty did not create jobs on a scale that matched unemployment in Newark. President Johnson and other policymakers opposed an explicit jobs program to boost substantial numbers of people into the working classes and hoped that, once trained, the unemployed would be absorbed into a robust economy.

In addition to criticizing the inadequate number of jobs produced by the War on Poverty, activists and scholars have also dissected its impact on class stratification. Steven Gregory argued that the antipoverty program increased the mobility of a small professional and semiprofessional class, which ultimately divided black communities and diminished the pursuit of common goals.[127] Others deemed the War on Poverty an intraclass transfer of wealth among the existing ranks of middle-class social service professionals.[128] Welfare rights activist Johnnie Tillmon forcefully questioned whether the millions spent on programs that created jobs for the already employed would alter the fundamental inequality the War on Poverty purported to address: "When all this poverty money is spent, the rich man is going to be richer and I'm still going to be receiving a welfare check."[129] Tillmon's observation speaks pointedly to the ways the poor were lost amid the very policies that purported to elevate them: during the city council's investigation, for example, it appeared that poor residents were only one marginal party in the debates over community action. The most heated and significant disputes of the War on Poverty's early years raged between municipal officials and the middle-class reformers, social service professionals, and working-class civic leaders who led the UCC.

Other critics pointed to the low turnout in area board elections to argue that the War on Poverty failed to empower the poor according to its own mandate.[130] While the Lilley Commission had praised the UCC, commissioners also conceded that "only a few area boards have been able to involve significant numbers of community people who were not previously active in community affairs."[131] Yet residents recalled that community action precipitated a distinct, if not universal, shift in civic life. Veterans of Newark's War on Poverty held intensive meetings that reenergized longtime neighborhood activists and drew newcomers—"housewives dragging their kids to meetings"—into dialogues that could last "to one, two in the morning."[132] Despite—or perhaps because of—bitter conflicts in city hall among the UCC, municipal officials, and residents, a survey conducted in 1967 found that a vast majority of Newark residents expressed familiarity with and approval of the UCC's role in the city.[133]

Municipal critics of the War on Poverty appeared to base their opposition on rickety evidence, deliberate misinterpretation, and stereotypes about the poor. But they accurately perceived that maximum feasible participation could upend the leadership and privileges they enjoyed. Antipoverty programs set out to explicitly confront the inequities of class, race, and representation in the day-to-day distribution of social services. As Annelise Orleck writes, "in an era when the language of civil and citizenship rights was on everyone's tongue and when a sitting U.S. president insisted that poor people deserved a slice of the pie, unintended consequences were inevitable."[134] The $12 million in federal antipoverty funds that came to Newark in the UCC's first few years underwrote organizations that became increasingly critical of the Addonizio administration. The issues at stake in area board deliberations lived on in electoral challenges, demands for the democratization of urban planning, and opposition to the displacement of poor and working-class Newarkers by urban renewal.

Antipoverty activism and civil rights shaped the electoral campaigns that black candidates waged in the mid-1960s by fostering black voters' growing influence and mobilizing them around increasingly ambitious goals. The War on Poverty, Robert Curvin argued, "gave the black community political resources, skills, and a degree of independence that would have been impossible without it."[135] In 1964 Donald Payne, who later served multiple terms as a US congressman from New Jersey's Tenth Congressional District, won a county committee seat running as a "New Breed Democrat."[136] The next year, a coalition of "dissident blacks, Puerto Ricans, and 'civil rights–oriented whites'"—many of whom developed their political visions in the city's more controversial community action programs—launched the United Freedom Party ticket. They drafted several other black candidates to run for offices, including former state assemblyman George Richardson—who had been involved in both the Newark Coordinating Committee and the UCC.[137] Richardson had broken with the Democratic establishment several years earlier, partly over Mayor Addonizio's failure to address job discrimination and police abuse. In 1966 Kenneth Gibson, then a civil engineer, first ran for mayor and received sufficient support to force a runoff election. Although the United Freedom Party ticket and Gibson were both defeated, these campaigns publicized frustration with slum housing, policing, and poor city services and portended more formidable challenges to come.[138]

In the years before the 1967 uprising, opposition to urban renewal also coalesced around residents' attempt to halt the construction of the New Jersey College of Medicine and Dentistry. Some Newark area boards joined the opposition, eroding the fragile coherence of the UCC's leadership. Tyson's replacement, a former Urban League director from Westchester, New York, named William Wolfe, objected to the area boards' plans to protest urban renewal, a decision that divided the UCC membership. Area board representatives—mostly black and poor or working class—believed maximum feasible participation should encompass protest against displacement and regarded the reassurances of Newark's municipal officials with suspicion. Heckel and the other moderate white and black trustees, many of whom were middle-class professionals, regarded the opposition to urban renewal warily and reluctantly advised compromise. In May 1967 the area board faction prevailed in a vote to suspend Wolfe and several other UCC trustees for interfering with their plans to organize against the medical school. Several other UCC trustees—including President Heckel—resigned in protest.[139] Community action may have lost federal support, but it remained viable—and volatile—locally, as area boards pursued their own versions of maximum feasible participation.

The War on Poverty may have contributed to Newark's political upheaval in the late 1960s, but it also fostered more subtle yet equally significant changes. Kent B. Germany's study of the War on Poverty in New Orleans emphasized its role in expanding "the soft state," a "public/private governing apparatus . . . dependent on soft money from grants, soft power from private and nonprofit organizations."[140] Andrew Morris has argued in a similar vein that the War on Poverty spurred "interpenetration of the nonprofit and the public sector" in ways that diminished the primacy of government agencies established in the decades after the New Deal.[141] Rather than posit a cohesive liberal welfare state diminished solely by a conservative backlash that accelerated after the 1960s, these scholars suggest that the public-private partnerships that became a hallmark of conservative and neoliberal platforms in the late twentieth century emerged during the "high tide" of liberalism itself. Morris calls the War on Poverty "a step in the fundamental reordering of the social service sector, . . . not the democratization that poverty planners had hoped; rather, it was the increasingly blurred line between public and private social provision."[142] The political theorist Barbara Cruikshank draws on Foucauldian concepts of governmentality to argue that community action made empowerment of the poor and the transformation of their individual subjectivity a goal policymakers and grassroots organizations could share. She disputes the concept of empowerment as an "unquestionably noble or radical political strategy" and suggests instead that the War on Poverty bequeathed a political legacy in which "relations of empowerment are simultaneously voluntary and coercive."[143]

Newark's fixers, chronicled in the second part of this book, responded to the spread of the "soft state." Their disillusionment with some aspects of the War on Poverty prompted some to pursue alternative means of addressing poverty.[144] They continued to seek out new federal urban and antipoverty programs, to be sure, but they also demonstrated deeply held commitments to local autonomy, as well as ambivalence about the efficacy of government policies. Such sentiments would be mobilized—and contained within—the spread of the soft state. But if the War on Poverty marked a new stage in the formulation of the soft state, it was nonetheless the "hard state" of police repression and displacement by urban renewal that black Newarkers confronted in 1967, and it is to that struggle that we now turn.

THREE

"Case City Number One": Urban Renewal and the Newark Uprising

In spring 1959 major Newark employers underwrote a conference convened by the American Committee to Improve Our Neighborhoods Inc. (ACTION Inc.). National business leaders had founded ACTION Inc. to guide and profit from federal urban renewal legislation, the scope of which had been expanded by the Housing Act of 1954. They wanted to showcase to the nation the benefits of urban redevelopment in Newark.[1] Mayor Leo Carlin told the assembled he pined for the days of his childhood when the wealthy and solidly middle class called Newark home. Now overwhelmed by "the malignant cancer of slum and blight," Newark required "the surgery of redevelopment, the most valuable tool in the entire kit of Urban Renewal."[2] H. Bruce Palmer, the president of Mutual Benefit Life Insurance Company, concurred: "Newark could be considered Case City Number One with respect to urban renewal problems and the application of existing tools toward their solution." With several years of rapid change behind them, Carlin, Palmer, and other city leaders were eager to show off to an appreciative audience.[3] ACTION Inc.'s president, James E. Lash, commended the city's progress from what he called "one of the worst situations that could possibly exist."[4] According to ACTION Inc., Newark was on the cusp of victory over blight.

Yet in the eight years that followed, urban renewal sharpened Newark's political and economic disparity. On the eve of the 1967 uprising, many black residents—especially those in the Central Ward—had not experienced urban renewal as the careful application of planning "tools." Instead they had witnessed the elimination of neighborhoods and the flattening of civic dissent in pursuit of a vision of progress that excluded them. Residential neighborhoods deteriorated under the shadows of new buildings, giving credence to the charge of Stanley Winters, a Newark civic leader and historian, that urban renewal boosterism "depended upon the myth of a city sedate, happy, and beautiful."[5] Such serenity eluded leaders as residents plotted against their plans with growing force.

In 1966 Newark city officials undertook their largest and most controversial urban renewal project yet: the construction of the New Jersey College of Medicine and Dentistry (commonly referred to at the time as the Medical College, now formally known as the University of Medicine and Dentistry of New Jersey). In June 1967 the Central Ward residents threatened by this undertaking assailed city officials—to no avail—at public hearings that lasted late into the night. The Housing Act of 1954 had made the airing of citizens' grievances a legally required phase of the urban renewal process, but that did not deter the city from pursuing a plan that would displace thousands.

To characterize what happened next in Newark as an uprising—rather than a riot or civil disturbance—is to name it as a political act. It is to conceive of the "long, hot summers" as collective responses to strikingly similar conditions around the country. It does not require proof of coordination by radicals or agent provocateurs, as some claimed, to perceive that the uprisings drew on shared grievances. In Newark, as in other cities, physical violence by police sparked the revolt. The protesters who threw bricks that night were not responding directly to urban renewal policy; they were "not sitting around talking about the medical school fight," emphasized one activist. "They were mad because the cops did what they did and they were generally mad for the same reasons people are mad today, because they're at the bottom of the well, looking up, all the time."[6] But it was the accumulated effects of urban renewal policies that helped maintain that deep well.

Urban renewal constituted a form of institutional violence that extended beyond law enforcement. Urban renewal came to encompass decrepit housing, lack of representation in municipal agencies, employment discrimination, the sidelining of resident opposition, all factors that furnished an explosive context for the Newark uprising. The negotiations over the Medical College that followed the uprising were consequently about more than a hospital. They unfolded alongside a quickening mobilization of black political power, and they raised larger questions about who would shape redevelopment policies, whose interests such policies would serve, and whether or not residents' own expertise would count.

The events of the uprising themselves are crucial, but my focus extends to the aftermath, when activists, residents, business leaders, and government officials disputed the meaning of what had happened. Among the outcomes of this contest over meaning was a fixer ethos that channeled the sense of urgency created by the uprising.[7] Urban historians have offered a rich context for understanding the long, hot summers, yet those uprisings remain, in many accounts of the 1960s, the confirmation of epic decline, rendering an urban future unimaginable for those who could leave the cities and escalating the crisis for those who remained.[8] But examining the Newark uprising through the Medical College reveals how the uprising acted as a claim—however inchoate—to a different kind of future. What sort? Many individuals and organizations demanded answers to this question; fixers sought them by seizing political leverage and wresting concrete gains in the uprising's wake.

In late 1967 and early 1968 a remarkable series of negotiations over the construction of the Medical College took place. The uprising lent momentum to the coalition opposing its construction, and they used this clout, combined with strategies drawn from the civil rights and emerging black power movements, to advance a new social contract. The agreement they won required the participation of citizen groups and private nonprofits in employment, housing, and clinical care in a way reminiscent of the War on Poverty's community action programs. But while it promised unprecedented grassroots intervention in the top-down politics of Newark's urban renewal, the agreement's implementation was fraught with backtracking and contention. The fixer ethos emerged as activists mixed the "protest" of public hearings and the "politics" of citizens' negotiating committees and advisory boards.[9]

The "New Newark" and the Costs of Urban Renewal

Despite ACTION Inc.'s optimistic predictions about Newark in 1959, city leaders were still deeply worried about their future. Commercial stretches of the Central Ward remained vacant, mired in what one report called a "private depression."[10] The city's tax rate—already the state's highest—was expected to rise, as were taxes in surrounding Essex County suburbs.[11] Mayor Carlin, a "good government" reformer, responded earnestly but unimaginatively, following the path of cities such as Philadelphia and Pittsburgh. Carlin appointed eighteen of the city's most prominent finance, corporate, and labor leaders to the newly formed Newark Economic Development Committee to cultivate private-sector support for efforts to retain major companies.[12]

If Carlin could not build a sufficient foundation for renewed growth, his administration nonetheless retained some important Newark employers. Mutual Benefit Life Insurance Company had considered joining the suburban exodus but stayed and in 1954 built a new skyscraper. Prudential Insurance Company signaled its commitment to Newark by replacing its 1892 headquarters with enormous office towers. The Port Authority poured money into Port Newark, while a massive modernization of the city schools began.[13]

It was not enough. At the ACTION Inc. conference, Mayor Carlin noted that public and tax-exempt institutions made up 65 percent of the city. The remaining 35 percent, he said, was located in the Central Ward, "consumed by slum and blight." With the help of federal funds and the city's business leaders—whom an ACTION Inc. leader described as "on-call consultants"—Carlin aimed to "restore purchasing power to our downtown areas" and the Central Ward to its "highest and best use."[14] Carlin's "New Newark," was one of many similar campaigns hatched in cities around the country. The passage of the 1949 Housing Act gave municipal housing agencies the right of "eminent domain," empowering them to condemn slum neighborhoods, compel residents to leave, and apply federal subsidies to demolish their homes and erect new housing.[15] For contemporary readers, the term "urban renewal" may conjure images of dystopian city landscapes: neighborhoods divided by impenetrable networks of expressways, interminably long and lonely city blocks, enormous parking lots crowned with isolated, hulking housing projects. Such images correspond to the potent critique of urban renewal mounted since the 1960s by community activists and some scholars, now reflected in the broad consensus that urban renewal projects often failed on their own terms.[16] But that obscures the allure urban renewal held for leaders of the 1950s. Urban renewal initially embodied a vigorous corporate liberalism: downtowns would be rebuilt and housing for the poor and working class improved, two goals unlikely to be met without massive public and private investment. Meanwhile, contractors would profit and municipal officials would shore up constituent loyalty.

This vision appealed not only to those who perceived poor and working-class neighborhoods as an obstacle to prosperity but also to those who conceived of themselves as advocates for these communities—some of whom had grown up in the very neighborhoods whose demolition they later supported. Recognizing the attraction and ubiquity of urban renewal requires an understanding of the many other postwar problems—suburban growth and central-city decline, poverty, and racial segregation—that urban renewal advocates claimed they could ameliorate. But as Newarkers discovered, urban renewal ultimately compounded the problems its proponents promised to solve.[17]

Urban renewal came to Newark's largely Italian American First Ward in 1952. The city planned to raze about fifteen blocks of two- and three-story tenements and replace them with a combination of publicly and privately funded high-rises.[18] The plan received some support from the community. The *Italian Tribune* argued that the dynamism of Little Italy's shopping district, with its specialty grocery stores, belied the reality of poor housing in the First Ward. "Many homes have no bathtubs, hot water, or toilets. The houses are old and to a large extent are firetraps."[19] But over four thousand First Ward residents stood to lose their homes, and some fought back by founding the Save Our Homes Council. They had few allies among the city's Italian American leadership: Congressman Pete Rodino, who had grown up in the First Ward, supported the plan, as did Father Gaetano Ruggiero of Saint Lucy's Catholic Church, the First Ward's "spiritual axis." Mayor Carlin's predecessor, Mayor Ralph Villani, had blustered, "May God strike me dead if I want to harm anyone. Nobody will be thrown out into the streets. Some day you people will build a monument to me for what I'm trying to do for this city."[20]

Down came the brick tenements; up went the Columbus Homes, designated for low-income tenants, and the Colonnade, a middle-class development designed by Bauhaus architect Mies van der Rohe. Many First Ward Italian Americans left, neither poor enough to meet the income requirements for the Columbus Homes nor sufficiently well-off for the Colonnade. Others found the high-rise apartments incompatible with the Italian American "way of life," according to Rose Marie Giannetta, a former resident. Monsignor Joseph Grenato of Saint Lucy's Church elaborated: elderly First Ward residents had cherished "their cellars, their backyard, their vines with grapes [to make] their own wine."[21] Two photographs of saints' feasts, taken twenty years apart, reveal the transformation urban renewal had wrought. At a 1939 procession for the Feast of Saint Gerard, a crowd assembled in narrow streets beneath a system of ropes and pulleys rigged to fire escapes. Children dressed as angels swung from the ropes, tossing down flower petals and whispering prayers. A photograph of the Feast taken twenty years later depicts parishioners standing in what appears to be a sprawling parking lot. Behind them looms a nearly featureless segment of the Columbus Homes, completely filling the frame.[22]

Some residents would later argue that they had been compensated for poor physical amenities by the sense of their neighborhood as an extended family. Romanticization colored their recollections as well: there was no acknowledgment of the racism that later became explicit in white residents' complaints about integrated housing and the reconfiguration of the city's racial boundaries.[23] And yet in other regards, accounts of the First Ward in the early 1950s point to an almost-textbook definition of healthy civil society—thriving small businesses, countless political, civic, and leisure associations—all of it drawn together by Saint Lucy's.[24] Leaders such as Father Gaetano Ruggiero and Representative Pete Rodino, both with deep affection for the First Ward and a clear stake in its survival, nonetheless supported plans to raze it. Ruggiero would come to regret urban renewal, but his early influence helped to diffuse strong opposition.[25] By 1963 the city had over a dozen projects in progress, encompassing 2,500 acres on which lived 50,000 people, about 12 percent of Newark's population. Most of the projects were clustered in a ragged rectangle of residential and commercial blocks in the city's center, surrounded by major roadways that carried travelers through and around the city. Routes 1 and 9 bordered this area to the far east, Central Avenue to the north, and Hawthorne Avenue to the south. The western border included several smaller streets—Osborne Terrace, Bergen Street, and Wilsey Street. A few examples illuminate the scope of the city's vision. Around Howard Street—inspiration for the best-selling eponymous novel of crime and poverty published by Nathan Heard in 1968—the city planned to demolish over 85 percent of existing housing. The Newark Colleges expansion project, meanwhile, would provide facilities for the Newark College of Engineering and Saint Michael's Hospital—but no housing. The Saint Benedict's project called for the elimination of all residential acreage in favor of institutional and commercial use. While seven of the projects included plans for either new or replacement housing, the proposals indicate a net loss of nearly four thousand units.[26]

The immense cityscape slated for urban renewal was the result of shrewd work by Louis Danzig, the formidable director of the Newark Housing Authority (NHA), and his team of housing experts, who had avidly pursued funding for slum clearance. The NHA had an admirable reputation for building public housing, but Danzig lamented legal restrictions that he believed encouraged rebuilding slums with a modern veneer.[27] Why, for example, replace the tenements of the First Ward solely with public housing while middle-class residents left for the suburbs, taking their assets with them? He aspired to enact the urban renewal philosophy percolating in cities like New York and Boston—huge, multineighborhood, multiuse projects. Like Mayor Carlin, Danzig wanted to maintain the middle class; he disparaged block-by-block replacement, aiming instead to "tear down the entire ghetto and build 'a city within a city.'"[28]

Such ambitions necessitated both federal funds and developer investment. Danzig had to work within "the tightly confined box" of the legislation. Its strictures and the realities of the market limited Danzig to a more piecemeal undertaking. Private developers, he found, doubted they would profit from building more affluent housing abutting the so-called slums.[29] The FHA refused to approve mortgages for plans that focused exclusively on neighborhoods rated poorly by the Home Owners' Loan Corporation. Danzig could not combine urban renewal funds for clearance with FHA loans to private builders unless he targeted neighborhoods that the Home Owners' Loan Corporation deemed "blighted" but not yet "slums."[30] Clinton Hill, an interracial neighborhood of homeowners and renters squeezed between wealthier and poorer neighborhoods, fit the bill. Yet to secure private financing, Danzig had to open these areas to the kind of large-scale development—typically requiring eminent domain—that would guarantee timely repayment of FHA loans and profits for private investors. The city collaborated with Danzig's plan, declaring Clinton Hill "blighted" in 1961 and slating seventy-four blocks for clearance.[31]

A neighborhood of mostly single-family homes, Clinton Hill had long included a mix of working- and middle-class residents: tenants and homeowners, whites and blacks, Protestants, Jews, and Catholics. In the decade before the 1958 blight declaration, the proportion of the neighborhood's white residents declined from 92 to 56 percent.[32] By the late 1960s Clinton Hill was distinguished by its high rate of black homeownership. Dr. Nathan Wright Jr., a leader in Newark's Episcopal Diocese and a co-organizer of the city's first National Conference on Black Power, saw Clinton Hill as model for anchoring black neighborhoods: "The Clinton Hills of our cities provide us with the opportunity . . . to help save ourselves from headlong self-destruction. Black people should own homes, not rent them." Yet he argued that such opportunities had been lost because of FHA policies and the federal government's reluctance to subsidize urban black homeownership as it had for suburban-bound whites.[33] In fact, Clinton Hill was also the destination to which the NHA had relocated many poor renters as they prepared vast swaths of the Central Ward for demolition.[34] Some Clinton Hill landlords responded to this heightened demand by charging exorbitant rents for dilapidated quarters. The Mayor's Commission on Group Relations determined that black and Puerto Rican newcomers to Clinton Hill paid higher rents than white tenants although they tended to earn lower incomes.[35] The quality of municipal services declined, while the NHA's lax enforcement of housing codes relieved owners of responsibility for repairing their properties, making blight a "self-fulfilling prophesy."[36]

Some Clinton Hill residents set out to bridge widening divisions of race and class and preserve their neighborhood. In 1956 they formed the interracial Clinton Hill Neighborhood Council and sought to unite disparate residents around "a program of self-discipline and self-help," writes David Gerwin.[37] The council appealed the 1961 designation of blight as far as the New Jersey Supreme Court.[38] While the group lost, their suit portended the broader opposition that would form in the late 1960s when officials pursued the largest urban renewal project in Newark history.

The Contested Origins of the New Jersey College of Medicine and Dentistry

"The city has bitten off more than it can chew," Mayor Hugh Addonizio warned upon surveying the breadth of the city's urban renewal plans for the 1960s.[39] But the determination of the more powerful and politically skilled Danzig overwhelmed Addonizio's fleeting admission of doubt.[40] In 1966 Addonizio offered the state 150 acres of municipal land for the construction of the Medical College. It would be the crowning achievement of the city's revival, Addonizio insisted: a first-rate medical training facility that would deliver a steady stream of federal and state funding. He claimed it would also provide urgently needed medical care to Newark's poor, who were primarily served by Martland Hospital, known in the black community as the "Butcherhouse."[41] For years, employees, patients, and some officials had complained about conditions that resembled those of a nineteenth-century hospital. In 1965, for instance, an outbreak of diarrhea killed eighteen infants—four in one day alone. Meanwhile, only a few miles away, New Jersey's suburbanites benefited from some of the country's highest-rated medical facilities.[42]

So it was no surprise when 76 percent of Newark residents surveyed by the United Community Corporation initially expressed support for the Medical College. A sizable minority approved even if they were forced to move. But many Central Ward residents—including those who had been relocated to the area in preparation for earlier urban renewal projects—were not so enthusiastic. Opposition grew as new details about the project emerged.[43] Even if there was support for a new hospital, some questioned why the plans had not been subject to any public debate. The plans depicted an insular research facility, not a superior replacement for the "Butcherhouse."[44] How would it benefit everyday people? Not many jobs seemed forthcoming, given how few black doctors the city employed and the ongoing exclusion of black and Puerto Rican workers from the city's construction trades.[45]

These Central Ward residents were not alone; many municipalities now confronted citizen demands for more participation and transparency in the selection of urban renewal sites.[46] To comply with the 1954 Housing Act, local authorities had to prove they included residents in urban renewal planning. Newark officials attempted to satisfy this requirement with a planning board made up of nine mayoral appointees. But the board's record of having never opposed a municipal proposal confirmed what residents suspected: such overtures were often little more than a chimera.[47]

Meanwhile, downtown institutions, including the Greater Newark Chamber of Commerce, Rutgers University, and a group called Citizens Committee in Support of the Medical College in Newark, lined up behind Addonizio—further evidence for critics who saw the Medical College as a campaign to oust the poor and working class.[48] Addonizio responded with boilerplate boosterism that came to represent to many Central Ward residents the arrogant and even punitive nature of municipal leadership.[49] Louise Epperson, who described herself as "the one who started all the crying and belly whining about the Medical College coming to Newark," recalled "what a shock it was to open the papers . . . and read that my home and many of my neighbors' homes were being taken away."[50] Officials' plans, Epperson testified, had already had dangerous effects. In anticipation of the city's seizure of Central Ward land, absentee landlords had sold their houses or re-fused to repair them, and insurers had refused to take payments from homeowners. "Hammering can be heard every night," Epperson said. Scavengers ransacked abandoned homes in search of pipes and other parts for salvage. The number of house fires climbed.[51]

Epperson joined with other residents to form yet another coalition, broader than previous attempts. It included Epperson's own Commit-tee against Negro and Puerto Rican Removal as well as the Newark Area Planning Association, Congress of Racial Equality (CORE), Student Nonviolent Coordinating Committee, and the state NAACP. Their ef-forts amplified opposition, but they won no concessions. Residents' anger mounted, and even some officials who supported the Medical College argued that the mayor had erred by failing to address their discontent.[52]

To Addonizio, grassroots opposition appeared at first as a minor an-noyance. A more critical conflict brewed between the city and Medi-cal College officials over how much land the Medical College truly necessitated. Talks had spun out of the administration's control, with Medical College representatives lauding the virtues of an alternative suburban location. Initially, when the Medical College site selection committee had considered Newark, city officials offered them a plot of about 30 acres already slated for urban renewal. This fell short of the 150 acres the site selection committee desired. They appeared to lean instead toward a much larger tract in suburban Madison, New Jersey. State officials pressured the Medical College to reconsider Newark. The Addonizio administration exceeded the committee's expectations by offering a 185-acre plot that included land already cleared for urban renewal. Medical College officials finally committed; then they refused to start building until the city razed yet another plot across the street. City officials were furious. "This, to us," complained one city official, "is insanity." Nonetheless, the Addonizio administration pursued the blight declaration necessary to clear the land.[53] The Medical College appeared determined to extract a premium; and Addonizio was willing to secure the facility whatever the cost. On the eve of the uprising, a massive land grab was under way.

Uprising

On the evening of July 12, 1967, two white policemen, John DeSimone and Vito Pontrelli, pulled over a black cab driver named John Smith for passing their double-parked car. "I thought you were working and I just made a normal pass," Smith recalled telling DeSimone. He had a fare in the car; he also had a suspended license and sensed DeSimone was "trying to play games" with him. After DeSimone told Smith he was under arrest, Smith forcefully pushed his door toward DeSimone. Pontrelli rushed to his partner's side and the two cursed as they dragged Smith to their car. "Stop beating him!" DeSimone recalled witnesses yelling.[54] Once in the cruiser, DeSimone subdued Smith with repeated blows, including one to the groin that left Smith unable to walk when they arrived at Fourth Precinct Station House. Inside, other officers joined the beating.[55]

The assault of a black man by white policemen was hardly uncommon in Newark. Civil rights activists in CORE and other groups had attempted since the early 1960s to organize a community review board to scrutinize police brutality.[56] Newark had been the recipient of federal funds to improve relations between police and the city's black communities, but little had changed.[57] The city council defeated a review board proposal, and the director of the Newark Commission on Human Rights (formerly the Mayor's Commission on Group Relations) resigned in protest.[58] In the months prior to Smith's arrest, police had shot Lester Long Jr., an unarmed black youth, during a traffic stop. The memory of Long's recent killing was fresh in many minds when news of Smith's beating spread across the city.[59]

Some witnesses had seen Smith dragged—seemingly unconscious—from the car and believed he was dead. Residents gathered around the precinct house. Esta Williams, a tenant activist, reminded those assembled that precinct officers had beaten others. Civil rights leaders persuaded officers to let them see Smith, whom they found "in great agony and pain."[60] At their insistence, Smith was taken to the hospital. Some favored immediate confrontation with police; others thought they should protest at city hall the next morning. As Amiri Baraka would later note, the tenor of debate was unlike "the lighter kinds of demonstrations" he had attended near the same precinct. "It was like the air itself was a container for something that was pushing against it trying to break out. People turned and looked at each other, sensing this presence. They grinned nervously or squinted up at the precinct at the mostly white police who stood outside frozen or the ones who would occasionally scowl through the windows."[61] A photo from that first evening shows CORE's Robert Curvin in a white T-shirt, one hand in the air, the other grasping the bullhorn police briefly permitted him to use. The camera's flash captures the sweat on the faces of police and residents in the hottest stretch of summer. Some in the crowd pay rapt attention to Curvin, others look away; one even smiles. Amid a group of mostly young men stands a small girl with short pigtails, waiting to see what would happen.[62]

Someone threw a Molotov cocktail at the precinct wall. Civil rights leaders argued with police to allow them more time to channel the crowd toward a focused protest, but their tenuous hold was unraveling. Rocks thrown from nearby buildings began to fall on the precinct and the people beside it. Some in the crowd retreated; others armed themselves with bottles and bricks. Police surged forth. A night of intermittent clashes in the surrounding streets and housing projects began.[63]

The next morning, officials minimized the clash as "an isolated incident." Addonizio suspended DeSimone and Pontrelli, appointed an independent panel to investigate Smith's arrest, and brought Smith's case to the FBI.[64] Nathan Wright Jr. recalled "an air of expectancy, but not of anger," as he drove near the precinct on Thursday evening, July 13, witnessing "clusters of thirty to fifty people, mostly men," on the corners of major intersections.[65] But Addonizio's strategy floundered. He dispatched James Threatt of the Commission on Human Rights to the Fourth Precinct to inform protesters that a black police lieutenant, Edward Williams, would be promoted to captain within days—if the crowd dispersed. Authorities perceived the promise as a major concession; protesters perceived it as worthy of rocks, bottles, and debris. "The authorities had been indifferent to the community's demand for justice," Tom Hayden would recall. "Now the community was going to be indifferent to the authorities' demand for order."[66]

As Newark's uprising accelerated, Amiri Baraka noted a sense of time out of time: "The spirit and feeling of the moment a rebellion breaks out is almost indescribable. Everything seems to be in zoooom motion, crashing toward some explosive manifestation." He witnessed people shot by police and drove an injured man to the hospital, where he saw "blood on the floors and wall, smeared on aprons, falling out of people in gasps." Then he, too, was beaten severely by police and imprisoned for several days on a trumped-up weapons charge. What he had seen and experienced remained as the city cooled: "The hottest rage had become a constant of my personality."[67]

Hayden, one of a handful of community activists called to consult with Governor Hughes as looting, fires, and arrests mounted, recalled Hughes's anger at the "carnival atmosphere" among looters. But from Hayden's perspective, the looting was distinguished by its orderliness and a latent sense of justice served: looters targeted stores with a history of price-gouging black customers and rarely fought with each other, as "there was, for a change, enough for all."[68] Hayden observed collaboration in the midst of chaos as "people on the street felt free to take shelter from the police in the homes of people they did not know. . . . What for Hughes seemed like 'laughing at a funeral' appeared more like a celebration, a refutation of an oppressive past. People felt as though for a moment they were creating a community of their own."[69]

Hughes saw nothing of the sort: "The line between the jungle and the law might as well be drawn here as any place in America," he declared, activating the New Jersey National Guard on Friday, July 14.[70] Over one hundred state police and four thousand ill-prepared young guardsmen rolled into the city that morning over the objections of activists who argued that their presence would only prolong the violence. Springfield Avenue, the commercial thoroughfare that cut diagonally across the city from the downtown toward the West Side Park neighborhood, emerged as the epicenter of the uprising. Residents and police also clashed at Bergen Street and Clinton Avenue and around the Scudder and Stella Wright housing projects. Guardsmen and state troopers had no maps and little understanding. All three branches of law enforcement employed different radio frequencies. At times, they were shooting at each other.[71]

Many police and National Guardsmen brought their own racist assumptions to the task of pacifying what Governor Hughes called the "jungle" of Newark. White Newarkers encouraged them, chanting, "go kill them niggers."[72] State police and guardsmen shot out store windows, including many marked with a "Soul" sign, shopkeepers' plea to looters to bypass stores owned by minorities.[73] Enez King reported waking to the sound of state troopers rifling through her dry-cleaning store and emptying the cash register, part of the "counter-riot" mounted by police and National Guardsmen as they rolled through Newark's Central Ward.[74]

By July 17, the police and the National Guard had crushed the uprising. Nearly 1,000 were injured and more than 1,500 had been arrested. Nearly 95 percent of those arrested were African American, mostly men in their teens and twenties. Twenty-six people had died. All but two of the dead, a police detective and a fire chief, were African Americans.[75] Among them were children: ten-year-old Eddie Moss, shot while riding in the backseat of a car, and twelve-year-old Michael Pugh, shot in front of his home. Some, like Eloise Spellman, a grandmother, were shot while taking refuge in their homes.[76] *Life* magazine photographer Bud Lee captured one of the most enduring images of the uprising:

twelve-year-old Joe Bass, bleeding and crumpled on the street after police shot him along with Billy Furr, twenty-four, who'd been carrying
stolen beer. Bass survived what appears in the photo to be a devastating
wound. Furr did not.[77]

Assigning Blame, Finding Meaning

When police retreated and the National Guard rolled out, they left a
city mourning these deaths and a nation speculating about the political consequences of another "long, hot summer." On the federal level,
"the riots threw Johnson into a mood of near despair." His aides had
been in behind-the-scenes contact with Governor Hughes throughout, but Johnson feared his own direct involvement could be widely
viewed "as a case of black rioters blackmailing the government into
giving them more federal money."[78] In conversations with Johnson,
NAACP director Roy Wilkins and Urban League director Whitney
Young shared the president's pessimism. A senior Johnson aide, Joseph
Califano, noted that the civil rights leaders appeared "numbed by their
lack of influence" with black youth. Like many local commentators
who had discovered that nearly three quarters of the arrested were employed, they concurred that poverty and joblessness were insufficient
explanations.[79] Young attributed the violence to "communists." Johnson focused his wrath on the Democratic Party ranks, excoriating liberals such as Robert F. Kennedy. The criticism of these "cannibals," as he
called them, had rendered the War on Poverty vulnerable to accusations that federally subsidized antipoverty activists had fomented the
riot, accusations already made by Mayor Addonizio and, in Congress,
by Gerald Ford.[80] Although federal and state investigations exonerated
United Community Corporation activists of incitement, perceptions of
their guilt lingered among police and officials.[81] Congressional reaction to the long, hot summers confirmed Johnson's fears that the advances of early civil rights and antipoverty legislation had now stalled.
Within a week of the Newark uprising, Congress passed an "antiriot"
bill "making it a federal crime to cross state lines to participate in or
incite a riot."[82]

Among state officials, one of the more revealing postmortems came
from Paul Ylvisaker, who headed New Jersey's newly formed Department of Community Affairs (DCA) midway through his long career as
a scholar, policymaker, and political adviser. A former program officer
at the Ford Foundation, Ylvisaker had overseen demonstration proj-

ects—the Grey Areas of New Haven, Connecticut, and Mobilization for Youth in New York City—that shaped the War on Poverty.[83] He was "passionately committed to the downtrodden, yet no ideologue, deeply religious in outlook and motivation, but not above shrewd internal politicking when necessary."[84] As head of the infant DCA, Ylvisaker was charged with mediating local conflicts in the aftermath of Newark's uprising and of another that erupted in nearby Plainfield a few days later.

The Newark uprising was only three months past when he spoke candidly about the urban crisis at a conference attended by management expert Peter Drucker, urban planner Edward Logue, and other elite professionals, many of whom saw the uprising as a harbinger of greater violence to come. So candid was the conversation that attendees concurred that the tape recording of it should be destroyed; a transcript nonetheless made its way to the archive, providing an intimate record of their fears and proposals for managing urban rebellion. In intense, often rambling and surreal meditations, Ylvisaker admitted how profoundly the Newark uprising had shaken his own confidence in government's efficacy.[85] "My life was discredited," Ylvisaker recalled feeling; "what I stood for was wrong."[86]

Echoing Governor Hughes's declaration about drawing a line between "the jungle and the law," Ylvisaker said he found New Jersey "about as rough a jungle as any place." He likened his job to opening an overstuffed closet. "Up on that shelf, when you open the closet, is more damn crap in our society just ready to pour down on the guy who almost accidentally triggers it."[87] In his view, racial inequality was the product of a clash between "the last group of immigrants and the next group," meaning competition between urban white ethnics clinging to municipal power and African American communities that had little. "We now have white ethnics running the Maginot Line right next to the black migrant, and the police force is the extension of the class and race war into law enforcement."[88]

Attendees agreed: some suggested that black rioters would soon attack white people en masse, possibly through coordinated campaigns. Ylvisaker turned the conversation toward escalating *white* violence. White Americans could press for an "ultimate solution to the Negro problem," he speculated, like "the apartheid of South Africa."[89] The ethnic pluralism these officials thought they knew, with its low simmer of manageable strife, was in meltdown. The only hope, Ylvisaker argued, were emergency orders, temporary measures while government leaders devised a more enduring peace.

For Ylvisaker and others at the meeting, that enduring peace required channeling black militancy in ways that would reinforce the legitimacy of the state. Immediate recruitment of minority men into the police and fire departments was among the solutions they floated. Black soldiers leaving active duty, one argued, could transition into domestic law enforcement, while black men with criminal convictions would be rerouted from recidivism to the policing of black neighborhoods. Radical black youth already constituted a "paramilitary force," another argued, capable of acting as "a national (colored) regiment in the South Side [of Chicago]."[90]

Ylvisaker led the conversation away from paramilitary speculation to the example of Secretary of Defense Robert McNamara's Project Transition, intended to smooth Vietnam veterans' reentry into civilian life.[91] Such a program could transform veterans of foreign conflicts into a stabilizing force in the cities, Ylvisaker suggested. His optimism contrasts sharply with the bleak reality many returning servicemen faced. But in 1967 such a plan struck Ylvisaker as mutually beneficial social engineering: it could potentially gain the approval of veterans seeking employment, officials worried about social unrest, and black youth committed to self-determination. "This relates to the notions of self-policing," he argued, "of making discipline our kind of thing."[92]

For Ylvisaker, incorporating young black men into policing, "making discipline our kind of thing," was key to diffusing the urban crisis. City officials, he recommended, should address radicalism preemptively by offering venues for its limited expression. He cited the case of H. Rap Brown, the Student Nonviolent Coordinating Committee chairman, whose 1967 visit to Camden had been feared by the city's mayor. Brown, a full-throttle advocate of black power, was alleged to have incited rioting in Cambridge, Maryland, in July 1967. But Ylvisaker convinced wary Camden officials not to arrest Brown and provide his supporters with a "provocation." Instead, he advised them to offer Brown a "legitimate theater." "[T]he emotional response to this guy is going to be fantastic—screams and hollering and jumping up and down," Ylvisaker recalled warning officials. "But that is not the trigger to riot. That is probably release from the feeling." Ylvisaker recalled with pride how closely events surrounding Brown's visit transpired according to his predictions. During Brown's electrifying speech, some in the audience jeered at police, but the officers restrained themselves, and according to Ylvisaker, "the evening evaporated . . . , the myth of Rap Brown disappeared in New Jersey."[93] In fact, bottle throwing and clashes between police and black teenagers did follow the speech, although police quickly quelled the disturbance without dispatching the legions of backup power arranged by the city.[94] Unlike Camden police, Ylvisaker did not believe that enthusiasm for H. Rap Brown's ideas was in itself predictive of rioting. Yet he still conceived of black people's political agency in strikingly patriarchal terms and perceived black militancy's appeal as a force to be "inoculated against."[95]

Ylvisaker did not mention—and perhaps did not understand—that divisions over Brown's ideas within Camden's black organizations no doubt influenced his reception. Howard Gillette notes in his study of Camden that the NAACP and some local leaders considered disinviting Brown because of his views on violence but decided to proceed once officials pressured them to cancel. Among the thousands attending Brown's speech was Charles "Poppy" Sharp, who became a prominent Camden activist. Brown's speech prompted Sharp's transformation from aimless youth to dedicated organizer of the Black People's Unity Movement. In 1972 the organization Sharp founded after hearing Brown negotiated with the city to open construction jobs and low-income housing to African Americans during an impasse over urban renewal that resembled Newark's Medical College dispute.[96]

As Ylvisaker and the conference attendees discussed H. Rap Brown and rechanneling black militancy, they were circling around a larger problem that encompassed not just police departments and black power rallies but the everyday institutions that anchored urban life, institutions like the contested Medical College in downtown Newark. How could they govern mobilized communities in the wake of the uprising? Could the very institutions targeted by the black freedom movement transform sufficiently to forestall violence? Ylvisaker had assumed that the Medical College was a marginal irritant until Oliver Lofton, a black attorney who headed Newark's Legal Services and later served on the Lilley Commission, explained that "it goes very deep, at the root of the discomfort and unhappiness of many of the people."[97] Lofton's explanation persuaded Ylvisaker that the Medical College offered state officials an urgent—if fragile—opportunity to restore stability and potentially a model for short-circuiting urban rebellion. For Ylvisaker, the answer meant not stubborn retrenchment but strategic engagement with community leaders. The goal of such community empowerment, political theorist Barbara Cruikshank has argued, was "to act upon another's interests and desires in order to conduct their actions toward an appropriate end."[98] Ylvisaker, who had trained as a Lutheran minister before veering toward political science, would have probably found such a formulation cynical. But as he faced his peers in the aftermath of the Newark and Plainfield uprisings, the scales seemed to fall from his eyes. For him, the Medical College negotiations would test new theories of power wrested from the chaotic summer of 1967.

Toward the "Magna Carta" of Newark

The causes of the Newark uprising were numerous, but the many accounts tumbling from the press in late 1967 nonetheless assigned major blame to the contested Medical College and the officials who had ignored residents' opposition to it.[99] Louise Epperson and the Committee against Negro and Puerto Rican Removal intensified their campaign with greater urgency in the wake of the uprising and found the ground was shifting. Officials who had previously deemed construction inevitable began taking opponents more seriously.[100] The dispute over the location of the Medical College was only a preview of the extraordinary act of bureaucratic choreography required to actually build it. The project's complexity, coupled with officials' fears of another uprising, provided shrewd activists with many points of leverage.

To compete for the Medical College, Newark city officials had harnessed plans for the massive development to the federal Model Cities legislation passed amid much contention in 1966.[101] Model Cities—originally called Demonstration Cities—emerged from the Presidential Task Force on Metropolitan and Urban Problems in 1964 and gained interest as the frequency of summer uprisings increased. Its creators envisioned Model Cities as an "urban TVA."[102] It diverged from existing antipoverty programs by offering cities more federal funds for major projects while requiring better coordination of their disbursement. Government agencies that had worked in isolation would now be expected to collaborate. Delegated to the newly created Department of Housing and Urban Development (HUD), Model Cities was to launch in a handful of major metropolitan areas, bringing what President Johnson called "all the techniques and talents within our society" to bear on the urban crisis writ large.[103] But the compromised version of Model Cities that Congress passed diluted funding across numerous cities, ensuring that none could afford "the sweeping, long-range strategies initially envisioned."[104]

Model Cities in Newark was swiftly embroiled in the Medical College dispute.[105] By the early 1960s, some urban planners and officials were criticizing how local redevelopment agencies had used the powers of eminent domain granted to them by federal housing acts. Urban renewal had expanded from the original purpose of replacing aging housing stock to underwriting other development schemes. Many met only vague criteria for spurring downtown growth and enriched private developers while exacerbating the problems housing legislation purported to solve.[106] Model Cities, in contrast, promised synthesis between the destruction and reconstruction of community, between the programs that had erased many older neighborhoods and the community action programs that were intended to knit them together.[107] But even as Model Cities stipulated community participation, notes Jill Quadagno, "final authority rested in the hands of the mayors, a strategy designed to avoid the controversy of community action."[108] In other words, Model Cities offered a selective intensification of the War on Poverty while channeling resident participation into conventional modes less likely to sideline municipal officials.

The promise of Model Cities would remain unfulfilled in the long term, but the opposition to the Medical College seized upon its provisions for community involvement to make short-term gains. The NAACP filed a complaint with HUD, insisting that the agency withhold funding for the Medical College. The lawsuit charged that the project fell short of HUD's own standards for urban renewal, having failed to guarantee services, housing, or employment for local people.[109] Critics of the Medical College were now more coordinated and energized than ever. So, too, were Medical College officials.

The impasse among residents, federal officials, and municipal leaders was initially broken by a pledge signed by Robert C. Wood, undersecretary of HUD, and by William J. Cohen, undersecretary of the Department of Health, Education, and Welfare (HEW), to withhold federal funds from the Medical College until all involved could prove the project would alleviate the problems of Central Ward residents.[110] This so-called Wood-Cohen letter reiterated with more specificity many of the principles of community involvement encoded in Model Cities, but it also insisted upon an unprecedented level of coordination among federal agencies. Even the executive branch intervened, with Johnson's aide Joseph Califano acting as a liaison among HUD, HEW, and Governor Hughes. The letter itself marked a victory for Medical College critics. It required that school officials, city leaders, and community groups negotiate a reduction of acreage; greater access to medical services; construction jobs for residents; and relocation aid. But it left the details to be resolved by these parties in a series of rapidly organized and remarkable public hearings chaired by New Jersey's chancellor of higher education, Ralph A. Dungan, a former special assistant to President Kennedy.[111]

Negotiations often revolved around the definition of "community" and who could legitimately serve as its leaders and spokespeople.[112] Hospital trustees equated their leadership of nonprofit institutions with the community's best interest. Trustees appeared perplexed by the opposition's doubts about their capacity to act in the best interest of a mostly black and largely poor and working-class population. An administrator from Beth Israel cited the uncompensated care his hospital delivered to thousands of poor patients each year and the accomplishments of the hospital's community services department.[113] This work, he argued, made hospital officials authentic members of the community and empowered them to act on its behalf. He noted that Medical College trustees had considered compromises in the face of community opposition, thereby affirming their "manliness and character."[114] Yet the very assertion of the trustees' "manliness" hints at their perception that they had barely prevailed over an unjust challenge to their expertise. Indeed, Medical College president Robert R. Cadmus claimed that officials and residents with no "interest in the school as a school" had cornered the leadership. Cadmus grew convinced that the very officials—like Ylvisaker and Governor Hughes—who had urged the trustees to select Newark now backed unreasonable community demands. His fears that the controversy would prevent the Medical College from opening grew as accepted students threatened to transfer. He pleaded with HUD secretary Robert Weaver to smooth the Medical College's approval as part of Newark's Model Cities plan.[115]

Cadmus correctly inferred that Ylvisaker had come to view the Medical College negotiations as imperative for the city's recovery. Ylvisaker argued that the Medical College presented officials with opportunities for inclusion and a strategy for managing black self-determination, perhaps the kind of inoculation against racial violence that he had discussed privately with his colleagues. Ylvisaker had also developed a keener appreciation of the depth of opposition. He acknowledged that residents now stood to gain concessions through the "social application of the art of jujitsu."[116] Even so, he wanted a hand in turning the abstract principle of community involvement into negotiations with actual people. The question of how "the people" of the Central Ward were to be represented had to be resolved before negotiations over the Wood-Cohen letter could proceed.

Medical College leaders complained frequently about the shifting cast of community representatives with whom they were expected to negotiate. Some of the discord reflected the predictable jockeying among individuals for leadership roles on the negotiating team. Other times, residents who had built the opposition movement expressed frustration at those whose sporadic involvement led to the retreading of old issues. "We been fighting for houses and schools, all of us, a long time and not one of you came out and said one word for it," Louise Epperson declared during one impasse.[117]

Another community negotiator insisted at the first hearing that the opposition "had agreement on our side" and recommended that officials approach the situation "as if we were a union in a union negotiating situation."[118] But Cadmus remained frustrated with the community groups because unlike conventional labor negotiations, community groups were quick to unseat chosen spokespeople they deemed ineffective.[119] But what Cadmus perceived as a chaotic approach was for the opposition evidence of a truly deliberative process that would keep their fractious coalition together. In this sense, community groups shouldered a burden of working through questions of representation among themselves that the other parties to the Medical College dispute—whose leadership roles were already formalized—did not.

The Medical College hearings exceeded the perfunctory attempts at citizen inclusion that municipal authorities had staged in the past, as some of Newark's most marginalized residents raised their voices, demanded answers, and shaped the direction of negotiations. Yet the negotiating committee itself comprised largely working- and middle-class people—ministers, college-educated activists, and steadily employed homeowners—who already possessed some sway.[120] Medical College leaders, such as Cadmus, were not alone in questioning whether the negotiating committee was truly representative. The obliquely expressed subtext of their concern was that the negotiating committee consisted of grandstanders and opportunists. Ylvisaker argued for public meetings "to go over the head of the 'self-appointed' negotiating team" and "get the pulse of the community."[121] Among the negotiators he questioned were Harry Wheeler, a minister, and Junius Williams, a young attorney who had been raised in Virginia and educated at Amherst College and Yale Law School. Williams had come to Newark years earlier at the urging of Students for a Democratic Society's Tom Hayden. He later engaged in the city's emerging black power movement and helped to organize opposition to the Medical College through the Newark Area Planning Association.[122] Ylvisaker, as head of the newly formed DCA, was obliged to consider how fairly the groups he dealt with were represented. But his objections to Wheeler and Williams also reflected his preeminent goal of shaping community representation itself.

Officials may have balked at the negotiating team, but residents affirmed the leadership of Wheeler and Williams in a referendum. Members of the Committee against Negro and Puerto Rican Removal and the United Freedom Party secured spots on the committee. So, too, did Reverend Sharper of the esteemed Abyssinian Baptist Church. Duke Moore of United Community Corporation and Oliver Lofton of Newark Legal Services also joined, rounding out representation of organizations affiliated with the War on Poverty.[123] They sparred frequently with Louis Danzig of the NHA, Donald Malafronte from the mayor's office, and a rotating group of representatives from HUD, HEW, Public Health Service, and Ylvisaker's DCA. Ralph Dungan, chair of the New Jersey Board of Higher Education, facilitated.[124]

Central Ward residents found government and hospital officials no less frustrating than their opponents found them. Community negotiators complained that officials wielded power through diffusion, citing Chairman Dungan's refrain when a concrete demand was made: "all the cards are not in my hands."[125] Why, Williams demanded, could none of the officials assembled approximate the number of workers required for the first phase of the hospital construction, so that they could begin negotiating over the hiring of black and Puerto Rican workers? "It seems that throughout this process . . . there is never anybody to blame," Williams said. "We come from the community and we ask a specific question . . . and then the people who are supposed to be representing the power structure say, 'it's not our fault.'"[126] Williams's claim overestimated the power held by any one of the officials at the table, let alone their influence over the trade unions.[127] But he had accurately diagnosed a source of the city's power to obstruct change: it ruled by making superficial appeals to include opponents, diffusing conflict, and obfuscating accountability.

When the negotiations accelerated beyond the questions of representation, they ranged widely from the construction of the Medical College to its mission. At stake were the ordinary medical services community members urgently needed and officials' insistence that the very presence of a Medical College would improve care. Residents rebuffed this argument: "It is a fallacy to assume that because a teaching hospital comes and takes over the municipal facilities that automatically health care for the community will be improved."[128] Williams cited the social medicine practice of Montefiore Hospital in the Bronx as a model for Newark, insisting that Medical College faculty "may not be interested in knife cuts, but it is a necessity."[129] Dungan and others countered that a state-sponsored teaching hospital had to treat patients from across New Jersey.

Medical College trustees and the Public Health Service argued that the school's location had to provide opportunities for students to practice medicine across a wide range of specialties. But "housing, relocation and land use problems are unrelated to producing good medical men," they contended.[130] Shortly before the hearings began, however, a perfunctory inspection of the Newark site by the Public Health Service had taken a surprising turn, reopening "the whole question of what is medical education?" The Surgeon General's office had insisted that the visit include observers from HEW, HUD, and Newark community groups. The presence of community leaders and some sympathetic officials from these other agencies challenged narrow views about the purpose of medical education, advancing instead a wider vision that explicitly addressed inequality.

As they attempted to realize this vision through negotiations, Williams and other Medical College opponents had at first perceived the divided nature of officialdom as an obstacle. But such divisions soon appeared to be a potential source of new alliances. For example, community representatives challenged the Medical College's sprawling design, arguing that a taller complex would displace fewer residents. Cadmus countered that the existing plan had won accolades from medical planning experts; he was unwilling to compromise on a design that would sacrifice possibilities for horizontal expansion. But community representatives gained traction on this point precisely because of the competition among officials to prove their expertise. After Cadmus asserted that Danzig was no expert on planning for medical facilities, Danzig upbraided him: "I had hoped Dr. Cadmus wouldn't get into personalities, like he knows what he is talking about. . . . The whole issue would never have arisen if these people had stayed out of my business, which is land and its use in the urban scene." Danzig cited Tufts Medical College in Boston and others built on much smaller plots as models for Newark. He called Cadmus's handling of the negotiations "absurd" and mocked his resistance to alternative designs.[131]

Danzig was an unwaveringly self-confident negotiator who appeared to revel in conflict. Yet the Medical College negotiations signaled for him a new and troubling phase of urban renewal during which years of methodical effort to insulate the NHA from effective criticism began to unravel. Early on, Danzig had secured the NHA's status as the city's "official" redeveloper and courted nationally prominent companies to partner with him. According to Howard Kaplan's account of Danzig's impressive rise, he positioned himself as "the interpreter of federal policies," taming a local press "baffled by the technical questions" urban renewal raised.[132] He negotiated projects discreetly "to avoid public defeats or open skirmishes" and waited until the last possible deadline to provide crucial details, when a deal's prospects were strong and officials feared rejecting it.[133] The obfuscation that Williams slammed during the hearings was in fact a part of NHA's well-honed strategy. Danzig and his staff saw themselves operating in an apolitical technocratic realm that could benefit the city only if protected from the digressive pull of outside interests. Developers spoke admiringly of how Danzig and his staff "own the slums. . . . They can sell any piece of real estate to a developer before it's even acquired."[134] They lauded the very qualities that many residents called undemocratic. Reverend Sharper of the community negotiating team railed against them as "undertable shenanigans" and "the kind of stuff that makes for riots."[135] The Medical College hearings threatened Danzig's reign, wrenching open for vigorous debate a process long obscured in secrecy.

City bureaucrats and Medical College officials would probably have clashed over a project of this scale and complexity even if they had not been under public scrutiny. But the hearings undermined the inviolability of their expertise. One architect and city planner reminded Cadmus and Danzig that expertise was "no magic or holy thing" and suggested that the untrained residents assembled could resolve many of the questions raised at the hearings.[136] Williams and Robert Curvin argued that residents' engagement with technical matters was imperative and should not be ceded to the conventional experts.[137] The process was by turns tedious—sometimes, Williams recalled, "we just told people to shut up and sit down"—and exhilarating. Residents analyzed proposals, consulted outside experts, and parsed the technical and political stakes of the decisions they faced.[138]

What came to be called the Medical College Agreement was finally reached at a jubilant meeting in March 1968, about six months after the uprising.[139] The first successful challenge to Newark's urban renewal regime since neighborhood protests had begun in the late 1950s, the agreement reflected residents' goals for health care, employment, housing, and their city's future.[140] Implementation and enforcement of the agreement were charged to interlocking review councils led by community members and government officials from city agencies like the NHA and the United Community Corporation, state agencies such as the Division on Civil Rights and the DCA, and federal agencies such as HUD, the Office of Economic Opportunity, and the Treasury Department.[141] Disparate community representatives had collectively produced a fixer framework, although they would not necessarily have claimed that at the time. But activists had made plain the intertwined nature of the city's problems and the unexamined impact of urban re-development. In so doing, they forged a template for negotiations with multiple levels of government and private-sector leaders, as well as a new network of organizations to sustain their goals and hold officials accountable.

The agreement cut by more than half the amount of land allotted to the Medical College, but relocation nonetheless remained an urgent issue for many in the Central Ward. It mandated a construction sched-ule to allow ample time for residents to move and called on the NHA to expand its rent subsidy programs. The parties involved also looked beyond the NHA, which had failed in the past to address complaints, and appealed instead for state oversight. The DCA and the Department of Institutions and Agencies were charged with ensuring rent subsi-dies for those pushed into higher-priced markets. A Citizens' Housing Council made up of housing advocates, HUD representatives, and DCA officials was charged with establishing a relocation review board to in-vestigate complaints.[142] Another body, the Community Housing Coun-cil, was tasked with devising a plan to expedite relocation and improve the quality of housing in the Central Ward. The council would also monitor the transfer of land from the NHA to "community based hous-ing corporations"—then a novel creation—that would help rebuild the residential neighborhoods abutting the Medical College.[143]

As the Citizens' Housing Council tackled displacement, a health council comprising community members and representatives of the United Community Corporation and local hospitals would develop a health plan to serve local, low-income residents, funded in part by the Office of Economic Opportunity and the Public Health Service. The Community Health Council was also assigned to work with the Medical College to create a scholarship program for minority medical students and establish career tracks for nurses and technicians. Essex County Community College, other vocational schools, and the city's Manpower Development Training Association were to train workers in a range of fields with the goal of staffing the estimated 2,600 positions to be generated by the Medical College with as many local residents as possible.[144]

But the most specific and urgent goals for minority hiring were set for the construction of the Medical College: "at least one-third of all journeymen and one-half of all apprentices." Their fulfillment would be a major test of the agreement. Yet another review council of community, union, government, and contractor representatives was to review contracts and monitor minority recruitment plans to ensure their efficacy.[145] Contractors would be required to report their anticipated workforce needs and plans for complying with the agreement. State officials consented to the hiring of nonunion minority workers if unions refused to hire and train from within their own ranks.[146] The agreement also permitted the review council to oversee the subdivision of larger contracts to ensure that small, minority-owned businesses would also contribute to the Medical College's construction.[147]

Activists had made few distinctions between the destructive consequences of urban renewal, employment discrimination, and the dearth of meaningful political representation in the Central Ward.[148] And it appeared that the coalition had won, that it had successfully drawn what appeared to be separate grievances together into a systemic critique. "For the first time the people had a voice in making policy that affected them," recalled Harry Wheeler, who deemed the Medical College Agreement the "Magna Carta of Newark."[149] The agreement was not just the result of sophisticated coalition politics. Staid language of quasi-legal obligations and overlapping review boards could not disguise the history of a document forged in blood and fire. Officials had ignored the Central Ward until the uprising made the stakes too high. Louise Epperson's inquiries about the Medical College had gone unanswered until the uprising, when, suddenly, "everyone wanted to talk to me."[150] Black activists have long referred to the "brother with a brick" dynamic (militancy, usually embodied by a black man who white authorities believed was behind all black collective action) at work in negotiations with white leaders. The uprising itself had been the "brother with the brick," a belief succinctly expressed by Junius Williams of the United Brothers and the Newark Area Planning Association as he reflected upon the outcome of the Medical College hearings: "None of this would have happened without last summer's rebellion, when black people tried to burn the town down."[151]

A Contentious Victory Demands Fixers

At first, the Medical College Agreement appeared to be the pinnacle of the organizing project begun during the 1963 Barringer High School demonstration and the realization of maximum feasible participation on a scale that had eluded many community action programs. But even as the agreement was widely praised, its actual enforcement remained a struggle.[152] In the midst of the Medical College hearings, Junius Williams had asserted that no matter how persuasively community groups laid out the evidence of unjust policies, "there was never anybody to blame."[153] Williams might just as well have said that there were too many targets sharing the blame for the state of the Central Ward. Accusations bounced from one to the other without any single entity accepting responsibility. The Medical College Agreement established a chain of responsibility for redressing the injustices of the past and a framework for the future that would have been unimaginable less than a decade before, when ACTION Inc. had praised Newark's progress as Case City Number One. But the fixing was never done: an emerging group of individuals and organizations would now have to push for implementation beyond the mere letter of the law. Constantly on the lookout for the next ally or the most effective point of leverage, they would have to remain clear-eyed about when and how to fight.

The ink on the agreement was barely dry before contractors and unions undercut it by failing or outright refusing to employ minority construction workers.[154] Work stoppages, accusations of bad faith by all sides, and several lawsuits unfolded over the next year. Union leaders insisted that they could not accept referrals for workers who had not received training from union tradesmen. Two black leaders who had aided the negotiations, Gustav Heningburg and George Fontaine, responded by raising funds to establish the Newark Construction Trades Training Corporation. Heningburg and Fontaine were pursuing a policy of parallelism, creating a separate black organization to challenge the segregated unions, much like black southerners had created the Mississippi Freedom Democratic Party or the Lowndes County Freedom Organization to run black candidates and sidestep the official, segregated Democratic Party. Heningburg, Fontaine, and their allies enlisted older union members to prepare young African Americans and Puerto Ricans for entry into a formal union apprenticeship program, but "pretraining" improved their acceptance rates only marginally. Union apprenticeship officials still used other criteria—mainly age—as a proxy to reject applicants.[155]

Citing the unions' and contractors' violation of the Medical College Agreement, community members pressured Governor Hughes to halt construction with an executive order. Hughes rejected their demand, choosing instead to pursue the less immediately disruptive strategy of a lawsuit in January 1969.[156] In 1970 Heningburg decried "two years of fruitless efforts to develop an acceptable plan" and called on the Labor Department and state officials to resuscitate the agreement.[157]

In December 1970 a district court decision finally upheld the legality of the Medical College's Affirmative Action Plan and asserted the prerogative of the court to enforce integration of the unions, requiring them to accept minority journeymen as members.[158] While this decision fortified the Medical College's Affirmative Action Plan as a model for minority hiring throughout the city, its implementation in subsequent projects still required grassroots vigilance, rooted in the recognition that irreplaceable opportunities were lost each day that construction continued without minority workers. The losses represented not just a few days' wages but opportunities for hundreds of workers to become apprentices and to learn trades that would provide stable incomes and the security of a union membership. In a city with an unemployment rate of 13 percent, these were immediate benefits that no drawn-out lawsuit, no matter how favorable the settlement, could replace. As Heningburg attempted to extend affirmative action to public construction projects throughout Newark, he would apply these lessons from the Medical College Agreement, as well as the resources of a new organization, the Greater Newark Urban Coalition.[159] He would emerge as a consummate fixer.

PART TWO

Fixers Emerge

FOUR

The Making of a Fixer: Black Power, Corporate Power, and Affirmative Action

On January 13, 1970, a neighborhood community center honored Gustav Heningburg, the executive director of the Greater Newark Urban Coalition, for his efforts to resolve conflicts over urban renewal, employment discrimination, and housing. It was less than six months before an eagerly anticipated mayoral election, the first since the uprising. The possibility that Newarkers would elect their first black mayor appeared strong. Though Heningburg's name would not attract national news like that of Kenneth Gibson, the cautious civil engineer he would help to elect that spring, Heningburg was also a pioneer. As an architect of the new alliances that were changing the city and mobilizing an influential black constituency, Heningburg would imbue "black power" with tangible meaning.

At the time, Heningburg—forty years old, a former military intelligence officer, linked to nearly every establishment African American organization in the country—was already enmeshed in Newark's elite. Companies such as Mutual Benefit Life Insurance and Prudential Insurance, whose office towers anchored the Newark skyline, underwrote the donations that supported his organization. But in his speech that night, Heningburg criticized his patrons. He accused Newark's business community of "practicing the most sophisticated form of political hypocrisy" because many denounced black militants and municipal corruption while refusing to support alternatives. He decried business leaders' emphasis on "planning" and "infrastructure" over communities and individuals.[1] He knew of what he spoke; Heningburg was the rare activist who had worked intimately with both corporate elites and everyday people. He drew on his many roles: civil rights activist, advocate for black trade unionists, champion of black middle-class leadership, mediator between Newark's corporate leaders and its emerging black power organizations, and fixer who moved among all these interests to consolidate black political and economic power.[2]

Heningburg came to his leadership position by dint of decades working with civil rights organizations and more recent forays into grassroots opposition to the Medical College. Tall and slim, with a dimpled chin and dark brows, Heningburg was laconic yet culturally nimble, fluent in the nuances of both corporate euphemism and activist rhetoric. He was born into the African American educational elite, the son of Alphonse Heningburg, a director of the Alabama Tuskegee Institute. When Heningburg was still a child, the family moved to North Carolina, where his father accepted a position as assistant to the president of North Carolina Central University (formerly North Carolina College for Negroes). They kept going north. After the National Urban League hired Alphonse, Gus completed high school in New York City. He graduated from Hampton Institute—and the Reserve Officer Training Corps—in 1950 and spent the next six years in the army. He came to Newark while serving in the Army Counter Intelligence Corps. After retiring his commission in 1957, Heningburg worked as a fundraiser for the United Negro College Fund and, later, the NAACP Legal Defense and Education Fund.[3] He served as vice president for the nationally prominent public relations firm Harold L. Oram Inc., which raised funds for a broad spectrum of liberal anticommunist organizations in the 1950s. In the 1960s and 1970s Oram counted many preeminent black institutions among its clients, including the National Council of Negro Women, the NAACP, Spellman College, Howard University, and the National Urban League. Heningburg was connected.[4]

And yet even as he ascended the ladder of respectable accomplishment, Heningburg was drawn to the increasingly militant civil rights and black nationalist ideas transforming Newark into a movement hub. Perhaps he did not fit the mold of Newark's homegrown radical, Amiri Baraka, but in black power Heningburg saw the potential to achieve changes of which the organizations he had worked with had barely dreamed. The struggles unfolding in Newark and the organizations cropping up to guide them increasingly commanded his attention. In the late 1960s Heningburg joined them—albeit in the cautious but influential role of executive director of a new group called the Greater Newark Urban Coalition (GNUC), for which he would organize in corporate boardrooms. But he also spent time in churches, on street corners, and in public housing complexes talking to people with little money or—up to that point—power.

Alarmed by the uprising, the mildly progressive businessmen and community leaders who formed the GNUC looked to Heningburg as a matchmaker, a fixer: a man with connections in every corner, an activist who could make deals with the many antagonistic groups—machine politicians, corporations, and black activists, among them—laying claim to Newark's future.

Most black organizations viewed Newark's white-dominated business community with suspicion. Amiri Baraka likened downtown to the "Gold Coast" of a developing country.[5] The president of the National Business League, a black trade association, called the city's corporate community a "plantationship." But some black power activists shared with Newark's businessmen a frustration with the city's corruption and the slow pace of reform.[6] Through GNUC, corporations and civil rights groups attempted limited partnerships to seek ends they agreed on: municipal reform, elimination of job discrimination, and support for black-owned businesses. These were relatively conservative goals, and yet Heningburg brought to their pursuit a subtle infusion of the more radical ideas that fascinated him.

The GNUC was an offshoot of the National Urban Coalition (NUC). Comprising former government officials, civil rights activists, and corporate executives, NUC founders argued that the urban crisis demanded the same kind of cooperation among public- and private-sector leaders as had World War II and the Great Depression. As the Democratic Party collapsed under Lyndon Johnson's distracted leadership, the NUC pulled examples from recent history—most notably, the Marshall Plan—to build consensus around the need for a more expansive urban policy that demanded private-sector investment. The NUC initially stumbled in its attempts to articulate legislative priorities, but the membership supported greater black electoral representation as a means of institutionalizing what they perceived as acceptable versions of black power.

Heningburg's work embodied those goals even as he used the resources of the Newark affiliate to set a precedent for sharpening the national organization's left edge. Rather than simply putting a business stamp of approval on minority politicians who managed to squeeze into preexisting establishments, Heningburg also worked with radicals such as Baraka, the Black Panthers, and the Young Lords to help build the broad black power front that emerged in Newark between 1966 and 1970, successfully electing a slate of black and Puerto Rican candidates to office. Heningburg also applied the GNUC's clout to the ongoing fight against employment discrimination in Newark's construction trades, extending it to the multimillion-dollar expansion of the Newark airport.

Although local electoral victories and new federal laws against employment discrimination provided momentum, Heningburg found that the implementation of federal policy demanded persistent local initiative and unyielding pressure. Situated between grassroots potential and corporate power, Heningburg acted as a middleman. But this term suggests neutrality and he was no neutral observer. He was also a fixer, bringing disparate parties together to forge something new. It was a strategy for leveraging power day by day.

Harnessing the Power

Heningburg was waiting for a flight home from Columbia, South Carolina, in late summer 1967, not long after the Newark uprising, when a page notified him of a phone call. Three powerful men waited at the other end of the line: Donald MacNaughton, chairman of the Prudential Insurance Company, the city's leading white-collar employer; Malcolm Talbot, dean of the Rutgers University Newark Campus; and James Pawley, director of the Essex County Urban League. "They had tracked me down to tell me that earlier that day they had created something called the Newark Urban Coalition, and they wanted me to run it," Heningburg recalled.[7] He declined; he was already employed.[8]

MacNaughton, Talbot, and Pawley pursued him nevertheless. Prudential's MacNaughton exemplified the businessmen determined to shape post-riot Newark. "The business community has done a great deal," he insisted to a reporter after the uprising, "and it isn't going to stop."[9] MacNaughton no doubt had in mind the businesses that engaged in some philanthropy, supported small-scale job training, or negotiated with activists to minimally improve hiring policies before 1967. But a "great deal" amounted to not much—especially given the enormous resources of Newark's business community. But moderate progressives such as MacNaughton saw themselves at the cutting edge of a racial reorganization of capitalism. They perceived the uprising as a new phase in the decline of northeastern cities and one they were ill equipped to confront with piecemeal concessions. Newark had recently become a majority black city, and it seemed likely that a black challenger would oust Addonizio in the next election.[10] Businessmen perceived the uprising not only as a threat to their investments but also as a harbinger of the political realignment to come. They wanted a hand in shaping it, and they wanted Heningburg to be that hand.

Heningburg actually agreed with much of MacNaughton's analysis. He believed no organization in Newark was both sufficiently influential and capable to guide the city's recovery.[11] The mayor, the city council, and established civic groups had been unable to prevent or short-circuit the riot, Heningburg reasoned; the chamber of commerce, meanwhile, was "hiding under the bed." The chamber's executive director, Henry W. Connor, a prime example of the head-in-the-sand white businessmen whom reformers such as MacNaughton wanted to leave in the past, had declared he was simply shocked by the uprising. Newark, he complained, had "done most of the things a city is supposed to, to avoid trouble like this."[12]

Other business leaders accepted no responsibility for Newark's condition. They insisted that militants committed to violence had hijacked the city's antipoverty agency. Or that black leaders and community action programs had heedlessly raised the expectations of "people without education and preparation."[13] MacNaughton wanted to mitigate these blunt reactionary forces by eliciting a more sophisticated response from the corporate sector—and he wanted Heningburg's help.

When Heningburg's plane landed in New Jersey, MacNaughton, Talbot, and Pawley were waiting. "You're not going home until you agree to take this job," they told him. With "no staff, no money, no nothing," and an ambitious, unformed plan to "fix Newark," the Greater Newark Urban Coalition did not inspire Heningburg's confidence.[14] But he believed Newark's crisis demanded action and experimentation. Instead of fighting white businesses, he wanted to harness their power— and so he took a leave from his NAACP position and accepted the offer.

The NUC, GNUC's parent organization, was itself an outcome of the Newark and Detroit uprisings, launched that August 1967 by 1,200 "leaders of American life." At an "Emergency Convocation" presided over by Andrew Heiskell, CEO of Time Inc., and A. Phillip Randolph, former president of the Brotherhood of Sleeping Car Porters and a leader of the 1963 March on Washington, participants discussed plans to devise a national model of urban leadership to relieve "the crisis in the cities."[15] The NUC sought to distinguish itself by the scope of its alliances. According to John Gardner, who had served as secretary of Housing, Education, and Welfare before assuming the chairmanship of the NUC, "some people think of the Coalition as just another organization tackling the tough urban problems of the day. . . . Our distinction is that we bring together segments of American life that do not normally collaborate in the solution of public problems." Gardner called on "the most influential citizens" to be "unsparingly honest in facing the toughest issues."[16] He envisioned executives, activists, union leaders, and clergy engaged in impassioned, uncomfortable, and—eventually—productive conversation.

Despite their claims to novelty, NUC leaders drew on concepts of individual uplift with deep roots in the nineteenth century as well as the contemporary "rediscovery" of poverty that animated Johnson's War on Poverty. New York City mayor John Lindsay instructed the assembled to envision just one unemployed man and to "make it your task to bring him out of the slums—to make him part of the other America, the one all of us live in."[17] The GNUC attempted this by leading mostly white businessmen and officials on tours through the so-called ghetto of Newark, which I discuss in more depth in chapter 7.[18] Some NUC members' assumptions reflected early twentieth-century models of corporate welfare, as well as the "soulful corporation" admired in postwar America.[19] NUC publications featured lavish photography and illustrations. NUC graphic designers faced the task of translating the organization's main activity—holding meetings—into dynamism and moral urgency. A pamphlet on state housing initiatives, for example, featured a charcoal drawing of businessmen in conversation, its rough rendering meant to convey fierce animation. In keeping with an aesthetic widely shared among nonprofits and foundations in urban uplift work, other publications' sharp geometric designs surrounded black-and-white photographs of corporate leaders seated at conference tables or crowded into auditoriums. These images were juxtaposed with the subjects of their conversations: children, teenagers, unemployed young men photographed against crumbling buildings, visually representing Lindsay's suggestion that each member envision the individual he would lift out of poverty.[20] Urban riots, by this narrative and aesthetic logic, resulted from business leaders' failure to fulfill their moral obligations. Such men churned out a great—some said excessive—number of speeches and newsletter articles as they attempted to address their guilt for this perceived failure and to clarify their collective responsibilities.

The inability of US businesses to confront the "crisis in the cities" represented not only a lapse of moral commitment but also a threat to business itself, according to Heiskell of Time Inc. "We ask ourselves how free enterprise can better participate in the social process," he warned, "not only because it should but because, surely, it stands to be the first victim of the failure of that process."[21] The new progressivism of such business leaders was, in Heiskell's reckoning, the familiar enlightened self-interest. In its pursuit, business leaders who were resentful of regulation became open to new arrangements. The NUC offered them space and encouragement to reconsider the relationship of government to private enterprise.

Gardner and several of the administrators who had come to the NUC from the Johnson administration urged members to articulate urgent legislative priorities and promote them with corporate philanthropy and lobbying.[22] Coalition members focused most consistently on unemployment. Lindsay reminded them to "hold each program up against the yardstick of the awesome need for jobs." In addition to a "Domestic Marshall Plan," others suggested a new Works Progress Administration or an "Emergency Jobs Program."[23] In January 1968 Heiskell called on Congress to "provide Government-generated employment to every citizen able and willing to work but unable to find private employment."[24]

But some of the NUC's most powerful members opposed direct federal intervention. Henry Ford II acknowledged that "the country faces its greatest internal crisis since the Civil War," but he warned businessmen not to let their sympathies for the poor cloud their judgment: "even more basic than the responsibility of business to provide equal job opportunities is its responsibility to stay in business," he argued. "Business cannot hire more people than it needs, or hire people who are not qualified to do useful work, or hire people for more than work is worth."[25] Gerald L. Phillippe, chairman of General Electric, flatly rejected the Works Progress Administration model: "jobs which will provide lasting satisfaction must come from the private sector and not from government make-work programs."[26] Phillippe argued that the private sector, not the government, held a "mandate" to create jobs. He predicted that companies that failed to do so would simply lose business to competitors that did.

The true source of unemployment, Phillippe insisted, was the unemployed themselves. Absenteeism and high turnover, he decreed, constituted the most formidable obstacles to redeeming the "hardcore" unemployed. His position echoed that of some conservative union leaders. Both emphasized the poor skills and substandard education of minority applicants, an analysis that boiled down to a tautology: the poor are poor because they are poor. Phillippe approvingly recounted General Electric's decision to move plants to the Southeast, without acknowledging that such shifts came at the expense of northern industrial cities, only rearranging the very problems he now insisted the market would solve.[27]

Although NUC leaders disagreed about employment policies, many agreed to support black empowerment, so long as it could be done without endorsing what they considered "separatism" or "extremism." Whitney Young Jr., president of the National Urban League, frequently addressed this issue. Although he ranked as a moderate within the spectrum of the civil rights movement, at NUC meetings—portrayed in photographs as a wall of black suits and middle-aged white jowls—Young's mere presence as a black man was radical.[28] But Young criticized black militants for polarizing the country, accusing them of contributing little besides "chanting" to the creation of actual black economic and political clout. Still, by 1967 even moderate black leaders recognized black power's appeal and attempted to incorporate it into their own politics.

For Young, this meant challenging the audience at the NUC Emergency Convocation to "suppress the crackpots among the white society" before criticizing black extremism. He described what he deemed a more palatable version of black power, one that bore a strong resemblance to the storied ethnic solidarity through which nineteenth-century European immigrants had moved into the middle class. "We get Black Power the same way the Irish, the Jews, the Italians, and everybody else got power," Young instructed, advancing a comparison also made by Malcolm X, Charles V. Hamilton, and Stokely Carmichael. "That is, by keeping your mouth shut and going ahead and mobilizing your economic and political strength, winning other people who will become allies, and rewarding your friends and punishing your enemies."[29] Young denounced "racial exclusivity," but he praised self-determination and uncompromising black leadership.[30] His insistent attempts to explain and defend the political dynamics within black communities marked him as one of the closest representatives of black power the NUC had.[31]

John Gardner, the NUC chairman, echoed Young's call. Gardner wanted to appeal to black power and also hoped to manage it within the coalition's structure. His defense of black power conveyed the rhetorical pleasure he experienced in a full-throttle attack against the very white elite he represented. Shortly after he assumed the chairmanship, Gardner warned an audience that black Americans would reject "solutions cooked up in the back rooms of the establishment and then served to them on a platter."[32] The same month, though, Gardner published an article in *Reader's Digest* in which he conflated militancy with hatred and called for "a revolt of the moderates—in offices, factories, homes, and clubs."[33] Like Young, Gardner coupled his endorsement of self-determination with denunciations of vaguely defined extremism, seeking to retain the support of diverse black organizations and predominantly white corporate donors.

Gus Heningburg would be called upon to balance those interests as director of the GNUC, although the political climate of Newark required more from him than the abstract appeals made by Young and Gardner. Indeed, Newark's experience had shaped the national dialogue on black power in which Young and Gardner participated, as shown in a 1967 *New York Times* editorial supporting the National Conference on Black Power. The conference, scheduled to take place in Newark at the end of July, became a source of conflict between Governor Hughes and its organizers, including Dr. Nathan Wright Jr., a director in the city's Episcopal Diocese and the author of *Black Power and Urban Unrest*. When the uprising occurred less than two weeks prior to the anticipated date of the conference, Hughes pressured organizers to cancel or postpone it. The *New York Times* disagreed, arguing that the Newark conference could shape race relations by allowing black leaders of whom they approved to define a moderate black power. "Up to now, the most shrill Negro voices have left the impression that 'black power' stood for a defeatist form of race separation and violence," the editorial read, proceeding to praise the version offered by Wright: "'It's only the whites who consider that black power is used only by Negro radicals,'" Wright had said. His definition centered on the nonviolent mobilization of "black economic and political power."[34] The editorial illustrated one of two dynamics at work: recognizing the resonance of black power, white liberals and black moderates attempted—often for very different reasons—to wring from this provocative and expansive concept a definition that corresponded to what they claimed were universal values.

Many historical accounts of this period emphasize the animosity between black nationalists and integrationists, radicals and moderates, but they obscure a second, competing dynamic. Amiri Baraka, for example, sought a nationalist ethos that was critical of moderate strategies and yet accommodating of moderates. Baraka wanted his nationalist framework to stem infighting among black organizations and enable what became the Modern Black Convention Movement.[35] He had returned to his hometown of Newark after achieving success as the author of *Blues People* and *Dutchman* and founding the Black Arts Repertory Theater in Harlem. Nationalism for Baraka figured into a larger revolutionary project of cultural, economic, and psychological liberation. But he advanced "operational unity" to include black people who did not perceive their actions in nationalist terms. The strategy of "operational unity" originated with Malcolm X but was further theorized by Los Angeles–based black nationalist Maulana Ron Karenga (Ronald McKinley Everett). In Baraka's formulation, it required black radicals to wring a "nationalist interpretation" from what they often dismissed as the most moderate institutions of black life—churches, municipal elections, fraternities, and organizations such as the Urban League and the NAACP. Through operational unity, all black people, from "welfare mothers" to "slick dudes," could be persuaded to "function as nationalists every day."[36] Baraka's emphasis on operational unity underscores the internal dialectic of black power at this time: as moderates such as Wright or Young sought to incorporate it into their own worldview, radicals such as Baraka similarly tried to draw moderate institutions into an explicitly nationalist project.

Though less well known outside the city than Wright, Young, or Baraka, Heningburg contributed vitally to these developments, shifting between the GNUC and the United Brothers, a cadre of diverse black leaders that convened in 1966 to unify the city around black power goals and develop an electoral strategy to realize them. The GNUC's founders had chosen Heningburg precisely because of his involvement with these developments and the Medical College dispute. Yet, taking on a new role in close collaboration with Newark's business elite pushed Heningburg into a constant fight for legitimacy in the eyes of both his white employers and the black activists wary of his new organization.

In the Image: Proving the Greater Newark Urban Coalition's Legitimacy

Heningburg fought one of his earliest battles as director of the GNUC over the location of the group's office. The group's executives planned to establish the office "in the ghetto," Heningburg recalled, but he objected, arguing that Newark's black residents would sense contempt.

"You're going to put this office right downtown where you are," Heningburg told Prudential's MacNaughton.[37] Heningburg also demanded an office large enough to accommodate the various groups he wanted to invite for meetings. MacNaughton acquiesced and installed Heningburg next door to his own office on the top floor of the Prudential Building. But the location proved problematic. "The Black Panthers were coming in at 10:00 and the Young Lords were coming in at noon," Heningburg recalled, "and the security people in the lobby were saying, 'Where you going again, who you going to see?'"[38] Ultimately, Heningburg opened a larger office downtown, but in that first year, he said, founders of the GNUC had to share their space.

Heningburg soon took on a fight with the battle-worn United Community Corporation (UCC), the coordinating agency for Newark's War on Poverty. By fall 1968 the GNUC and the UCC were competing for federal grants and private-sector contributions.[39] Since the departure of the UCC's first executive director, Cyril DeGrasse Tyson, in 1966, the UCC had cycled through several executive directors and was led at the time by L. Sylvester Odom. He joined with Reverend Levin B. West—both were established black leaders with ties to Mayor Addonizio—to question the GNUC's motives. They charged that Heningburg had funneled $12,000 from the Ford Foundation to a voter registration drive led by the more militant United Brothers. Although the United Brothers' candidates had narrowly lost their bids for several city council positions, they had mounted a memorable challenge to Newark's Democratic leadership, with which Odom and West were aligned. West argued that by funding Heningburg's GNUC instead of the UCC, white businessmen had further polarized the black community and perpetuated an attack on its rightful representatives.[40]

West and Odom's position must be viewed within the context of Newark's crumbling Democratic machine. Many other black leaders cheered the machine's weakening, having long condemned the incompetence, condescension, and hostility with which the largely white leadership treated Newark's emerging black majority. And yet, white officials needed black voters and courted them with promises of equality, a handful of high-profile black appointments, and, after 1964, strategic distribution of War on Poverty funds. Some black Newarkers who worked in the municipal government or depended upon its resources for their neighborhood projects, such as Odom and West, maintained loyalty to the Addonizio administration.[41] Heningburg recognized a familiar pattern, whereby black leaders who might have united around shared goals fought one another over scarce resources distributed by white benefactors. But from Odom and West's perspective, the GNUC was an untested interloper.[42]

Numerous speakers defended Heningburg at a GNUC rally held in response to the UCC's attack. In so doing, they confirmed Odom and West's fears: Newark's political landscape was about to undergo a tremendous reconfiguration. Even the formidable Central Ward Democratic chairman, Eulis "Honey" Ward, told the crowd, "This is the beginning of a fight in 1970 to elect a black mayor and as many black councilmen as we can." Fliers distributed at the rally reflected the new alliances in the works: they pitted Newark's black majority and its allies in the white business community against a swollen municipal social service bureaucracy staffed by "paid professionals," "over-compensated individuals," and "black profiteers who, out of envy, have put self over city."[43]

Heningburg's fundraising experience had prepared him for controversy of this sort. He expected that the UCC would automatically rebuff a new entity, such as the GNUC, that threatened to upset established philanthropic relationships. Heningburg arranged a meeting with the UCC's leaders at which he pressed them not to waste time with internecine battles. The meeting—and, months later, an invitation to join the GNUC board—evidently cooled the UCC's criticism. But the fight wasn't over. By winning a truce on one front, Heningburg was freed to step up the battle on another.[44]

Not long after his successful showdown with the UCC, Heningburg proposed throwing "the biggest party this city has ever seen." He wanted to bolster the GNUC's reputation as a rising power and disprove outsiders' views of Newark as a crime-ridden wreck. Officials told Heningburg that his "Love Festival"—a daylong series of concerts, speakers, and children's attractions in Weequahic Park—would end in another riot. They denied his request for police protection. So Heningburg solicited volunteers from among the black officers of the Newark and New York City police forces and, testing a freshly brokered alliance between the Young Lords and Black Panthers, enlisted both groups to guard parked cars. Interns from Newark hospitals and members of the Essex County Welfare Rights Organization ran first-aid and childcare stations beneath tents he borrowed from a military connection at Fort Dix. He persuaded Tony Lawrence, producer of the Harlem Cultural Festival, to host the event and attracted producers from WNBC.[45]

But as the event approached, Heningburg learned that the Addonizio administration had put political muscle into its opposition to the Love Festival, asking black ministers to discourage congregants from attending. Many churches, Heningburg knew, "were beholden to the mayor only because of the money they wouldn't have otherwise for their senior program and their food program and their daycare program."[46] A statement signed by a number of them questioned the morality of the scheduled performances and the choice to hold the event on a Sunday.[47] The Love Festival had become another contest, Heningburg realized, "between me and the mayor." He told the board of the GNUC that the organization's survival depended upon the festival's success. "If I'm going to be useful in the future, I've got to immobilize the mayor so he'll stop messing with me, and, by extension, you." He requested fifty buses from the chairman of Public Service, who also served on the GNUC board, to shuttle festival attendants between downtown and Weequahic Park. Heningburg also supplied a list of "pick-up points" at city churches, recalling, "I want to empty these black churches right in the middle of the collection. I want to make these black preachers understand there's a force in this town in addition to the mayor."[48]

On October 5, 1969, over 35,000 people gathered at Weequahic Park to hear Bobby "Blues" Bland, the Magnificent Men, the Commanders and Ruth McFadden, and the Branford Gospel Singers perform throughout a peaceful sunny afternoon.[49] Although one deputy mayor attended, the rest of the administration and the city council shunned the festival, and the press offered scant coverage. But Bernice Bass, a local radio host popular for her blunt appraisals of city leaders, applauded Heningburg.[50] That endorsement reflected another aspect of the change overtaking Newark: the erosion of the traditional media's ability to produce and control the public narrative.

The GNUC had defied the municipal administration and won. "Although it was just a party," Heningburg said, the Love Festival had "serious political overtones." It revised "the image of the Urban Coalition from being a corporate-created social service agency"—which, of course, it was—"to being a potentially powerful political and economic reality in the city."[51] Heningburg—a product of the black elite, a public relations expert, and a veteran of the Cold War's propaganda battles—believed that power lay in perception. "Image is very important and if the image is that I'm the type of person who can turn out 35,000 people in a park without anything happening, then you have to pay attention."[52] In Heningburg's initial confrontations he emphatically denied any intention to pursue electoral politics himself. Yet he was in effect mobilizing a constituency, directing the GNUC's resources to challenge city leaders. He was positioning himself as an unusual figure in urban politics: not a strongman or a demagogue, neither a new boss nor a kingmaker—rather, a middleman. Not so much a movement leader as the movement's agent, a man who could fix a rigged machine to produce new outcomes.

The conflict between Heningburg and Addonizio culminated two months later. Addonizio recognized that Heningburg had crafted a potential alliance among civic leaders, corporate executives, and black power activists that could undermine his reelection. The United Brothers had emerged from semisecrecy to claim a bold role, most publicly in their sponsorship of a Black and Puerto Rican Political Convention in November 1969. The month after the convention, the city council voted down a $7,500 grant to the GNUC for youth programs, and Addonizio, a GNUC board member in name only, abruptly resigned. The organization had fallen under the influence of "divisive" elements, Addonizio charged, claiming that his board affiliation conflicted with his duty to serve all residents "with equal consideration and concern."[53]

The source of Addonizio's complaint was Heningburg's participation in the Black and Puerto Rican Political Convention, which had been largely planned and carried out by Baraka and other nationalists.[54] Intended to winnow a contentious pool of candidates down to a slate capable of attracting broad support, the convention represented the tangible application of black power and advanced a tenuous alliance between blacks and Puerto Ricans around their shared opposition to Addonizio. The convention also demonstrated Baraka's vision of operational unity in its diversity; attendees ranged from established groups such as the National Federation of Negro Women's Clubs, the NAACP, and the Urban League, to new, more militant groups such as the Rutgers Student Puerto Rican Organization, Baraka's Committee for a Unified Newark, and the United Brothers themselves.[55]

Heningburg told Addonizio that he had attended the convention as a "private citizen," not a representative of the GNUC. Robert Curvin, a leader of the Congress of Racial Equality (CORE), took a stronger stand, arguing that Addonizio did not respect Heningburg's right to participate in the political life of the city, singling him out for criticism when many leaders of Newark organizations had attended.[56] Both defenses seemed to confirm Addonizio's suspicion about the event: there was no denying that he had lost his once-solid support among the city's black electorate and his attempt to retaliate only highlighted his diminished status.[57]

Heningburg negotiated his various roles pragmatically, deploying the themes of black power while adapting his message to diverse audiences. In December 1969 Heningburg spoke to an audience of five hundred, mostly white, Newark businessmen and civic leaders upon receiving the Greater Newark Salvation Army Red Shield Award. His appeal was at odds with the expressions of black nationalism percolating through Newark politics: "The leadership is going to have to come from white America to solve the problems of black and Spanish-speaking Americans," he said. "No black man can provide the leadership. Martin Luther King failed because the task was impossible."[58] His comments seemed calculated to persuade white leaders that black political victories would not absolve them of all responsibility. His references to King, whose vision for interracial cooperation perhaps awakened some longing among white liberals puzzled and alarmed by the black power movement, prepared them to accept Heningburg's implicit invitation for white men to pick up the reins—and then hand them over to a new black leader. The speech he delivered the next month confirmed this view: he castigated business leaders and suburbanites for "political hypocrisy" when they denounced black militancy but also rejected black electoral challenges to the dysfunctional status quo.

Yet Heningburg also returned to the self-help ethos of older black nationalist traditions in other speeches. He called for the creation of black capital through the cultivation of black-owned businesses and support for black candidates. At an Organization of Negro Educators meeting about Newark's mayoral election, Heningburg echoed the comparison between African and European Americans that Young had made during a speech for the NUC. For Europeans, he argued, ethnic businesses may have served as a "wellspring" of economic and political clout. For African Americans, however, "those sources which have financed the political aspirations of the ethnic groups in this city have been turned off."[59] He exhorted the black middle class to take a more aggressive role in contributing to black candidates' campaigns and to electing a black mayor who could restore the city's credibility and draw private-sector resources back to Newark.[60]

The contrast between Heningburg's speeches before mostly white and mostly black audiences no doubt reflected his appraisal of what each needed to hear to support what Heningburg saw as the first step in saving Newark: the election of African American and Hispanic candidates and the organizing of dedicated constituents to support them in office. With Kenneth Gibson's election in 1970 came expectations for wholesale change of the sort Heningburg had envisioned.

The Newark Plan

Kenneth Gibson's 1970 victory elicited celebration across the city, but it also threw the entrenched patterns of discrimination encountered by black Newarkers into sharp relief. The unprecedented Medical College Agreement, for example, existed mostly on paper, prompting Heningburg to describe the 250 million dollars' worth of new construction under way in Newark as "a continuing source of friction and hostility."[61] In response to government failures to enforce affirmative action, Heningburg and longtime activist George Fontaine launched the Black and Puerto Rican Construction Coalition. The group targeted the massive expansion and renovation of the Newark airport. Over the next few years they participated in hearings, lawsuits, and negotiations; issued threats and attempted to shut down construction sites where discrimination prevailed.[62] Their efforts were alternately bolstered and hampered by developments at the federal level. Once again, Heningburg was both provocateur and middleman.

The Black and Puerto Rican Construction Coalition took on the airport during what promised to be a milestone year. Arthur A. Fletcher, assistant secretary of labor and the highest-ranking black official in the Nixon administration, announced that the Department of Labor had adopted the "Philadelphia Plan"—originally devised to integrate the construction trades—as a model for half a dozen cities where civil rights groups demanded federal oversight.[63] The Philadelphia Plan required contractors to include in their bids on federally funded projects goals and timetables for recruiting skilled minority workers. To liberals, it seemed too good to be true. Nixon's initial support for the Philadelphia Plan confounded his supporters. Unions, meanwhile, protested. AFL-CIO president George Meaney called affirmative action a "concoction and contrivance of a bureaucrat's imagination to offset the Nixon's Administration's bad civil rights record."[64]

The Philadelphia Plan also generated conflict within the federal government. It had been sidelined in 1969 by arguments, voiced most prominently by Comptroller General Elmer B. Staats, that the plan's hiring goals and timetables too closely resembled hiring quotas, which the Civil Rights Act of 1964 prohibited. Attorney General John N. Mitchell disagreed with Staats, distinguishing the goals of the Philadelphia Plan from "hard quotas."[65] But as implementation began, unions, employers, and activists continued to replay the debate. Like Staats, many unions resisted the plan, while activists, following Mitchell, argued that the goals and timetables they advocated were permissible.

Government officials, meanwhile, sought affirmative action plans in the construction industry as a kind of de facto economic measure and means to rein in union power. Inflation and declining productivity were coming to define the economy of the new decade, and the Nixon administration blamed union wages.[66] Nixon actually suspended all federally financed construction between September 1969 and March 1970, citing wage inflation caused by the tight labor market in skilled trades.[67] Postmaster General Winton M. Blount, speaking for Nixon, insisted on the connection between union wages, inflation, and affirmative action, denouncing the "outrageous wage settlements" unions had won and advocating legislation that would expedite training, bypass apprenticeships, and compel unions to welcome minority members. Blount predicted, "If we don't bring more people into these high-paying trades, it will be very dangerous for our country."[68] Union members correctly feared that the Nixon administration would try to use affirmative action to sow discord among Democratic constituencies and undermine union power.[69]

This national picture establishes the context in which the Black and Puerto Rican Construction Coalition sought to extend the affirmative action provisions promised (if only weakly enforced) in the Medical College Agreement to other projects. As an intricate rhythm of protest and negotiation played out during the early 1970s, officials at the Departments of Justice and Labor proved to be unreliable, alternately pledging and retracting support. Their inconsistency compelled local activists to devise their own "Newark Plan" and their own enforcement mechanisms. In an ironic twist, the coalition ultimately rejected federal intervention on behalf of affirmative action when it was finally offered, too little, too late.

In March 1970 John Wilks, assistant secretary of the Office of Federal Contract Compliance in the Department of Labor, came to Newark at Heningburg's insistence to investigate discrimination on publicly funded construction sites.[70] Witnesses at the hearing Wilks convened presented a "picture of almost all-white skilled trades unions" (see table below).[71] Heningburg testified that "only eight of the almost 2,000 union plumbers, pipefitters and steamfitters are black or brown. . . . Only 18 of the 1,130 union electricians are black or Spanish-speaking."[72] Among the skilled trades, the ironworkers had the highest percentage of minorities, but since they sponsored only 22 apprentices, this amounted to a mere five workers. All of their 546 journeymen were white. The roofers had no minority journeymen, either. Only the laborers' unions—whose members were typically among the least-skilled and lowest-paid in the construction trades—proved exceptions. Activist George Richardson reported that there had "been no bargaining in good faith" since 1962, when the US Commission on Civil Rights first held hearings on discrimination in Newark.[73] In the meantime, Newark's workforce, over 60 percent of which was black and Puerto Rican, had declined from 176,000 in 1960 to 157,000 in 1970, while its unemployment rate had increased from 8 to 13 percent.[74] Heningburg urged the government to cancel contracts on jobs where discrimination had been established until affirmative action measures could be enforced.[75]

Nathan Duff, secretary of the Ironworkers' Union, employed a familiar defense among trade union officials, insisting that failure to apply for apprenticeships explained the low numbers of black and Puerto Rican workers. As evidence, Duff cited his effort to recruit minority apprentices, which had yielded only twenty-four applicants. But Duff's claims were undermined by the testimony of black tradesmen, who had been denied union membership despite decades of experience, and the records of employment agencies, which indicated over five hun-

Composition of Essex County Building Trade Unions

Trade	No. of minority workers	Total no. of workers	Percentage minority
Electrician (apprentices)	11	211	5.2
Electrician (journeymen)	18	1,130	1.6
Electricians (combined)	**29**	**1,341**	**2.1**
Plumbers, pipefitters, and steamfitters (apprentices)	5	204	2.5
Plumbers, pipefitters, and steamfitters (journeymen)	8	1,974	0.4
Plumbers, pipefitters, and steamfitters (combined)	**13**	**2,178**	**0.6**
Roofers (only journeymen)	**0**	**247**	**0**
Sheet metal workers (apprentices)	4	212	1.9
Sheet metal workers (journeymen)	2	1,103	0.2
Sheet metal workers (combined)	**6**	**1,315**	**0.4**
Ironworkers (apprentices)	5	22	22.7
Ironworkers (journeymen)	0	546	0
Ironworkers (combined)	**5**	**568**	**9**
Carpenters (apprentices)	12	149	8
Carpenters (journeymen)	234	2,999	7.6
Carpenters (combined)	**246**	**3,148**	**7.6**
Glaziers (only journeymen)	**2**	**165**	**1.2**
ALL TRADES	301	8,862	3.3

Source: Data supplied for hearings conducted in Newark, March 1970, *Joyce v. McCrane, Bricklayers, et al.*, 1970 U.S. Dist. Lexis 9004.

dred unskilled and slightly fewer skilled minority workers had sought employment in the construction trades.[76]

The hearing supported claims made by both Secretary of Labor George Shultz and Wilks that Newark's building trades were ripe for a federal Philadelphia Plan.[77] Shultz initially selected eighteen cities for federally imposed plans and then narrowed the selection to six, including Newark. Shultz also shifted his stance on the type of plan he recommended. Instead of the Philadelphia Plan, Shultz now promoted the Chicago Plan. The Chicago Plan permitted unions leeway to negotiate so-called hometown affirmative action plans and to avail themselves of what Assistant Labor Secretary Arthur Fletcher called an "escape hatch" to avoid federal intervention of the more stringent Philadelphia variety.[78] Shultz's revision reflected the Nixon administration's wariness of imposing affirmative action plans and the risky political trade-offs they required. Meanwhile, contractors and unions in Newark, eager to use the "escape hatch," devised their own Chicago Plan. It emphasized publicly funded remedial education and preapprenticeship training, while supplanting project-specific goals and timetables with a five-year integration plan. The advocates of this "Chicago" option promoted it to Labor Department officials over the objections of Newark civil rights activists, who deemed its substitution for the Philadelphia Plan, which the groups had already accepted, as a bait-and-switch.[79] The result was no plan: federal officials retreated from Newark for a time, and its status as a target city for any sort of federal intervention remained unclear despite the evidence of discrimination revealed at the 1970 hearing. The challenges of implementing and enforcing these laws fell once again to groups, such as the Black and Puerto Rican Construction Coalition, that worked project by project to define what equal employment would mean in their city. Their next step was the Newark airport.

The airport, growing in size and regional prominence, was an ideal target for an antidiscrimination campaign.[80] By asserting a right to jobs there, the coalition also waded into a decades-old and highly imbalanced relationship between Newark and the Port Authority of New York and New Jersey.[81] A powerful, quasi-public entity comprising state officials, developers, and urban planners, the Port Authority oversaw the financing and construction of the states' shared infrastructure. Heningburg petitioned the Port Authority to take decisive action on employment discrimination, but his efforts went nowhere for months. "The Port Authority has so many layers of people," he recalled, that "[it] can negotiate until hell freezes." His failure to even initiate talks with the Port Authority prompted Heningburg to consider a more public

strategy: "One morning, without a plan, I walked out on the runway."[82]
It was a dangerous move, literally and tactically. Heningburg could
have been killed; he might also have marked himself as an "extremist"
and beyond the reach of negotiation. Airport security guards promptly
arrested Heningburg, but his spur-of-the-moment protest worked. The
director of the Port Authority, Austin Tobin, decided it would be better
to meet with leaders of the Black and Puerto Rican Construction Coalition than to let one black man get on the runway.[83]

When the Port Authority finally responded to Heningburg, they
presented a new challenge to his coalition: they seemed to want to kill
them with kindness. At their meeting, Port Authority officials greeted
each member of the coalition personally. Heningburg found himself
surrounded by "pretty little girls in short skirts and aprons running
around, 'Can I get you some coffee? Would you like a doughnut?'" He
had anticipated a battle. Now he feared his group had instead become
the target of "a seduction just short of being screwed." When Tobin
appeared, he further surprised Heningburg by reading a prepared statement in which he fully acknowledged the activists' demands. Employment discrimination was a national, not local, problem, Tobin insisted.
He invited Heningburg to accompany him to Washington to meet with
Attorney General John Mitchell. Heningburg was shocked. "I came to
fight and he's embracing me and saying let's go off and see the attorney
general." Tobin went further: he reminded Heningburg that not only
skilled construction workers but also minority vendors were underrep-
resented at the airport. Heningburg assured Tobin that he could find
him "ten qualified minority concessionaires in two days." Privately,
Heningburg worried that he could not keep such a pledge. "But it was a
stage," he recalled. "There was a performance going on."[84]

Why did the famously independent and ungovernable Port Authority, after ignoring Heningburg for months, suddenly adopt the cause of
affirmative action? Given the highly disruptive protests over discrimination in the New York and New Jersey building trades that had been
ongoing since the mid-1960s, Tobin may have intended his meeting
with Heningburg as a preemptive gesture, asserting the Port Authority's control over the implementation of new employment policies he
believed inevitable. Tobin knew that the Port Authority's lease for the
Newark airport allowed it to profit handsomely from the property.[85]
Tobin may have predicted (correctly) that Kenneth Gibson, newly
elected to govern a city in severe fiscal distress, would soon revisit the
arrangement. Perhaps Tobin hoped that a cordial relationship with the
Black and Puerto Rican Construction Coalition would help him main-

tain the Port Authority's advantages in future negotiations with the city's first black mayor.[86]

With a prize as big as the airport on the line, Tobin's motivations mattered less to Heningburg and the coalition than the action he was prepared to take. "You begin to realize the power and the influence that Austin Tobin has," Heningburg recalled thinking as he boarded a flight to Washington, DC, with Tobin, Republican governor William T. Cahill, and MacNaughton. At the Justice Department, Attorney General Mitchell sat silently smoking his pipe while "Tobin made the most emotional speech." He impressed upon Mitchell the intensity of employment discrimination in Newark and the willingness of its black and Puerto Rican residents to bodily block the airport's construction. Tobin warned that "women and children" would be killed trying to stop planes on the runway if the attorney general did not intervene. Since his arrest, Heningburg had not made any new threats to interrupt air traffic, but his failed attempt had apparently so alarmed Tobin that he painted for the attorney general a frightening portrait of the chaos and tragedy that would ensue if Heningburg's walk on the runway became the model for mass direct action.[87]

Mitchell promised he would send Justice Department officials to the airport in the fall.[88] He said he could take no action before Election Day that could possibly hurt the US Senate campaign that Nelson Gross, New Jersey's Republican Party chairman, was waging against the Democratic incumbent, Harrison Williams. The Republicans did not actually want credit for enforcing the law, but Mitchell kept his promise. On November 4, the day after Gross's defeat, Justice Department officials arrived in Newark.[89] Facing stiff penalties, union leaders negotiated consent decrees under which they agreed to employ minority apprentices on the airport project. This was a victory for the Black and Puerto Rican Construction Coalition, but the fight was far from over.

In response, white union members walked off construction sites to protest minority workers they believed were unqualified; contractors protested that they were being asked to violate longstanding contracts; airlines insisted they supported minority hiring but were powerless to impose conditions on contractors; and the Port Authority halted construction.[90] As a result, little was accomplished in 1971.

Behind this apparent impasse, however, Heningburg was laying the groundwork for the breakthrough that occurred in January 1972. Nearly two years after Secretary Shultz had threatened—and then failed—to impose a federal plan on Newark, Heningburg announced that major public agencies and several private companies had agreed to what became a "Newark Plan." Modeled after the Medical College Agreement and described as a superior, homegrown alternative to both the Philadelphia and the Chicago Plans, the Newark Plan stipulated that minority workers would compose 30 percent of journeymen and 50 percent of apprentices on the 650 million dollars' worth of construction projects under way.[91] February 1972 marked a second victory when six airlines agreed to enforce similar minority hiring goals among their contractors, contribute $2 million toward basic construction training for minority workers, and fire noncompliant contractors.[92] Participants in the airport negotiations also agreed to abide by the decisions of the Review Council. Composed of community leaders, union officials, contractors, airline representatives, and Port Authority officials, the Review Council resembled the system of accountability activists had pursued in the Medical College dispute.[93]

By mid-1972 there were around one hundred blacks and Puerto Ricans on the airport terminal jobsite. Such numbers hardly reversed Newark's abysmal unemployment rate (over 13 percent) or redressed historical patterns of discrimination. But *Business Week* nonetheless predicted the Newark Plan "could set precedents not only for Newark but for the nation."[94] Voluntary "hometown" plans were now the standard, and Newark's performed well in comparison to those in Los Angeles and Detroit.[95]

Just as the efforts of the Black and Puerto Rican Construction Coalition bore fruit, however, Secretary of Labor J. D. Hodgson, who had replaced Shultz in July 1970, announced that a weaker federal version of the Newark Plan was about to be imposed on a dozen trades in Essex County and all federally financed projects over $500,000. Heningburg opposed it.[96] Why did Heningburg, who had originally demanded federal intervention in 1970, now find himself fighting against it? Hodgson's proposal came two years after the Black and Puerto Rican Construction Coalition had first been promised a federally mandated Philadelphia-style plan and after they had then painstakingly forged a local alternative. Hodgson's intervention threatened the hard-fought successes of the fledgling Newark Plan: Hodgson's version lacked penalties for violators and training components, and it stipulated significantly lower hiring goals. The flurry of plans had been hard enough to keep straight when their names stood for distinctly different approaches. The federal Philadelphia Plan had given way to the weaker Chicago Plan, to which Heningburg and the coalition had responded with the strong—and successful—local Newark Plan. Now, it appeared that the federal government was trying to hijack that success, rebranding its own weak plan with a homegrown label. From the coalition's perspective, it would be a disaster; not only would the plan undermine the work they had accomplished, but it would also render useless the name by which their successful approach was known.

Heningburg declared the federal government's faux Newark Plan "deficient in every category."[97] He predicted it would produce confusion, fortify white union members' resistance, and justify backsliding among his corporate allies.[98] Joined by a contingent of labor officials and businessmen, Heningburg persuaded the Labor Department to withdraw the proposal. The department's retreat was ironic: "the first time anyplace in the country," Heningburg noted, "a community has been able to fight off a federal plan."[99] Proponents of affirmative action had typically favored the imposition of federal plans in their cities rather than voluntary, less stringent "hometown" plans. But developments in Newark inverted this situation, as the Black and Puerto Rican Construction Coalition sought to protect their achievements from an inferior plan and federal officials they suspected were insufficiently committed to minority hiring.

Small but significant gains in employment at the airport—what Heningburg called "the most important project in town"—may have bolstered enough confidence in the homegrown Newark Plan to forestall Hodgson, but its implementation remained a challenge throughout 1972.[100] Some union officials skipped meetings with the Review Council and rejected portions of the Newark Plan that hinged on the category of "trainees." The term pertained to workers who had been referred to the site by a source other than the union local, such as the Newark Construction Trades Training Corporation. The Ironworkers were most resistant to trainees, claiming they could supply adequate numbers of minority workers through their hiring hall.[101]

In late August the Black and Puerto Rican Construction Coalition, the Port Authority, and several airlines jointly pressured Kidd-Briscoe, a major contractor on the terminal extension, to assign some black trainees to crews on the site.[102] But when six of the workers referred to Terminal C by the Newark Construction Trades Training Corporation reported for work, Kidd-Briscoe told them they would be paid for doing nothing, forbidden to work because they did not meet union qualifications. In fact, members of Ironworkers Local 11 had threatened to strike if the trainees picked up a tool. The general contractor had responded with a compromise, hoping to quietly satisfy the trainees by permitting them to show up to the work site, while keeping white workers on the actual job. But the trainees promptly filed a suit with the Equal Employment Opportunity Commission.[103]

Marty Schwartz, a white electrician who worked on the airport extension, recalled white workers' hostility. But although Schwartz acknowledged that racism played a role, he insisted that union members also had a legitimate grievance. Trainees had not gone through the standard union apprenticeship program, but they were compensated at journeymen levels. The union, in turn, expected them to come on the job with some experience. "The idea was they [advocates of the Newark Plan] just wanted them to become union members as journey persons," Schwartz recalled. "The trainee was supposed to have all the qualifications, the work on the site, the ability and all. Obviously, there were some that did, but there were many who had no ability of a journeyman nature." From the perspective of many white workers, Schwartz said, the "trainee" category undermined any "working model" for integration. "The guys that were in the local wouldn't show them anything because they were stuck there; they were getting paid the same and they didn't know anything."[104]

For many white workers, concerns about trainees' experience were compounded by fears that they were losing control of their locals and attendant privileges, such as unions' preference for apprentices related to members. According to Schwartz, "those who were in the trade would say, 'That's a job one of our guys could have had, or my son could have had.'"[105] For a decade, Essex County unions had claimed they could adequately integrate locals through their own apprenticeship programs. But given white resistance to black and Puerto Rican workers from all sources and the familial preferences built into the membership structure, no substantial integration had occurred.

The conflict over the six Ironworker trainees extended into autumn 1972, and the Port Authority briefly halted construction.[106] In response, Local 11 agreed to employ the six workers and to accept trainees if it was unable to recruit adequate numbers of minority apprentices by its own methods.[107] Returning to the job, black workers maintained a wary optimism. "It's too early to tell whether they are giving us the maximum instruction we could get," Jeffrey Benson said, "but we are being taught something."[108]

Benson and the others were reinstated amid reports that Nixon had further distanced himself from affirmative action. Arthur Fletcher, who had left his post at Labor in 1971, confirmed that Nixon, to attract the support of affirmative action opponents in organized labor, now disparaged Philadelphia-style plans as indistinguishable from quotas. It was the double-dealing that Nixon critics had feared. "This is an indication that blacks and minorities are being excommunicated from this society. They're moving against the goals and timetables of the Philadelphia Plan and if it goes, the others will go too," Fletcher warned. "It is very popular this year to run against everything black Americans stand for. . . . [T]he new code word is quotas, and it means whites don't want to see any systematic way to deal with minorities."[109] Fletcher's comments suggest that the Labor Department's decision to forgo intervention in Newark may not have simply reflected the modest success of the locally negotiated Newark Plan, as Heningburg believed. It likely signaled Nixon's calculated retreat from affirmative action as well, and the flagging capacity to implement the policy among those in his administration—such as Fletcher—who had supported it.[110]

Back in Newark, though, the lack of a federal plan—whether successfully "resisted" by Heningburg or never offered in good faith—allowed the local approach to flourish. The original, local Newark Plan created under the auspices of the GNUC and the Black and Puerto Rican Construction Coalition proved influential. The drawn-out struggle at the Newark airport was a local turning point. Once institutionalized within the Port Authority, the Newark Plan soon extended—informally and formally—to other construction projects in the region.[111]

"There was no heyday for attempts by federal regulatory agencies to impose affirmative action on U.S. industries," Trevor Griffey writes, assessing the combination of union resistance and calculated federal reluctance that characterized local struggles. "There was no pristine origin against which a backlash could define itself, because enforcement of affirmative action had accommodated its opponents from the beginning."[112] Newark's experience reveals the responsibility that black civil rights and labor organizations—and their allies—assumed in documenting discrimination, pressing for federal intervention, and devising their own plans when it was not forthcoming. It was a moderately successful model, but not an easily replicated one. Similar approaches in other cities often came up short. Crucial to the relative success of the Newark Plan was the role of fixers such as Heningburg, local actors who could play the part of a militant in the eyes of white establishment figures and the role of representative for actual militants and others willing to negotiate for the power found in small gains, job by job.[113]

Fixing Capitalism

Heningburg's role as a fixer also shaped his engagement with black capitalism. As historian Laura Warren Hill argues, scholars have "relegated to footnotes and brief sidebars" the history of black capitalism. But the fraught relationships between black power and corporate power produced complex, locally driven approaches to economic inequality that—for a time—redirected business as usual.[114] Black capitalism also stands as an influential variation of US social movements' perennial quest to tame or humanize capitalism.

While Heningburg's efforts to implement the Newark Plan had been contested as the airport's new terminals rose, a much quieter change was taking place inside these buildings, as vending contracts for minority businessmen multiplied. Benjamin Books, one of the first minority vendors at the airport, became a national chain, soon followed by EBON Services International Inc., which provided maintenance in Terminal B, and a minority-owned bus company that signed a contract with Eastern Airlines in 1975.[115] Minority concessionaires, starting with the dozen whose contracts stemmed from Heningburg's meeting with Tobin, formed the Airport Minority Advisory Council (AMAC), which grew into a national association, another offspring of Heningburg's efforts.[116]

The proliferation of minority concessionaires at the Newark airport reflected the centrality of black entrepreneurship to some strands of black power.[117] Both black activists' enthusiasm for black capitalism and Newark businessmen's plans to guide minority contractors through the government bidding process elicited comparatively fewer protests than had the Newark Plan. The local affiliate of the Interracial Council for Business Opportunity (ICBO) furnished loans of over $1 million in its first five years for minority businesses.[118] In 1969 the ICBO and the GNUC collaborated to secure another $2 million from local banks that underwrote groceries, trucking companies, data-processing services, and dry-cleaning establishments. By 1970 local corporations and the Ford Foundation had expanded funding for what they called "entrepreneurial education." The grant supported courses at Rutgers Graduate Business School that drew dozens of minority businessmen and revolved around mentoring relationships between established black business owners and less experienced entrepreneurs.[119]

Assessing these developments in 1970, Heningburg shifted from his role as the tarmac-trespassing voice of black tradesmen to an advocate of black capitalism. "Businessmen give leadership in our society," he said. "When you want things done, you ask businessmen." While conceding that capitalism was not the antidote to all of Newark's problems, Heningburg echoed Whitney Young's celebration of white immigrant entrepreneurialism with little acknowledgment of the historical differences this bootstrap history glossed over. "If it was good for others," Heningburg declared, "it should be good for blacks."[120]

To the extent that "black capitalism" constituted a movement in Newark, it was largely professionals with antipoverty and civil rights experience who attempted to codify it. Dairy Williams, for example, had worked for two New York antipoverty agencies and the New Jersey Department of State before taking a post as economic development director of the GNUC. He left the GNUC in 1969 to lead the Ebony Businessmen's Association. Williams launched Ebony Manor, a catering business intended to train young workers and serve as a private club for black businesspeople. The Ebony Businessmen's Association disparaged "charity," according to Williams, and preferred self-help to what he called the "artificial process" of government subsidies.[121] Beyond his criticism of subsidies, Williams's position reflected many African Americans' disillusionment with federal antipoverty policy.

The ICBO and the GNUC also celebrated independent businessmen, but they emphasized mutual cooperation between government experts, banks, and minority entrepreneurs, arguing that black capital accumulation could be best advanced by preparing business owners to seek Small Business Administration loans and to bid for public contracts. While Williams talked about the creation of a distinct, black entrepreneurial space comprising clubs, associations, and seminars, the GNUC and the ICBO focused on integrating individual minority entrepreneurs into an existing system. They also sought to correct the racially exclusive nature of government contracts, which had historically delivered giant public subsidies to white-owned businesses.

These efforts to cultivate a black economy in Newark overlapped with the ambitious goals of Newark's cultural nationalists, who gravitated to the Spirit House, a theater and community center operated by Amiri Baraka and activists affiliated with the Committee for a Unified Newark. Baraka and the disciplined young activists around him published books and periodicals, operated cafeterias, and crafted jewelry and African clothing. Their businesses both disseminated their beliefs and underwrote independent black political institutions, such as African history and language schools, music and theater performances, and a childcare center.[122] Newark activists played a central role in popularizing the holiday of Kwanzaa, developed by Los Angeles–based black nationalist leader Maulana Ron Karenga in 1967. In the early 1970s cultural nationalists veered toward socialism in their calls for more equitable division of property and profits and in their belief that economic development must contribute to the global solidarity of African people, but many also embraced an entrepreneurial ethos strikingly similar to the black capitalism espoused by Heningburg.[123] Yet they rejected the comparison: "We see no negative contradiction in the creation of small business as providing an economic base for the cadre. To call this 'capitalism' is not to know what capitalism is."[124] They instead committed themselves to *ujamaa*, cooperative economics. Forays into business ownership, they claimed, were strictly to achieve economic independence and fund political goals.

Such examples fueled a larger debate in activist circles and the mainstream press over the place of capitalism in a black freedom movement that encompassed economic reform, entrepreneurship, and anticapitalist revolution.[125] Calls for independent black economic power excited officials in the Nixon administration, who attempted to exploit that enthusiasm for private enterprise with new policies and rhetoric. Black capitalism reflected Nixon's own admiration for self-made businessmen, and supporting it offered him a less controversial method of courting black voters than embracing the movement.[126] But many activists perceived Nixon's stance as a cynical political maneuver, meant to compensate for Nixon's aggressive criticism of affirmative action and to exploit disputes within the movement. For example, Martin Luther King Jr. had deemed black Americans' full integration into corporations and labor unions a more effective strategy for black economic empowerment than the cultivation of a distinct black capitalism.[127] Many black power thinkers rejected "black capitalism" because they opposed capitalism outright. Some denounced it as a fraud or, even worse, a strategy that would further stratify black communities and eclipse the possibility of a more radical, redistributive movement attuned to both class and race.[128] But in practice, many black power activists embraced black businesses as instrumental to self-determination: a longstanding means of sustaining communities within a segregated society and a way to finance the movement. For others, the cultivation of "black capitalism" appeared to be less a choice than a reality. As African Americans accurately anticipated the increasingly segregated nature of many cities, experimentation with every possible type of black capital accumulation and institution building became the order of the day. But even as black capitalism took hold, as it fueled debate about capitalism and racial inequality, white capitalists' support for the GNUC waned.[129]

Disintegration of the Greater Newark Urban Coalition

The "political hypocrisy" of local business leaders that Heningburg had diagnosed in his 1970 speech only seemed to accelerate amid Newark's sustained fiscal problems and the federal retreat from the urban crisis. These same factors contributed to the weakening of the National Urban Coalition, although harbingers of its undoing were present in its earliest meetings. At the NUC Emergency Convocation in 1967, John Lindsay had criticized the short-lived nature of so many urban programs, a factor that prompted anger and cynicism among their purported beneficiaries. The NUC soon found itself conforming to that very pattern. Many projects languished and its legislative agenda stalled, while its leadership struggled to fundraise. Within four years of the NUC's founding, John Gardner had resigned and the NUC reduced its national staff. Internal dissent immobilized many local coalitions.[130]

Corporate support for the NUC began to collapse as donors complained that the organization was long on plans, short on action.[131] But some complaints seemed little more than excuses for corporations' own declining commitment to reform, as urban uprisings subsided and the threat of black power seemed to fade. A fundraising firm bluntly informed the NUC that the organization "has lost its credibility with both givers and leaders. . . . A philosopher might ask, was there ever really credibility or was it from the beginning nothing more than a gut reaction to panic, fear, conscience?"[132] American Standard Inc. complained, "NUC has no program, nothing to sell." Jones and Laughlin Steel Corporation, known for its conservatism, complained that it had received "no gratitude from Black community."[133] The sense of urgency and sweeping liberal idealism with which Gardner had launched the NUC had clashed with the motivations of those donors who perceived the NUC as a penny-pinching public relations strategy.

These differences emerged forcefully among the NUC's prominent members. Although the organization claimed employment discrimination as a core concern, fundraising consultants recommended that its leaders avoid "integration" in their conversation with certain companies—Kroger Company and Great Atlantic and Pacific Tea Company, for example—in favor of less politically charged issues.[134] Conservative donors also rejected the NUC's "Counter-Budget." Aiming to reorder national priorities, the NUC had prepared an alternative federal budget for 1972 that drastically increased funding for urban programs and decreased military spending. Some executives denounced the Counter-Budget as ineffective grandstanding; many more bluntly decried its politics. AT&T and Equitable Life Insurance Society, whose donations surpassed $500,000, both complained about the Counter-Budget, and its call for national health insurance incensed the latter. "The National Urban Coalition is finished," said one executive. "Many other companies know it and agree."[135] General Motors recommended that NUC "cut out the b.s. about Counterbudget" and concentrate instead on local coalitions.[136]

In 1971 Sol Linowitz, the new chairman of the NUC, appeared to take this advice. He conceded that "caught in the squeeze between soaring prices and a sagging economy, individuals and institutions alike seemed to have little time and less money to spend on urban problems." The NUC, he said, would now focus on local affiliates, helping them "develop alliances between the racial and blue-collar minorities of our cities in order to overcome hostilities that prevent them from working together."[137] This plan reflected a conviction among many policymakers that civil rights and antipoverty legislation had alienated white urban Democratic voters: the Irish, Jewish, Italian, and Slavic Americans subsumed under the term "white ethnic."[138] As Republicans and Democrats competed for the loyalties of these voters, they became only one of NUC's diffuse concerns. The organization tempered the urgent, comprehensive recommendations that had characterized its launch. Instead, NUC shifted again, this time to studying regional metropolitan alliances and filling gaps in federal housing policy. They championed some organizational fixers, such as those discussed in part 3, and attempted to stem urban decline through housing rehabilitation and homeownership programs for tenants.[139]

When measured against the multitude of problems the NUC set out to address, its accomplishments were likely to be modest even in the best possible scenario. NUC members favored disparate goals; some resisted even its gentlest affront to the assumption of capitalism's virtues. Gardner and his successors could not build a sufficiently powerful consensus among them. In this way, the short history of the NUC and its involvement in Newark echo previous attempts by business leaders to address capitalism's fallout: seeking alliances with government and civic leaders in a contentious attempt to influence social movements, shape federal policies, and redefine the extent of "corporate responsibility" to the cities in which they operated. Their attempts at "reorder-ing national priorities" flourished briefly, but at a time when US cities most needed steady, persuasive advocacy; their retreat signaled a return to the myopic liberalism they once condemned.

Like the NUC, the GNUC also struggled to raise funds in the early 1970s. At the same time, it faced a new round of political conflicts simi-lar to those that had characterized Heningburg's first year with the or-ganization. The GNUC's attempts to influence the course of the Gibson administration continued to arouse some residents' suspicion that it was ultimately a front for the business establishment. Donald Mac-Naughton persuaded the chamber of commerce that it should subsidize the salary of Newark's new municipal business administrator in order to attract a wider pool of highly experienced candidates. Although MacNaughton insisted that the offer did not entail the chamber's in-volvement in the hiring process, some Newark residents opposed the use of private-sector philanthropy to underwrite municipal functions. MacNaughton reacted with frustration. "Would they rather we didn't do anything? What do they want from us?"[140] MacNaughton's protes-tations must have struck many residents as disingenuous: from the wards to city hall, from the housing authority to community action programs, money in Newark rarely changed hands without activating a vast network of expectations and obligations.

Heningburg, like his counterparts at the NUC, also noticed that support had diminished among local corporations—many of whom had been "dragged kicking and screaming" into the GNUC in the first place. At one point, Heningburg reported that the GNUC's balance dipped so low it could barely meet payroll expenses.[141] Despite Gibson's insistence that his election alone was not a silver-bullet solution to en-demic inequality—"I am not a narcotic," he said at one point—many former donors believed the black mayor would relieve the conditions that contributed to the 1967 riot and justify a reduction in their sup-port for the GNUC.[142]

The GNUC staggered into the late 1970s but ultimately dissolved against a municipal backdrop of persistent fiscal problems, inadequate city services, and high poverty rates that lent a particularly dire cast to the claim Gibson had made upon his election as mayor: "Wherever American cities are going, Newark will get there first."[143] Heningburg's career with the GNUC had crested on the tensions and alliances that developed between the private sector and the grass roots in the late 1960s and 1970s. He mediated between a diverse spectrum of civil rights, black power, and antipoverty activists and the corporate executives seeking to contain the urban crisis, adapt to new federal policies, and reestablish corporate leadership over the city. He sought a third way: an uneasy coalition of black power's conservative wing and corporate power's progressive margin, allied against the city machine that had long suppressed Newark's black residents and no longer served the interests of the corporations that demanded a stable environment for their operations. In negotiating these two largely contradictory impulses, Heningburg emerged as an influential and widely respected middleman. Heningburg's career encompassed the heady rise and development of grassroots black power politics into a broad-based constituency that secured unprecedented electoral victories. He helped to mobilize an urban constituency that made sustained demands for political power and jobs. He translated the momentum of black power into policies for which the city's business interests briefly lent institutional support. But his experience also illustrated the limitations of activists' attempts to realize black self-determination within an economy still shaped by white-owned corporations and to realize civil rights gains when the federal government ultimately retreated from enforcement, abandoning cities such as Newark to the new black power and leaving the old "plantationship" around them largely intact.

Dismantling it, Heningburg argued, meant looking beyond the city limits. As Newark's problems overwhelmed Gibson's administration, Heningburg focused his criticism on the suburbs and the tax structure that punished the state's oldest and largest city. "If the city of Newark closed down on a Monday, the 300,000 suburban residents who make their living in Newark would have to go on welfare the next day. . . . It is the only city that gives more employment to nonresidents than residents," Heningburg told a meeting of the Newark Airport Businessmen's Council, at which Nikki Giovanni, the celebrated writer of the Black Arts Movement, saluted him with a poem.[144] The celebration testified to Heningburg's success as a fixer, but his comments made clear that the "most sophisticated form of political hypocrisy," against which he'd raged in 1970, persisted.

Conclusion

Within the National Urban Coalition, civil rights and corporate leaders debated the future of cities and the role that the private sector and civil society would play in their regeneration, while the Greater Newark Urban Coalition magnified the dialectic between black power and white corporate executives. Heningburg sought to deploy the financial and political capital of the GNUC, and at the same time, he brought legitimacy to the GNUC by virtue of his experiences in the civil rights movement and his affiliation with more militant groups such as the United Brothers. The "strange bedfellows"—black power advocates and white Republicans—who jointly supported some affirmative action programs, contract set-asides for minorities, and the concept of "black capitalism" make provocative, if fleeting, appearances in scholarship on federal legislation and policymaking.[145] Yet the experiences of fixers such as Heningburg reveal how such alliances actually took shape and influenced the "half-life" of black power—the way that interracial alliances with the private sector could be used to adapt and amplify black power but also to co-opt and rechannel it. A mobilized black constituency pursued ambitions to remake the city's business, civic, and political life and sent public officials and corporate leaders scrambling for a response. Black power unified African American residents around seemingly disparate goals, from building separate institutions to integrating existing ones. In the pursuit of these goals, one found the tactics and strategies developed by Heningburg, the consummate middleman.

1. Women host meeting of soldiers' club in this image of black Newark from January 1, 1918. Photograph from FPG / Hulton Archive / Getty Images.

2. Aerial view of Newark in the 1960s. Photograph courtesy of the Newark Public Library. Licensed by Media General Communications Holdings LLC.

3. Pickets against job discrimination at the building site of Rutgers University School of Law, January 30, 1965. Photograph from Afro American Newspapers / GADO / Getty Images.

4. Activist Rebecca Doggett (Andrade) in 1964. She fought racial discrimination in employment and worked with the Newark Preschool Council to launch Head Start in Newark and in Puerto Rico during the War on Poverty. In the 1970s she led the Tri-City Citizens Union for Progress and its People's Center. Photograph courtesy of the Newark Public Library. Licensed by Media General Communications Holdings LLC.

5. National Guard and residents face off during the uprising, July 14, 1967. Photograph from Neal Boenzi / New York Times Co. / Getty Images.

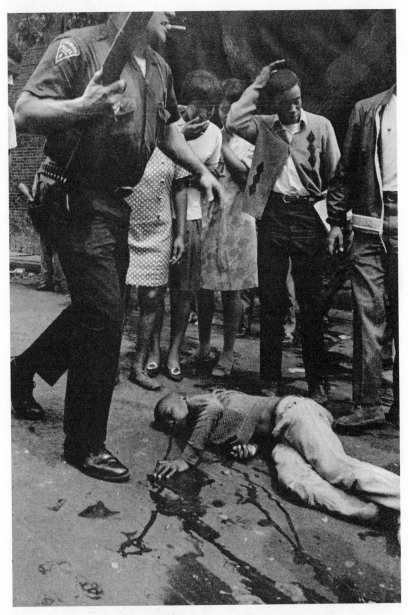

6. Joe Bass Jr., age twelve, July 1967. Police shot Bass while pursuing twenty-four-year-old Billy Furr for stealing beer. Bass survived his injuries, but Furr did not. Photograph © Bud Lee Picturemaker.

7. Willie Wright leads business and government leaders on a "ghetto tour" through Newark's Central Ward in 1968. Photograph courtesy of the Newark Public Library.

8. Business and government leaders participate in "ghetto tour" of the Central Ward in 1968. Photograph courtesy of the Newark Public Library.

9. Gustav Heningburg overlooks construction in the late 1970s. Photograph courtesy of the Newark Public Library.

10. Toby Henry, at center with cap, coordinating activities of Stella Wright Tenants Association members as they try to keep Stella Wright Homes open, March 8, 1974. At right, a stove provides the only heat for the offices at 254 Prince Street. Photograph from *New York Times* / Neal Boenzi.

11. Headquarters, Committee for a Unified Newark, October 31, 1972. The top billboard refers to the weekly "Soul Sessions" led by Amiri Baraka, involving poetry, music, and dance. The middle billboard defines the Nguzo Saba, the seven principles of Kawaida. Photograph from Fred W. McDarrah / Getty Images.

12. Workers amid protesters at Kawaida Towers site, 1972. Photograph from *New York Times*.

13. A father at Babyland daycare center, April 6, 1975. Photograph from Fred R. Conrad / *New York Times*.

14. Mayor Kenneth A. Gibson shows President Jimmy Carter's domestic policy adviser, Stuart E. Eizenstat, the progress of New Community Commons, a development created by the New Community Corporation, August 7, 1979. Photograph from *New York Times* / William E. Sauro.

15. Mary Smith, a founder of Babyland and leader of the New Community Corporation, speaks while William Linder, director of the New Community Corporation (seated far right) and Governor Tom Kean (seated center) listen, 1985. Photograph from *Star-Ledger*. Courtesy of the Newark Public Library.

FIVE

Fixers for the 1970s? The Stella Wright Rent Strike and the Transformation of Public Housing

Oliver Todd and his wife were so excited about their apartment that they moved in before the furniture arrived. That first snowy night at Stella Wright Homes, Newark's new public housing complex, they slept on the floor.[1] In the 1940s and 1950s tenants expressed relief at finding themselves in "heavenly" replacements for the city's dilapidated cold-water tenements and liberated from the slumlords, who capitalized on poverty and segregation.[2] Washing machines, hot water, toilet facilities, elevators, health clinics, and plans for on-site job training promised an elevated quality of life for residents of the city's most hard-pressed neighborhoods. Public housing was "one of the greatest things that ever happened in the U.S. for the poor class of people," a tenant declared. Every time she unlocked her door, she remembered, "I felt like screaming with joy." A woman who had moved into public housing after losing a home to foreclosure wrote, "I could embrace every piece of cement that forms this virtual paradise on earth."[3]

But by the 1970s what had once felt like liberation had become a trap. The squalid conditions in many high-rise buildings evoked any word but "paradise." By the 1990s complexes like Stella Wright Homes were boarded up and vacated. The New Jersey–based hip-hop group Naughty by Nature set their 1993 video for their song "Everything's Gonna Be Alright (Ghetto Bastard)" in front of Newark's abandoned Columbus Homes: "If you ain't ever been to the ghetto / Don't ever come to the ghetto."[4] Few mourned and many cheered in 2002 as city leaders, community activists, tenants, and Newark children helped a team of engineers demolish Stella Wright Homes. Mayor Sharpe James joined the crowd—among them Gustav Heningburg and his granddaughter—in yanking the handle that triggered the explosives. "Within seconds," wrote a demolition engineer, "a forgettable chapter of the venerable city's past gently melted into oblivion."[5]

But Stella Wright did not go gently. In between the opening of new buildings that promised a better life and their implosion lie four decades of history grounded not in condemnations of public housing but in tenants' collective struggle to shape it.[6] Few events encapsulate that struggle more than the Stella Wright rent strike. On April 1, 1970, public housing tenants across Newark launched what became the longest, largest, and most expensive rent strike in US public housing history. Tenants positioned themselves not only as protesters against housing authority malfeasance but also as fixers, advancing their own diagnosis of a system in crisis and insisting on a voice in its resolution. Tenants issued demands; they also devised solutions that encompassed education, employment, and a voice in housing management. At its peak the rent strike in Newark involved about ten thousand tenants and over $6 million of withheld rent, exceptional even in an era marked by tenant revolt. But it also reveals the common struggles for power that reverberated nationally when tenants attempted to salvage—then transform—this bulwark of the New Deal state.

Newark's public housing rent strike benefited from and lent momentum to a national wave of tenant activism in the 1960s and 1970s.[7] Like the rent strikes organized by tenement dwellers against private landlords in the 1910s and 1920s, public housing rent strikes spoke to the everyday challenges—both brutal and pedestrian—faced by the residents of deteriorating, overcrowded buildings. Implicit in tenant complaints was a claim to decent housing as a right.[8] As in earlier rent strikes, women often led protests and emphasized the deleterious effect of substandard housing on their domestic labor—cooking, cleaning, budgeting, and caring for children and elderly family members.[9] Progressive Era strikers had often pressured a welfare-state-in-the-making for legislation that would produce decent low-priced housing. In contrast, the tenants of the 1970s fought to hold public housing authorities—the products of earlier housing activism—accountable. Beyond that, they attempted to maintain the promise of the Housing Act of 1949 amid a growing consensus that it was doomed.

Recent histories of public housing have illuminated tenants' historical agency and challenged a record dictated largely by officials, planners, and housing advocates. Rhonda Williams's groundbreaking study of poor black women's activism in Baltimore offers a template for rewriting the history of public housing. Poor black women defended their communities, Williams shows, in the face of hostile bureaucracies and even putatively sympathetic social movements—such as civil rights and black power—that often diminished women's leadership.[10] D. Bradford Hunt has argued in his illuminating study of the formidable Chicago Housing Authority that the neglect of tenants' perspectives constitutes "a distinct element of public housing's tragic downfall."[11] By adding an analysis of the Newark rent strike to this body of work, we see how tenants built upon a preexisting—if overlooked—civic life and employed strategies from community action, civil rights, and black power activism. Tenant activism is part of these movements' histories that has often gone unrecognized as such. Newark strikers' appeal to self-determination also kept alive a version of the War on Poverty that had elsewhere already been scaled back by the early 1970s.

Like the Central Ward residents who challenged the Medical College, rent strikers briefly found allies in the Department of Housing and Urban Development (HUD), in Mayor Kenneth Gibson, and among civic and religious groups. Federal authorities and the judges who intervened affirmed the tenants' position (though not necessarily their tactics). And while tenants themselves sometimes disagreed about strategies, they displayed solidarity throughout much of a long strike. Tenants were not simply victims of an institution in headlong decline; as fixers in their own right they mustered resources and coordinated action among themselves. They won several critical legal victories and contributed to the increasingly powerful criticism voiced by tenant and welfare rights activists around the country.[12] Small victories—though often buried or outright dismissed in the historical record—secured more tenant representation and directly informed the organizational fixers who proliferated over the next three decades. But their attempts to act as fixers on a broader scale were thwarted as government authorities divested from public housing. Even some tenants imagined "tearing it all down." Ultimately, tenants found it difficult to succeed as fixers within the funding and legal constraints of the public housing system.

Dissatisfying to Dangerous: The Plummeting
Quality of Public Housing

Newark residents were not alone in their early admiration of public housing. A Baltimore woman in Rhonda Williams's study called subsidized housing "a little heaven for poor people."[13] In Chicago, as D. Bradford Hunt writes, "early public housing residents responded with an intense affinity for their new communities, and the word 'paradise' surfaces repeatedly."[14] What became perhaps the most notorious public housing development—the modernist behemoth Pruitt-Igoe—was described by its early tenants as a "resort hotel"; its crisp design, lawns, and amenities were like an "oasis in the desert" of Saint Louis's tenements.[15] It was not just the physical improvements but also the self-help organizations, mothers' groups, sports clubs, and children's programs that combined with informal neighborly ties to sustain a durable civic life.

Newark's housing was initially a source of pride. Newark officials were eager applicants for housing funds following the passage of the Housing Acts of 1937 and 1949.[16] The pace of demolition and construction quickened in the 1950s and early 1960s. Newark built 18,000 units, approximately 9,000 designated for the poor. Stella Wright Homes, completed in 1959, was part of that boom. Yet even as the city built new low-income units, over 7,000 were demolished in the name of urban renewal. Thousands more fell into an uninhabitable state. In terms of units built, the quantitative success of the Newark Housing Authority (NHA) belied a history of unmet need.[17]

Tenants who moved into high-rise buildings with anticipation faced immediate problems: leaky ceilings, exposed wires, and malfunctioning elevators compromised public housing from its earliest years.[18] By the 1960s lack of security dominated tenants' concerns. They joined with civil rights organizations such as the Congress of Racial Equality (CORE) to criticize the Newark Police Department. Tenants, the majority of them African American, found themselves victims of crime and police brutality on the streets and neglect in their own buildings. Few projects had more than part-time security. In May 1964 tenant Mary Smith told a Newark City Council meeting that a child had been raped near Scudder Homes. Robberies were daily occurrences.[19] "Our children see addicts, drunks, people making love in the hallways. We can look out our windows and see pocketbooks snatched. People throw wine bottles and whiskey bottles from the roof," Smith told another meeting.[20] She feared that crime would undermine many tenants' hard-won respectability.[21]

The NHA and the city had sparred for years over who was responsible for policing the housing projects. Chicago public housing residents were at the mercy of housing authorities and police who expressed indifference: "Foot patrols of public housing superblocks were rare, and 'vertical patrols' inside buildings were nonexistent," according to Hunt. Tenants demanded that authorities hire more security or train tenants to provide it, while the *Chicago Defender* publicized the pervasive fear curtailing tenants' lives.[22] In Newark, two years of tenant complaints, combined with a 1963 court ruling, prompted the city council to reassign housing project security to the police. They assumed the responsibility with reluctance.[23] Long after Smith had moved out of Scudder Homes, residents continued to press the NHA on the safety of what the *Newark Evening News* called the "crime-haunted housing projects."[24] Tenants' efforts to maintain security were overshadowed by political and cultural narratives that blamed them for rising crime.

In addition to disrepair and weak security, other factors exerted heavy pressure on Newark's public housing in the 1950s and 1960s: migration from the South, urban renewal dislocation, and suburban segregation. The income and occupation profile of tenants changed as the city's fortunes declined. Across Essex County, the number of people receiving Aid to Families with Dependent Children doubled between 1960 and 1965.[25] Part of the increase may have been the result of War on Poverty legislation that expanded eligibility for such programs. Even so, tenants in 1970 were more likely to be unemployed, recipients of Aid to Families with Dependent Children, and single parents than in previous decades. They were also younger.[26] In Newark, as in other cities, working-class tenants left public housing. "Numerous policy choices and external forces," argues Hunt, "converged to both push and pull the working class out of public housing—and kept others from entering altogether."[27]

In Newark this public housing population participated in the War on Poverty as well as the campaigns against Clinton Hill slumlords carried out by members of CORE, Students for a Democratic Society, and some of the more radical community action programs.[28] In the early 1960s NAACP Youth Council activists recruited public housing tenants for construction jobs as part of the campaign to desegregate the trades. Black nationalists also organized extensive voter registration drives in the projects.[29] By 1970 tenants' ambitions were bolstered by the new alliance among blacks and Puerto Ricans that helped to elect Kenneth

Gibson. Their visions for public housing were shaped by black nationalists' plans for empowered communities. By 1970 they had expanded the scope of their goals and the strategies they were willing to use to meet them.[30]

Origins of the Rent Strike

In spring 1969 Gladys E. Dickinson, president of the Newark Public Housing Joint Tenants Association, led a conference at Rutgers University Newark Campus during which activists developed the platform that later defined the strike: advisory committees, participation in housing policy, security, on-site health care, and a newsletter.[31] Councilman Calvin D. West, the younger brother of NAACP chairwoman Larrie Stalks, persuaded Mayor Addonizio and agency leaders to scrutinize deficiencies in public housing. After several tours, they insisted that the NHA increase maintenance services, called on tenants to clear litter, and promised vigilance in the form of unannounced inspections.[32]

Dismayed by this weak response, tenants led by Constance Washington broke with the Newark Public Housing Joint Tenants Association to affiliate with the more militant National Tenant Organization. Washington and other activists called their new group the Poor and Dissatisfied Tenants Association (PDTA), rejecting the euphemistic terms—"hope," "opportunity"—that characterized antipoverty nomenclature of the time.[33] They would not bow to expectations that the poor accept benefits—whatever the quality—humbly and with shame.

In November 1969 the PDTA confronted Mayor Addonizio and the NHA's executive director, Joseph D. Sivolella, about anticipated rent increases. The change was dictated not by the NHA, Sivolella told them, but by the federal government, which had set rates at an average of 21.8 percent of tenant income. That average meant little to residents who already struggled to pay. "It's about 31 percent," a tenant activist named Lucille Peterson insisted, referring to her own budget. "We're suffering mister, you hear me?"[34] Such confrontations with housing authorities rallied residents across the public housing system in the months leading up to the strike.

Newark tenants were not alone in asserting themselves. In San Francisco, black Americans joined with Chinese Americans to help oust the director of the San Francisco Housing Authority, who had long repressed organizing. Residents of the Hunters Point neighborhood struck from 1966 to 1967, channeling rent money into their own renovations until the housing authority and mayor stepped in with funding to finish the job.[35] In 1969 Saint Louis tenants protested the housing authority's decision to raise rent. They opposed the blurred administrative line between public housing and urban renewal. The arrangement, they argued, would always work to the detriment of public housing.[36] When officials ignored them, they responded with the first public housing rent strike to gain system-wide momentum, involving over two thousand tenants. The Saint Louis protesters, Clarence Lang shows, were largely women conversant with the city's black power movement but often sidelined by it. Yet black women made public housing a major front in poor and working-class people's contest with the state over economic citizenship. "At a time when both white liberal and Black Nationalist discourses associated matriarchy with the black community's poverty," Lang writes, "these women claimed the right to respect, fair rents, and the ability to maintain autonomous households."[37] The Saint Louis strike ended with more tenant control at both the housing authority and building level. Tenants won limited rent increases and the separation of urban renewal and public housing functions.[38] Union, civic, business, and religious leaders were also prevailed upon to hold the housing authority accountable.[39] That outcome would influence Newark's strike in the years ahead.

On April 1, 1970, Newark tenant leader Constance Washington launched a strike alongside activists Toby Henry and Father Thomas Comerford. Henry was twenty-five, a fifth-grade dropout who had spent years of his childhood in a series of juvenile detention centers. Prior to the strike, he had run a small record company out of his apartment in Stella Wright Homes.[40] Until the summer of 1969, Comerford had been a priest at Queen of Angels Catholic Church. At the urging of his mentor, Father Thomas Carey, he had studied with Father Leo Mahon at San Miguelito Mission in Panama, one source for the emerging liberation theology. Comerford left the rectory to live and organize among public housing tenants.[41] Newspaper articles made much of Comerford as the sole white Stella Wright tenant.[42]

Rent strikes were common in the private sector, but public housing tenants had rarely tried them. Newark's striking tenants had cause for optimism, however. The National Welfare Rights Organization had just formed in 1967, led by an African American woman named Johnnie Tillmon, who honed her organizing skills in tenant groups at her Los Angeles public housing complex.[43] In 1969 the National Tenant Organization formed in the wake of massive rent strikes in Chicago and

Harlem, which had won rent protections for tenants.[44] The accomplishments of both organizations challenged the widespread view of poor people as incapable of self-representation.[45] Closer to home, the state of New Jersey passed stricter tenant protection laws in 1970. And striking tenants' cause was boosted by the NHA's early concession to one major demand: officials postponed an increase in the maximum rent for families on welfare.[46] The Black and Puerto Rican Political Convention also endorsed the strike. They called on voters in public housing to overturn political leadership that had compounded segregation and held poor residents captive to a negligent housing authority.[47]

Throughout the spring of 1970, tenants and officials debated the strike.[48] The NHA director of management, Allan Rizzolo, defended his agency's efforts to improve maintenance and meet other demands, and he insisted that they were powerless to authorize tenant participation on the board since membership was determined by the mayor and the governor.[49] The strikers won a victory in mid-May, however, when Judge Ward J. Herbert, of Superior Court, issued a temporary restraining order that prevented the NHA from evicting them. Public housing, Herbert argued, constituted the last resort for many residents; eviction violated their rights.[50]

As the strike deepened, tenants sought—and received—support from multiple sources. Although this coalition of poor and working-class people was challenging the city's most powerful agency, they had help. HUD supplied the NHA with most of its funding and yet gave measured support to the tenants. State and city officials were more vocal: in August 1970 the state Department of Community Affairs and the mayor's office encouraged tenants' organizations across the city to combine. Officials even suggested that tenants could secure HUD and state funds, perhaps perceiving the strike as a potential catalyst for establishing greater oversight of the powerful and autonomous NHA.[51] Constance Washington of the PDTA agreed with Gladys Dickinson of the Newark Public Housing Joint Tenants Association that a merger of their previously antagonistic groups could give tenants the kind of clout city labor unions wielded. But the two groups decided to work in concert without merging. Many tenant activists perceived their public housing residences as idiosyncratic cities within cities. While they wanted to benefit from the collective power of the citywide and national movement for tenants' rights, they also prized flexible alliances that deferred to local leadership. Tenants relied on a dizzying array of organizations to represent them through the four-year strike. Out of the PDTA emerged the Stella Wright Tenants Association. Led by Washington, Toby Henry, and Father Comerford, the Stella Wright Tenants Association contributed some of the most committed activists, while the residents of Stella Wright Homes maintained the highest level of support for the strike—at its most successful point, a majority of tenants withheld rent.[52] The conflict is commonly referred to as the Stella Wright strike, but thousands of public housing tenants across the city participated after November 1970, when the six-month-old strike extended beyond Stella Wright and Scudder Homes to fourteen other projects. Tenant representatives in each building collected rent and deposited it in an escrow account managed by the Newark Legal Services Project, a practice common during private-sector tenant disputes.[53]

National Reckoning and Local Intervention

As the rent strike escalated, the NHA fell under increasing scrutiny by city and federal officials. In the fall of 1970 health inspectors found more than two thousand violations in Columbus Homes alone. The city's Health and Welfare Department pressured the NHA's Sivolella to participate in joint inspections of the authority's other properties, followed by a maintenance team that made immediate repairs.[54] Once again, short-lived improvements could not resolve an impasse that had been building since the birth of public housing.

The Housing Act of 1937, Hunt argues, marked "a major expansion of state responsibility for the welfare of its citizens."[55] It reflected some foresight about US cities and had been passed amid legislative calls for housing, transportation, and metropolitan planning. While these elements did not coalesce in a "fully developed urban policy," according to Raymond Mohl, they signaled "an activist and interventionist approach that produced quick results."[56] But that foresight was eclipsed by public housing's funding structure. Tenants in 1970 struck against a public housing system that had been stressed not only by recent developments but also by the unspooling consequences of the 1937 Housing Act and subsequent compromises.

Real estate interests, lenders, and other businesses leaders had sought to curtail housing legislation during the New Deal. They ensured that its passage was "belated, begrudging, and beset with conceptual contradictions" and made its elimination a goal of post–World War II conservatism.[57] The 1937 Housing Act and subsequent legislation that they influenced stipulated that subsidized units must not add to or compete with offerings in the private rental market.[58] Nor could public housing siphon from the market of working- and lower-middle-class renters. But business interests alone did not determine these strictures: even some public housing advocates favored housing reforms that only narrowly addressed market failures.[59] Public housing putatively existed outside market forces but was in fact sustained by its own economy of federal subsidies, local contributions, tax exemptions, and rents. The federal government subsidized low-interest loans for the construction of housing and made annual payments to housing authorities to offset the income-adjusted rents of tenants. Housing authorities determined rents on the basis of what they required—within certain guidelines—to afford maintenance and a portion of operating costs. At first this worked: public housing expanded during the acute housing shortages of World War II. But in the long run, this combination proved unsustainable for many housing authorities.[60]

After the war, many better-off tenants left public housing, joining the largely white suburban exodus underwritten by low-cost mortgages—also federally subsidized—and lower taxes. This eased the housing shortage, but it required public housing authorities to take more concerted action to avoid competition with private landlords, so they barred higher-earning tenants. The rent limits incorporated into the 1949 Housing Act, writes Rachel Bratt, reserved public housing "for people who were more or less separated from society's mainstream."[61] Newark's striking tenants rejected that stigma. They believed that their expectations that the housing authority fulfill its obligations were comparable to those of any private renter or homeowner.[62] Still, Bratt's comment speaks to the fact that in Newark, as elsewhere, housing authorities contended with an increasing proportion of poor tenants, the accelerating maintenance costs of older buildings, and city economies in decline. The system could not provide housing of last resort to those unable to pay market rates and at the same time generate sufficient revenue. Rising costs were not the sole problem. Public housing's subsidy structure set decline in motion, argues Bratt, by permitting "developers to underestimate operating costs" and by maintaining "a subsidy formula that did not increase when additional resources were needed."[63] Housing policy, Hunt concurs, "was frozen in place during much of the 1950s, even as insiders recognized misguided strategies and predicted future failure."[64] As a day of reckoning approached, tenants were on the front lines.

Housing authorities in Chicago, Baltimore, Saint Louis, and other cities contended with accusations of chronic mismanagement, decaying physical plant, and demands for tenant control. By 1969 the Senate could not ignore the system's unraveling. Hearings revealed public housing authorities that ran up deficits in the millions yet failed to maintain decent housing. The Senate mandated that HUD evaluate local housing authorities in about twenty cities, including Newark.[65]

HUD released the results of its investigation in early 1971, largely confirming tenants' complaints and recommending a massive reorganization of the NHA. Work orders for leaking pipes, smashed windows, and broken doors had accumulated over months, even years. The report noted halls and basements blocked by garbage and unwanted furniture. The "mutilated doors" and smashed windows of Stella Wright Homes looked out on grassless lawns.[66] Residents knew their building by its stench: the incinerator in the basement—urgently in need of repair—spewed smoke into the building twice weekly, staining walls and permeating halls with the smell of burning garbage. Scudder Homes was characterized by dark, trash-strewn hallways, its so-called "recreation area" consisting of "unrelieved asphalt." Columbus Homes compared favorably to other buildings inside but was surrounded by a carpet of dog feces, broken glass, mud, and litter. Even projects that investigators deemed "generally good" were often diminished by poor lighting, little space for playing and socializing, and severely damaged lawns. Their trees had slowly asphyxiated, the result of protective guards that had been secured too tightly around their trunks. [67]

HUD determined the lack of services to foster "self-sufficient families and individuals" just as dire as the physical deterioration. The NHA had created a Community Relations and Social Services (CRSS) program to offer tenants referrals, collaborate with other community groups, and mediate disputes. But CRSS staff complained to HUD investigators that understaffing, overcrowding, and inadequate budgets prohibited them from reaching "a growing project population of less stable, less easily motivated, less upwardly mobile residents." Although the CRSS failed to deliver on its promises, it nonetheless had some strengths. The quality of social services in each project often reflected the abilities of individual CRSS staff, including tenant aides. In Scudder Homes, for example, residents endured one of the city's worst buildings but benefited from a particularly motivated community service aide and a CRSS manager who welcomed staff opinions. Sometimes tenants bypassed ineffective CRSS programs altogether, relying on a larger network of civic groups. "With little apparent input from the CRSS," investigators wrote of Seth Boyden Court, "the tenants and the manager have set up a program of community activities for all ages, education programs for high school equivalency and for the Spanish-speaking, an active tenant league which works with the manager on common problems." HUD similarly deemed Babyland, the pilot daycare program organized at Stella Wright, worthy of emulation.[68]

The HUD report revealed that insecurity ranked high among tenants' complaints: it created a mood of fear and interfered with their access to social services. HUD investigators acknowledged that additional police patrols were unlikely; Newark's police were already "too hard-pressed." So HUD looked to the tenants themselves, encouraging the NHA to seek funds from the state and the Department of Justice to create tenant security forces, similar to the one developed by tenants at Scudder Homes. HUD made the case for greater tenant involvement in all aspects of management to alleviate some of the dissatisfaction contributing to the strike. There was "an urgent need," HUD claimed, for the election of tenant representatives to influence management within buildings and contribute to the NHA's citywide housing policies. HUD investigators called on the NHA to "plan immediately for such an election with the assistance of existing tenant groups" and insisted that a third party monitor it.[69]

Stepping back from the details of the NHA's operations, HUD concluded that the NHA's overall organization was "top-heavy," characterized by "wasteful" levels of management. Budget deficits had prompted the NHA to rely on extra subsidies from HUD to maintain solvency.[70] Yet at the same time, the agency had spent only half of the $7 million modernization fund granted in 1969, which could have covered some of the repairs and renovations long requested by tenants and recommended by HUD. Federal officials insisted on a major reorganization of the NHA before it could even begin to meet the project-level requirements of the report. They called for NHA's division into two entities—one for urban renewal and one for housing management—each with its own director and board. HUD also called for the elimination of about forty-five positions, many of them filled by well-paid managers.[71]

Even as the HUD report conceded that tenants had reason to protest, federal officials' empathy with the rent strikers evaporated when it came to the NHA's growing deficit. In the press, tenants and NHA officials disputed the extent of the strike and the toll it had exacted on the NHA, but the HUD report left little doubt as to the strike's impact. Between 1966 and 1970, tenant receivables had doubled from $97,437 to $180,026, but this increase over several years paled beside the changes experienced in 1970. During the first eight months of the rent strike, delinquent accounts climbed steadily after April, reaching $876,947 in December 1970 and "approaching 100 percent of the monthly rent roll." Strategizing for ways to defuse the strike, HUD officials sought to intervene in the transfer of cash benefits from the Essex County Board of Welfare to striking tenants. "We urge the Local Authority to continue its efforts to negotiate with the Welfare Department to pay rents directly to the Authority," the report recommended. HUD even recommended that the NHA call for the amendment of New Jersey laws to ease the transfer of direct payments between welfare departments and housing authorities.[72] HUD officials approved of limited tenant control in the service of discrete, shared goals, but the strike was a step toward tenant empowerment that alarmed them. HUD officials had affirmed the complaints fueling tenants' actions, but they simultaneously encouraged the NHA to pursue legal action to disarm tenants of their most powerful weapon.

The NHA reeled from the report at the same time that it scrambled to meet dangerously delinquent utility payments. Director Sivolella successfully appealed to HUD for a $600,000 subsidy to ensure utility service for several months, during which local officials promised a response to HUD's report.[73] But the report had soured the NHA's relationship with federal authorities and starkly revealed its diminished state to the city. Newark's public housing system had taken shape in the 1950s, under the imperial rule of Louis Danzig. During the fifteen years he led the NHA, Danzig garnered millions in urban renewal funds and paid scant attention to residents' concerns. His successor, Joseph Sivolella, never matched Danzig in skill or stature, but he jealously defended the NHA's autonomy and his own management.[74] Sivolella was also constrained by the new problems facing Newark's public housing. He confronted the consequences—deficits, overcrowding, displacement—of Danzig's choices, choices that had been partially conditioned by the funding structure of public housing. In the shadow of Danzig's legacy, Sivolella rejected the criticism of both HUD and Newark's tenants. He painted HUD officials as fickle and uninformed, claiming that they had originally endorsed many of the staffing policies now under attack. So HUD punished Sivolella by withholding $400,000 from the NHA pending its compliance. Sivolella then begrudgingly attempted to comply with HUD's demand that the NHA separate urban renewal from housing management functions. But HUD officials rejected his proposal because it too closely resembled the NHA's old managerial structure.[75]

While the NHA denounced the HUD report, the Stella Wright Tenants Association seized upon it as a catalyst for their own plans to relieve overcrowding and improve security. The modest security provisions at Stella Wright in 1971 will perhaps surprise contemporary city dwellers. In a building with over 1,200 units, there was no buzzer system and only one security guard, who split his time between two complexes. Entrances remained unlocked, allowing drug users to turn hallways and stairwells into "shooting pads." Police cruised by the parking lots but rarely ventured inside. Tenants called for locks on the entrances and the training of a part-time, paid security force—consisting of building residents—that would have direct radio contact with the NHA and police. Acknowledging that twenty-four-hour security was likely beyond the means of the housing authority, the tenants would arrange to supplement the formal force with volunteers, creating a system they estimated would cost $250,000.[76] In this proposal, as in many others, the improvement of the projects was linked to tenant employment. Their demands also prefigured the 1973 Comprehensive Employment and Training Act. This legislation empowered the Labor Department to provide local agencies with funds to offset the costs of training and hiring the so-called hard-core unemployed, especially in areas suffering high unemployment. By 1975 nearly $1 million in Comprehensive Employment and Training Act funds supported over one hundred employees working in security, maintenance, social services, and office support for the NHA.[77] Tenants also sought to relieve the overcrowding blamed for the "deplorable and uninhabitable conditions" of the projects. They acknowledged Newark's affordable-housing shortage but insisted that the answer was not to overcrowd housing to the point that it became "destructive of human life and development."[78] Tenants argued for the relocation of large families from Stella Wright to more spacious rehabilitated townhomes owned by the NHA. They also suggested combining about eighty currently vacant apartments to accommodate large families or communal space for tenant groups.[79]

But the stalemate between HUD and the NHA sidelined any hope that these plans would be implemented. By the end of April 1971, Sivolella and the NHA commissioners—under pressure from Republican senator Clifford Case and Mayor Gibson—had inched toward accepting HUD's major recommendations on a "trial basis." Gibson urged the city council to endorse them, but council members sided with Sivolella. It was soon clear to HUD officials that the city ordinance permitting the reorganization of the NHA was headed for defeat.[80]

As Mayor Gibson faced the intransigent opposition of the NHA and its city council allies, he insisted that HUD yield ground. By August, Gibson's administration had mediated a compromise. The NHA agreed to eliminate forty-five managers, earning a combined $500,000, and to implement the modified reorganization plan. HUD restored some of the NHA's funding to prevent the layoff of several hundred more workers. Sivolella agreed to resign in March 1972. Mayor Gibson appointed Pearl Beatty, a black woman with ties to the NAACP and local antipoverty programs, to the NHA's board. Beatty's appointment met with some disapproval from strikers; they thought she was too close to city officials.[81] But with a compromise between HUD and the NHA established, officials on both sides now focused on ending the strike.

To the Courts

HUD's tolerance of the rent strike waned throughout late 1971 and 1972. Although federal officials still affirmed tenants' aims—especially their desire to influence policy—they rejected many of the tenants' proposals.[82] HUD officials also continued to explore methods of short-circuiting the strike by arranging to transfer welfare benefits for housing directly from the Essex County Board of Welfare to the NHA, although this effort stalled in 1971.[83] HUD also welcomed the NHA's decision to sue tenants over the escrow account, anticipating that a decision in the NHA's behalf would end the strike and expedite its transformation.[84] The NHA estimated that it had lost nearly $2 million in rent, nearly one-third owed by Stella Wright tenants alone. In February 1972 Judge Herbert ordered the Stella Wright Tenants Association to provide a full accounting of the escrow accounts. As tenant receivables grew, both HUD and the NHA were brought into a provisional alliance, pressuring the tenants association for information on the size of the fund and the identity of its contributors.[85]

Toby Henry of the Stella Wright Tenants Association expressed tenants' fears that HUD and the NHA wanted the information to "move more effectively and more swiftly against individual tenants." They also feared that the NHA would confiscate the fund.[86] Tenants lashed out at HUD: "HUD doesn't allow these monstrosities to be built anymore," Father Comerford said, "but it wants to ignore past mistakes and keep news of the unlivable conditions here from getting out."[87] Judge Herbert did not force tenants to transfer fund ownership—estimated at only $94,000—but he prohibited additional deposits and withdrawals. As an alternative, tenants were permitted to pay rents to a safe deposit account managed by Comerford and Henry, who were under court order not to withdraw any deposited funds.[88]

The dispute over the fund cemented the increasingly bitter relationship between tenants and HUD officials. Both had once shared the goal of reorganizing the NHA, but now the director of the Newark area office of HUD warned that the rent strike had paralyzed it. Tenants, the official insisted, stood to benefit from elevator repairs, new incinerators, a half-million-dollar emergency repair fund, and $12 million in modernization funds, if they would only reach a settlement with the NHA. Instead, he alleged, tenants had "boycotted" a HUD budget planning session, which was prohibited by law from proceeding without their participation.[89]

Modernization funds were at the core of much wrangling between federal officials, local housing authorities, and mobilized tenants in the 1970s. HUD infused local housing authorities with these funds to achieve the dual purpose of restoring buildings and redressing complaints about tenants' lack of influence. As a condition of funding, HUD required housing authorities to include tenants in determining priorities. In Baltimore, Williams found, tenants used that leverage when housing authorities failed to include them by demanding that modernization funds be withheld, prompting the creation of the Resident Advisory Board, led largely by black women. Tenant leader Shirley Wise remarked that the modernization requirements gave leaders tangible gains around which to organize their fellow tenants and offered the possibility of more transparent operations.[90] Tenants in Chicago also prevailed upon HUD to withhold modernization funds until they could reach an agreement over tenants' involvement in governance, budgeting, and hiring that was "unheard of in private housing management and radical even by War on Poverty standards."[91] But withholding modernization funds offered tenants only fleeting leverage and required them to exert persistent pressure on HUD.

In Newark, striking tenants contended that HUD wanted to secure only superficial tenant representation. Meanwhile, tenants' attorney J. Michael Callan claimed that HUD and NHA officials failed to respond to tenants' proposals.[92] As the promise of working with HUD to bring the NHA into compliance evaporated, tenants turned to the courts. Harris David, another tenant attorney, filed for an injunction to compel the NHA to repair Stella Wright's elevators and incinerators under court supervision.[93]

From this point on, the story of the rent strike could be told through the gradual abdication of each level of government. Negotiations with HUD stalled as federal officials grew frustrated with the NHA's intransigence, tenant demands they deemed unreasonable, and Gibson's ineffectiveness. New Jersey Governor William T. Cahill, a liberal Republican, resisted involvement; Republican senator Clifford Case retreated.[94] The Archdiocese of Newark insisted that Mayor Gibson was "the only man who can precipitate meaningful negotiations," but the NHA had shut him out of deliberations over the hiring of a new director to replace Sivolella.[95] Also, the rent strike was only one among many conflicts that had depleted the mayor's influence by the early 1970s. Public transit workers and teachers struck repeatedly, while the city's deficit blossomed.[96] Gibson campaigned for a wage tax increase and lost in a bruising battle with his city council opponents. His irritation with tenants grew evident. "If this rent strike had occurred in private housing, it would have been over in four days," he angrily declared. "But because it is public housing, some people believe they should live rent-free."[97] His frustration signaled a retreat from reform that Laura Maslow-Armand noted a decade later in her assessment of the strike's impact. Like municipal officials in other cities, Gibson had "not centered his attention on living conditions in the projects"; nor had he wanted to expend more political capital on challenging the NHA.[98]

As officials at all levels of government retreated, civic organizations continued to support the strikers and to insist that Newark would again rise up if housing conditions did not improve. Members of the Black and Puerto Rican Political Convention sided with the tenants and criticized the apparent inability of Gibson—the mayor they'd helped elect—to corral the NHA. Komozi Woodard, who worked with Amiri Baraka to build Newark's black nationalist movement, spoke at a rally on behalf of tenants. The stakes were impressed upon him as he looked across the audience of angry tenants, many strapped with barely concealed weapons.[99] And yet, though tensions boiled, the strike was characterized by little violence and few arrests compared with the simultaneous Newark teacher strikes.[100] Fixers may explain the difference. The Greater Newark Urban Coalition, Gustav Heningburg's organization, already acted as a depositor and financial steward for one of the rent strike escrow funds; tenants asked Heningburg to mediate the dispute. A group called Operation Understanding also backed the tenants and cultivated support from local leaders. Founded after the riot by suburban and urban residents, Operation Understanding sought to tackle the city's problems through interracial, cross-class alliances. It drew Catholics associated with Father Comerford's Central Ward church, Queen of Angels, and suburban residents who volunteered in Newark. Operation Understanding's spokeswoman, a white suburban mother named Pat Foley, voiced approval of tenants' strategy when they refused to relinquish control of their rent fund.[101] But as 1972 drew to a close, supporters and opponents of the strike were sidelined by the judiciary, which began to assume a more prominent role.

In October 1972 Judge Herbert decided that the funds collected by the Stella Wright Tenants Association had remained "idle" too long.[102] He ordered tenants to present a case for why they should be permitted to maintain control over the fund. Press reports anticipated that Herbert's October decision would compel tenants to pay their rent—effectively ending the strike. NHA officials resumed eviction proceedings against striking tenants, stopping only when residents of Archbishop Walsh Homes and Scudder Homes smashed the windows of NHA offices, threatening to shut them down.[103]

Over the next month, tenants debated strategy with their attorneys at the Newark-Essex Joint Law Reform Project. The looming court battle sparked a dispute among tenants: only some of the strikers had deposited their rent into the fund, and they asserted that the court order unfairly targeted them instead of tenants who had simply not paid. Still, tenants agreed that the NHA's quest for the rent fund diverted attention and resources from addressing the very problems all tenants shared, regardless of whether they had paid. The rent fund in fact composed a very small portion of the total amount withheld from the NHA. But it was a formidable symbol of tenants' leverage, and its seizure threatened to undermine the strike. Two years in, the court now forced tenants to answer an urgent question: what to do with the fund?

The answer came on November 17, 1972, when Stella Wright tenants crowded into Judge Herbert's courtroom. The attorney for the NHA was deep into his argument for taking possession of the fund when the tenants' attorney, J. Michael Callan, suddenly stood to announce that there was no longer any strike fund to be taken over. Three days before, Toby Henry and Father Comerford had withdrawn the safety deposit box and, following a near-unanimous vote, redistributed the fund to its owners. Callan's announcement flabbergasted Herbert and the NHA attorneys. Tenants laughed and applauded. Judge Herbert decried the "flagrant, brazen and unequivocal defiance of the laws of this country." He abruptly adjourned.[104]

A month later, Comerford and Henry returned to court to defend their action to Judge Irwin Kimmelman, a Republican and former Essex County assemblyman, who later became New Jersey's attorney general. Comerford told Kimmelman about the tragedies experienced by tenants living in high-rises: one tenant had found her elderly husband beaten to death in an elevator; a second tenant, forced to descend ten flights of stairs when she went into labor, lost her child. "Was I going to give the money back to the Newark Housing Authority, which didn't fix the elevators, or to those women?" asked Comerford. Judge Kimmelman acknowledged that conditions were "deplorable" but attacked what he described as their aspirations for "martyrdom." "To allow your action to go unpunished because you profess to follow a higher moral authority will lead only to anarchy," Kimmelman declared. He sentenced Comerford and Henry to forty-five days.[105] The tenants' attorneys, Callan, David, and Clark, who had disapproved of the tenants' decision and tried to persuade them to restore the fund, were also found in contempt of court and sentenced to similar jail terms. They had, Kimmelman wrote, "turned their backs on the court, . . . the very forum and institution of government which in recent years has been singular in extending its aid and protection to that very segment of society which Callan, David, and Clark and the Newark-Essex Joint Law Reform Project here represented."[106] Kimmelman, unlike other judges who arbitrated the dispute, delved little into housing policy. He instead focused considerable wrath on how Henry, Comerford, and especially their lawyers had endangered the legitimacy of the court. Kimmelman's martyrdom comment conveyed his assumption—more or less true—that Henry and Comerford would use their punishment to build solidarity among striking tenants and to secure the support of sympathizers who perceived imprisonment as unreasonably harsh.

The tenants had rebuffed the NHA's attempt to reclaim the rent fund, but this was no enduring victory. Meanwhile, the NHA withdrew even more maintenance, accelerating the buildings' physical and social decline. Between 1970 and 1972 Stella Wright residents documented "47 violent deaths, 33 rat bites, 179 people hospitalized for pneumonia or other bronchial ailments, 27 heart seizures suffered by elderly residents forced to walk up the stairs to reach their apartments when elevators ceased to function."[107] At the start of the strike, tenants filed proposal after proposal, testifying to such terrible conditions and their solutions. Long after officials had begun to declare high-rise public housing a total failure, tenants insisted they could not just salvage but transform it. Their persistence had evinced some optimism that tenants' involvement in setting managerial policies would significantly improve residents' lives. After 1972, however, strike leaders increasingly spoke in favor of demolishing Stella Wright altogether and replacing it with low-rise apartments and townhomes. The widely publicized decline of the Pruitt-Igoe housing complex in Saint Louis was one among many factors prompting some Stella Wright tenants to favor the demolition of their own homes. A pioneering behemoth with vaulted hallways, express "skip-stop" elevators, and wide lawns, Pruitt-Igoe opened in 1954. By the late 1960s it had come to symbolize the growing consensus among municipal officials, urban planners, and some tenants that the much-lauded high-rise products of midcentury urban renewal—many barely two decades old—did not work. Louis Danzig, who had directed the NHA through its most productive years, acknowledged that high-rises had been a concession to price and space constraints and "probably the worst housing that you can build" for the young families that would occupy the buildings.[108] In 1972, a month before Pruitt-Igoe's demolition, Stella Wright tenants advised the NHA to "follow the lead of St. Louis Housing officials," who had planned to replace Pruitt-Igoe with garden-style apartments.[109]

By the early 1970s the spatial critique of high-rise housing was widely accepted, and its implications are worth considering. Attributing the decline to mismatched design or the architectural hubris of midcentury modernism had the potential to open a discussion about how tenants' actual experience should be considered in the creation of future housing. Yet the spatial critique also had the potential to depoliticize public housing. The discussion turned inward, toward the broken elevators and lawless halls, rather than outward, toward the economically diminished, often segregated, cities that surrounded these buildings; toward the lack of political will to sustain safe and decent housing for the poor and working class; and toward a funding structure long ago set to self-destruct.

Striking tenants, however, had more urgent worries. In December 1972—as Henry and Comerford sat in jail—the NHA resumed its attempts to evict strikers. Over two thousand tenants throughout the public housing system received notices, including five hundred in Stella Wright Homes. This strategy, pursued by the NHA's new director, Robert Notte, compelled several of the tenants' groups to engage in multilateral negotiations with the NHA, seriously straining their alliances with one another.[110] The Stella Wright Tenants Association held out for months, but as the third year of the strike passed in early April 1973, they arrived at a tentative settlement during a sixteen-hour meeting with the NHA. The agreement, filed with Judge Joseph Walsh of the Essex County District Court, required tenants to pay $300,000 in April and May, which NHA officials would apply to emergency repairs. The NHA agreed to include tenants on its board of commissioners, and both parties appealed to HUD to release funds to the NHA. Significantly, both sides concurred in their diagnosis: "High-rise housing," the agreement read, "has failed miserably in the City of Newark." Tenants and

NHA officials stated that HUD should assist municipalities in "phasing out the projects" and developing alternatives to the high-rises.

Toby Henry commended the agreement reached under Walsh but emphasized its provisional nature. "Temporary relief is ok. Other than that they've got to tear them down. The judge is right. Tear them down. Now that's my only goal."[111] By July, however, the agreement had broken down: Henry claimed that the NHA had made no attempts at improvement, while Notte alleged that tenants had continued to withhold rent.[112] A health inspector had identified four thousand violations at Stella Wright Homes and declared the buildings "uninhabitable," but he acknowledged that the NHA did not have the capacity to relocate tenants to better buildings.[113] By fall, the NHA had resumed its campaign to evict strikers.

Judge Walsh once again intervened in November 1973. Tenants won a decisive victory in *Newark Housing Authority v. Aiken*, when Judge Walsh prohibited their eviction and laid the groundwork for what many believed would be a resolution.[114] Attributing the strike to the national crisis in subsidized housing, Walsh wrote that "[i]t must be apparent from comparison with Pruitt-Igoe and from the despair of all witnesses in projecting any hope of solution; that there are just too many people in too little space under conditions that are incapable of management." Walsh blamed HUD, calling the agency "Newark's and Essex County's largest absentee slumlord." Acknowledging that the court could offer no "clear remedy," Walsh required the NHA to give tenants an 80 percent abatement on past-due rent and required the tenants to pay the remaining 20 percent to cover utilities in the buildings during the strike.[115] Comerford and Henry deemed this a victory, "a sign to other tenants," said Comerford, that they had the power to hold the NHA accountable. Henry hoped that other judges contemplating tenant cases would follow Walsh's lead, bolstering the "movement that is continuing to spread all over the nation."[116] In fact, news of Newark's housing crisis was also spreading, thanks to the results of a thirty-city survey issued in November that indicted Newark's housing—public and private—as the country's "worst." The report offered an opportunity for both the NHA and Gibson to bemoan the state of city housing, with Robert Notte assigning blame to inadequate federal support and Gibson indicting the NHA for years of "inept" management.[117]

William Green, the regional administrator of HUD, disputed Walsh's decision. The comparison between Stella Wright and Pruitt-Igoe in Saint Louis did not stand, he argued, because Newark had a much lower vacancy rate, which would inhibit the relocation of thousands of high-rise tenants. The 20 percent payment Walsh recommended would not even cover steadily rising utility expenses, Green said. He doubted that Walsh understood federal officials' relationship to the NHA, emphasizing that HUD did not have the legal authority to compel the NHA to reorganize its operations.[118] Walsh had delivered an impassioned opinion that was deeply sympathetic to tenants, but Green made a compelling point: Walsh's simplistic diagnosis of the relationship between HUD and the local authorities offered little hope for resolving the conflict. As 1974 dawned, the *Aiken* decision seemed less definitive. As Gustav Heningburg acknowledged, "the strike is over but nobody knows how to end it."[119]

In January 1974 the NHA requested emergency funding from HUD, lest it be forced to close Stella Wright and possibly Scudder and Columbus Homes. HUD rejected the plea. In February the NHA announced that the strike, which had cost the agency over $6 million and occasioned a pending suit for $1 million in unpaid utilities, had compromised the entire public housing system. Its commissioners agreed to turn off utilities at Stella Wright in early April, relocating about 350 rent-paying tenants to other projects and offering the remaining 650 rent strikers referrals to apartments outside the NHA system.[120] "They're threatening to cut off things we don't have anyway," Toby Henry told a reporter. "We'll just bring in kerosene lamps and have our own back-to-nature movement."[121] Although Henry insisted that the strike would continue, tenants submitted another settlement proposal modeled after one HUD had helped to implement in Saint Louis.[122] Notte dismissed this attempt to restart negotiations. "We must recognize that we are responsible for the well-being of not only those who live at the Stella Wright Homes," he said, "but for all 12,000 families who live in Newark's public, low-income homes." Notte also feared for the future of the NHA, which employed hundreds of Newark residents in the maintenance of public housing and thousands in its construction projects: nearly three hundred employees had been dismissed over the previous two years.[123] With these pressures in mind, Notte appeared to desire a final confrontation.

By March 1974 Stella Wright Homes stood half-empty as hundreds of nonstriking tenants departed in anticipation of its closure.[124] Henry reported that half of the 684 remaining tenants had resumed collecting rent and begun to create a budget to manage the project themselves.[125] HUD tacitly approved of NHA's decision to close Stella Wright by refusing requests for additional funding or intervention, insisting that closure was within the NHA's power. On April 2 Judge Frederick B.

Lacey delayed the closure, insisting that NHA commissioners first participate in a hearing about Stella Wright's future.[126] Lacey also threatened to make striking tenants pay their utility bills while the NHA plan for closure was suspended, a condition that moved both parties closer to settlement. In July 1974 Lacey handed down a final decision that derailed closure and laid the groundwork for tenant management. Citing the $6.5 million in rent tenants had withheld by February 1974, Judge Lacey declared that "it is not hyperbole to state that NHA is on the brink of bankruptcy." Lacey acknowledged the terrible conditions underlying the strike, but his sympathy appeared to lie with the NHA. Thirty percent of NHA tenants had "indulged" in the rent strike, he said, contributing to a disastrous cycle whereby the already cash-strapped NHA was compelled to reduce its services and repairs. "Whatever efficacy this device has in the private sector," Lacey said of the strike, "it failed miserably here." In public housing, Lacey argued, a strike had "vastly different consequences from a rent strike in the private sector, where parties, dealing at an arm's length, exchange items of equal value. In the public low-income housing context, the very nature of the relationship between landlord and tenant presupposes that the tenant will receive premises of greater value than that which he can afford to pay." Since public housing generated no profit from tenants, he argued, the withholding of rent immediately impaired operations.[127] "[W]hether the rent strikers are or are not warranted in the action they have taken," Lacey wrote, "other tenants who are paying rent to the NHA are subsidizing those who are not." Even as Lacey doubted Stella Wright could be improved, he called the NHA's proposed closure of Stella Wright and other complexes "intolerable." Closure would dislocate thousands of families, and the NHA had no immediate plans to replace the buildings. Lacey insisted he could not simultaneously allow the rent strike to continue while preventing closure of Stella Wright Homes. He ordered the parties to accept a settlement that provided an infusion of funds from HUD for the immediate renovation of Stella Wright and other buildings once tenants ended the strike. Even as he insisted that "history is made by this unprecedented agreement," he warned that in the end, tenants could be left with "brick and mortar, but little else."[128]

In fact, this settlement was hardly groundbreaking: variations on such an agreement had already been attempted and discarded. But Lacey actually addressed many tenant demands despite his criticism of their methods. His settlement ensured the continued operation of Stella Wright, included tenants in decision making, and set aside funds for repairs. It gave tenants two years to repay the NHA slightly over a year's worth of back rent.[129]

The settlement ended the strike but hardly resolved the inequalities that fueled it. Judges struggled to acknowledge tenants' complaints without endorsing the strike; they alternately blamed the conflicts on the tenants, their lawyers, the NHA, HUD, and the "urban crisis" more generally. They could not agree on whom to hold accountable. At the same time, the insurgencies of black power, the War on Poverty's emphasis on participation of the poor, and the specter of urban uprisings made it seem dangerous—and politically unpalatable—to outright suppress tenant agency. Stella Wright tenants, acting as both protesters and fixers, brought a simmering conflict to a boil and then seized the moment to wrest some power from competing authorities.[130]

Lacey admitted to having feared that the conflict was irresolvable, and he commended all involved for bringing to an end the "longest, most crippling rent strike in the history of this country." Lacey singled out the negotiating work of Gustav Heningburg, in particular. The end of the strike, he optimistically wrote, cleared the way for the achievement of the "lofty and noble goal of the United States Housing Act of 1937."[131] The settlement provided for $1.3 million in aid from the Federal Target Project Program, which supported the development of tenant management corporations. It also included a pledge by Gibson to appoint a public housing tenant to the NHA's board of commissioners. Tenants agreed to transfer most of their $100,000 emergency fund, currently held by the Greater Newark Urban Coalition, over to the housing authority. Under oversight from HUD, the Ford Foundation also contributed funds to the tenant management program.[132] After a five-year freeze on federal urban development funds, HUD restored $41 million to the NHA. According to NHA officials, the resolution signaled "the start of a new era in the rebuilding of the city."[133] But while the settlement almost immediately benefited the NHA, the "new era" it promised tenants remained in question.

The first year saw few successes: tenant attorney Harris David lamented that "every party to the agreement had been lax in living up to its terms."[134] There were few tenant management precedents to follow, so Newark tenants and the NHA sought the advice of consultants who had helped Saint Louis tenants transition to managers. That city's public housing tenants had established a widely influential model for tenant management in 1973.[135] By the late 1970s there were about a dozen public housing complexes under tenant management. In the most successful cases, tenants built alliances with civic groups, churches, unions, and even local business organizations that could offer technical support or political pressure.[136] Soon, Stella Wright residents had cleaned up buildings, improved landscaping, installed a new security system, and trained as supervisors and managers. They formed standards committees for each floor.[137] With HUD funds, they began renovating apartments, the gleaming new units standing as a promise for what awaited.[138]

Meanwhile, the NHA proceeded with plans to rehabilitate the buildings. It wanted to seal off the top six floors of each, effectively depopulating the project to five hundred families.[139] Two years later, newly trained tenant managers assumed responsibility for the project, working alongside building directors, floor captains, and maintenance clerks. A journalist who had covered the strike noted that the clean hallways and freshly painted walls contrasted starkly with the conditions HUD had condemned six years earlier. A building director testified that the strike had mostly strengthened tenants' sense of solidarity and their enthusiasm for the experiment.[140] Her observation was confirmed by subsequent research on tenant management: while tenants' distrust of housing authorities could impede tenant management, it also provided the solidarity required to slog through the minutiae of self-management. Although one administrator surmised that "the essential fuel for tenant management may be 'pure hatred' of the housing authority," leaders had to moderate their animosity because tenant management was hardly a matter of pure self-determination: it ultimately required a stable relationship with the local housing authority.

A short-lived but critical chapter in the history of public housing, tenant management defied common tropes of decline, social pathology, and disfranchisement.[141] Though the research on tenant management is thin, the few studies that exist demonstrate that tenant management often proved successful, if not radically transformative. Tenants arranged or provided security, mediated conflicts, vetted prospective renters, collected rent, and maintained buildings better than, or at least as well as, the housing authorities they supplanted. But there were major impediments to the expansion of tenant management: the long and costly training and transition period and the presence of a stable core of tenant leaders who could rally their neighbors and make the initial transition.[142] And not all organized tenant groups desired self-management or perceived it as the ideal end of tenant activism.

Several years out, most Stella Wright tenants agreed that the improvements in their buildings had been worth the hardship of the strike. Tenants carved out for themselves a small universe for experimentation amid the accelerating decline of the city's overall public housing system. But most feared that the improvements could not be sustained as support for public housing waned and the costs of maintaining the buildings climbed.[143] Tenant management continued into the 1990s, although the housing authority maintained a heavy hand over Stella Wright's governance, and conditions were never wholly reversed.[144] As political opposition to high-rise public housing gained force, the line between abandonment and self-determination thinned.

On the Eve of Demolition

Rent strikers had radical visions for public housing, but they were also deeply pragmatic and willing to endure considerable hardship for often quite moderate reforms. They mounted an unprecedented and formidable movement that forced their issues into the courts.[145] If they met only modest success as fixers, it's worth remembering that their accomplishments were achieved against extraordinary and unrelenting odds.

Ira Katznelson argues in *City Trenches*, his foundational study of class and racial struggle in Upper Manhattan, that class identity in the United States rarely extended beyond the workplace. Identity rooted in one's experience as a wage earner was muted, if not displaced, by identities forged at home in racially segregated neighborhoods and in civic, religious, or ethnic associations.[146] What impeded effective radical—or even vigorous reformist—movements in the United States, he argued, was "the radical separation in people's consciousness, speech, and activity of the politics of work from the politics of community."[147]

But public housing activists of the 1970s functioned as fixers precisely because they challenged the separation between housing and employment. Katznelson does not explicitly address the black freedom movement in public housing, but in writing about the multiple insurgencies of the 1960s, he argues that black power in particular "produced demands . . . radically different from the usual articulation of urban issues. . . . School, welfare, police, and housing were treated together as aspects of a total condition."[148] His analysis of the education and social service bureaucracies that wielded growing clout in urban politics could certainly extend to housing authorities like Newark's. Among public housing tenants, diagnosis of the "total condition" took the form of a racially conscious working-class politics informed by the persistent reality of joblessness and of single mothers caught between low wages and the indignities of a welfare system that denied them respect and distorted their agency. Such holistic views may have been common to black politics, but the exigencies of the 1960s and 1970s briefly amplified them.

Like Heningburg, Louise Epperson, and fellow opponents of the Medical College, striking tenants shaped and seized this moment to protest a dysfunctional order and create a new one. But the leverage and momentum that fixers sought depended upon a direct engagement with the market. For example, the Medical College received federal, state, and municipal funds, but as the centerpiece of the city's urban renewal agenda, its success was also of vital importance to Newark's private sector. Similarly, Gustav Heningburg's work with the Black and Puerto Rican Construction Coalition proved successful in part because of his corporate backing through the Greater Newark Urban Coalition. Numerous airlines and the city of Newark stood to profit from the expansion of the Newark airport.

In the case of public housing, the rent strike prompted HUD to withhold funds from the NHA, stalling urban renewal projects and imperiling the future of one of the city's largest employers. And the construction of public housing had enriched many contractors over the years. But ultimately, public housing tenants sought to salvage a system toward which the private sector had been historically ambivalent. Though a floundering public housing system imperiled the city's health, from the perspective of those in power it did not constitute the same kind of crisis or offer the same potential for profit as these other examples. From this perspective, tenant management may not have prevailed as a widespread model in part because it did not promise private-sector opportunities.

The gains won were small in terms of the number of tenants who directly benefited from tenant management and physical improvements. Such an outcome would not have surprised Katznelson. He argued that the radical mobilizations of the 1960s were ultimately contained by symbolic concessions and the devolution of administration *without* a concomitant redistribution of wealth and political power. Very few of the original claims of these insurgencies survived, Katznelson argues, to leave behind what Frances Fox Piven and Richard Cloward called the "residue of reform."[149] In the short term, neither the rent strike nor tenant management sparked the transformation—or even deep reform—of public housing for which many tenants had fought. But tenants' attempts to act as fixers did influence housing activism outside the scope of the NHA, as we shall see in the subsequent chapters, while tenant organizing endured within the NHA as well.

In subsequent decades, tenants fought to keep low-income housing even as the federal government retreated. Doris McCray, who moved into Stella Wright in 1968 when her parents were displaced by the Medical College, continued organizing tenants long after the strike. She earned a reputation for persistence and frank confrontation with officials. In the 1990s she led the Newark Tenants Council and joined the NHA's board of commissioners, a position won by striking tenants two decades earlier.[150] Activists like McCray witnessed public housing's transformation as new federal incentives drove private developers and landlords into the subsidized-housing market. Chief among these changes was the NHA's greater reliance on private housing vouchers under the expansion of Section 8 in the Housing and Community Development Act of 1974.

In the 1990s, Newark received funding through the HOPE VI program to demolish high-rise public housing and replace it with smaller, garden-style apartments.[151] When the NHA again seized upon massive demolition as a solution to its expensive, partially shuttered high-rises, the Newark Coalition for Low Income Housing opposed the plan. Nevertheless, the NHA demolished over seven thousand units in the 1990s without replacing them.[152] Most displaced tenants received Section 8 vouchers but did not always find better conditions in the private market, according to one tenant who remarked that "people are going from the worst to hellholes."[153]

The Newark Coalition for Low Income Housing pursued the singular goal of forcing the NHA to rehabilitate enough housing to prevent a net shrinkage of units from demolition. In so doing, they were represented by attorney Harris David, who had counseled striking tenants decades before. The NHA initially agreed to Stella Wright tenants' demands for a rehabilitation guarantee but "proved utterly unable to implement its provisions." Once again, the court turned to Gustav Heningburg, designating him "special master." Heningburg determined that Stella Wright was too damaged to repair, too expensive to maintain, and too notorious to attract sufficient tenants. So tenants shifted course: instead of insisting on renovation, they called on the NHA to apply for HOPE VI funding to cover demolition and reconstruction. They prevailed. The Newark Coalition for Low-Income Housing obtained a Settlement Agreement that compelled the NHA to replace those units lost to demolition.[154] Stella Wright tenants had become fixers of a different sort: instead of saving high-rise public housing, they attempted to gain access to low-income housing for poor Newarkers as policy shifted decisively to a semiprivatized footing.

During the Stella Wright strike, some of the tenants' allies had begun developing alternative sources of low- and middle-income housing outside the realm of the NHA. Indeed, as the Stella Wright strike unfolded in the Central Ward, black nationalists across town were facing off with white trade union leaders and city officials over the construction of Kawaida Towers, a complex of mixed-income apartments, theaters, and businesses through which they would give black power tangible meaning. A few blocks from Stella Wright Homes, parishioners at Queen of Angels—Father Comerford's church—raised $1 million for their own experiment in low-income housing. These groups combined an incremental strategy of fixing cities neighborhood by neighborhood with much grander ambitions for resolving the urban crisis. Their own strategy for organizing neighborhoods and meeting residents' needs for housing and employment had to engage with new federal legislation that encouraged private investment. Newark's new organizational fixers would flourish—and encounter new impediments—between the utopian and the pragmatic.

PART THREE

Institutionalizing
the Movements

SIX

Black Power, Neighborhood Power, and the Growth of Organizational Fixers

Few organizations came to embody the fixer ethos more than the community development corporations (CDCs) that formed across the United States in the 1960s.[1] Buoyed by claims to self-determination issuing from the black power movement, the CDC vision of communal economic advancement straddled a line between reformism and radicalism. Their pursuit of local power as an antidote to federal overreach and incompetence intersected with the politically diffuse "backyard revolution,"[2] what Suleiman Osman calls "the hidden drama in a decade remembered as dead air between the tumult of the 1960s and the economic revival of the 1980s."[3]

More than that, the journeys of these early community development organizations map the uneven institutionalization of broader social movement demands. Often begun as grassroots, volunteer experiments, they were shaped and amplified by federal legislation—Special Impact Projects, the 1968 Housing Act, the 1974 Housing and Community Development Act—that constituted the newest iteration of the "patchwork welfare state." As the United States shifted rightward under Nixon's New Federalism, they responded to the devolution of funding to states and localities.[4] The philosophies and commitments of many community economic development activists endured, even as the structures of their organizations and the political context in which they operated changed between the 1960s and the 1990s. CDCs offered an imminently pragmatic and ideologically flexible approach that appealed to people of diverse political commitments who were urgently motivated to fix Newark. The work of activists Rebecca Doggett, Lydia and David Barrett, and Pat and David Foley reveals the circuitous paths that led to a movement in Newark.

From Uprising to Community Development

By 1967 Rebecca Doggett had spent a decade protesting racial discrimination. She had run a campaign to elect a black commissioner in her hometown of Orange, New Jersey, when she was a college student. She and her husband, Edward Andrade, had protested the exclusion of black workers in the construction trades during the brutal winter of 1965, when she walked a picket line with her two-month-old daughter in her arms. After she graduated from Upsala College, Doggett had taught in Newark's first Head Start program and designed a remedial math program through Rutgers University to prepare African American and Puerto Rican youth for jobs in the building trades.[5]

Doggett's early forays into activism were influenced by Ernest Thompson, a black labor organizer who cast a long shadow over New Jersey politics. Thompson's career began in the 1930s when he organized a union at the American Radiator Company in Bayonne, New Jersey. Throughout the 1940s, Thompson served as a field organizer with the newly formed United Electrical, Radio, and Machine Workers of America (UE). In the 1950s he led the UE's Fair Practices Committee and the National Negro Labor Council in coordinating joint attacks on race and sex discrimination. The UE, having long defined the labor movement's Left, came under increasing federal scrutiny as anticommunism took hold. Threats from federal investigators prompted the National Negro Labor Council to dissolve itself, while anticommunist purges within the labor movement precipitated the union's split, bringing Thompson's career to an end in 1956. Essentially blacklisted, Thompson moved to Orange, New Jersey, where he advised political candidates and promoted municipal reforms with the goal of consolidating an African American voting bloc.[6]

Thompson and Doggett met in the late 1950s on opposing sides of an election for the Orange City Commission. Doggett sought Thompson's aid in electing the only black candidate for the office. Thompson refused; he supported a white candidate he believed more likely to win. When Doggett's candidate lost, as Thompson had predicted, she decided she could learn from him. Thompson later worked with Doggett, Andrade, and others in the Newark Coordinating Committee to end discrimination in the building trades. In the late 1960s Doggett and Andrade joined Thompson and others to adapt a labor model to organize residents of Newark, Patterson, and Jersey City into the Tri-City Citizens Union for Progress. These three cities, they argued, would "be pivotal for the nation in terms of Negro acceptance in significant numbers at all levels into existing or projected enterprises."[7] Advancing what they called an "anti–urban renewal plan," the Citizens Union sought to transform residents into effective advocates for their cities by rehabilitating existing houses and saving them from demolition. Thompson's commitments to cultivating black leadership and interracial organizing around electoral politics, civil rights, and the labor movement had sustained traditions of the Communist-influenced Left through the early Cold War. With the leadership of younger activists, he now sought to adapt them to Newark, neighborhood by neighborhood.

Lydia Davis Barrett and David Barrett watched the Newark uprising on television from their apartment in Pittsfield, Massachusetts. Newly married, the two had met at Rutgers University in Newark, where they were both leaders in the student NAACP. David had grown up in a cold-water flat in the North Ward, the son of a housewife and a clothing presser who had migrated to Newark from Virginia. Shortly after David graduated from college with a math degree, General Electric recruited him to work in its Western Massachusetts division.[8] Lydia grew up west of Newark in the middle-class suburb of Montclair, the daughter of a teacher and an IRS accountant, who had quietly disapproved of her early marriage to a working-class man. Before moving to Pittsfield, neither Lydia nor David, both black, had lived in such a homogenously white community. They found it lonely, especially since their NAACP work at Rutgers-Newark had primed them for civil rights activism. Now David was designing software for weapons systems. Lydia, who had studied psychology, applied for a job as a social worker with the county welfare department. She was rejected in favor of a young white man who had fewer academic credentials. Barrett filed a discrimination complaint and it wound its way through the federal bureaucracy. Meanwhile, Lydia found herself in a life that seemed familiar from Betty Friedan's *Feminine Mystique*, which she had read in college—depressed, unemployed, and encouraged by doctors to ease her worries with Valium.[9]

Newark's televised destruction served as a catalyst for the Barretts' return to the city. They hungered for Newark news, receiving newspaper clippings from Lydia's mother and phone calls from a friend, who described the tanks rolling by her office window on Bloomfield Avenue. David's mother alerted him to a job opening at Lockheed in New Jersey. By November they had arranged to move back. The day before they left, Lydia received a call informing her that she had won her job discrimination case and that the Berkshire County Department of Welfare planned to offer her a job. It was too late to change her plans. The Barretts were Newark-bound.[10]

David and Lydia spent barely an hour at their new home in East Orange before heading off to a Congress of Racial Equality meeting in Newark, and then a United Brothers gathering later that night. During the flurry of meetings the Barretts attended, they met Amiri Baraka, who had also recently returned to his hometown of Newark after years living and writing in New York City. Although five months had passed, the uprising was at the center of every conversation: "We found . . . a number of people who were struggling, still trying to figure out what to do," David recalled. "How do we respond to this in a positive way?"[11]

Over the next seven years, the Barretts took Swahili names for themselves and the two children they had. David became M'tetezi; Lydia became Staarabisha. They became deeply involved in the constellation of cultural nationalist organizations that Baraka had helped found—the Committee for a Unified Newark, the Temple of Kawaida, and the Congress of African People (CAP). These organizations advanced a wide-ranging community development strategy that called on nationalists to transform existing institutions—municipal government, schools, businesses, and social service agencies—or build new ones. David and other nationalists successfully campaigned for the leadership of the United Community Corporation (UCC), allowing them to fund youth programs in journalism and media criticism. Lydia worked alongside Baraka's wife, Amina, to start a vegetarian restaurant, community center, and daycare center.[12] They also created the Black Women's United Front with fellow nationalist women around the country. They anticipated that these institutions would be cornerstones of a new wave of black economic and political development. Kawaida Towers, the high-rise housing development and theater that would become the target of violent opposition, was only one among the many projects reflecting cultural nationalists' determination to set forth a liberating black aesthetic in concrete—a black utopia rising from the ashes of urban New Jersey.

Pat Foley spent much of the early evening of July 13, 1967, multiplying recipes she typically cooked for her husband and eight children. She had to feed fifty additional teenagers who were running a day camp in Scudder Homes, one of Newark's huge subsidized-housing complexes. Foley, a blonde, Irish Catholic native of the Bronx, lived in the middle-class suburb of Woodcliff Lake, New Jersey. Her husband, David, com-muted to Newark for his job as a partner in the international account-ing firm Arthur Young and Company. That summer, the Foleys and their five school-age children had relocated to Saint Bridget's Parish in Newark to supervise the camp. David arranged evening workshops on budgeting for housing project tenants. On that hot July night, David and Father Thomas Kleissler accompanied a fellow parishioner to Scud-der Homes for a presentation on home economics. The parishioner had only begun speaking to a group of tenants when David heard gunshots outside. Engrossed in her presentation on coupons, the woman did not notice until David and the priest abruptly escorted her to the elevator. On their way down, the car stopped and its door opened, admitting a young man with a rifle strapped to his back. He rode silently with the three of them.[13]

Upon returning to the house where they were staying, David told Pat a riot was under way. They instructed the teenagers to pack their clothes. A restless night followed, Pat stationed at the door to make sure none of the children ventured outside. The teenagers protested the adults' decision to return to the suburbs the next morning. But the adults had decided the situation was too dangerous to stay.[14]

As the Foleys drove out of the Central Ward in their station wagon, their children were absorbed by the sight of men and women with armfuls of groceries or balancing stolen mattresses between them as National Guard tanks rolled into the city.[15] Although the Foleys left Newark that day, they would soon return as representatives of a group of mostly white, suburban residents who sought to bring their profes-sional and economic clout to bear on Newark's recovery. In the after-math of the uprising, the Foleys contributed to the politicization of the Catholic laity around urban inequality. They attempted to forge a role for white advocates of the civil rights movement that acknowledged the new political landscape wrought by the black power movement.

Rebecca Doggett, a black teacher and civil rights activist; the Barretts, a young black couple radicalized by cultural nationalism; and Pat Foley, a white middle-class housewife, were just a few of the many drawn to the practice of community economic development in the late 1960s and early 1970s. They followed different routes to a similar conclusion: that fixing Newark required a new kind of organization. Out of their disillusionment with the public housing system and their awareness of municipal government's limitations—even when it came under putatively sympathetic black leadership—they created Newark's first generation of CDCs. The three organizations profiled in this and the following two chapters—the Tri-City Citizens Union for Progress (Tri-City), the Congress of African People/Kawaida Inc.,[16] and the New Community Corporation (NCC)—acted as fixers by crafting a holistic response to the urban crisis. They sought to address the failures of the public housing system, reverse the devastation of urban renewal, and close the widening imbalance between city and suburb.

Activists in early CDCs recognized flaws in existing antipoverty programs, much like Cyril DeGrasse Tyson, UCC's first executive director, had in 1965. The War on Poverty offered ample job training, Tyson noted, but few actual jobs beyond running the antipoverty effort itself. These jobs provided mobility for some poor people, but they also fueled municipal patronage and competition among the very residents community action was supposed to organize. Tyson recognized that the antipoverty programs had no economic development function, no means for the poor to begin accumulating capital.[17]

If federal antipoverty policies were insufficient, Tri-City, CAP/Kawaida Inc., and the NCC sought alternative ways for poor and working-class communities to amass the economic and political clout to produce jobs, revive neighborhood commerce, and exercise self-determination. In so doing, early CDCs veered between individual and collective programs. They embraced homeownership in the context of a broader neighborhood solidarity modeled on labor unions; they aimed to elevate entire neighborhoods, not spur mobility for a fortunate few. Housing anchored their diagnosis of poverty and its solution: the construction of low-income homes would equip residents with skills and prepare them to manage collectively owned developments. They argued that aesthetically appealing and affordable housing would attract new businesses, stem the departure of existing ones, and promote stability.[18] The NCC and Tri-City especially praised the homeowner's dignity as a citizen, echoing Nathan Wright's insistence in *Ready to Riot* that homeownership was key to economically stable black communities and vital cities: "Black people should own homes, not rent them," he wrote. Wright, in fact, served as a consultant to Tri-City.[19] Homeownership was not only a foundation of class mobility. In New Jersey, where political power had long been situated in the suburbs, it appeared a necessary element of any plan to reclaim the city. As fixers cast about for an organizing model that would provide leverage to poor and working-class people, they attempted to adapt a labor movement model to organizing for neighborhoods and housing. Medical College negotiator Junius Williams had foreshadowed this strategy when he likened Central Ward residents to workers engaged in collective bargaining. He told officials they should approach the situation "as if we were a union in a union negotiating situation."[20] Tri-City's Ernest Thompson expressed this union strategy most explicitly: Tri-City aimed to demonstrate not only an alternative housing strategy but also a more politically unified community and, with their sister organizations in Patterson and Jersey City, to create a more powerful advocate for the state's working-class neighborhoods. The NCC did not incorporate union metaphors in the same way, but one of its leaders, Father William Linder, argued that organized labor offered a model for communities facing the vagaries of federal authority and market forces.[21]

Tri-City, CAP/Kawaida Inc., and the NCC positioned each of their neighborhood experiments within a larger civic network and sought to prove that stable inner-city communities were crucial components of a healthy regional economy. They were three of about half a dozen organizations formed in the late 1960s and early 1970s that constituted Newark's first generation of community economic development corporations.[22] They represent a diverse—though hardly exhaustive—range of motivations that drew activists together at the intersection of multiple social movements. Tri-City attempted to rehabilitate multifamily homes in Newark, Patterson, and Jersey City. Black cultural nationalists associated with Baraka and CAP proposed Kawaida Towers, one in a series of housing and business developments that would meld African aesthetic and ethical influences while anchoring new nationalist institutions. The NCC was the product of an interracial alliance between members of Newark's predominantly black Queen of Angels Catholic Church and white Catholics from the surrounding suburbs. The novel strategies—some successful, some not—that early CDCs pursued for fixing Newark reveal the nuanced influence of black power on neighborhood politics beyond the familiar—often-exaggerated—narrative of masculine militancy and separatism. All three organizations brokered new alliances—with officials in New Jersey's recently created Department of Community Affairs, for example, and with federal officials who could provide the grants, loan subsidies, and tax breaks necessary to keep housing costs down and permit experiments in communal ownership. Meanwhile, the Housing and Urban Development Act of

1970 apportioned funds for CDCs to build housing, in addition to conventional subsidized-housing programs. In contrast to the now widely criticized excesses of urban renewal in the 1950s and 1960s, the 1970s, it seemed, might deliver locally controlled revitalization on a more humane scale.

All three groups drew from different experiential roots and reflected distinct intellectual currents that often clashed, even as they shared concerns and a common connection to the early civil rights movement. Rebecca Doggett and Edward Andrade's work with Tri-City was shaped by Ernest Thompson's experience in the labor movement, the social gospel of their mainline churches, and Rebecca's experience working for the War on Poverty, specifically Head Start. For the Barretts, projects such as Kawaida Towers made tangible the ideas of African anticolonialists, such as Tanzania's Julius Nyerere, and, closer to home, black power theorist and former Student Nonviolent Coordinating Committee leader Stokely Carmichael, cultural nationalist Maulana Ron Karenga, Malcolm X, and Baraka. For the Foleys the NCC drew inspiration from the Poor People's Campaign set in motion by Martin Luther King Jr. before his assassination and built upon the politicization of the Catholic laity.

Indeed, the community economic development experiments that flourished in Newark were not solely responses to specific policy and market failures. They also tapped deep wells of ambivalence about the massive, anonymous scale of urban life and the conviction that a renewed focus on neighborhood and family promised residents the most humane interaction. In this sense, they reflected some elements of not only the neighborhood movement but also the counterculture of the 1970s.[23] These groups' disparate ideological and religious commitments shaped fixers' diagnosis of the urban crisis and the strategies they pursued to relieve it.

The first-generation Newark CDCs analyzed herein were only three among the hundreds of community economic development corporations founded across the country with similar goals.[24] "The significance of this movement," wrote Stewart E. Perry in 1971, "has not yet been adequately described in the near-revolutionary terms it deserves."[25] Though their emphasis resembled that of some federal policies, many CDCs proceeded without well-established public support or even an agreed-upon vocabulary. Their growth was ad hoc, deeply contingent on the opportunities that presented themselves. Although CDCs came to vary widely in structure, they typically began as nonprofit organizations. They combined private grants and donations with public funds to construct low-income housing, provide services, and employ local residents in neglected neighborhoods. Some CDCs perceived themselves as alternatives to capitalism; others, as facilitators of local markets. Many started businesses with the goal of reinvesting their earnings in other CDC projects or redistributing them through collective ownership. Some pursued for-profit ventures in the hope of offsetting dependence on unreliable government funding or philanthropic whimsy. Many provided low-interest loans in neighborhoods neglected by banks.[26] For some activists, CDCs offered a prospective resolution to the debates over "black capitalism" discussed in chapter 4: they embodied the unfulfilled promise of community action and the potential of black self-determination, and they blended locally responsive decision making with entrepreneurial vigor. This was especially the case in neighborhoods where residents contended with the closure of basic businesses such as grocery stores, pharmacies, and health clinics.

CDCs had plenty of critics as well, who pointed out that economic redevelopment in older manufacturing cities stood little chance of succeeding in an economy bent on corporate consolidation. This argument provoked broad debate in the late 1960s and the 1970s as early CDCs countered claims that reinvestment in troubled cities amounted to "gilding the ghetto," a losing strategy grounded on "the false analogy of the ghetto to an underdeveloped country" and programs "based on the permanence of the central ghettos." In the then center-Right journal *The Public Interest*, John Kain and Joseph P. Persky pointed out that the "ghetto," by the late twentieth century, did not constitute a colony, because it maintained economic connections to the regional political economy, "strong linkages that tie the ghetto to the remainder of the metropolis."[27] But few who concurred with the domestic colonialism thesis denied these ties; they knew that the development of ghetto economies would not happen in an economic vacuum, so they sought the resources and policies to enable economic self-determination.

Kain and Persky recommended low-income housing construction in the suburbs and subsidized rentals in the private market—similar to the dispersal policies and Section 8 voucher program that became mainstays of low-income housing in the 1970s.[28] Yet the success of such a plan depended on the uncompromising enforcement of anti-discrimination laws, which seemed unlikely. The suburbanization of low-income black urbanites that they championed was certainly occurring, but it happened unevenly, as did the anticipated return of middle-income whites to the city. Other critics did not believe community-based development could alter structural poverty. They perceived

CDCs as a petit bourgeois extension of "black capitalism" thinly veiled in social justice claims. Yet even some of these critics withheld their fire until the infant CDCs could be judged. In his widely cited *Black Awakening in Capitalist America*, Robert L. Allen accurately predicted that many CDCs would come to be controlled by "a professional bureaucratic elite," despite their grassroots origins; but otherwise, CDCs escaped his searing and exhaustive criticism.[29]

Around the country, CDCs multiplied at the intersection of black power and the community action programs of the War on Poverty. In Philadelphia, Reverend Leon Sullivan exercised the economic potential of that city's black freedom movement with "selective patronage" campaigns that channeled buying power away from companies with discriminatory hiring policies. A few years later, he launched the Opportunities Industrialization Centers, which drew on War on Poverty funds to train black workers. Sullivan raised funds to invest in black-owned businesses, residential developments, and housing rehabilitation programs. "[T]he communal basis and sense of social responsibility that lay at the root of Leon Sullivan's version of capitalist development," writes Guian McKee, "provided an alternative to the increasingly rootless economic model that came to dominate the American economy in the last decade of the twentieth century."[30] Activists both in the United States and abroad replicated the combination of protest, job training, and black-led economic development Sullivan honed through the Opportunities Industrialization Centers.[31]

Mexican American activists evinced similar motivations when they founded The East Los Angeles Community Union (TELACU) to organize East LA neighborhoods, "like a union organizes plants."[32] Starting with antipoverty programs for youth, TELACU expanded their offerings to include job training and financial services. TELACU's founders, according to Robert Bauman, wove together their trade union experience with internal colonialism theories popular among black and Chicano radicals and an ethos of economic self-help reminiscent of Booker T. Washington. Coordination, militant neighborhood solidarity, and economic clout were the necessary foundation of political power for TELACU. The Office of Economic Opportunity (OEO) recognized it as one of several dozen official CDCs in 1970.[33]

But when it came to CDCs with federal imprimatur, none achieved a status comparable to the Bedford-Stuyvesant Restoration Corporation of Brooklyn, New York. One of the earliest and most lauded organizations, the Bedford-Stuyvesant Restoration Corporation (BSRC) traced its roots to a coalition of neighborhood and civic groups, many led by black women. For years, they had organized loan pools for housing re-habilitation and furnished youth recreation programs in their sprawl-ing city within a city, all the while pressing officials for a share of ur-ban renewal funding.[34] Unlike most early CDCs, which struggled in obscurity, the BSRC attracted the attention of federal and state officials as well as private-sector leaders. New York senator Robert F. Kennedy heralded the BSRC as the necessary evolution of the War on Poverty and—it was implied—an improvement over President Johnson's ver-sion. Kennedy's team collaborated with Brooklyn judge Thomas Rus-sell Jones, a power broker in Brooklyn's Democratic Party, to secure bipartisan support from Governor Nelson Rockefeller, Senator Jacob Javits, and Mayor John Lindsay. Lauding the BSRC as "a new national response to the whole urban crisis," they also recruited private-sector heavyweights like IBM to reinvest in the neighborhood.[35] The BSRC received millions from the Ford Foundation and the federal Special Im-pact Program, an amendment to the Equal Opportunity Act that was secured by Senators Kennedy and Javits in 1966 with the BSRC in mind. The Special Impact Program provided an infusion of funds—a sort of miniature, warp-speed War on Poverty—in defined areas characterized by high unemployment, vacancies, and disinvestment. In keeping with BSRC's model, the Special Impact Program focused on manufacturing, housing, and job training, embodying what Guian McKee calls "'lib-eral federalism' because of its emphasis on direct federal provision of resources to local, community-based initiatives." Unlike existing War on Poverty programs, McKee notes, "[r]egional OEO offices, state and local governments, and local Community Action agencies had no in-put at any stage of the process."[36] BSRC-type community development may have received more unfettered access to funds and enjoyed more local flexibility because of Kennedy's influence, but this hardly avoided high-stakes conflict over community development goals locally.[37]

Nishani Frazier shows how one of the OEO's most heavily funded CDCs, Hough Area Development Corporation in Cleveland, Ohio, en-compassed such debates. This CDC was one of many activist groups challenging the racist franchise policies of the McDonald's Corpora-tion. But the Hough Area Development Corporation aimed to take the lead in purchasing local restaurants and combining their profits with substantial OEO funding to hire locally and offer much-needed com-munity services. Activists tried to build upon their gains, but they split over other issues, including whether to favor collective ownership by a black community organization or ownership by black individuals.[38]

Activists' disparate priorities sometimes proved irreconcilable. Meanwhile, federal funders and private-sector collaborators introduced demands that heightened internal divisions of ideology, class, and, especially, gender.[39] Brian Purnell shows how white and black men involved in the BSRC delegitimized the perspectives of the black women who had built and sustained the original organization before Kennedy's involvement. In press interviews, these men rarely acknowledged the substance of women's criticism of the new BSRC. Instead, they summarily dismissed longtime organizers as "matriarchs" and "obstructionists." These references conjured damaging stereotypes that blamed black women for perpetuating inequality by usurping men's roles as breadwinners and community leaders.[40] Similarly, the Mexican American women in TELACU in Los Angeles and African American welfare activists who formed Operation Life in Las Vegas had to fight the assumption—shared by fellow activists, private-sector funders, and policymakers—that "business is man's work."[41]

While scores of CDCs emerged out of the community action agencies of the War on Poverty, others arose out of local organizing prior to this legislation taking hold.[42] In Rochester, New York, working-class black activists and church leaders responded to the inequalities laid bare in that city's 1964 uprising with FIGHTON, which created manufacturing businesses to train and employ black workers. FIGHTON received support from the Xerox Corporation but rejected the paternalistic corporate philanthropy model that had dominated Rochester's civic life. Instead of accepting short-term, unskilled work doled out by corporations, FIGHTON contracted with the city's high-tech sector. This provided stable demand to sustain their larger mission of steady employment and training in skilled occupations.[43]

Many CDCs reflected residents' frustrations with inadequate urban, antipoverty, and civil rights policies. But they also built on the anticipation that these developments—however halting or limited—provided momentum and perhaps an opening for more dramatic transformations. The strand of community economic development sustained by the black freedom movement—as well as other groups in Asian American, Chicano, American Indian, and white working-class communities around the country—reflected the ethos of fixers in their attempts to address urgent problems. These communities desired a reordering of political power beyond the pluralist tinkering that electoral politics could provide on its own. In cities ruled by distant bureaucracies and perfunctory political machines, CDCs were small islands of resources, local expertise, and organizing passion that could be used to disrupt—or at least sway—politics as usual. Liberals, radicals, nationalists, conservatives, and those who defied categorization could be found in the ranks of first-generation CDCs.[44]

Early CDCs believed that fixing Newark required the democratization of expertise. They attempted to hone the technical skills and build the institutional clout they hoped would enable poor and working-class residents to reverse the decline of neighborhoods or alter the course of state- and private-sector development. Their holistic vision of neighborhood renewal encompassed architecture, city planning, real estate finance, political organizing, cultural production, and social services. Members sought expertise in these fields—in the form of licenses, degrees, skills, and other credentials—to carry out their plans and achieve legitimacy in the eyes of municipal officials, lenders, and state and federal regulators. In the broadest sense, community economic development organizations acted not only to widen residents' avenues of participation but also to prepare them to act as mini–state builders.

Residents involved in Tri-City, CAP/Kawaida Inc., and the NCC sought to democratize expertise in four ways. First, they demanded more accountability to local residents by the urban planners, housing developers, and physicians who served them. Residents educated themselves to better communicate with experts and challenge technical language used to obfuscate the political nature of urban renewal, zoning, and housing finance.

Second, CDCs served as a career ladder for activists, many of whom continued to work in these organizations after they acquired professional credentials.

Third, resident activists in CDCs offered alternative notions of expertise based on their own experiences, expertise that was increasingly seen as legitimate. "In almost every facet of a community's existence," read one planning document, "there will be someone there around whom the life of the community revolves." This approach rejected what Tri-City founders called "bad social science" and the assumptions of ghetto residents' passivity that colored influential scholarship on urban poverty.[45]

Fourth, the CDCs positioned the communities they represented as corporate entities prepared to borrow money and finance professional housing and business development. The new civic organizations that emerged after the 1967 uprising no longer sought merely to hold officials accountable for development policies in their neighborhoods: they wanted to control the nature of development itself.

The previous chapters show the fraught prehistory of devolution in policymaking. Devolution is commonly associated with conservatives' goal of shrinking the welfare state by decentralizing control of urban and social programs and eventually defunding them.[46] Although devolution accelerated from Nixon to Reagan, it is a process for which the community action programs of the War on Poverty—a signature of 1960s liberalism—actually provided some precedent. In this sense, devolution was not solely a top-down, partisan phenomenon. Organizational fixers, such as CDCs, initially embodied a persistent urban populism born of both necessity and a commitment to self-determination; they proliferated precisely because they managed the consequences of devolution and secured resources for local communities in this tumultuous political transformation.[47] Tri-City, CAP/Kawaida Inc., and the NCC sought to refashion a more responsive social safety net for poor and working-class people. As devolution became a way of cutting federal funding for cities and shifting more of the burden for maintaining affordable housing and social services to the voluntary sector, the stakes rose for fixers.

Tri-City Citizens Union for Progress: Old Left, Black Power, and "Anti–Urban Renewal"

Ernest Thompson, Rebecca Doggett, Edward Andrade, and about a dozen others created Tri-City Citizens Union for Progress in 1966 to prove that organizing residents around the rehabilitation of older homes could preserve working-class neighborhoods. If the Medical College dispute had challenged the massive demolition necessitated by the city's urban renewal agenda, fixers like Tri-City would forge alternatives. Tri-City originally targeted Patterson and Jersey City as well as Newark with the aim of coordinating branch offices in the soon-to-be-bustling neighborhoods of each city. Episcopal minister and black power advocate Nathan Wright Jr. influenced the founders' emphasis on homeownership, although most were to his left politically.[48] Residents would teach each other how to maintain their homes, resist careless city policies, develop cooperative ownership of apartment buildings, and, eventually, expand into a regional network of neighborhoods with the strength to reverse their cities' decline.

Thompson extended the tactics of the shop floor to the city block. As a founding member of the National Negro Labor Council, he perceived civil and economic rights as inextricably bound and promoted unions as the best means of achieving both. A neighborhood union would "organize Negro people of all classes" and release them from "crippling powerlessness."[49] Tri-City easily reconciled fresh calls for black power with more conventional commitments to self-determination. Tri-City founders interpreted "Negro initiative" and "self-development" as the "true meaning of Black Power" and argued that these goals "were a wish conceived within the context of American democracy and tradition."[50] But while Tri-City conceived of itself as a black power organization and some members participated in Newark's National Conference on Black Power, it was not directly aligned with the more heavily publicized national movement taking shape around Baraka's Committee for a Unified Newark.[51] Tri-City also drew on the Protestant affiliations of some members, positioning the organization as an instrument through which New Jersey's black churches could "redeem the cities."[52]

Tri-City focused almost immediately on housing. In the autumn of 1967 founders met with Walter Berry, a real estate agent and a member of the Foundation for Negro Progress, and Lucille Russell of New Horizons Development Corporation, to weigh options for housing in several Newark neighborhoods. Berry knew Thompson through their shared history in the labor movement. Berry had some money he wanted to invest. At Berry's suggestion, Tri-City selected West Side Park, situated at the westernmost part of Newark's Central Ward, along the Irvington-Newark City Line. Tri-City perceived this choice as an experiment in "anti–urban renewal," but it was also a pragmatic one based on the anticipation that the Department of Community Affairs and the New Jersey Housing Finance Agency would make rehabilitation funding available. Tri-City deemed rehabilitation a more expedient solution than new housing construction, which necessitated more upfront funding and a time-consuming approval process.[53]

Between 1967 and 1973 Tri-City purchased and rehabilitated several hundred units of housing in West Side Park. This fifty-block neighborhood of wood-frame multifamily homes and well-kept, tree-lined streets contained some of the city's oldest, most densely packed housing.[54] Tri-City's founders believed that a rehabilitation plan that succeeded there could be easily replicated elsewhere.[55] West Side Park exemplified the demographic transition under way in neighborhoods across Newark as white residents departed for the suburbs and were replaced by African Americans and Puerto Ricans. By 1970 African Americans made up a majority of the neighborhood's 17,200 residents. Many—a larger percentage than the city average—lived in or on the cusp of poverty.[56]

Tri-City raised money for its initial project internally, soliciting

$3,000 investments from among its founders and mostly other black professionals. Fundraising was already under way in 1966, but the 1967 uprising brought new urgency to Tri-City's mission and galvanized potential supporters among some state officials. Commissioner Paul Ylvisaker of the Department of Community Affairs offered an especially enthusiastic response. With his support, Tri-City secured a $1.4 million, thirty-five-year mortgage from the New Jersey Housing Finance Agency for acquiring, rehabilitating, and establishing cooperative ownership of ninety-seven units, called Amity I.[57]

Tri-City spun off a construction company, called Priorities, under the direction of Oliver Lofton, the former Legal Services attorney who had helped negotiate the Medical College Agreement and served on the Governor's Select Commission on Civil Disorder (Lilley Commission). Priorities drew together black architects, contractors, and tradesmen with the goal of creating an autonomous development network. But union business agents rebuffed their initial requests for black tradesmen. So they depended on nonunion tradesmen and often poorly financed contractors.[58] Construction subcontractors traditionally "carried" the general contractor during the construction, meaning that they covered the costs of materials, equipment rental, and workers' wages until the job was completed. But minority contractors who bid on construction jobs did not have access to sufficient capital, requiring Priorities to furnish more frequent cash payments.[59] Priorities planned to rehab the units according to the "Levittown" method of simultaneous construction, named after the famous subdivisions that seemingly appeared overnight in the suburbs of New York, New Jersey, and Pennsylvania.[60] But the construction company encountered frustrating delays and rising costs that called into question the ease with which the Levittown model could be widely replicated.[61]

Even with these challenges, Tri-City attracted attention from outside Newark for its novel approach. Tri-City's use of housing rehabilitation to cultivate black economic self-sufficiency in the face of urban disinvestment was variously described as "black capitalism," the "social approach," and a "hybrid." A building industry magazine gushed over Tri-City's success in maintaining middle-class homes in what "may be the most hopeless of the big cities."[62] By stabilizing neighborhoods like West Side Park, housing cooperatives would transform urban black residents into "a more potent group of voters" and enable them to "exert political influence in the way that other minorities have," a position that mirrored Stokely Carmichael and Charles V. Hamilton's recommendations in *Black Power: The Politics of Liberation*.[63] To be sure, the ninety-seven-unit development, called Amity I, also had its critics. Training workers in construction and management, some urban planners argued, would delay production and ultimately undermine the goal of efficient, affordable housing. Still, Tri-City's approach was cautiously promoted by both public policy analysts aware of the vast need for affordable housing and construction industry professionals curious about what kind of markets remained in the riot-torn cities.[64]

Tri-City's organizers experienced some ambivalence about the Amity project, but for reasons that differed from those of their critics. Rebecca Doggett recalled the incessant demands of coordinating a major construction project. Some of the early tenant meetings were "bitter lessons," with "a lot of people yelling at us" about unfinished repairs. Tri-City's founders, steeped in black trade union radicalism, were essentially becoming landlords, absorbed in the everyday demands of property maintenance and a losing battle against escalating costs, while the community-organizing goals at the heart of their mission began to languish.[65] As Tri-City considered adding a second phase to the development, which came to be called Amity Village, the North American Development Corporation (NADC) approached Tri-City about collaborating. The NADC was one of a growing number of companies taking advantage of new federal tax breaks to build affordable housing. The company sought hundreds of units in Newark that it would rehabilitate and resell.[66] The NADC wanted a local partner; Tri-City needed liquidity. Tri-City reached what appeared to be a favorable arrangement: the NADC would continue construction and management of the second Amity development while overseeing the transformation of Amity I into cooperatively owned housing. Thompson grew seriously ill during the negotiating process and fought for Tri-City's future from his hospital bed, establishing a trust fund from the proceeds of the sale and ensuring that the NADC would give Tri-City the first option to buy back the Amity homes and preserve the cooperative ownership option should the NADC ever decide to sell them.[67] But shortly after his death in 1971, Doggett and Andrade left Newark; Head Start hired Doggett to direct a preschool program in Puerto Rico. In their absence, Tri-City's accomplishments began to unravel as local and national developments drew Amity into precisely the kind of crisis Thompson had hoped to avoid.[68]

By the summer of 1972 the NADC had sold a couple hundred of the units to absentee owners who had no plans to pursue cooperative ownership. Meanwhile, its relationship to tenants in the remaining units deteriorated, evidenced by rent strikes, lawsuits, and vandalism.[69]

Tri-City's vision for decent housing and a politically potent West Side Park was further jeopardized by a moratorium on subsidized housing imposed by President Nixon in 1973. Subsidized housing had come under attack for the very problems highlighted by the tenants' strike. The Department of Housing and Urban Development (HUD) also pursued production goals that many legislators deemed mismatched to a time of high inflation, property abandonment, and declining urban populations.[70] But fiscal concerns were not the sole, or even most important, justification for the moratorium. HUD-directed subsidies for new construction were supposed to promote the desegregation of cities and the opening of interracial housing in suburbs. The moratorium indirectly allowed Nixon to fulfill his campaign promises to roll back—or at least delay—the implementation of civil rights reforms.[71] Tri-City's housing goals for the majority black and Puerto Rican West Side Park did not explicitly involve desegregation, but it nonetheless suffered from the moratorium. The NADC had staked its business on partnerships with groups that received federal subsidies and now lost investors. As the NADC failed to meet its obligation and Amity floundered, Tri-City was once again forced into the role of landlord to protect itself.

Tri-City's board members persuaded Doggett and Andrade to return to Newark to help save the organization.[72] The couple was able to stave off collapse by negotiating for state intervention. Alarmed by the mismanagement of Amity under the NADC, the New Jersey Department of Community Affairs arranged a loan from the New Jersey Housing Finance Agency; Tri-City finally purchased Amity Village from the NADC with the intention of selling the units to tenants.[73] Doggett, Andrade, and other Tri-City founders reluctantly reassumed management. With funds from the Comprehensive Employment and Training Act of 1973 (Title VI), they hired residents to carry out basic maintenance, household repair, and collective management.[74]

As Andrade worked with state officials to resolve the NADC's broken agreement with Tri-City, Doggett and volunteers transformed the People's Center—a Ukrainian church renovated with proceeds from the sale of Amity I to the NADC—into a hub for social services, daycare programs, workshops, and community meetings. West Side Park lacked basic medical facilities, prompting the People's Center to open a women's health clinic in 1974 with prenatal care, abortion referral, weight loss and nutrition programs, and cervical cancer screening.[75] Volunteer "block workers" supplemented the clinic's work by advising residents in their homes. Educating women about preventative healthcare reflected the Center's emphasis on grassroots expertise and emboldened them to ask questions of their providers. A photograph of the Tri-City medical clinic depicts a young African American doctor clad in a denim jacket, turtleneck, and oversized glasses inspecting the ear of a black child during Saturday office hours at the People's Center. Another image features the same doctor with a group of black and Puerto Rican women seated on a couch and chairs. The caption identifies them as nurses and block workers, but their casual clothing and intimate seating arrangement suggest an organization with little use for traditional hierarchy between expert and volunteer.[76]

In addition to democratizing health care expertise, Tri-City also incorporated youth into the People's Center. They operated preschool and after-school programs to compensate for the deficits of the public school system. The People's Center called their methods the "whole child approach," similar to that embraced by Head Start: they devised activities and set goals for children at all stages.[77] Tri-City's teachers, counselors, and volunteers believed that citizenship skills had to be taught to children from a young age and reinforced through everyday tasks.[78] They taught young children African American and Puerto Rican history to instill community pride. As West Side Park children grew into teenagers whose idleness was deemed "potentially explosive," they worked summer jobs arranged by the People's Center and led neighborhood beautification teams.[79] Tri-City's "ideology of self-help and independence" extended beyond children to require the participation of parents. Surveying the high high-school dropout rate and the demand for remedial education, the People's Center concluded that teaching parents to be effective advocates for their children was as important as providing supplemental education.[80]

As these programs suggest, Tri-City initially forged alliances between African Americans and the growing Puerto Rican community of West Side Park. This goal receded as the organization sunk its energy and resources into housing rehabilitation. But the People's Center revived it in response to Puerto Ricans' demands for inclusion. Although Puerto Ricans had long been active in Newark's civic life, September 1974 marked a major turning point: police in search of gamblers interrupted the enormous Labor Day picnic at Branch Brook Park that had become an annual tradition among Newark's Puerto Ricans. Mounted officers wielding clubs plowed into the crowd, injuring many in their attempt to clear the park. Two men later died, but despite witnesses, no one was blamed. Mayor Gibson himself led a march to city hall, but smaller-scale skirmishes continued.

Puerto Ricans' attempts to repel police at Branch Brook confounded

the black and white binary through which many Newarkers understood their city and were perceived by outsiders. Findings of the Newark Commission on Human Rights demonstrated high unemployment
and systemic underrepresentation of Puerto Ricans in public agencies,
although their population—and that of other Spanish- and Portuguese-
speaking communities—had been growing. Ike Hopkins of the Greater
Newark Community Workshop noted that the fruitless commission
hearings resembled those held during the height of the civil rights
movement over a decade earlier: "The same folks that had the cake still
have the cake," he told the commission.[81] Jose Rivera, a Rutgers University professor, said Latinos in Newark received only "the scraps of
housing that Blacks have left behind," contributing to a yawning gap
in the two groups' experiences that inhibited collaboration.[82] "We have
to make changes for ourselves," Leopoldo Santiago Sanchez told the
commission.[83] In the North Ward, Ramon Rivera was doing precisely
that. Influenced by Puerto Rican nationalism and the militancy of the
Young Lords, he founded La Casa de Don Pedro, which would become
one of Newark's largest CDCs by the late 1990s.

Meanwhile, in West Side Park, Tri-City Puerto Rican activism was
made visible through "bicultural" children's programs. Block workers
and the health clinic also addressed the challenges faced by Spanish-
speaking women in securing health care. By the late 1970s Tri-City
had stipulated that a third of its programs target Spanish-speaking
residents, while staff enrolled in Spanish classes, hired interpreters for
community meetings, and recruited more Puerto Rican residents.[84]

The People's Center and the Amity developments advanced Tri-
City's goals of linking housing to neighborhood political organizing.
Like some of the more radical area boards created during Newark's War
on Poverty, Tri-City leaders explicitly acknowledged how class could
foreclose political involvement: "Unlike middle class participation,"
they explained, "the neighborhood people do not have the kind of
jobs that permit them to use part of their work time to get their volunteer work done."[85] In this way, Tri-City responded to the complaint of
Cyril DeGrasse Tyson, the United Community Corporation's first director, that the community action programs of the War on Poverty had
mobilized residents to make demands of those in power but did little
to actually build their political clout and economic leverage. As fixers,
Tri-City attempted to use rehabilitation and cooperative homeownership as a platform for political consciousness-raising, a practical means
through which poor and working-class people could acquire political
and economic capital. But did they succeed?

Long after Thompson's death, Tri-City spoke in the rhetoric of black self-determination and employed the organizing techniques he had championed. But it did not achieve the level of self-sufficiency its founders had envisioned. They had anticipated that they would evolve into a self-sustaining organization by 1970, run by volunteers and paid staff, funded from a combination of Tri-City business ventures and community contributions. But their goals proved too ambitious. A decade later, Tri-City employed a staff of forty-five professionals and paraprofessionals and relied on individual contributions, grants, and social services contracts.[86] One critic questioned Tri-City's reliance on Andrade and Doggett, whose formidable skills as activists and professionals remained indispensable.[87] Indeed, it is unlikely that Tri-City would have survived the 1970s had they not returned to Newark. More than a decade into its operation, the collapse of the Jersey City and Patterson branches and the overwhelming challenges presented by its twelve-block section of West Side Park had compelled Tri-City to abandon the regional vision reflected in the organization's title. Even so, Doggett and Andrade recognized that tiny self-sufficient communities could not stem the decline of the city. In the late 1970s one evaluator predicted that Tri-City's success in the future would require "a powerful neighborhood coalition throughout the greater Newark area" and federal infrastructure "dealing with neighborhood reinvestment."[88] Tri-City had attracted favorable attention from HUD. President Carter's National Commission on Neighborhoods, meanwhile, included Tri-City in a national study of promising community development organizations on which to model a new national urban policy. But while Tri-City met with the favor of federal-level policymakers, its relationship to local powers was fractious.

Like many CDCs, Tri-City formed partly to challenge municipal policies and never enjoyed much support from officials in its efforts to cultivate neighborhood power. Indeed, Tri-City's founders chose the West Side Park neighborhood because it was close enough to the city core to serve as what Lofton called a "firewall against the spread of blight" but was outside the perimeter of the Model Cities neighborhood with its "red tape" and "political rivalries."[89] One evaluator warned the National Commission on Neighborhoods that Tri-City's contentious relationship with Mayor Gibson was its most pressing liability: the organization was unlikely to win Gibson's cooperation in applying for federal programs requiring his approval.[90] In fact, the People's Center did win contracts from Newark to provide childcare and administer aspects of the Medicaid program, but municipal officials excluded Tri-City from the Community Development Block Grant program, which offered funds for the sort of health and children's services Tri-City had already successfully established in the People's Center.[91]

Over the next couple decades, the People's Center continued to provide much-needed health services, as well as culturally attuned educational programs. It also offered Spanish- and English-language classes and fostered cooperation among African Americans and Puerto Ricans. Even after Tri-City disengaged from housing development, the Amity projects endured, although their status remained in legal limbo for years and they were never transferred to cooperative ownership. The organization's strength waxed and waned, but it survived. Tri-City continued to organize West Side Park around housing issues, advising residents who faced foreclosure during the financial crisis of 2008. The impetus behind Tri-City's formation—the commitment to organizing residents to advocate for their communities—was sustained into the twenty-first century, stabilizing West Side Park even as many of the communities around it deteriorated.[92] It was, in some sense, an island. The Carter administration had cited Tri-City as a national model for urban redevelopment in the late 1970s. But federal officials never devised a coherent urban policy to support such organizations—that would evolve later, and in piecemeal fashion. Had it happened earlier, perhaps the "anti–urban renewal" model Tri-City advocated would have been replicated beyond West Side Park, as Ernest Thompson had imagined. But in its absence, other organizations were joining the ranks of Tri-City, offering their own ambitious plans to fix Newark.

SEVEN

From Redeeming the Cities to Building the New Ark: Black Nationalism and Community Economic Development

Early community development corporations (CDCs) embodied the indistinct boundary between protest and politics. They deployed the direct action tactics of the civil rights movement, adopted black power's diagnosis of the inadequacy of reform, and embraced self-determination. But these institutional fixers also depended upon influence accumulated behind the scenes. Radical goals often inspired their work, yet their strategies tended less toward outright revolt against established authority and more toward the cultivation of alternative institutions and strategies that would subvert it. Even so, such fixers' work could be fiercely contested. Among the fixers in Newark during the late 1960s and 1970s, the community development efforts associated with Amiri Baraka and his advocacy of black power were most vigorously advanced as part of a national liberationist project; they also met the most violent resistance.[1] Decades on, the growth of CDCs across the United States may suggest a simple narrative of political moderation enabling greater institutionalization. Returning to the historical moment clarifies how these institutional fixers desired ends more radical than the gentle

honing of the status quo in the aftermath of reform. When black nationalists' work as fixers was misconstrued and rebuffed, they did not
respond with further concessions but struck out further toward the
revolutionary Left.

Amiri Baraka's poetry called his readers to arms. In "Black Art"
(1965) he demanded "Assassin Poems, Poems that shoot."[2] Radicalized
by Malcolm X and the Cuban Revolution, Baraka transformed from a
disaffected bohemian to a leader of the Black Arts Movement. In 1960
the US-based Fair Play for Cuba Committee invited Baraka to view the
revolution firsthand. With fellow black intellectual and movement vi-
sionaries he embarked on a trip that looms large in the history of late
twentieth-century radicalism.[3] Among them was Robert Williams, the
renegade NAACP leader from North Carolina who had blended militant civil rights protest with self-defense and embodied black power
before the Student Nonviolent Coordinating Committee or the Black
Panthers had raised their fists. The historian John Henrik Clarke, a
founding theorist of Africana studies, also joined them, as did Harold
Cruse, the social critic and author of *The Crisis of the Negro Intellectual*.
Young Cubans avidly challenged what they deemed Baraka's limited
and apolitical view of himself as a poet. He found himself on the de-
fensive; his politics, he wrote, "seemed puny" compared with the politics of his Cuban peers, "for whom Cuba was the first payoff of a world
they had already envisioned and were already working for." Upon his
return, he noted, "[t]he arguments with my old comrades increased
and intensified. It was not enough to write, to feel, to think, one must
act! One *could* act."[4] Baraka's authorial voice was changing, his artis-
tic center of gravity shifting when he encountered Malcolm X, who,
Baraka wrote, "charged me in a way no one else had ever done. He
reached me." Watching Malcolm X prevail in his debates with moderate civil rights leaders or reading about his stand against police in Harlem, Baraka recalled, "made my head tingle with anticipation and new
ideas. He made me feel more articulate and forceful myself, just having
seen him."[5] Baraka's conviction that artists should play a crucial role
in forging revolutionary culture energized his work in the Black Arts
Movement, even as he sometimes evinced doubt about whether or not
poetry would rise to the challenge.[6]

Baraka's profile as a provocateur was in many ways at odds with fixers' capacity to forge unlikely alliances or navigate polarizing politics.
For example, Baraka famously rebuffed Office of Economic Opportunity director Sargent Shriver when Shriver attempted to visit Baraka's
Black Arts Repertory Theater in Harlem in response to critics who had

blasted Shriver for funding theater with an explicit black power orientation. Yet as an activist in Newark and in the national black power
movement of the 1970s, Baraka combined his role as a black power in-
surrectionist with that of a fixer, enmeshed, as we glimpsed in chapter 4, in a broad spectrum of black organizations. Placing Baraka and
the organizations he led in the spectrum of fixers brings to mind the
arguments of literary scholar Gene Jarrett, who frames African American literature by recourse to "deans," those whose work consolidates literary conventions around race and realism, and "truants," writers who
reject, fracture, and digress from them. Jarrett identifies Baraka as a
dean, an institution builder and gatekeeper. To be sure, Baraka's prolific
body of work pulsed with idiosyncrasies, but Jarrett's characterization
of Baraka as a literary dean could also be said to extend to the roles
Baraka played nationally through the Congress of African People (CAP)
and, in his hometown, through the Committee for a Unified Newark
(CFUN), where he briefly sought to act as a fixer.[7]

Turning Black Power into Bricks and Mortar: The Fight for Kawaida Towers

Baraka's rise and fall as a fixer centers on his attempts to build housing
in Newark and join the ranks of first-generation CDCs with perhaps
the most ambitious plan of them all. Baraka and fellow activists originally aspired to construct new homes, businesses, theaters, and cultural institutions in a one-hundred-acre stretch of the Central Ward,
referred to as "NJ-32," that had been cleared for urban renewal. The
tremendous scope of their plans reflected, according to Komozi Woodard, "Baraka's admiration of the Tanzanian President Julius Nyerere
and his socialist vision of Ujamaa, African communalism." For cultural
nationalists—and supportive local residents who contributed ideas to
the plan—it constituted "the first attempt to flesh out what the Black
Power experiment could mean for a new community life in a 'liberated
zone.'"[8] When municipal stonewalling sidetracked the NJ-32 project,
Baraka and his collaborators decided to instead test their development
model on a smaller middle- and low-income high-rise called Kawaida
Towers. But the project, located in a racially mixed neighborhood on
the periphery of Newark's predominantly white North Ward, barely
advanced beyond the foundation before falling under unrelenting attack by white protesters. They set off a clash over the building's future
that illustrated the limits of black political victories in the early 1970s

and the depth of white residents' commitment to segregation. But to understand how the erection of a single building in a residential section of Newark erupted into a four-year struggle that even a group attempting to act as fixers could not resolve, one must first show how Kawaida Towers reflected the aspirations and increasing political clout of black cultural nationalists in Newark and the often-neglected economic thrust of black power activism writ large.

After returning to his hometown from the Black Arts Repertory Theater in Harlem, Baraka established himself at the intersection of several organizations in Newark. Through his involvement in the United Brothers' campaign to elect Kenneth Gibson mayor in 1970 and his participation in a series of black power conferences, Baraka drew many young people into the CFUN. The CFUN seized upon the possibilities for redressing the inequities of urban renewal and making black power principles tangible in the redevelopment of the NJ-32 parcel. Black power organizing in Newark was extensive and heterogeneous, as exemplified by the numerous organizations that formed, disbanded, or evolved in the late 1960s and early 1970s. As Woodard explains, participants in both local and national black power conferences formed the CAP, a "broad, working federation of Black nationalists," to translate the nationalist platforms they devised into tangible economic and cultural liberation on the ground and to serve as "a new national vanguard organization."[9] During the period on which this analysis focuses, the Newark branch of the CAP subsumed the CFUN, although many of the same people remained involved.

In Newark, Baraka and the CAP pursued their goals through street-level organizing around housing, jobs, and urban renewal. Baraka's strategies for remaking the Central Ward of Newark into what he called the "New Ark" were shaped for a brief but influential period by the prominent theorist of black cultural nationalism Maulana Ron Karenga (Ronald McKinley Everett). Karenga, a scholar, civil rights activist, and founder of the US Organization in Los Angeles, forged an ethical system, which he named "Kawaida," from his study of African languages, religions, and mythologies. "Kawaida" itself was adapted from a Swahili term connoting a tradition of reason; Kawaida's adherents pursued liberation from the racism endemic to the United States, seeking instead a new cultural and social framework that would prepare black communities for political revolution.[10] Baraka's Newark branch of the CAP sought new institutions that would unite Kawaida theory and practice, integrating political organizing and economic life with cultural production. To that end, they established a nationalist network across the Central Ward: dancers, poets, and musicians from around the country performed at the Spirit House on Sterling Street, where Baraka frequently produced his own plays. From an office on the second floor, activists fanned out across the city to register voters, campaign for candidates, and organize residents to oppose police brutality and poor management of the city's schools.[11] By the early 1970s they had established a network of African Free Schools throughout the city as well as businesses that sold clothing, jewelry, and "kits" for the celebration of Kwanzaa (the holiday Karenga had created), and that printed and sold books.[12]

Activists sought to extend this nationalist geography through housing, specifically "a Black nationalist alternative to the white supremacist policy of urban renewal," but the Newark Housing Authority indefinitely delayed the CFUN's plans for the NJ-32 urban renewal plots.[13] Newark's black cultural nationalists instead pursued the construction of Kawaida Towers on an empty lot in the North Ward recommended by their architecture firm. Although it was not their ideal choice, the site was one of the few readily available and met their requirements. They took advantage of the Department of Housing and Urban Development's (HUD) Section 236 program, which subsidized construction and rent to keep the building within the range of low- to middle-income renters. The New Jersey Housing Finance Agency also provided funding and negotiated the purchase of land.[14] Although smaller in scope than the CFUN's original plan for NJ-32, Kawaida Towers still reflected black nationalists' commitment to spatial and political transformation. Building design would promote community gatherings and cultural production: plans included a professional theater; broadcast equipment; and space for community meetings, art exhibitions, and recreation.[15] CAP/Kawaida Inc. intended to provide the sort of amenities typically unavailable to low- and middle-income renters and to offer a more aesthetically pleasing design than the typical modern highrise. Majenzi Kuumba (Earl Crooms), who modified the design of an existing building in nearby Jersey City, wanted to avoid the featureless hulks "we have become accustomed to in Newark." Plans called for sixteen stories with ample windows and two columns of inviting balconies.[16] Like Amity I, the high-rise development built by the Tri-City Citizens Union for Progress (Tri-City), Kawaida Towers sought to unite a network of black architects, planners, contractors, and tradespeople in preparation for a future of increasingly ambitious development projects. Baraka and the other officers of Kawaida Inc. arranged "mix and match" mentoring relationships, pairing "a few Black people with white experts as a step toward developing an autonomous African-American development team."[17] North Ward councilman Frank Megaro agreed to introduce a tax abatement for Kawaida Towers, which the city council unanimously approved in the fall of 1971, signifying a hesitant, highly pragmatic step toward interracial cooperation on the city's acute housing problems.[18] Although white residents, city officials, and some journalists would later condemn Kawaida Towers for provoking one of the most racially divisive conflicts in the city's history, its early planning proceeded with little controversy.

But support for Kawaida Towers was upended during the ground breaking when the young director of the North Ward Education and Cultural Center, Stephen Adubato, questioned whether black nationalists should be permitted to build a project in the heavily Italian American North Ward without residents' approval. "What would happen if the Italians got funds to build an apartment in the Central Ward and called it the 'Garibaldi Building'?" he asked. Adubato, a political upstart establishing his own role as a fixer in Newark's North Ward, implied that Kawaida Towers represented a betrayal of the North Ward's white residents.[19]

One answer to Adubato's rhetorical question was that one of Newark's first major urban renewal projects had, in fact, been named for an Italian: Christopher Columbus Homes, an initially segregated mixed-income project had been named to reflect the Italian heritage of many residents and the Italian American neighborhood that had been partially demolished to make room for its construction.[20] Adubato became a locally and nationally known representative of the so-called "white ethnic" revival, anchored by institutions like the National Center for Urban Ethnic Affairs, helmed by Monsignor Geno Baroni. Adubato's North Ward Education and Cultural Center received funding from Baroni's organization.[21] The Ford Foundation underwrote the larger white ethnic movement partly in response to the fracturing of the working class but also to soften public officials' criticism of the foundation and their threats to revoke its tax-exempt status because of its support for some black power organizations in the late 1960s.[22] Grass-roots white ethnic groups—even as they often saw themselves competing with black organizations—also sought to appropriate elements of black power, particularly its critique of assimilation, and to adapt its focus on community control and self-determination to their own embattled enclaves. In many cases, this produced a politics of aggrieved whiteness allied with law-and-order conservatism, but in others, such groups embraced the strengthening of a more inclusive New Deal–style social safety net attuned to local variance. White ethnic leaders occasionally reached out to black power organizations, claiming that their situations were not all that distinct given that the decline of US cities redounded to all its working-class residents. More often, white leaders glossed over the occupational and residential advantages from which whites had historically benefited. At the same time, Malcolm X's famous speech "The Ballot or the Bullet" and Stokely Carmichael and Charles V. Hamilton's *Black Power: The Politics of Liberation* assembled striking examples to warn against coalitions with white groups.[23]

At the national level white ethnic leaders like Geno Baroni might have called for expanded, more inclusive urban policies to help working-class people, and indeed, Adubato presented himself as an advocate for working- and lower-middle-class residents struggling with underemployment, declining cities, and poor education. But he outlined an impasse at the local level—one he'd helped create—in a letter to his adviser and benefactor. Adubato said he had "established lines of communication with Newark's black and Puerto Rican communities" but found that "the pre-conditions for meaningful interracial cooperation . . . do not exist at present. This situation is attributable in part to the racial discord, which was generated by the school strike, to a vacuum of leadership in the city, and to the mounting frustration of North Ward whites because their needs remain unmet. At present there is no program in the North Ward which is relevant to the white residents of the area."[24] Adubato's insistence on "no program" for whites seems overstated given the influence of North Ward leaders, the dominance of white representatives in local government, and the fact that the city had had a white majority until the mid-1960s. Still, Adubato's comments at the ground breaking proved explosive. Not only did they underscore the crisis among some Italian American civic leaders in the wake of Gibson's victory over incumbent Hugh J. Addonizio. His comments also implicitly addressed a sense of loss and marginalization that some whites harbored and soon channeled against Kawaida Towers. In that struggle, noted David Barrett (Kaimu M'tetezi), local leaders appeared to be "jockeying for who would be the 'white horse' of the North Ward."[25]

The outspoken Anthony Imperiale seized that role.[26] A Korean War veteran, karate instructor, and butcher, Imperiale had risen to regional prominence as the leader of the North Ward Citizen's Committee.[27] Following the 1967 uprising, Imperiale organized vigilante groups of armed men to guard the streets. His warning "when the Black Panther comes, the white hunter will be waiting" catapulted him to national fame as a symbol of the white backlash against the black freedom struggle.[28] In 1972 the same year construction on Kawaida Towers began, Imperiale's explicitly racist platform helped win him a seat in the New Jersey General Assembly. Adubato was considered "moderate" in comparison to Imperiale, with his explicit vigilantism, but his statement at the ground breaking was perceived as a challenge to Imperiale and Councilman Megaro to prove their loyalty to whites in the North Ward.[29]

Soon after, Imperiale stationed himself in front of the Kawaida Towers site, bullhorn in hand, while Megaro backtracked on his approval for the tax abatement, claiming he had been deceived into introducing it. Over the next year, opposition to Kawaida Towers snowballed. Imperiale organized pickets of off-duty policemen, young mothers, elderly women, and students that reached into the hundreds.[30] Picketers complained about Baraka's involvement and equated the construction of Kawaida Towers to an invasion that would bring crime to the neighborhood, disorder to schools, and erosion of Italian American autonomy. When these complaints failed to shake the project's legal standing, opponents filed a suit that claimed its tax abatement was illegal. Meanwhile, Imperiale also leaned on the trade unions—already resisting pressure to integrate their ranks—to respect white-community picket lines, withholding their labor from the project and blocking workers who attempted to report to the site.[31] Workers who persisted did so through jeering, spitting crowds.[32] Blanton Jones recalled that "it was just like going to Korea in '50," when he attempted to report for his first day on the job in late November 1972 after a long stretch of unemployment.[33] While Jones escaped a throng of protesters under Imperiale's leadership, he was the sole worker who made it to the site that day. Judge Irwin Kimmelman—the same Superior Court judge who intervened in the Stella Wright tenants' strike—shut down construction. From that point unfolded a series of baseless but time-consuming lawsuits, city council interventions, and white appeals for community control.

Playing the role of a fixer, Baraka tried to navigate the crisis coolly, rejecting the idea of organizing black opposition at the construction site as both dangerous and misguided. Although the Kawaida Towers conflict became popularly associated with black "extremism," Woodard shows that Baraka was in fact drawing on the same narrative power that the nonviolent protests of the early civil rights movement had employed, calling attention to the contrast between black workers steadfastly proceeding with the construction of much-needed housing amid threatening crowds of white protesters.[34] Reflecting his antipathy to the New Left at the time, Baraka also condemned efforts by the predominantly white Progressive Labor Party and Students for a Democratic Society to organize counterprotests against Imperiale's faction. He argued that they would interfere with black people's "right to self-determination" and essentially manifest "the same kind of racism which is expressed in another way by the Imperiales."[35] While Baraka spurned some white radicals, Kawaida Towers did seek and find support from other interracial groups, clergy, civic organizations, and trade unions.[36] Baraka had demanded that the US secretary of labor, Peter Brennan, intervene in the dispute, citing union leaders' breach of contract and the threats they issued against black workers. Brennan refused, but Kawaida activists identified sympathetic unions who supported the project and identified union tradesmen willing to cross Imperiale's picket.[37] FIGHT BACK, a New York City–based organization that pressured unions to integrate and supplied skilled tradesmen for projects stalled by discriminatory work stoppages, offered to help but their workers were turned away from the site by the contractor for Kawaida Towers, who seemed to side with the picketers.[38] Some unions outside the construction trades also supported Kawaida Towers, including Local 837 of the United Steel Workers of America, a predominantly black and Puerto Rican union with many Newark members. The union's secretary, Anthony Cascone, rejected the notion that Italian Americans were unified in their opposition to the project. "We come from an immigrant background and have been denied our share of decent housing and jobs. We are just one step removed from the blacks and should try to enlist them as our allies to help elevate our own condition."[39] Religious leaders also called for Kawaida Towers to rise: over seventy clergy signed a letter that described the controversy as "a retreat from Christian commitment—a retreat from the biblical call 'to do justice,'" while a group of Presbyterian, Baptist, Lutheran, and ecumenical leaders proposed a Kawaida-community liaison committee that would meet with North Ward residents to resolve concerns about the building and encourage them to apply for apartments.[40]

Baraka's attempts to keep his plan for the New Ark intact were bolstered when Judge Kimmelman affirmed that Kawaida Inc. had met all legal requirements to qualify for a tax abatement.[41] But Kimmelman's decision did not diffuse local opposition. Baraka drew on the facilitating acumen he had demonstrated on the national stage only months earlier to hold together the fractious National Black Political Convention in Gary, Indiana. Yet in Newark, Baraka's attempts to both mobilize militant black power and channel its contentious strains in the interest of "operational unity" frayed.[42] Allies defected amid the onslaught of North Ward protesters, including Mayor Gibson. His very victory had depended upon black nationalists' efforts to register voters and translate Baraka's fame and connections to other black artists and performers into electoral momentum. Yet a political chasm had opened up after the election, as his administration began to distance itself from black nationalist influences.[43] The Gibson administration's newspaper, *Information*, ran articles that seemed intended to subtly diffuse the conflict. One, entitled "Kawaida: It's More than a Dispute," described the Kawaida philosophy and its adherents in favorable terms, and a set of columns depicted Italian Americans whose views ran counter to Imperiale's.[44] But *Information* primarily attempted to transpose a violent contestation over political power and the boundaries of the ghetto into a mild dialogue about cultural difference. After a tepid attempt at mediation, Gibson's administration appeared to retreat, and the Kawaida Towers conflict accelerated into a clash unlike any the other early community development organizations had experienced. And in February 1975 Councilman Earl Harris, another black candidate who had benefited from nationalists' organizing efforts, led the council in rescinding the tax abatement that had been granted for Kawaida Towers.[45] This vote decisively severed the coalition that had propelled many black leaders into office five years earlier—fostering enmity that Baraka later expressed in biting, barely fictionalized depictions of Newark's new black officialdom.[46] Bulldozers crushed and buried Kawaida's foundation, a physical manifestation of this bitter blow to black nationalists' expansive vision for the city and their philosophy of operational unity through diverse coalitions.

The defeat of Kawaida Towers marginalized—but did not eclipse—black nationalists' community development efforts in the city. Smaller-scale ventures proliferated in the early 1970s, including stores, cafeterias, a printing press, and housing for the elderly. The black power geography that took shape around the CAP and CFUN politicized many young Newarkers and altered the tenor of the Central Ward, carrying over into other organizations.[47] But during the years that the Kawaida dispute unfolded on the streets and in the courts and newspapers, women and men in Baraka's circles had pursued other projects with contributions from individuals, grants from the United Community Corporation, and donations from the Episcopal Church. Facing considerably less opposition, women in the nationalist movement had

pursued a separate community development agenda that at first conformed to—but soon challenged—common gender divisions in economic development.

Gender and Community Building

Both the implicit and the explicit gendering of community development functions shaped early CDCs. Some black nationalists, in particular, promoted a gendered division of labor with antecedents in West
African history. They argued that the promotion of black men's leadership was tantamount to a defense of black families—and, by extension,
their communities—from discrimination and racial violence. At a time
when debates about the past, present, and future of the black family
raged in the media and in social scientific literature, black men's dominance at home and in the political sphere defied enduring cultural
stereotypes of familial dysfunction. But the privileging of men's leadership also dovetailed with the very same punitive social theories that
blamed black women for usurping men's roles as workers and household heads. Yet even as black feminists criticized the social science of
the embattled black family, the maintenance of patriarchal gender roles
remained deeply entangled with the work of community development
and debates about what revolutionary gender ideals should entail.[48]

Rejecting the definitions of equality embraced by the emerging feminist movement, nationalists like Baraka and Karenga called instead
for an enlightened "complementarity" between men and women. This
concept bore some resemblance to the argument made by intellectual
and reformer Anna Julia Cooper, who wrote that "there is a feminine
and a masculine side to truth," "complements in one necessary and
symmetric whole."[49] Cooper proposed the concept of complementarity
in her 1892 book, A Voice from the South, to emphasize black women's
social, spiritual, and intellectual contributions to progress in all phases
of human endeavor. It was part of her multifaceted argument in favor of women's unfettered access to education during the height of Jim
Crow. Among cultural nationalists in the 1970s, however, "complementarity" was in practice often used to justify men's authority over
women and children.

That the gender ideals embraced by nationalists overlapped so
closely with the separate spheres of nineteenth-century American do-
mesticity rendered them a ripe target for critics. Karenga's conviction

for the appalling abuse of women activists also called these ideas into question, fractured his own organization, and repelled some of his allies.[50] Meanwhile, the celebration of militant black masculinity within the broader black power movement—and its fetishization by outsiders—contributed to black women's marginalization both within the movement and in its historiography.[51]

Still, Lydia Barrett recalled that for many women nationalist gender divisions did not at first differ substantially from those practiced by families outside nationalist circles when it came to the everyday reality of work, marriage, and childcare. To be clear, gender roles among Newark's black nationalists were tied to a more explicit ideological project founded on the restoration of men's leadership.[52] But on a practical level, a conventional division of labor characterized Tri-City, CAP, and the New Community Corporation (NCC) to some degree. With some exceptions, men generally focused on the finance and construction of housing and women focused on education, nutrition, childcare, and domestic life. Like the health block workers of the Tri-City People's Center, some of the women activists, such as Amina Baraka and Lydia Barrett, settled on nutrition as a site for political organization. They scrubbed clean and renovated a building donated to the group into a vegetarian cafeteria to serve fresh, low-priced food to a neighborhood that had lost its supermarket after the riot and would not have a new one for two decades. They instituted communal childcare, establishing a nursery and clinic where portraits of revolutionary heroes from around the world peered down on sleeping children, while women took turns caring for them, organizing in the streets, or working in the Spirit House.[53] They participated in a long history of women's attempts to meet the demands of childcare and political labor through collective arrangements, in some ways challenging bourgeois versions of the nuclear family.

The women's early adherence to "complementarity" may have rendered many of their political goals invisible, hence less controversial to the world outside nationalist circles, even though opposition was brewing within. As disputes over women's revolutionary roles erupted among men and women, especially between Amiri and Amina Baraka, the cultural nationalist version of "complementarity" gave way to literal separate spheres. In pursuing their own community development priorities, women had revised their position on gender and black nationalism. They pushed CAP to the radical Left and overturned earlier convictions about gender that Baraka later conceded had been "a great deal of unadulterated bullshit in the name of revolution."[54]

From Fixers to Revolutionaries

Many community economic development corporations across the country tended to follow a predictable trajectory: once energized by radical critiques of a system seemingly immune to conventional reform, they settled into a more comfortable relationship to existing power. Success in housing development or the provision of social services not only anchored them to communities they wished to serve but also entangled them in government contracts and philanthropic grants that diluted their radicalism and nudged them toward long-term stability. Yet the activists associated with Baraka defied this trajectory—though they had some small-scale success, Kawaida Towers had revealed the limits of fixing Newark, and they set their sights on the long-term vision of revolution.

More than either Tri-City or the NCC, CAP/Kawaida Inc. most directly challenged—and paid a high price for challenging—municipal leadership and the Newark Housing Authority. Not only did the defeat of Kawaida Towers underscore the differences between the cultural nationalists' and the Gibson administration's visions for the city, but nationalist achievements—electing black officials and successfully lobbying for the appointment of black officials, including a new police director—proved consistently disappointing. Activists were disillusioned not only by Gibson's apparent powerlessness over the recalcitrant, often-hostile city council but also by Gibson's decision to exclude from his administration many of the young adults who had worked alongside Baraka to elect him. Indeed, key to Baraka's work as a fixer was the training of young people in political mobilization and community development, preparing them to remake the Central Ward on a massive scale. Lydia Barrett recalled that shortly after the election, Baraka proposed that Gibson establish internships and mentoring programs to cultivate an experienced cadre of black professionals. Baraka was concerned that the euphoria occasioned by the election of the city's first black mayor had disguised the fact that the new administration was inexperienced and thus perilously close to wasting its momentum. The proposal would also have given young activists in Baraka's circle a hand in the transition. Barrett recalled being "stunned and hurt when it got turned down. . . . I remember realizing, 'man, this is bad.' I was profoundly disappointed." Groomed by parents, teachers, and mentors for professional careers, the Barretts had anticipated that they would find a way to reconcile their professional goals with social activism, to "work for our people," as Lydia expressed it. But in the aftermath of the election, as Gibson "stopped returning our calls," the sacrifices the nationalist vision would require became more evident.[55]

The dissolution of the United Brothers alliance and Earl Harris's crushing opposition to CAP suggest the fragility of "united front" alliances. As the momentum and euphoria of Gibson's election, amid a spate of victories across the country, dissipated, the difficult work of governing deeply troubled cities divided former allies along ideological and even generational lines. Some of the older members of United Brothers recognized the organizing power that the generally younger cultural nationalists contributed, as well as the national support for Gibson's election that they could mobilize through Baraka's contacts with celebrities like Dick Gregory, Ossie Davis, Ruby Dee, and other musicians and artists. But, as Lydia Barrett argues, "they had already been there and resented the idea that at a moment in history when they were going to get their chance, somehow they found it superimposed by this artist/writer/poet living in a red, black and green house."[56]

At the same time, the city moved to write black nationalists out of Newark's future, as city bulldozers razed Kawaida buildings and interred what remained of Kawaida Towers.[57] "They just systematically went about doing things that would wipe out any recollection as well as capacity for that kind of organizing," Lydia Barrett recalled, "and that was what we hadn't counted on and what drove us to the left."[58] CAP/Kawaida Inc.'s defeat crystallized the limits of a nationalist strategy focused on electoral politics and collaboration with local authorities, and it accelerated CAP's leftward shift. In the early 1970s Amiri and Amina began to lead activists in a transformation from what Baraka called "Revolutionary Kawaida" to Marxism.[59]

All three of the organizations analyzed here—Tri-City, CAP, and NCC—required all-consuming efforts from their leaders in terms of organizing residents, attending countless meetings, fundraising, and educating themselves in the minutiae of construction and housing finance. But Baraka's CAP also required a further level of discipline and commitment from its members that proved unsustainable for some. Upon his election to the United Community Corporation, Newark's antipoverty organization, David Barrett alluded to his own variation on W. E. B. Du Bois's concept of double consciousness when he described his "double life." After a black power slate won control of the United Community Corporation, David advanced the movement's goals as the organization's president. Meanwhile, he commuted to his white-collar job at GE, fielding curious white coworkers' questions about his opinions of William Styron's provocative first-person novel *Confessions of Nat Turner.*[60] The use of his Swahili name encapsulated the worlds he crossed every day: "Although the very, very close people in the community would call me Mteteaji, in public gatherings they would call me David. So it was something, psychologically, kind of halting every now and then for me. But those were the two identities that I walked with."[61] Activists like David and Lydia Barrett asserted new identities and challenged conventional forms of domestic life in an effort to revolutionize their relations with others as well as with politics.

To be sure, all the individual and organizational fixers discussed here—individuals like Gustav Heningburg and the leaders of CDCs such as Rebecca Doggett—found their work intensive, often all-consuming, no mere job but a vocation. But the constellation of nationalist organizations surrounding Baraka demanded an even greater level of commitment that eroded the boundary between the personal and the political—and not always with liberating results. Black nationalists—like other radicals in the 1960s—have been criticized for ideological rigidity.[62] But the term "rigidity" is in many ways inaccurate, as black nationalists were often in flux, constantly theorizing their own revolution and drawing from, revising, and discarding historical models. Their work required intensive self-education (and reeducation)—reading in history and political theory, group discussion, and revolutionary catechism. But this regimen of self-education alternately unified and polarized the group. The Barretts, for example, not only worked in the childcare center and on political organizing but also attended weekly target practice with the American Rifle Club and sang with the Anti-imperialist Singers. They were expected to keep pace with a rigorous schedule of political theory readings and discussion groups. When David ran for office, first for the Essex County Board of Freeholders and then for the New Jersey General Assembly (Twenty-Ninth District), he campaigned from early morning to late at night, with little time for Lydia and their two sons.[63] His campaign also distanced David from the ideological realignment under way in classes and reading groups. In the aftermath of his election defeat, he felt depressed, alienated from his organization and his family, and frustrated with Baraka's leadership, which left increasingly little room for dissent.

Baraka conceded that the pace and discipline he demanded exacted a toll on activists' relationships, including his own marriage to Amina, which temporarily settled into a "weary perfunctoriness." In the political urgency of the struggle, he recalls, "the organization became a fanatical driving thing that tended to remove us from our community and even from each other."[64] The Barretts' marriage could not withstand this pressure and they split in 1972. Lydia continued to work long hours alongside Amina and other women in the organization, cooking, developing daycare and clinic facilities, managing the cafeteria, and dealing with tedious conflicts of communal life. In contextualizing what might seem a shocking transition from middle-class college graduate and housewife to Marxist-Leninist revolutionary, Barrett notes many of the mitigating continuities in her life: "[P]eople tend to overlook that we were raised in the 1950s, World War II babies, children of parents who had been in this military environment and teenagers in the 1950s, where life had a lot of structure." As she noted, even in the midst of the liberating and disconcerting tumult of the 1960s, "I think structure was still very appealing. . . . [I]f you take a hard look at that stuff, we were just creating a new one."[65] Lydia occasionally found this structure repressing or infuriating, but she remained committed to the larger goals and to an organization that offered crucial support to a young divorced mother raising two children. She eventually left the CAP after the Barakas instituted elements of self-criticism gleaned from Maoism and the Cultural Revolution in China that she found irrelevant to her own life and the organizing of black Newark.[66] Lydia and her former husband, David, both continued to pursue the goals of the black freedom movement in other organizations over the decades that followed.[67]

In the wake of the Kawaida Towers defeat, Baraka's organizations seemed increasingly wary of pursuing the imperfect political goals of a provisional black collective and more devoted to internal consistency. They shifted away from nationalism and sought to distinguish reliable revolutionaries from their accommodationist imitators. In this sense, they diverged from fixer organizations that were often influenced by similar black power critiques but that tolerated, even welcomed, ideological inconsistency. They also diverged in focus: while early CDCs around the country channeled their resources more exclusively into housing, Baraka's organizations shifted to labor. They concluded that the working classes had to be organized before they could recapture a revolutionary moment, and they attempted to do so by moving members into manufacturing jobs.

As the scholarship on black power—on both its ideological complexities and the breadth of its expression—has flourished, discussion of black radicalism continues to concentrate on organizations with shared ideologies or the struggle among starkly opposing groups. While generating crucial insights, the scholarship must also be brought into conversation with the other organizations affecting the political economy of cities. Examining how Kawaida Inc., Amiri Baraka, and activists such as Lydia and David Barrett functioned as fixers sheds light on black nationalism's possibilities, its inroads into existing power structures, and the political alliances and barriers assembled to contain it.

EIGHT

The New Community Corporation: Catholic Roots, Suburban Leverage, and Pragmatism

Pat and David Foley, the white suburban couple who had fled Newark mid-uprising with their family and the Catholic youth campers they supervised, did not stay away for long. At home in Woodcliff, New Jersey, friends who had watched Newark burn on television inundated the Foleys with calls about what could be done to help. Pat knew that Queen of Angels Catholic Church was located near the uprising's epicenter, so she called to offer assistance. Father Thomas Comerford warned her that black residents were not eager to see "white faces." But Pat and David returned seven months later, joining more than eight hundred people from Newark and its suburbs who crowded into Queen of Angels for "Days of Study," a series of conversations to formulate responses to the uprising. Newark's problems were not solely urban but also suburban in origin, attendees concluded. Inadequate housing in the city, segregation in the suburbs, and unaffordable housing across the state could be addressed only if urban blacks and suburban whites developed alliances that transcended paternalism.[1]

The result of these meetings was the creation of a new organizational fixer: the New Community Corporation (NCC). The NCC crossed boundaries between urban and suburban, religious and secular; its founders alternately spoke in the rhetorics of moral suasion, bootstrap capitalism, and black self-determination. They combined the practices of real estate developers with grassroots direct action. They both criticized and reinvented a role for Catholic institutions in the city. The NCC exemplified the institutionalization of fixers as they came to run a parallel state within cities, housing and employing thousands. In the three decades after its founding, the NCC grew to become one of the largest and most successful community development corporations (CDCs) in the United States—what one scholar called a "small empire that offers services government has been unable to provide."[2]

Renegade Catholics

The civil rights movement had energized church members and leaders alike in the 1960s, as had calls for the Catholic Church to respond directly to the problems of modern life in the wake of the Second Vatican Council in the early 1960s. These factors emboldened priests and nuns to make new demands on the church hierarchy, as did younger congregants who embraced black power. But it was not just recent developments that influenced Queen of Angels. As a church built by black Catholics—mostly women—with a fraught relationship to the diocese, Queen of Angels was perhaps more prepared than other churches to grasp the new realities reshaping Catholic life.

The church traced its roots back to three black women who met for prayer, catechism, and discussion in the 1920s. Over the years, they were joined by other black Catholics and new converts, but even as they sought to honor the universal promise of the church's covenant, they contended with racism at the diocesan level. So they pursued their own church.[3] Although they successfully petitioned the archdiocese to serve the Central Ward's growing black population, church leadership still slighted them. In subsequent years the survival of Queen of Angels thus depended on savvy, persistent lay leadership, and a corps of dedicated priests and women religious.[4]

Queen of Angels appealed to both recent converts and cradle Catholics such as Cecelia Faulks. As a teenager, Faulks migrated to Newark from Georgia in 1957. She found worship at predominantly white Saint Columbus Church perfunctory; at Queen of Angels, though, black parishioners showed up early and lingered after. Young church members participated in a theater company that mounted elaborate productions. While other Catholic churches ran similar programs, Faulks had never before been invited or expected to join.[5] But to compete with the preeminent churches of Newark's black middle class and attract converts, Queen of Angels offered lively social programs and incorporated some black Protestant traditions, including call-and-response, a gospel choir, and a modified social gospel. Members combined sacred and public space, using the church for meetings at which priests were mere observers.[6]

These elements shaped the spiritual and political coming-of-age of a migrant from West Virginia named Joyce Smith Carter. Carter joined Queen of Angels as a teenager. She recalled how black congregants and young white clergy reinforced one another's political education in the heady 1960s. Intense conversations about moral philosophy and social justice consumed Catholic Youth Organization meetings. The church had become a hub of Newark civil rights activity and Carter was at its center. She met Martin Luther King Jr. when he visited Newark and coordinated the caravans traveling to Washington, DC, in 1968 for the Poor People's Campaign.

Carter's experience demonstrates how young people reconciled elements often compartmentalized in the historiography of the era. Black nationalism, Catholicism, and her devotion to the "beloved community" envisioned by Martin Luther King Jr. shaped her identity as a young adult. Following King's assassination, Carter gravitated to Newark's black nationalists even as she remained active in Catholic youth groups. She participated in the Committee for a Unified Newark—another of Baraka's organizations—to register voters and elect black candidates. She wore her hair natural and donned African-inspired clothing. For Carter, as for the Barretts, the years between the uprising and Kenneth Gibson's first election were a time of exhilaration and political ferment. As she walked to work one morning, Carter heard music— percussion and saxophone—arching over the walls of Scudder Homes. Baraka and the Committee for a Unified Newark had driven a flatbed truck into the courtyard of the housing projects, from which the composer Sun Ra played a crack-of-dawn serenade.[7]

As black power flourished, Carter developed a more critical awareness of her relationship to her white mentors in Queen of Angels. When they arranged a scholarship for her at New York University, she was both tempted by and wary of the offer, suspecting that some in the church opposed her nationalist leanings and sought an opportunity to push her out. Carter decided that Newark's struggles demanded her full attention and she turned down the offer.[8]

Queen of Angels never identified itself as a black power organization. Congregants were more likely to speak a language of Catholic universalism. Yet many embraced black power's diagnosis of institutional racism, its emphasis on self-determination, and its militant strategies. Given their distinctly independent history, it is perhaps unsurprising that Queen of Angels congregants drew from these multiple discourses; or that they attracted priests and women religious who preferred an active laity and believed the church should reflect the aspirations of the Central Ward's black residents, not the white archdiocesan leadership. Their ranks came to include Father William Linder, who would attack the archdiocese for perpetuating institutional racism and emerge as an NCC leader.[9]

The suburban white Catholics involved in the NCC's creation came to activism through a circuitous route. Some established their connection to Queen of Angels through the Cursillo Movement. Started in Spain in 1949, the Cursillo Movement sought to transform the role of the laity by bringing modern psychological and sociological insights "into harmonious fusion with the traditional doctrine of the church."[10] At spiritual retreats Cursillo participants would experience what amounted to a second baptism, rediscovering the "fundamentals" of their faith: in the words of Paul, "I live, no, not I, but Christ lives in me."[11] Some Cursillo participants chose to fulfill their spiritual commitments through activism. Cursillo theorists such as Father John Randall deemed each participant "a leader" poised to bring "Christian renewal" to churches and cities. Randall told members of Queen of Angels, "There can be no sheep in our movement, just shepherds."[12] Randall's exhortation echoes that of Student Nonviolent Coordinating Committee leader Ella Baker: "strong people don't need strong leaders."[13] While the Cursillo Movement shared some of the democratizing thrust of the Student Nonviolent Coordinating Committee, it focused less on elevating the marginalized than honing existing lay leadership. Organizers preferred affluent or solidly middle-class participants, such as the Foleys, or working-class people "recognized and legitimated by others."[14] Through the Cursillo Movement, the Foleys met some of the early leaders of the NCC, including Joseph Chaneyfield, a black Queen of Angels member and president of AFL-CIO Local 305, a maintenance union representing workers at the Newark Housing Authority (NHA).[15]

The Foleys' involvement with Newark intensified when they publicized the Days of Study findings to suburban Catholics through the City-Suburban Liaison Committee of the Christian Family Movement.[16] At first, suburban Catholics rehearsed an approach to racism based on moral suasion and individual psychology. "Perhaps," the Foleys wrote, "the white man does not understand the problems and the frustrations of the Negro because he does not really know them as individuals."[17] To this end, the Foleys and others at Queen of Angels recruited members of churches and synagogues to participate in a massive "Walk for Understanding" to demonstrate black-white, urban-suburban solidarity. But days beforehand, Martin Luther King Jr. was assassinated in Memphis. As grief and anger turned to rioting in some cities, Mayor Addonizio urged Father Thomas Carey of Queen of Angels to cancel the walk for fear it would ignite violence. Carey refused. On Sunday, April 7, 1968, over twenty-five thousand people marched through the Central Ward in tribute to King. The majority were white, many suburban. Newark was by this time a mostly black city, the Central Ward around 80 percent black.[18] The infusion of white people from segregated suburbs to commemorate interracial unity posed some uncomfortable questions about what vision of racial justice—beyond marches—could prevail in the aftermath of King's assassination.

The Foleys and others extended the city-suburban collaboration through a longer-term campaign called "Operation Understanding." Interracial teams of Catholics, Protestants, and Jews volunteered to lead discussions on race and the urban crisis in living rooms, synagogues, and church basements.[19] But black volunteers were routinely shouted down and threatened; white suburbanites such as the Foleys were called "nigger lovers." Fifty people joined the group, but the threats took their toll: only a core of about a dozen continued into the early 1970s.[20]

Operation Understanding, along with the Greater Newark Urban Coalition, also sought to expose suburban residents to the urban crisis with tours of Newark and its housing projects. Organizers believed that familiarity would enhance empathy between suburban whites and poor and working-class blacks. The burden and privilege of knowledge gathering were placed on white participants, in part because it was assumed that armed with the correct information, they would be able to wield their power as suburban taxpayers and voters for the benefit of their urban neighbors. The organizers also believed that tours would prepare philanthropically minded suburbanites to cede some control over the city's recovery to the poor, whose firsthand experience was rarely acknowledged as a legitimate source of expertise.[21]

Willie Wright, a black member of Queen of Angels, organized what was probably the first "ghetto tour" of the Central Ward. In collaboration with the Greater Newark Urban Coalition, he recruited participants from among the state's power brokers, including former governor Robert B. Meyner. Organizers and participants desired authenticity. Yet this stance also rendered black Newarkers' lives into spectacle. Participants prepared for a cold reception from riot-torn neighborhoods. During one walk Wright gestured to the vista of abandoned buildings and charged that "the men who control the economy of this city have not taken a stand." Wright argued that to "change the picture of a decaying, deteriorating, dying city," Newarkers must oust Addonizio.[22]

Central Ward residents responded variously to the tours. Some welcomed the interest, and others were eager to voice their frustrations. Yet others projected "suspicious stares and muttered comments." As an opponent of the Medical College and director of a group called the Afro American Association, Wright had an activist's reputation. Yet some activists denounced him as an "Uncle Tom" as he led columns of white men in suits through the Central Ward.[23]

According to Gustav Heningburg, the tours prompted the city to make minor improvements: more frequent trash collection, a sweep of abandoned cars. Yet most dispatches chronicled accelerating decline. Businessmen who toured the Central Ward shortly after the uprising and again a year later noted an increase in abandoned buildings. John J. Magovern, president of Mutual Benefit Life Insurance, declared most of the housing to be beyond repair.[24] While Wright had seized the opportunity of a captive audience with New Jersey power brokers to demand political change, officials seemed to perceive the tours as an index of inexorable decay.

Operation Understanding confronted a moment deeply inhospitable to interracial collaboration. But Pat Foley's thinking, as expressed in her newsletter, *Understanding*, had shifted. She less frequently focused on individual prejudice and, instead, implored her predominantly white readership to consider how institutions like the Catholic Church reproduced racism and how they could overcome inequality between city and suburb. Increasingly, *Understanding* examined the insufficient response of the church to the civil rights movement and grappled with the demands of the black power movement. She referred to the Black Clergy Caucus's diagnosis of the Catholic Church as "primarily a white racist institution" and to the caucus's deep skepticism about the willingness of white Catholics to accept assertive black leadership. White Catholics and clergy, the caucus insisted, had to embrace the roles of "supporter and learner."[25]

In the pages of *Understanding*, Foley also implored readers to translate the relationships forged between city and suburb, black and white, into tangible political victories. Yet Operation Understanding avoided endorsements even as they pressured legislators to pour resources into

Newark. In 1968 Foley, a lifelong Republican, reminded readers to press their elected officials to send additional aid to Newark, even if it required higher taxes: "If you are not willing to pay for this aid, how can you ask your neighbor to? The example is in your hands and so is the power. Newark is fundless. . . . Tell them you want that report on Civil Disorder implemented," she wrote, referring to the *Report for Action* produced by the Governor's Select Commission on Civil Disorder.[26] Over the next few years, *Understanding* advocated for school construction, welfare funding, and urban property tax relief.[27] The organization also called for a state income tax, a proposal that stalled numerous times until the state passed it under court pressure in 1976.[28] But out of all the actions Operation Understanding took in the years after the riot, perhaps its most significant was bringing together the urban and suburban activists who created the NCC.

"Doing Today Those Things": Launching the New Community Corporation

Like the proponents of Kawaida Towers, NCC members approached black economic development with a plan for the reconstruction of an entire neighborhood—a forty-five-acre portion of Newark's Central Ward, located a block to the north of Queen of Angels—complete with shopping plazas, offices, parks, and schools surrounded by lush landscaping and connected by wide pedestrian throughways. The NCC's plan also included two thousand units of housing they initially planned to transfer to tenant ownership.[29]

Like Tri-City and Kawaida Inc., the NCC blamed the city's urban renewal policies for offering superficial "bricks and mortar" progress that did not address—and in some cases worsened—residential inequality. The city was afflicted both physically and psychologically, NCC leaders argued, with residents "rapidly being swept downward into the whirl-pool."[30] NCC sought to short-circuit this cycle. "Personal ownership of something as valuable and symbolic as one's own house will, NCC is certain, instill pride—and more importantly, hope," read an early NCC pamphlet.[31] Homes would give residents a greater stake in their community's future, much as homeownership was a foundation for political power in New Jersey's suburbs. The NCC also shared with other CDCs the goal of using home construction as a career ladder, offering skilled work to local residents and elevating the neighborhood economies with well-paying jobs.[32]

The NCC planned to finance housing with private and public funds. In 1968 the New Jersey Department of Community Affairs offered the group a $10,000 planning grant, while the Newark Archdiocese agreed to act as a guarantor for $40 million in venture capital required to complete the NCC's entire plan.[33] The initial board of the NCC included Newark activists such as Joseph Chaneyfield, president of AFL-CIO Local 305, Robert Curvin of the Congress of Racial Equality, Elma Bateman, Willie Wright, and Father Linder of Queen of Angels, and emerging political leaders such as Kenneth Gibson. Suburban professionals such as David Foley established a fundraising arm, the New Community Foundation. NCC leaders believed that the participation of suburban professionals would convey the group's legitimacy to the corporations and banks from which they hoped to secure loans.[34]

Even as the NCC leveraged the authority of the Catholic Church, it set off a scandal within the archdiocese. Linder and an interracial group of dissident priests called the Newark 20 revolted after Archbishop Thomas Boland reneged on an agreement to provide funding promised to the NCC and diversify the archdiocesan housing committee by appointing black leaders recommended by Queen of Angels.[35]

In a missive that ricocheted between anguished betrayal and almost sneering contempt, the Newark 20 deplored the failure of the archdiocese to mobilize its vast capital on behalf of suffering congregations. Many of the signatories had welcomed the changes heralded by the Second Vatican Council, but they now questioned what their implementation meant to the lives of their parishioners. "The Official Church's concept of involvement is to change the liturgy from Latin to English," they wrote. "The poor are cold, hungry, housed in rat traps, largely ignored by the affluent society, denied employment opportunities, denied legal and moral rights and the Official Church responds by changing the direction of the altar."[36] They accused the church of leaning on the "promising rhetoric" of pastoral letters on the poor while actually doing little to change policy or living conditions. "We love you, Brothers and Sisters, but we'll love you better over there—out of our sight," they wrote, mocking the language of a pastoral letter. "We love you, but you make us feel guilty. Certainly, we love you." Parish priests, they insisted, must coordinate "the assets and contributions of concerned Christians" on behalf of the city.[37] Elements of the Newark 20's public letter to Archbishop Boland bore a resemblance to James Forman's "Black Manifesto," issued to churches and synagogues in 1969, which demanded reparations to be reinvested in black-owned institutions.[38] The "Black Manifesto" sparked similar protests in congregations around the country. In Saint Louis, for example, protesters turned up at Sunday services to demand that churches scrutinize their investments in substandard housing and in local companies with a history of employment discrimination.[39] The Newark 20 did not identify themselves with the black power movement, but they had nonetheless employed arguments and tactics popularized by the movement.

The NCC employed less explosive language than the Newark 20, but the organization also challenged church leadership in pamphlets, speeches, and newsletters. The NCC emphasized that the organization was "conceived in Black minds and organized by Black leaders."[40] But in the NCC's orbit, respect for black power mixed with paternalistic views of charity. "This is a white-help-Black project," Herman G. Haenisch, a suburban engineer and president of NCC's fundraising arm, tried to explain to a crowd of NCC supporters. "It is not a white-tell-the-Blacks-what-to-do project."[41] To reach their goal of raising $1 million to purchase and prepare land for the construction of one hundred units of housing, the NCC sold five-dollar "shares" of the Central Ward to residents of Newark and its surrounding suburbs, symbolically transforming neighbors into shareholders in the city's future.[42]

The NCC's expansive outreach was reflected in the mix of somewhat-incongruous ideological inspirations from which it drew in defining a mission. The NCC struggled to establish itself as a new phenomenon, an organization rooted in the Catholic Church yet independent of it. Auxiliaries like Operation Understanding supported legislation—especially concerning taxes—that affected Newark, yet attempted to sidestep electoral politics. The NCC raised funds aggressively by urging the middle class and wealthy to remember their obligations to the poor at the same time that its leaders criticized conventional charity and the paternalism it often entailed. *Doing Today Those Things*, a 1969 pamphlet that outlined the NCC's plan for the city, took its title from Edmund Burke: "The public interest requires doing today those things that men of intelligence and good will would wish, five or ten years hence, had been done." Quoting Henry David Thoreau—"There are a thousand hacking at the branches of evil to one who is striking at the root"—the NCC positioned itself as an organization that probed the structural causes of the urban crisis. Other quotations, such as Baroness Bertha Von Sutter's assertion "After the verb 'to love,' 'to help' is the most beautiful verb in the world," suggested an organization that depended upon and honored charitable acts. But citing Maimonides's insistence that self-sufficiency was the "highest step and the summit of charity's golden ladder" and Henrik Ibsen's assertion that "the most crying need in the humbler ranks of life is that they should be allowed some part in the direction of public affairs" revealed an organization that was impatient with the top-down methods of traditional charity. Although the NCC promoted black self-determination and emerged from a church historically dependent upon the organizing efforts of black laywomen, their role was not made plain. W. E. B. Du Bois was the lone black intellectual quoted, suggesting that the pamphlet was crafted for a suburban audience rather than for black Newarkers themselves.[43]

For the NCC, like other organizational fixers, immediate action was imperative. Like Tri-City, the NCC chose for its first project a neighborhood that bordered but was not included in an urban renewal tract. The NCC planned to develop outside the structure of urban renewal programs and pay market rates. The completion of the project, they hoped, would prove the capabilities of the NCC and the Central Ward residents and attract additional federal and state grants for rebuilding the neighborhood.[44] In May 1969 the Department of Community Affairs provided a $23,000 loan to help the NCC obtain federal grants for demolition.[45] In 1970 another suburban fundraising campaign relied on the canvassing skills of a group called Teens Concerned about People to raise $20,000.[46] Later that year, the New Jersey Housing Finance Agency provided the NCC with a $250,000 interest-free loan out of their revolving grant fund to buy land and begin construction. Engelhard Industries offered to donate to the NCC, but Linder and other leaders instead asked the company to lend $190,000 to help the NCC build credit and legitimacy with banks.[47]

The NCC, like CAP/Kawaida Inc. and Tri-City, argued that community activists and residents should participate in planning usually reserved for experts. Busloads of Newark residents traveled to Reston, Virginia, and Columbia, Maryland, to tour innovations in planned communities.[48] They likewise drew inspiration from Habitat 67, the pyramid-shaped development of interlocking modular homes built on the banks of the Saint Lawrence River for the 1967 World's Fair. They sought examples of high-density, affordable housing that combined residential with commercial space, avoided high-rises, and incorporated parks and pedestrian-only avenues.[49] NCC's leaders' resistance to "public housing orthodoxy"—high-rise designs—came at a cost. Their plans for low-rise buildings that incorporated potential residents' recommendations elicited protests from state and federal housing officials and caused delays in construction. The eventual compromise between housing officials and the NCC featured mid-rise buildings with open courtyards. The NCC broke ground on its first project, a 120-unit apartment building costing $4.5 million, in 1972.[50]

The NCC recognized that the community they were building would require its own governance structure.[51] For Mary Smith, who devised standards for NCC housing, community development required strict codes of respectability. Like tenant managers in Stella Wright Homes, the NCC vetted tenants rigorously and imposed behavioral codes. But the NCC also conducted unannounced inspections, the very sort of invasive policy that many welfare rights activists fought to eliminate during the 1970s.[52] As a former resident of Scudder Homes in the mid-1960s, Smith had organized other tenants to demand security improvements. Now, as she had a decade earlier, Smith argued that it was a small minority of irresponsible tenants whose behavior stigmatized the majority, and she had harsh words for them: "New Community is for people who want to live decently. If you want to live like a pig, we're going to kick you out and you can go live like a pig in the substandard housing you came from." Smith bristled at the claim made by some opponents of public housing that tenants could not be trusted to maintain their buildings. "I refuse to let what happened to public housing happen to New Community."[53]

Babyland and Women's Networks

While leading an Operation Understanding session, Smith met a group of white, suburban women who were casting about for a Newark project. "Operation Housewives" decided to collect used clothing and housewares and open a thrift store to raise money for summer recreation programs. Discussions among the women often turned to the difficulties that poor mothers had keeping jobs because of the lack of daycare. Suburban women, heeding Foley's call, had sought to persuade their husbands—many of them professionals and managers—to hire more of Newark's unemployed. But they resisted, claiming that the city's poor workers were too unreliable. The suburban women reasoned that daycare would make poor women more employable, and they began to plan for a daycare center.[54]

Smith's training in social and volunteer work with a host of Newark organizations, including United Community Corporation, made her a desirable leader for such a project.[55] Smith and other black women had already attempted to establish daycare centers in the city's public housing system, but their outreach to the NHA went unheeded. She was a fierce advocate for her cause, a self-described "big mouth."[56] When Operation Housewives predicted it would take two years to plan and raise funds for the first Babyland, Smith threatened to quit if the group could not expedite the opening.[57] The collective effort of black and white, urban and suburban women yielded concessions from the NHA in the form of a basement room for the daycare at Scudder Homes. The first Babyland opened in 1969 with a combination of loans and private donations. Smith and Madge Wilson, a member of Queen of Angels, devoted a staggering number of hours to Babyland, spending early mornings and evenings at the center while working full-time jobs elsewhere. Another volunteer from Operation Housewives persuaded her husband, a physician, to run a health clinic.[58]

Parents clamored to place their children in Babyland. The Department of Housing and Urban Development (HUD) praised the operation and called for it to offer more spaces to residents.[59] Despite the pressing need for its services, Babyland had to fight off near-constant threats to its existence between 1970 and 1975. As conditions in Scudder Homes deteriorated, Babyland became a target of multiple break-ins, but NHA officials offered little protection. Babyland also endured a contentious relationship with the state's Bureau of Children's Services, which rebuffed its request for state funding. When Babyland opened, New Jersey had not yet developed standards for infant daycare. Yet most federal and private philanthropic grants for daycare programs required that applicants comply with local regulations. Since there were none, Babyland was limited to soliciting donations from individuals and companies. Under persistent questioning from Babyland's directors, officials admitted that no state-level standards for infant daycare existed. Babyland advocates leaned on their allies in the suburbs, who pressured officials to define standards.[60]

Meanwhile, Babyland II opened in 1973 under the auspices of a federal demonstration project, a designation that exempted the center from state regulations.[61] Nonetheless, state officials still used the absence of state standards to withhold support. Smith criticized the state for neglecting childcare, lobbied for Babyland at public hearings, and appealed to the local business community, arguing that "the mothers who leave their infants with us make better and more efficient workers."[62] Echoing the NCC's familiar line, Smith told the New York Times, "We were trying to pull ourselves up by our bootstraps but we didn't have any boots."[63] Through its networks of private funders, Babyland was finally able to meet federal matching requirements and stave off closure.

The participation of middle-class suburban women in Operation Understanding, Operation Housewives, and Babyland replicated some longstanding class and gender patterns relegating middle- and upper-class women's engagement in charitable work to motherhood and childcare.[64] But these middle-class white Catholic women found that their work in Newark redounded to the suburbs and challenged gendered expectations in subtle ways. A profile of Foley and other women in the *Advocate*, a Catholic newspaper, generally sunny in tone, still suggested that these women's work was a potential threat to domestic tranquility. "How do you manage?" the author asked. "How do you keep your home livable, your children happy, your husband in clean socks, and still have time to be active on a weekly basis helping in the inner city?" Delores Duggan, who had taught adult education classes in Newark public housing projects, responded, "You can't neglect your home, but I do think you're a better wife and mother if you go outside the home—out to others." Pat Foley added, "you can go out to work for yourself, you can do a lot of things for yourself, but you can't do work for Christ without the cooperation of your whole family." Foley distinguished paid labor outside the home as an individual pursuit—"work for yourself"—while volunteer work was "work for Christ" and a justifiable extension of her religious commitment. Yet she implicitly rejected a division of labor that left women alone to tackle domestic chores and fulfill religious commitments. Her eight children did not live in a domestic vacuum with a mother servant at their beck and call but instead cleaned, cooked, and cared for their younger siblings, thus enabling Pat to do "Christ's work" in Newark.[65] As with Tri-City and Kawaida Inc., the women in the NCC's orbit found that to organize around poverty in Newark, they had to shift between the public realm of housing and jobs programs and the private realm of childcare. In so doing, they, too, sought to account for the often-invisible, taken-for-granted work of housekeeping and parenting. At the same time, the press attention bestowed upon white middle-class women's work as mothers and volunteers contributed to the very invisibility of poor black women's work. Such women were described as simply disadvantaged, their own work as parents mentioned mostly as an impediment to gainful employment. In the late 1960s and early 1970s, the welfare rights movement rejected such narratives and demanded recognition, respect, and even compensation for poor women's work as mothers.[66] Organizational fixers were part of this new ethos, often making "women's work" visible.

Explaining the Growth of the New Community Corporation

In the 1980s, two decades after the NCC's founding, Father William Linder pursued a graduate degree in sociology. In his dissertation, Linder codified the fixer ethos, distilling from the minutiae of NCC management a broader analysis of community development in urban crisis—articulating the shift of a diffuse social movement into a distinct model of economic development. Linder's thesis sweeps over purely structural explanations to consider instead issues of trust, accountability, social coherence, and alienation among neighbors. Citing Durkheim's theory of anomie in modern urban life, Linder asserted that suburbanization, migration, and forced relocation had severed social bonds in Newark's neighborhoods. Those who remained fought over the vestiges of a once-prosperous city, betrayed by a corrupted government.[67] Linder found early examples of community action worthy of emulation, particularly the use of schools as social service hubs for residents of all ages. But he criticized the War on Poverty for decentralizing services and exacerbating redundancy. Citing Cyril DeGrasse Tyson's discouraging tenure at the United Community Corporation, he argued that the War on Poverty had fueled competition among community action programs, municipal officials, and federal bureaucrats that ultimately worked to the detriment of the residents most in need of influence.[68] Linder, whose appreciation for a smoothly functioning machine was perhaps born of his engineering education, mourned what he saw as the War on Poverty's lost potential to create "supermarkets of service."[69] "It makes sense to apply the best of American business know-how in creating the delivery system," he wrote.[70] The NCC would pursue the unfulfilled potential of War on Poverty programs, in his view, by incorporating market mechanisms into all aspects of Newark's redevelopment. Over a decade into its existence, the NCC still sought to nourish neighborhood-based responses to government and market failures. But its earlier vision of interlocking housing, employment, and service provision had been recast by Linder into a sort of entrepreneurial pragmatism focused on piecing together a political economy of service. This point is worth considering in terms of what distinguishes fixers from similar kinds of social movement actors. CDCs often began as critics of capitalism. Locally controlled businesses were for many merely a means to the end of stable employment and urgently needed services in poor communities. But as federal policymaking increasingly emphasized privatization of social services to compensate for smaller budgets, CDCs that embraced market models often received the most support from funders.[71]

Pulling back from debates over efficient service provision, Linder delved into the political stakes of community economic development. He filtered Newark's history of racism and inequality through his graduate reading, arguing that Weber's evocation of "the process by which power is institutionalized and legitimated" clarified the problems of the urban crisis more persuasively than Marx's analysis of "the illegitimate use of power."[72] The New Left's fascination with bureaucracies and the means through which their legitimacy was cultivated also shaped Linder's intellectual development, but his interest more likely reflected the dilemma of a man often stuck between church and state, at the periphery of the market. After two decades of trial and error, Linder argued, the NCC had arrived at a position similar to that advanced decades earlier by sociologist Ralf Dahrendorf's *Class and Class Conflict in Industrial Society*: power, not property, was the source of conflict.[73] Poor Central Ward residents, even when they had created disciplined organizations to claim land and pursue housing development, required politically influential suburban allies leveraging influence behind the scenes to accomplish anything. Linder argued that urban and suburban alliances could best be cemented with an appeal to residents' collective antigovernment frustration, a position that had echoed across the ideologically disparate ranks of the neighborhood movement in the 1970s.[74]

Community Development Corporations and Public Policy

In the 1970s what remained of the War on Poverty and Model Cities was diminished by the introduction of Richard Nixon's New Federalism—a policy of reducing the federal government's obligations by devolving authority to states and localities. New Federalism prefigured the privatization of government services and the thinning of the social safety net that became cornerstones of neoliberal governance from Ronald Reagan to George W. Bush. David Harvey paints the federal retreat from floundering cities in the United States during the 1970s as a global dress rehearsal for the full-throttled neoliberalism embraced by Reagan and Margaret Thatcher.[75] Yet drawing such a taut causal line across the decades obscures the muddled early relationship of community development and devolution, which was not a completely partisan project. Vestiges of community action survived and mixed with New Federalism. Raymond Mohl argues that Nixon's urban policy sustained some elements of midcentury liberalism because it was heavily influenced by his Democratic adviser Daniel Patrick Moynihan and was implicitly shaped by the expansion of federal power that spanned Nixon's own career.[76] Surely New Federalism's emphasis on local decision making was geared toward municipal leaders, not community activists, but it resonated with demands for more responsive policies that had propelled community action out of the control of its authors, animated black power's demand for community control, and ricocheted across the political spectrum. As one HUD official remarked with dry bureaucratic understatement, "It is becoming increasingly apparent that citizen participation is being institutionalized as an integral part of local government."[77]

The early ambiguity of devolution is evident in a promotional film HUD made in 1972, *Cities Are People: How Dare We Not Save Them?* It featured Democratic mayor Gibson promoting the Nixon administration's "Planned Variations" as an innovative solution to the urban crisis. Planned Variations was an intermediate step toward Nixon's New Federalism, a strategy for phasing out what remained of Johnson's Model Cities by offering municipalities funding with fewer restrictions and the freedom to disburse it according to local priorities. The administration targeted a group of test cities, intending to reward successful Planned Variations with larger block grants through Model Cities' replacement, the Community Development Revenue Sharing program.

"The cities are the vital organs of the country," Gibson reflects in a voiceover as he jogs through Newark in the film's opening shots. "And if the heart or the brain dies, the body dies." Gibson contrasted infrastructural investment—signaled by shots of highways and the airport—with the dearth of resources for Newark's people, represented in a montage of residential abandonment. "I can't even get people from one end of Newark to the other," he said. "Not because we can't do it, but because we haven't dedicated the resources of this country to doing it."[78] Gibson's example of government's failure to deliver a basic service reflected the murky interval between Great Society liberalism and New Federalism. Gibson urged officials to muster the political will to make public infrastructure effective for the people it was supposed to serve; he did not offer the sort of wholesale denunciation of government incompetence that would fuel devolutionary politics a decade later.[79] In Gibson's scenes, Planned Variations is not so much a rightward departure in policymaking as an exercise in technocratic liberalism. He declares it "a way to more rationally solve problems."[80] Planned Variations also permitted city authorities greater scrutiny of local applicants for federal funds and more authority to direct their disbursement. Nixon's policy thus continued the thrust of the Green Amendment to the War on Poverty and other attempts to reassert municipal control over the unruly landscape of semipublic agencies, civic organizations, and nonprofits.[81] Here neoliberalism's historical roots are clearly visible, entangled in the receding tide of midcentury liberalism.

Gibson was not alone among Democratic mayors who saw in the coming of revenue sharing a way to secure more unrestricted funding for their hard-pressed cities. The National League of Cities and the United States Conference of Mayors called revenue sharing "by far the most promising concept of fiscal support for local government."[82] Outlays for 1972 showed that of the twenty cities chosen for Planned Variations, Newark already ranked among the more highly funded cities and stood to gain more than all but four, bringing its total from $5.7 to $12.7 million. Although many mayors embraced revenue sharing, it worked, they insisted, only if funding was "even, sustained, dependable, and long-term—augmenting, not replacing, Model Cities.[83] But reality quickly extinguished any modest promise of Planned Variations as federal aid to cities dropped, once again highlighting the need for local resourcefulness.[84]

In contrast to the fiercely polarizing views on the urban crisis and the black freedom movement that characterized the late 1960s, the rhetoric of CDCs seemed uncontroversial. Who would oppose community development? CDCs had appeal across the political spectrum. Community development aligned with conservatives' preference for self-help strategies and entrepreneurialism. For cold warriors—liberal and conservative alike—it was a domestic echo of the international pursuit of soft power. For radicals, it emphasized grassroots-based strategies against the "domestic colonialism" paralyzing US cities. Proponents, Kimberly Johnson writes, perceived in the CDC "almost mystical powers."[85] In response to stark disparity between city and suburb, they emphasized balanced growth and regional planning that incorporated impoverished areas. Yet appeals to community development were often conceptualized only vaguely to avoid frank acknowledgment of the entrenched dimensions of racial segregation. Discussions of enhanced "human opportunity," for example, focused on individuals, while officials' declared priority of "strengthened local self-government" actually departed from the goals of many CDCs. Organizations like Tri-City, CAP/Kawaida Inc., and the NCC certainly wanted to improve individuals' health and economic prospects, but they understood racial and economic discrimination as problems with vast spatial dimensions and collective consequences. Federal policymakers may have echoed the holistic claims of many early CDCs when they advanced revenue sharing to better attend to "every section of the community and every phase of its life."[86] But local activists had called not merely for an infusion and reorganization of resources among local officials; they wanted community development propelled from the bottom up, not administered from the top down.

Two years after Gibson's involvement in *Cities Are People: How Dare We Not Save Them?* Congress passed the 1974 Housing and Community Development Act, which codified the changes the film anticipated in the Community Development Block Grant program. As Wendell Pritchett writes in his biography of HUD secretary Robert Weaver, this legislation marked an unsatisfactory compromise and end point: "policymakers debated how much of a role the federal government should play in helping cities rebuild and urban areas manage the problems of growth. They never resolved the question, and in 1974, Congress gave up trying."[87] But in the wake of this forfeiture, programmatically malleable block grants endured. They "can be considered developmental, redistributive, or a combination of both approaches," writes Michael Rich, "depending upon the kinds of decisions local officials make."[88] Although urban policy may have diverged from CDCs' original vision, they were positioned to withstand such shifting political currents.

While the federal government retreated from the urban crisis, state officials seized an expanded role in housing policy in the 1970s and sought to partner with CDCs. Joseph Feinberg, who directed housing policy for the New Jersey Department of Community Affairs, argued that President Nixon's 1973 moratorium on subsidized housing had weakened an affordable-housing landscape already hobbled by fewer subsidies and unfinished urban renewal projects. Feinberg recommended that officials enter this "state of flux" with rehabilitation and other plans to "hold the line" until more funds were forthcoming. Feinberg's sketch of New Jersey's housing dilemmas in 1975 was pessimistic. While 50,000 new units of housing were constructed each year, Feinberg estimated that twice that many were needed. He acknowledged that physical rehabilitation itself would not suffice: the idea "that physical and social rehabilitation should operate in concert," he assured state officials, "is now generally accepted by urban experts." It was a consensus extracted from earlier failures and one that owed much to the community economic development activists who had attempted to concretize such convictions.[89] CDCs such as the NCC grew and even flourished in the absence of more comprehensive federal involvement. But this vacuum of federal involvement also resulted in a landscape of parallel agencies, competition, and neglect.

Maturation of the New Community Corporation

In the late 1970s the NCC grew swiftly, constructing 2,300 housing units between 1975 and 1983. The group renovated Saint Joseph's Church, opening new offices and a restaurant beneath a soaring atrium and stained-glass windows.[90] But the commercial life of the Central Ward atrophied. Residents had to travel long distances or rely on street vendors for goods as basic as toilet paper. In 1990 the NCC helped bring a Pathmark supermarket to the Central Ward. Joseph Chaney-field, the NCC's first president, supervised its construction and after-ward installed himself near the cashiers in the front, chatting with shoppers and overseeing the market's operation, unofficial mayor of the Central Ward.[91]

By the mid-1990s the NCC ranked among the city's largest private employers, with a workforce of 1,200. It rivaled the NHA as a provider of low-income housing and together with other CDCs around the country outranked public housing authorities and conventional developers as a producer of low-income housing.[92] Its daycare franchise, Babyland, had restored infant childcare to the city under Mary Smith's leadership. The aggressive advocacy and visionary leadership of Smith and Linder fostered the NCC's growth into one of the largest and wealthiest CDCs in the United States.[93] Its successes were renowned in the burgeoning ranks of community economic development practitioners; activists from around the country toured NCC projects, while foundation executives and policymakers looked to the NCC as a model.[94]

There is irony worth exploring in the fact that the NCC, the organization that identified least explicitly with the black power movement, actually achieved some movement economic goals on a scale other groups did not. The NCC's interracial activism was the target of occasional criticism from both white and black residents over the years.[95] But its redevelopment plans for the Central Ward never faced the violent opposition from white residents that Kawaida Towers had. The NCC—like Tri-City—initially stayed within predominantly black neighborhoods.

NCC founders may have embraced aspects of black power internally, but their public self-presentation was couched in the language of interracial cooperation by Father Linder, a white priest, and Mary Smith, a black social worker, who emerged as the organization's most indefatigable spokespersons. Many suburban donors, government officials, and philanthropic funders no doubt associated Smith and Linder with King's beloved community vision, a vision they perhaps found more appealing than the black power commitments of Kawaida Inc. The political landscape and racial ideologies through which funders and officials assessed the NCC no doubt worked to its advantage.

Most important, even though Linder had clashed with the archdiocese, the NCC still benefited from Catholic networks, the use of buildings owned by the Catholic Church, and the legitimacy that these associations lent. Even as the NCC promoted economic self-determination, the organization also cultivated the political and financial support of well-connected suburban Catholics. Given the abiding inequality between city and suburb that divided New Jersey, it is not surprising that for the NCC the business of black power would have to follow the money, to suburban coalitions. While Linder had at one time been threatened with dismissal, he led an organization that in many ways made the Catholic Church relevant to the Central Ward. The NCC brought black children into the parochial school system and offered a model for a Catholic Church whose foothold in the country's older cities had eroded.[96]

From its provision of low-income housing to its role generating new regulations for infant care in the 1970s, to employing thousands in its efforts to reconstruct the Central Ward during the 1980s and 1990s, the NCC often acted as a parallel state—operating its own city in the shadow of Newark's municipal government.

The New Community Corporation and City Leaders

Few entanglements proved as fraught for the NCC as its relationship with Newark's municipal government. In its first decade, the NCC enjoyed strong relationships with the city council and the Gibson administration. Like Baraka's CAP/Kawaida Inc., the NCC had a relationship with Gibson before he ran for mayor, when he briefly served as one of its board members. Yet unlike CAP/Kawaida Inc., the NCC sustained cordial relations with Gibson throughout his first three terms. At the same time, the NCC's success generated complaints from some Newark residents who felt the group had departed from their original mission. Others questioned why a group led in large part by a white priest in a majority black city should receive such overwhelming proportions of federal housing funds for low-income housing development. From Linder's perspective, Gibson occasionally sided with the critics to immunize himself from accusations that he had drifted from his black constituents. By the mid-1980s, the NCC had begun to clash with municipal officials, who unsuccessfully attempted to rescind several of its tax abatements. The conflict with the city escalated after Sharpe James unseated Gibson in 1984. Newspapers bear witness to James's appearance at the opening of every new NCC facility, but relations between James and the NCC remained cold.[97] By the 1990s the NCC provided counseling and drug addiction therapy and supervised housing through contracts with the federal government, making it increasingly vulnerable to budget cuts at the national level and political rivalries closer to home.[98]

Ideology and Pragmatism

Newark's first-generation CDCs—Tri-City Citizens Union for Progress, Congress of African People/Kawaida Inc., and the New Community Corporation—emerged from shared motivations and intersecting ideologies, producing a fixer ethos that shaped urban development on a national scale even as they remained locally focused. If the early generation had conceived of themselves as the antidote to destructive policies and the culmination of hard-fought struggles for political and economic justice, the fixer ethos—translated into a de facto urban policy—positioned community development as an alternative to the familiar and seemingly exhausted politics of the 1960s.

Linder asserted that "American pragmatism" expressed the NCC's philosophy, evident in the highly contingent and politically malleable nature of CDCs more broadly. The NCC, Linder argued, was not the product of what he termed "rational-abstract" theorizing on the meaning of community but rather the product of the accumulated decisions made in day-to-day "efforts to meet human needs." He indirectly compared NCC's approach to that of the US labor movement after its leadership "rejected the idea of the ultimate goal and accepted the idea of a series of steps in gradual change." Though evidently proud of the NCC, Linder was no full-throttle booster, typically measuring the organization's accomplishments against Newark's mounting needs. In the years since the revolt of the Newark 20, Linder had tempered his rhetoric and lowered his expectations.[99]

Linder's analysis could be extended more broadly to community development politics, but the pragmatism he invoked was not solely political mellowing or adaptation of market models to social services and low-income housing. For Tri-City, pragmatism meant investing in the People's Center and other programs when housing consumed too much of the organization's resources and diverted its original mission. For over four decades, Tri-City organized in West Side Park and beyond precisely by responding to community needs as they evolved, offering counseling to homeowners in foreclosure, for example, during the housing crisis in 2008. Though many in Newark would have placed Baraka and CAP on the radical end of the political spectrum in the early 1970s, Kawaida Towers represented a concrete expression of a larger black nationalist vision pursued within the existing framework of municipal tax abatements and affordable-housing policy. But opponents were able to obscure its pragmatism by framing it as a racially divisive invasion into the North Ward.

These organizations' histories speak to the kind of urban populism that undergirded the growth of early CDCs in distressed cities nationally. For all three groups, community economic development was not just a response to structural crisis but also a religious or spiritual intervention. The NCC's leaders drew inspiration not only from a long history of black Catholics' institution building but also from King's "beloved community," the Cursillo Movement, and even early experiments in liberation theology, all of which cultivated strong lay leadership. Even the comparatively secular Tri-City appealed initially to Protestant churches to make the social gospel a reality on the streets of West Side Park. Cultural nationalists freely borrowed religious metaphors in their efforts to adapt Kawaida ethics. Baraka described the cornerstone of Newark's black nationalist movement as faith—*imani*—in black people: "The same way your grandmamma used to weep and wring her hands believing in Jeez-us, that deep, deep connection with the purest energy, that is what the Nationalist must have."[100] One could cite Baraka's swift transformation from Kawaida to Maoism in the early 1970s to dismiss his spiritual entreaties as fleeting, perhaps opportunistic. But such arguments only underscore the power of religiously tinged metaphors about a utopian village in the heart of the city: even those who did not accept them as a matter of faith still employed that language. All three organizations sought community governance on a scale that was considered humane and authentic, even if the explicit discussion of such motivations was often overwhelmed by the practical demands of pushing building projects through city bureaucracies and by the recognition that money often smoothed the way.

CDCs in Newark also embodied the search for tight-knit, authentic social life and responsive government noted in the diffuse neighborhood movement of the 1970s. Harry Boyte locates CDCs in a larger movement to salvage "organic relations that modern life has not completely collectivized, rationalized and refashioned in the image of the marketplace."[101] Similarly, Suleiman Osman locates CDCs within the constellation of neighborhood groups that were "hostile to centralized control, ambivalent about government intervention, based in protest politics rather than backroom dealing, preoccupied with cultural authenticity, and rooted in a belief in neighborhood self-determination rather than in integration." Osman highlights the ideological range of the organizations that fell under such auspices: "Neither exclusively Left nor Right, the politics of the 1970s was militantly local."[102] Osman's characterization of the neighborhood movement applies in part to Newark. Yet the first-generation CDCs emerging from the black freedom movement manifested important distinctions: these organizations recognized the limitations of the local even if they could not transcend them, and they did not purport to carry out their aims in a vacuum of oppositional purity. Fixer organizations may have criticized machine politics, but they succeeded insofar as they were prepared to mix protest politics with backroom dealing and to leverage disputes among the powerful.

All three embraced a vision for community economic development that extended beyond their target neighborhoods. Tri-City's very name served as a reminder of its original, unrealized goal of uniting troubled cities across northern New Jersey. For CAP/Kawaida Inc., the city Baraka called "New Ark" would boast new models of urban redevelopment that other black communities would emulate, a step toward liberation from internal colonialism in all its forms. The NCC also drew on international examples and attempted to cull inspiration from the most innovative planned communities. Closer to home, the NCC raised money by selling "shares" of the Central Ward to build not simply a donor network but also a regional consensus—especially among suburban Catholics—on Newark's significance.

Unlike many other organizations within the neighborhood movement, Newark's CDCs did not uniformly condemn the federal government. Indeed, their experiences fighting against discrimination and for antipoverty measures had proven that federal power could be crucial in overcoming or circumventing intractable municipal opposition. As black or interracial organizations that understood how putatively race-neutral policies and bureaucratic stalling protected white power, they were more wary than disillusioned and were prepared to work parallel tracks.

Gender and Community Development

Fixers tended to discreetly advance feminist claims, such as influence over neighborhood clinical services, through the more generic notion of democratization. Early efforts often reflected a conventional gendered division of labor, with men leading the economic development efforts and women focusing on children, health, and domestic life. None of the three organizations—at least in the early years—explicitly challenged that division. But women such as Rebecca Doggett of Tri-City and Mary Smith of the NCC often crossed these boundaries, exercising decisive leadership roles over their organizations. Still, there were important distinctions among the three. For the NCC and CAP/ Kawaida Inc., gender roles were intimately tied to idealizations of community. Two of the NCC's influences—the Cursillo Movement and liberation theology—were subtly gendered projects, designed to involve more laymen in the activities of the church and solve a problem articulated by generations of clergy as they surveyed their predominantly female congregations.[103] The NCC did not set out to bring more men into the church, but priests, black laymen, and white male professionals appeared to dominate the organization's early economic development agenda even though black laywomen had played the leading role in building Queen of Angels.

Though CDCs did not explicitly embrace second-wave feminism, the positions they took overlapped with more self-consciously feminist goals and reveal the indirect ways that feminist claims were institutionalized.[104] The democratization goals of CDCs, for example, often paralleled the many feminist organizations' attempt to dislodge the traditional social movement hierarchy and appeared to encourage women's leadership. Members also brought to Tri-City, CAP/Kawaida Inc., and the NCC a similar democratic organizing principle born of the black freedom movement and community action's doctrine of maximum feasible participation. Residents crossed the boundaries between expert and nonexpert and challenged the very definition of expertise by insisting on the authority of their own experiences.

All three organizations fell short of their original goals, but they also adapted to new demands. Kawaida Towers met the most public defeat on the bricks-and-mortar front, but black nationalists created other organizations and businesses that continued the work of community building, albeit on a more modest scale, into the late 1970s. As in other cities, the greatest gains for Newark CDCs came in housing, although the emphasis on homeownership—both individual and collective— was not easily realized and low-income rentals prevailed. Still, CDCs attempted solutions where government had retreated. Both New Jersey's *Report for Action* (Governor's Select Commission on Civil Disorder, also known as the Lilley Commission) and the federal Kerner Commission report, which addressed the long, hot summers of rioting across the country, called for many of the changes that Newark's fixers advanced. They recommended aid to those displaced by urban renewal, rehabilitation of older homes, and alternatives to high-rise housing. They also called for the training and hiring of tenants to manage public housing and the extension of health and childcare. CDCs pursued these recommendations at the local level while these reports, commissioned with great fanfare, languished upon publication.[105]

CDCs helped to institutionalize the expectation that ordinary residents were entitled to collectively alter urban redevelopment. They also promoted the idea of publicly accountable development at a time when privatization eroded competing notions of the public. Yet while CDCs continued to reinvest in local communities, the calls for collective ownership that echoed through the black power era were fulfilled on mostly symbolic terms. The goals of collective wealth building, pursued quite literally in the early years, slid into metaphor. Meanwhile, some conservative advocates promoted CDCs precisely because they were seen as a means of privatizing urban policy and eroding the welfare state. In 1992 Republican HUD secretary Jack Kemp would champion CDCs as part of his proposed "conservative war on poverty."[106] Nearly all community development activists would have abhorred conservative appropriation of their cause.

Their fixer orientation mixed two goals: they sought self-determination of communities marginalized by poverty and lack of political power while they also pursued the related strategy of meeting immediate needs by doing for neglected or exploited communities what the state and the market would not. This parallelism reflected a deep-seated self-help ethos, but in the context of civil rights and antipoverty reforms, it was also a challenge to the state to guarantee full citizenship and economic rights. As political momentum swiftly turned against the liberal and radical experiments of the 1960s, CDCs institutionalized what they could, persevering as parallel cities.

Conclusion

Gustav Heningburg was often immersed in the nuances of power at the local level, but even so, he seized opportunities to identify the larger, acutely felt constraints under which he worked. In a 1969 speech at a high school in suburban Millburn, NJ, he told students—and, through them, their parents—that the advances of the civil rights movement hardly guaranteed a better future for their urban peers: "You and your parents are a major part of Newark's problems," Heningburg said. He pointed to high unemployment rates among New Jersey's black youth and deepening segregation; he asked students to consider their own families' complicity in a seemingly bleak future. He insisted on Newark's importance to the state's economy and condemned the unequal tax structure that imperiled it. "The people with the training, education, job security and financial stability, who extract their full financial resources from Newark, will not provide any leadership," he said. "Go home and ask your parents what responsibility they have to Newark beyond extracting money and I'll bet you get the strangest set of Mickey Mouse answers you have ever heard."[1] The following year, he sharpened his charges, accusing business leaders who blamed Newark's decline on municipal leadership of displaying "the most sophisticated form of political hypocrisy."[2] In 1974, at a dinner held in his honor, he put the problem in the bluntest economic terms: "If the city of Newark closed down on a Monday, the 300,000 suburban residents who make their living in Newark would have to go on welfare the next day."[3]

Heningburg was not alone in his analysis. The New Community Corporation's Pat Foley demanded that suburban voters see the city's future as their own, while Rebecca Doggett of Tri-City Citizens Union for Progress attempted to organize neighborhoods across city borders and around shared goals. By the mid-1970s the mainstream media, Congress, and state legislators had retreated from urgent deliberations over racial equality and the future of the cities, but Newark's fixers did not.

Meanwhile, the eastern cities of Newark, Patterson, and Jersey City continued to shed manufacturing jobs through the 1970s and 1980s. They found themselves at the losing end of what political scientists Barbara G. Salmore and Stephen A. Salmore call an "internal sunbelt migration" of businesses to the south and west of the state, a regional microcosm of the national trends that produced the Rust Belt. Still, New Jersey as a whole remained one of the country's wealthiest states.[4]

Newark's experience as a struggling city in a wealthy state received more specific analysis by political scientists Neil Kraus and Todd Swanstrom, who revisited Paul Friesema's "hollow prize thesis" to assess how some two dozen cities fared in the three decades that followed the black electoral victories of the 1960s and 1970s. Though their research confirmed many of Friesema's predictions, Kraus and Swanstrom concluded that the "hollow prize" metaphor masked stark internal inequality. Such cities actually remained prizes for some: "dynamic components of the growing service sector" that employed skilled, educated workers at higher wages than their suburban counterparts. But those passed over for jobs and forced to cope with diminished public services and atrophied public institutions experienced the hollowing out of the city acutely. Equitable development and tax policies required state legislation that rarely passed.[5]

So it is perhaps no surprise that fixers doubled down to attack inequality by alternative means. Yet even as the numbers of fixer organizations grew and they occupied their own realm of the nonprofit world, fixers encountered opposition and constraints. The simultaneous emergence of CDCs and the election of Kenneth Gibson on a broad reform platform were rooted in some shared social movement goals. Yet Newark's CDCs and its municipal government settled into a relationship of mutual dependence and, often, hostility in the years that followed.[6] It was not simply a story of ambitious expectations for grassroots reform thwarted by the regeneration of an urban political machine. Activists' visions for neighborhood renewal—both grand and intensely local—ranged beyond electoral challenges. But as city officials struggled with perennial shortfalls, CDCs came to act as managers of an almost-parallel city-state. And yet even as cities depended upon their services, officials sought to rein them in.

In 1985, during Kenneth Gibson's final term, local leaders revived citywide efforts to bring parallel civic organizations into tighter coordination through the Newark Collaboration Group (NCG). Newark was at a turning point: the urgency that gave rise to the Greater Newark Urban Coalition in the late 1960s had long faded, but a renewed civic boosterism took hold as new construction appeared and many officials celebrated—prematurely—the thousands of jobs they believed that companies occupying new buildings would bring.[7] But the city had not really recovered. Newark "is a 19th century industrial city that missed out on the 20th and is now preparing for the 21st," wrote Robert Curvin, the former Congress of Racial Equality activist who was, at the time, a Ford Foundation executive. Promoters of the NCG, including the *New York Times*, argued that it could be the organization to push Newark into that future.[8]

With a dizzying panoply of working groups and task forces, the NCG aimed at the full scope of the city's problems. They took the pulse of residents and businesses with a series of polls and focus groups. Newarkers struggled to find steady work in a low-wage, service-driven economy. A bustling transportation system, vital airport, and new office towers belied the reality that Newark had one of the country's highest poverty rates. Yet given these conditions, residents' opinions of their neighborhoods were surprisingly positive. Over 75 percent cited their "friendly and caring" neighbors as one of the city's strengths; a majority emphasized the value of "intangible" resources—including their deep social ties, which sustained "commitment to a common survival" at the neighborhood level.[9] These responses suggest the extent to which Newarkers relied on local networks and institutions, including those that CDCs had sustained since the 1960s.[10]

Based on these surveys, the NCG devised an elaborate plan of action, which it then vetted through public forums in each of Newark's wards. Residents at these meetings avidly debated the plans, asking questions and demanding revisions that reflected their own experience. The very fact that the NCG held such extensive hearings reflected the vestigial participatory thrust of the city's earlier movements. In the North Ward, home to the grave of Kawaida Towers, residents complained about the deterioration of local housing stock. They wanted the city to help Newark residents start businesses downtown. West Ward residents wanted to know how individuals, not just professional developers, could best influence the city's future. They called for housing cooperatives and homeownership programs to keep their assets in the community. Newark's Central Ward—the site of the 1967 uprising—met late into the night and called for additional sessions. People's questions and suggestions ranged far beyond the topic at hand, giving "the impression that the residents of the Central Ward have few opportunities to express their grievances publicly," wrote one observer. Residents had specific concerns about the efficacy of the NCG's plan: Could the NCG guarantee a percentage of minority set-asides for new developments in the city? Would it expedite the transfer of abandoned properties and foreclosed homes to local owners, who could refurbish them? Residents also questioned officials' unsustainable use of tax abatements to attract business. Many corporations in Newark benefited from abatements yet reneged on pledges to employ city residents. People in three of the four wards also pointed to the lack of supermarkets in Newark and the poor quality of the food available in the existing stores. Many exhorted the NCG to support new, better-quality small businesses through loans and rent subsidies.[11]

Participants expressed guarded support for the NCG's efforts, but pessimism abounded about its prospects. "What section of the community did you have in mind when you put together these initiatives?" asked a South Ward resident. "The middle class? Property owners? The affluent can take care of themselves. How about the poor, who need the help?" A Central Ward resident questioned whether the plan would help large corporations at the expense of Newark residents. Junius Williams, who had helped to coordinate opposition to the Medical College in the late 1960s and had also worked on the NCG's plan, answered the questions with one of his own: "Yes, someone is going to make some money," he acknowledged. "That is how things tend to get done in America. . . . [W]e all know Newark is coming back. The question is, Newark is coming back for whom?"[12]

The NCG did not offer a clear answer. Political, business, and civic leaders wanted to persuade residents that they could benefit—and should therefore support—the multiple revitalization efforts under way. But they also opened up an undoubtedly heated dialogue about whose needs would prevail. For Richard Cammarieri, a longtime community activist who worked with both the New Community Corporation (NCC) and the Newark Community Development Network, the NCG was inordinately focused on consensus. He recalled being privately rebuked by foundation executives for being an "obstructionist" when he called for more grassroots participation. He and the handful of other community organizers felt "like our presence was being used to justify something over which we have no control."[13] Roland Anglin, deputy director of the Community Development Resource Unit of the Ford Foundation, oversaw some of the NCG's efforts. He asserted that the city's political climate ultimately impeded collaboration among CDCs, government, and the private sector. Cooperation from the city was "always a fight and a question," Anglin recalled decades later.[14]

Newark was not the same place in 1986 that it had been in 1970, when Gibson argued that the city was a harbinger for urban America. But many of the residents who gathered for the NCG meetings that autumn were armed with familiar plans from those earlier struggles. Though the NCG ended with much of its agenda unfulfilled, it prompted avid public debate about economic justice and the role of the neighborhoods in the city's anticipated revitalization. This debate made visible fixers' often-unacknowledged influence, as well as their unfinished work.

The late twentieth-century history of fixers unfolded in three stages. First, early civil rights and antipoverty activists confronted officials unwilling to enforce antidiscrimination laws or sustain antipoverty programs even when they had new legislative tools to do so. Facing stalled or inadequate reforms in the public and private sector, activists took on fixer roles themselves. In the wake of the 1967 uprising, neighborhood and civil rights groups entered a second phase. They emphasized the interconnected nature of political powerlessness, economic exploitation, and displacement as they fought construction of the Medical College. Adopting a fixer ethos, residents channeled their opposition into influence over the conditions under which the Medical College would be built and operated. They established a framework for a third phase, characterized by individual fixers, such as Gustav Heningburg, and organizational fixers, such as Newark's first generation of CDCs. They attempted to hew an independent line, taking advantage of federal urban, antipoverty, and civil rights legislation even as they institutionalized an intensively local approach to fixing the city.

At each stage they found themselves taking on occasionally surprising, even unintended roles. The NCC, for example, achieved exceptional growth but also embodied the maturation of community economic development strategies more broadly. The NCC achieved sustainability through a combination of grants, government contracts, businesses, and housing loans. But like most CDCs, the NCC earned significant income through social service contracts with the government, not self-perpetuating enterprises, as its founders initially envisioned.[15] Managing government contracts requires organizations to hone administrative systems at the expense of other goals, such as community organizing.[16] The NCC maintained a reputation for operating well-managed and desirable housing, for example, but after the first generation of tenants in NCC buildings were gone, new tenants lacked the sense that they were part of an important housing alternative or a partnership with the organization.[17]

The NCC, like Tri-City, Kawaida Inc., and other CDCs around the country, began with a sense of themselves as part of a regional, national, even international movement. But the technical demands of housing development and competition with other organizations forced them to turn inward.[18] Conservatives seized upon the community economic development model as part of the shift toward localism and voluntarism that would enable the shrinking of the state. CDCs did establish crucial national support networks, such as the Local Initiatives Support Corporation, during the 1980s and 1990s, but they functioned more as trade associations than social movements.[19] On the local level, many groups pursued their goals individually. The minutiae of coordinating individual projects and competition for funding discouraged the creation of effective coalitions.[20] Rather than challenging municipal government and established social service agencies, they had become a part of what Jennifer Wolch calls the "shadow state."[21]

Wolch applies the term to a constellation of nonprofit social service agencies, philanthropic and voluntary organizations, and CDCs, which had, in the wake of the neoliberal transformation in the 1980s, come to offer entitlements of citizenship "formerly provided by the Keynesian, fordist state."[22] Nationally, the numbers of these entities doubled between the early 1980s and the late 1990s, and Newark reflected this trend. Political scientists Robert W. Lake and Kathe Newman argue that the devolution of state functions coupled with the neoliberal emphasis on market-based approaches to social problems imperiled many already-disadvantaged groups. Their study of about two dozen nonprofits in Newark shows the effects of the so-called shadow state on the city's most marginalized residents. These people turned to the shadow state to claim their rights to "the life of a civilized being according to the standards prevailing in society," yet it offered a scattered and inconsistent response. The typically small budgets and staffs of shadow state organizations are not sufficient to meet demands for housing, job training, and social services. Lake and Newman do not focus on the history of CDCs, but their analysis reveals contrasts between the first generation analyzed here and what prevailed by the late twentieth century. Committed to local development, early CDCs had nonetheless aimed for a wider, nationally influential strategy. But four decades later, Newman and Lake found CDCs immersed so deeply in their immediate neighborhoods that "a sense of protectionism and turf conflicts among organizations" prevailed, alongside a sort of second-class citizenship for those outside their scope. CDCs' earlier insistence that social needs, employment, and housing be addressed in tandem did not withstand the pressures of diminished budgets, growing need, and funders' restrictions.[23]

When we consider that CDCs proliferated during a time of increasing privatization, fixers' resemblance to the classic capitalist middlemen seems apparent. Crucial to the growth, spread, and consolidation of capitalist enterprises, middlemen identify new niches and secure access to new markets. They are then eliminated in the interest of efficiency, the act of elimination itself becoming a kind of commodity. We see a similar pattern in urban and antipoverty policy as localized, responsive services of the sort CDCs offer are touted one moment as the best response to economic and social problems. Next come complaints about redundancy and competence, followed by calls for consolidation and specialized expertise.

But viewing fixers through the lens of recent neoliberal policy cycles provides an incomplete analysis. Early fixers also reflected African American organizing traditions. The so-called de facto segregation of the North required that black communities work parallel tracks— pressing for a guarantee of full rights and protections while dealing with the reality of second-class citizenship. These dual requirements may explain why fixers appeared to shift easily between calls for radical redistribution of power and narrow reforms. They underscore the entrepreneurial vein that ran through many organizing strategies, as activists sought to meet black communities' immediate needs and also secure the capital to sustain their protest—and their independence— over the long run.

CDCs acted as a parallel government. They emerged from multiple activist traditions to provide services and advocacy while sustaining a critique of the state's failures to serve all citizens equally. But their successes as fixers then became the basis for a "shadow state" in which they became entrapped in an atomized status quo. This is not a time-worn explanation premised on tarnished ideals or the inevitable political mellowing of once-radical activists. Fixers have been essential to institutionalizing elements of the black freedom movement and vestiges of the War on Poverty, but fixers cannot remain institutionalized too long and still function. To be effective, fixers need to move along a wide political spectrum. Black power mobilizations, urban uprisings, and economic and political realignments in the late 1960s and 1970s opened up space for them to act.

Nearly half a century after the Newark uprising, escalating housing costs have fueled gentrification of some of the most persistently depressed cities.[24] Smaller-scale developments that house fewer poor and working-class people replaced demolished public housing complexes. Some of the urban displaced move to older suburbs, joining new struggles over education, employment, affordable housing, and policing. Deep in the suburbs, the inequality at the heart of the urban crisis is perhaps less visible, but it is no less destructive. From where will the new fixers emerge?

Acknowledgments

So many have helped me find sources, generate ideas, and finish this book. Here are a few:

I'd like to thank Thomas Sugrue for his encouragement. His electrifying ability to dissect a primary source continues to influence me. Michael B. Katz indelibly shaped my trajectory. I'm grateful for his warmth, his criticism, and the opportunities he offered to collaborate on research. His ability to shift between trenchant wide-angle critique of social policy and the minute humanity at stake was unparalleled—and is deeply missed.

I'm also indebted to Komozi Woodard. His scholarship fueled a necessary and exciting transition in the historiography of the urban black freedom movement to which I hope to contribute. When he agreed to offer some suggestions for my research, I anticipated a brief chat over lunch. Instead, I returned six hours later with a notebook full of Newark stories and a long list of people to contact—just one example of the intellectual generosity he has extended to me and countless others.

This project depended upon the willingness of Newarkers to set aside time to share their experiences and even their personal papers. The aid of numerous archivists and librarians was also essential. I owe special thanks to Bob Vietrogowski of the University of Medicine and Dentistry of New Jersey Archives and to the staff of the Newark Public Library, who went the extra mile to help me find sources.

Thanks to my father, Donald Rabig—my New Jersey connection—for everything. Vital support came from him and Jude Rabig in the form of meals, discussion, childcare, and love. My mother, Barbara Rabig, died years before I became a historian, but I will always remember the fury she expressed at the Reagan administration when I asked her about the boarded-up high-rises of Newark on childhood trips to my grandmother's in Elizabeth, NJ. I didn't fully understand at the time, but I wish she could see where it all led.

Thanks to Robert Sharlet for his unyielding support—and for sending books, helping with research, and commenting on some of these chapters. Adele Oltman generously shared her own research with me. She and Jordan Stanger Ross, Leah Gordon, Laura Warren Hill, David Goldberg, and David Rabig deserve my gratitude for commenting on parts of this book.

My incredible students and colleagues at Boston University, the University of Rochester, Amherst College, and Dartmouth College have helped me refine my arguments and consider new ways to write the history of social movements.

I'm grateful for the support of the New Jersey Historical Commission and a postdoctoral fellowship from the Center for the Study of African American Politics and the Frederick Douglass Institute of the University of Rochester. Thanks especially to Valeria Sinclair-Chapman, Jeffrey Tucker, and Gerald Gamm for their guidance and cross-disciplinary perspectives.

Thanks to the deans of Interdisciplinary Studies and Social Sciences at Dartmouth College, who helped in the licensing of images for this book. I'm also thankful for the remarkable generosity of Sergio Waksman of the Bud Lee Archive.

I deeply appreciate the insights and encouragement of Timothy Mennel and Rachel Kelly at the University of Chicago Press as they patiently guided this book to the finish line.

The reliable and loving care to my kids provided by the incredible teachers at Sarah McDonnell Family Daycare, the Dartmouth College Childcare Center, and the Child Care Center in Norwich made this work possible.

Thanks to the sustaining friendship of Gretchen Aguiar and Jeff Allred from Philadelphia to Brooklyn to Goshen. Aimee Bahng, Bill Boyer, and Dara: thanks for keeping the communal spirit alive in this frigid outpost.

Roxana and Malcolm: You're the best reason to keep writing history and the most compelling excuse to procrastinate.

My gratitude to Jeffrey Sharlet is immeasurable. His love, patience, and belief in me—even in my self-defeating moments—have been true gifts. There are no words to express my thanks, except, perhaps: you were right.

Notes

INTRODUCTION

1. Gustav Heningburg, interview by the author, Newark, NJ, July 13, 2004.
2. Tara Fehr, "Gus Heningburg Has Recently Donated Several Volumes to the Newark Public Library," *Star-Ledger*, February 11, 2010.
3. Arthur M. Louis, "The Worst American City," *Harper's*, January 1975, 67–71.
4. *Joyce v. McCrane, Bricklayers, et al.*, 1970 U.S. Dist. Lexis 9004.
5. Heningburg, interview, 2004.
6. Gustav Heningburg, interview by the author, Newark, NJ, December 6, 2006.
7. On Hague, see Barbara G. Salmore and Stephen A. Salmore, *New Jersey Politics and Government: Suburban Politics Comes of Age*, 2nd ed. (Lincoln: University of Nebraska Press, 1993), 27–44.
8. The term "urban crisis" has become amorphous. Thomas Sugrue illuminated its historical roots in housing and employment discrimination, regional disinvestment, discriminatory federal lending policies, and white opposition to black equality; see Thomas Sugrue, *The Origins of the Urban Crisis: Race and Inequality in Postwar Detroit* (Princeton, NJ: Princeton University Press, 1996). David Rusk, in *Cities without Suburbs* (Washington, DC: Woodrow Wilson Center Press, 1995), emphasizes urban/suburban wealth gaps and the isolation of urban residents. Frances Fox Piven and Richard Cloward, in *Regulating the Poor: The Functions of Public Welfare* (New York: Pantheon, 1971), and Ira Katznelson, in

City Trenches, Urban Politics, and the Patterning of Class in the United States
(Chicago: University of Chicago Press, 1981), argue that the urban crisis
was ultimately "a crisis of social control" over marginalized people. Kevin
Mumford argues that the racialized phrase "urban crisis" can suggest that
the problems facing majority black cities are unconnected to capitalism
and globalization; see Kevin Mumford, *Newark: A History of Race, Rights,
and Riots* (New York: New York University Press, 2007). The term "crisis"
implies a brief but intense escalation of factors beyond human control or a
departure from cyclical norms, yet the urban crisis was the product, not of
a fleeting catastrophe or a dip in the business cycle, but of specific policies
enacted, then reconfigured, over decades.

9. On Gibson's victory, see "Gibson—Newark's New Mayor," *Chicago Daily
Defender*, June 18, 1970, 15; Leroy Thomas, "Sees New Sanity in Newark
Vote," *Chicago Daily Defender*, June 18, 1970, 2; Whitney M. Young Jr.,
"The Lesson in Newark's Triumph," *Chicago Daily Defender*, July 4, 1970, 8;
and Ronald Sullivan, "Gibson Defeats Addonizio in Newark Mayoral Race,
Voter Turnout a Record," *New York Times*, June 17, 1970, 1. Newark's race
was followed across the country; see Peter J. Bridge, "Country Eyes Newark
Vote," *Newark Evening News*, April 15, 1970, 1.

10. Fred J. Cooke, "Mayor Kenneth Gibson says—," *New York Times*, July 25,
1971. Donald Malafronte, an aide for former mayor Hugh J. Addonizio,
was the original source of this quotation, but Gibson adopted it as his
own. John T. Cunningham, *Newark* (Newark: New Jersey Historical
Society, 1988), 330.

11. Max Herman, *Fighting in the Streets: Ethnic Succession and Urban Unrest in
20th Century America* (New York: Peter Lang, 2005), 77-79.

12. Until the 1950s, the Central Ward was called the Third Ward. I have used
"Central Ward," except when quoting sources. See Robert Curvin, *Inside
Newark: Decline, Rebellion, and the Search for Transformation* (New Bruns-
wick, NJ: Rutgers University Press, 2014), 10-13, 34-48.

13. Governor's Select Commission on Civil Disorder, *Report for Action* (Tren-
ton: State of New Jersey, 1968), 45-48. For corroborating accounts, see
Tom Hayden, *Rebellion in Newark: Official Violence and Ghetto Response*
(New York: Vintage Books, 1967); Ron Perambo, *No Cause for Indictment:
An Autopsy of Newark* (New York: Holt, Rinehart, and Winston, 1971);
Mumford, *Newark*, 125-48; and Nathan Wright Jr., *Ready to Riot* (New York:
Holt, Rinehart, and Winston, 1968). Lydia Davis Barrett, interview by the
author, Montclair, NJ, April 2005. The term "uprising," rather than "riot"
or "civil disturbance," encapsulates the forms of resistance evident in the
"long, hot summers" and the opportunities that opened for fixers in their
aftermath.

14. H. Paul Friesema, "Black Control of Central Cities: The Hollow Prize,"
American Institute of Planners Journal 35 (March 1969): 75-79; Neil Kraus
and Todd Swanstrom, "Minority Mayors and the Hollow Prize Problem,"

PS: Political Science and Politics 34, no. 1 (March 2001): 99–105; and Jesse Jackson, "Why We March," *Chicago Defender*, May 23, 1970, 1.

15. In 1982 an advertising campaign for haute couturier Christian Dior enraged Newark officials by asking, "What would New York be without Dior?" "Newark." Michael Norman, "Dior Makes Formal Apology to Newark for Reputed Slur," *New York Times*, September 15, 1982, B2.

16. Author's notes from "The Long Hot Summers in Retrospect: Urban Unrest in 1960s New Jersey" conference, New Jersey Historical Society, Newark, November 13, 2004. Other sources corroborated Smith's perceptions: Barrett, interview; and Joyce Smith Carter, interview by the author, Newark, NJ, February 27, 2007.

17. On earlier civil rights activism in Newark, see Mumford, *Newark*; Clement A. Price, "The African American Community of Newark, 1917–1947: A Social History" (PhD diss., Rutgers University, 1975), 63–66; and Rutgers University School of Social Work, *When I Was Comin' Up: Life Histories of Elderly Black People in Newark* (Hamden, CT: Archon Books, 1982).

18. On these developments, see Peniel Joseph, "Black Power Movement: A State of the Field," *Journal of American History* 96, no. 3 (December 2009): 751–76; Sundiata Keita Cha-Jua and Clarence Lang, "The 'Long Movement' as Vampire: Temporal and Spatial Fallacies in Recent Black Freedom Studies," *Journal of African American History* 92, no. 2 (Spring 2007): 265–88; and Jacquelyn Dowd Hall, "The Long Civil Rights Movement and the Political Uses of the Past," *Journal of American History* 91, no. 4 (March 2005): 1233–63. Scholarship that significantly expanded the frameworks for understanding black power includes Matthew J. Countryman, *Up South: Civil Rights and Black Power in Philadelphia* (Philadelphia: University of Pennsylvania Press, 2007); Hasan Jeffries, *Bloody Lowndes: Civil Rights and Black Power in Alabama's Black Belt* (New York: New York University Press, 2009); Robert O. Self, *American Babylon: Race and the Struggle for Postwar Oakland* (Princeton, NJ: Princeton University Press, 2005); Jeanne F. Theoharis and Komozi Woodard, eds., *Freedom North: Black Freedom Struggles outside the South, 1940–1980* (New York: Palgrave-Macmillan, 2003); and Komozi Woodard, *A Nation within a Nation: Amiri Baraka (LeRoi Jones) and Black Power Politics* (Chapel Hill: University of North Carolina Press, 1999).

19. Black Panther Party, "What We Want, What We Believe: Black Panther Party Platform, 1966," in *Modern Black Nationalism from Marcus Garvey to Louis Farrakhan*, ed. William L. Van Deburg (New York: New York University Press, 1996), 249–51.

20. Alice O'Connor, "Swimming against the Tide: A Brief History of Federal Policy in Poor Communities," in *Urban Problems and Community Development*, ed. Ronald F. Ferguson and William T. Dickens (Washington, DC: Brookings Institution Press, 1999), 113–14.

21. Mary Pattillo, *Black on the Block: The Politics of Race and Class in the City* (Chicago: University of Chicago Press, 2007), 18, 113–18. Pattillo's analysis

builds on her critical reading of E. Franklin Frazier's *The Black Bourgeoisie* (82–83). Middlemen and middlewomen are entrepreneurial, investing in renovating the neighborhood and expending social capital to address poor schools, inadequate public facilities, and hostile treatment by police. They often act effectively in concert with their poor and working-class neighbors, although they also clash (116).

22. Nancy Roberts and Paula J. King, "Policy Entrepreneurs: Their Activity Structure and Function in the Public Policy Process," *Journal of Public Administration and Research Theory* 1, no. 2 (1991): 148, 158–59; and Thomas J. Sugrue, "Affirmative Action from Below: Civil Rights, the Building Trades, and the Politics of Racial Equality in the Urban North, 1945–1969," *Journal of American History* 91 (June 2004): 145–73.

23. Robert Halpern argues that community development corporations acted most powerfully as mediating institutions, shaping residents' interaction with markets, charities, and government agencies. I prefer the term "fixers" to "mediators," however, because it conveys the urgency and fierce critique of existing institutions that initially characterized these groups and heightened their political complexity. I agree with Halpern's claim that CDCs were ultimately more successful as mediators than as creators of community-run businesses, housing collectives, or employers, but I aim to re-create the historical context out of which CDCs' more ambitious goals emerged and analyze the process through which they were narrowed. Robert Halpern, *Rebuilding the Inner City: A History of Neighborhood Initiatives to Address Poverty in the United States* (New York: Columbia University Press, 1995), 221–33.

24. Amiri Baraka, *Afrikan Revolution* (Newark, NJ: Jihad Press, 173).

25. Susan E. Hirsch, *Roots of the American Working Class: The Industrialization of Crafts in Newark, 1800–1860* (Philadelphia: University of Pennsylvania Press, 1978).

26. Cunningham, *Newark*; and Paul Anthony Stellhorn, "Depression and Decline in Newark, NJ: 1929–1941" (PhD diss., Rutgers University, 1982).

27. Barbara Kukla, *Swing City: Newark Nightlife, 1925–50* (New Brunswick, NJ: Rutgers University Press, 2002).

28. Thomas W. Hanchett, "Financing Suburbia: Prudential Insurance and the Post-WWII Transformation of the American City," *Journal of Urban History* 26, no. 3 (2000): 312–18; and Elihu Rubin, *Insuring the City: The Prudential Center and the Postwar Urban Landscape* (New Haven, CT: Yale University Press, 2012), 15.

29. Rubin, *Insuring the City*, 15; and Heningburg, interview, 2004.

30. Stellhorn, "Depression and Decline in Newark, NJ," 172.

31. Ibid., 25–28, 386. In 1921, 71 percent of officers and directors of the Newark Chamber of Commerce lived within the city, but twenty years later, only 14 percent did.

32. Richardson Dilworth, *The Urban Origins of Suburban Autonomy* (Cambridge, MA: Harvard University Press, 2005), 158–93. Dilworth's explanation for the consistent deferral of investment that made officials' options increasingly unpalatable focuses on a "mechanic's ideology" of "limited government action." Identified in Hirsch's study of Newark's nineteenth-century working class (*Roots of the American Working Class*), the "mechanic's ideology" bridged divisions of class and ethnicity. It offered "the major point of consensus in Newark's political arena," as residents' wariness of expanded government dovetailed with leaders' desire to contain costs (*Urban Origins of Suburban Autonomy*, 161).

33. Price, "African American Community of Newark," 6; Salmore and Salmore, *New Jersey Politics and Government*, 47; and Stellhorn, "Depression and Decline in Newark, NJ," 33–34.

34. Kenneth T. Jackson and Barbara B. Jackson, "The Black Experience in Newark: The Growth of the Ghetto, 1870–1970," in *New Jersey since 1860: New Findings and Interpretations*, ed. William C. Wright (Trenton: New Jersey Historical Commission, 1972), 40–41.

35. Stellhorn, "Depression and Decline in Newark, NJ," 34; and John P. Farmer, "Jersey Suburbs Get Most U.S. Aid," *Newark Evening News*, March 5, 1970, 1. A study of federal aid to New Jersey determined that most of it favored suburbs.

36. Governor's Select Commission on Civil Disorder, *Report for Action*, 48.

37. Ibid.; and "Record City Budget," *Newark Evening News*, February 6, 1964, 18.

38. Salmore and Salmore, *New Jersey Politics and Government*, xviii.

39. Ibid., x.

40. Ibid., 6. These dynamics would emerge in the legal battles over education funding and affordable housing in the *Abbott* and *Mount Laurel* cases. See also Lizabeth Cohen, *A Consumers' Republic: The Politics of Mass Consumption in Postwar America* (New York: Alfred A. Knopf, 2003), 235–50.

41. Rubin, *Insuring the City*, 36–38.

42. "Westinghouse Keeps Faith in Newark, Will Stay," *Newark Evening News*, March 18, 1958.

43. Rubin, *Insuring the City*, 39–41.

44. Salmore and Salmore, *New Jersey Politics and Government*, 56.

45. See Bruce Schulman, *From Cotton Belt to Sunbelt: Federal Policy, Economic Development, and the Transformation of the South, 1938–1980* (Durham, NC: Duke University Press, 1994).

46. Salmore and Salmore, *New Jersey Politics and Government*, 57.

47. Robert Curvin, "The Persistent Minority: The Black Political Experience in Newark" (PhD diss., Princeton University, 1975), 20–21. On the shift from manufacturing to white-collar service-sector employment, see Adele Oltman, "'A Diabolical Scheme': Urban Renewal and the Civil Rights Movement in Newark in the Early 1960s" (paper presented at "The Long Hot

Summers in Retrospect: Urban Unrest in 1960s New Jersey" conference, New Jersey Historical Society, Newark, November 13, 2004).

48. David Gerwin, "The End of Coalition: The Failure of Community Organizing in Newark in the 1960s" (PhD diss., Columbia University, 1998), 42–43.

49. Curvin, "Persistent Minority," 14; and Governor's Select Commission on Civil Disorder, *Report for Action*, 2.

50. City of Newark, "Newark Neighborhood Survey," 1958, Charles F. Cummings New Jersey Information Center, Newark Public Library. See table 5, "The Length of Time White, Negro and Puerto Rican Households Have Lived in Newark"; table 6, "Places from Which People Have Moved to Newark"; and table 26, "Birthplace of Head of Household."

51. Arnold Hirsh, *Making the Second Ghetto: Race and Housing in Chicago, 1940–1960* (Chicago: University of Chicago Press, 1988), 1–25; and Sugrue, *Origins of the Urban Crisis*, 21–23.

52. Jackson and Jackson, "Black Experience in Newark," 52; and Price, "African American Community of Newark," 57–59.

53. Jackson and Jackson, "Black Experience in Newark," 40–41.

54. See Kenneth T. Jackson, *Crabgrass Frontier: The Suburbanization of the United States* (New York: Oxford University Press, 1985), 198–220.

55. Cohen, *Consumers' Republic*, 213.

56. Price, "African American Community of Newark," 38, ii–iii, 31–33.

57. Ibid., 18.

58. Ibid., 66.

59. Ibid., 92–100; Mumford, *Newark*, 7–10, 16–24; and Michael Nash, *Islam among Urban Blacks: Muslims in Newark, New Jersey; A Social History* (Lanham, MD: University Press of America, 2007).

60. Price, "African American Community of Newark," 74–85, 92–94. For more on the secularization of leadership and its complications, see Adele Oltman, *Sacred Mission, World Ambition: Black Christian Nationalism in the Age of Jim Crow* (Athens: University of Georgia Press, 2007).

61. Price, "African American Community of Newark," 100–133, 140–50.

62. Malcolm X, "Message to the Grassroots."

63. Kraus and Swanstrom, "Minority Mayors and the Hollow Prize Problem," 102, quoted in James H. Cone, *Martin and Malcolm and America: A Dream or a Nightmare* (Maryknoll, NY: Orbis Books, 1991), 226.

64. Governor's Select Commission on Civil Disorder, *Report for Action*, 18.

65. Ibid., 5, 6, 51, 60, 67, 84, 90. Self's *American Babylon* links the history of the urban black freedom movement to deindustrialization, housing, and taxation in the suburbs. According to Mumford (*Newark*, 4–7), the reality of urban decline and suburban ascendance should not obscure the parallel manifestations of black agency.

66. William H. Simon, *The Community Economic Development Movement: Law, Business, and the New Social Policy* (Durham, NC: Duke University Press, 2001), 3.

67. Entitlements such as social security, unemployment, and Veterans Affairs loans were only inconsistently available to racial minorities in the twentieth century. To speak of the 1970s as the definitive fall of the New Deal order and rise of neoliberalism misrepresents conditions with which many urban residents had long contended.

68. Philip W. Smith, "Gibson Urges Caution on Citizen Group Roles," *Star-Ledger*, February 1, 1978.

69. On the decline of a national black power infrastructure and reform coalitions, see Cedric Johnson, *Revolutionaries to Race Leaders: Black Power and the Making of African American Politics* (Minneapolis: University of Minnesota Press, 2007), pt. 2; Adolph Reed, *Stirrings in the Jug, Black Politics in the Post-segregation Era* (Minneapolis: University of Minnesota Press, 1999); and J. Phillip Thompson, *Double Trouble: Black Mayors, Black Communities, and the Call for Deep Democracy* (Oxford: Oxford University Press, 2005), 39–74.

70. With the exception of Cory Booker, Newark's subsequent mayors were elected on reform platforms and ended their terms with indictments. See, e.g., Charles Grutzner, "Newark Indicts Mayor of Newark, Nine Present or Former Officials on $253,000 Extortion Charges," *New York Times*, December 18, 1969, 1; and Cunningham, *Newark*.

71. David Harvey, *Spaces of Hope* (Berkeley: University of California Press, 2000), 133.

72. Ibid., 150–54.

73. Ibid., 154, 178.

74. Lester K. Spence, "The Neoliberal Turn in Black Politics," *Souls: A Critical Journal of Black Politics, Culture, and Society* 14, nos. 3–4 (March 2013): 140.

75. On the variety of neoliberal experiments, see Neil Brenner and Nik Theodore, "Cities and the Geographies of 'Actually Existing Neoliberalism,'" *Antipode*, 2002, 349–79.

76. Kenneth T. Walsh and Joseph P. Shapiro, "'They Are Not Our Issues,'" *U.S. News and World Report*, May 18, 1992, 26.

CHAPTER 1

1. Milton Honig, "Racial Job Clash Erupts in Jersey," *New York Times*, July 4, 1963, 1.

2. Harry Burke, "Clash Brings Request to Halt Barringer Job: Mayor Asks Study of Bias," *Newark Evening News*, July 3, 1963, 1.

3. *Hearings Before the United States Commission on Civil Rights: Newark, New Jersey, September 11–12, 1962* (Washington, DC: GPO, 1963), 18, 52. An estimated fourteen African Americans were among the nearly four thousand apprentices enrolled in New Jersey's federally registered programs. See similar statistics for other cities in "Racial Discrimination in the Nation's Apprenticeship Training Programs," *Phylon* 23 (Fall 1962): 215–23.

4. Hearings, 6.

5. Robert F. Palmer, "Building Trades Unions Include Few Negroes Here," *Newark Evening News*, September 11, 1962, 1, 21.

6. See tables 24 and 25 in Mayor's Commission on Group Relations, *Newark: A City in Transition*, vol. 1, *The Characteristics of a Population* (Newark, 1959), Charles F. Cummings New Jersey Information Center, Newark Public Library (hereafter NPL).

7. Alexander Mulch, "Contractors Fear Wage Boosts May Brake Construction Growth," *Newark Evening News*, September 30, 1962, 4; *Hearings*; and Advisory Committees to the US Commission on Civil Rights, "Reports on Apprenticeship" (Washington, DC: US Commission on Civil Rights, January 1964), 91–92.

8. Division of Business Research, Seton Hall University and Newark Housing Authority, "Economic Base Study of Newark, New Jersey," November 1964, x, Gustav Heningburg Papers, Charles F. Cummings New Jersey Information Center, NPL; "Labor Force and Business Establishments," Newark, New Jersey, County and City Databooks, Historic Edition, http://fisher.lib .virginia.edu/collections/stats/ccdb/; and Newark Coordinating Committee to Vincent J. Murphy, President of New Jersey AFL-CIO, September 11, 1964, folder 3 (Employment Committee, Bi-partisan Conference on Civil Rights, Apprenticeship Training), box 4, Ernest Thompson Papers, Rutgers University Special Collections, New Brunswick, NJ (hereafter Thompson Papers).

9. Amiri Baraka, *The Autobiography of LeRoi Jones* (Chicago: Lawrence Hill Books, 1997), 41–51; and David Barrett, interview by the author, Columbia, MD, January 29, 2005.

10. On the national impact of Philadelphia protests, see Thomas J. Sugrue, "Affirmative Action from Below: Civil Rights, the Building Trades, and the Politics of Racial Equality in the Urban North, 1945–1969," *Journal of American History* 91 (June 2004): 146–50, 170–73; and Palmer, "Building Trades Unions Include Few Negroes Here."

11. See Brian Purnell, "Revolution Has Come to Brooklyn: Construction Trades Protests and the Negro Revolt of 1963," in *Black Power at Work: Community Control, Affirmative Action, and the Construction Industry*, ed. David Goldberg and Trevor Griffey (Ithaca, NY: Cornell University Press, 2010), 23–47.

12. Hugh Davis Graham, *The Civil Rights Era: Origins and Development of a National Policy, 1960–1972* (Oxford: Oxford University Press, 1990), 51–54.

13. Sugrue, "Affirmative Action from Below," 164.

14. Jacquelyn Dowd Hall, "The Long Civil Rights Movement and the Political Uses of the Past," *Journal of American History* 91, no. 4 (March 2005): 1233–63.

15. Lizabeth Cohen, *A Consumers' Republic: The Politics of Mass Consumption in Postwar America* (New York: Alfred A. Knopf, 2003), 212–13, 219.

16. The commission system dates back to 1871 and emerged from a clash between reformist and nativist Republicans in the New Jersey Senate and Irish Democrats who wielded power in the cities. Stanley N. Worton, *Reshaping New Jersey: A History of Its Government and Politics* (Trenton: New Jersey Historical Commission, 1997), 56–57.

17. Robert Curvin, "The Persistent Minority: The Black Political Experience in Newark" (PhD diss., Princeton University, 1975), 27–30.

18. John T. Cunningham, *Newark* (Newark: New Jersey Historical Society, 1988), 305–6; and Stanley B. Winters, *From Riot to Recovery: Newark after Ten Years* (Washington, DC: University Press of America, 1979).

19. John O'Shea, "Newark Negroes Move toward Power," *Atlantic Monthly*, November 1965, 97.

20. On municipal reform and Turner's political career, see Robert Curvin, *Inside Newark: Decline, Rebellion, and the Search for Transformation* (New Brunswick, NJ: Rutgers University Press, 2014), 48–68. When Newark's urban renewal plans necessitated the displacement of several churches, Housing Authority director Louis Danzig relied on Turner's influence. He negotiated higher prices for church property in exchange for the clergy's support of urban renewal policies. Robert Curvin, interview by the author, Newark, NJ, September 16, 2004; Leila Meier Rice, "In the Trenches in the War on Poverty: The Local Implementation of the Community Action Program, 1964–1969" (PhD diss., Vanderbilt University, 1997), 184; and "Turner Seeks $60 Weekly for the Jobless," *Newark Evening News*, February 27, 1958. Turner supported greater relief payments, medical assistance to the poor, and benefits for working mothers during their pregnancies.

21. A September 19, 1964, editorial in the *New Jersey Afro-American* blasted Turner for exaggerating his own power in Newark's black community when he claimed his leadership prevented riots in Newark in 1964, during what turned out to be the first "long, hot summer" of civil unrest. Ralph Matthews, "Who Will Handle Newark's Anti-poverty Funds? An Editorial," *New Jersey Afro-American*, September 16, 1964.

22. Mayor's Commission on Group Relations (later called the Newark Commission on Human Rights), *Newark Points the Way*, undated pamphlet, NPL; and Chairman David M. Litwin's testimony in support of S. 692, US Senate Subcommittee on Civil Rights, Committee on Labor and Public Welfare (March 6, 1954), NPL.

23. Mayor's Commission on Group Relations, *Newark Points the Way*; and "DAD Church Program on Religion and Human Relations," *Human Relations News* 1, no. 4 (February 1957), NPL.

24. Human Relations News 1 (August 1956); and Human Relations News 2 (March 1958).

25. By the mid-1960s activists were criticizing the commission's director Daniel Anthony for his ineffectiveness. Meanwhile, Anthony clashed with the mayor and police when he supported a civilian review board

to address police brutality. Memo, Ad-Hoc Committee for Improving
the Operations of the Newark Commission on Human Rights to Mayor
Hugh J. Addonizio, March 5, 1963, Daniel S. Anthony Papers, container
10, NPL (hereafter DSA Papers). Upon his resignation, Anthony praised
the Barringer protesters for energizing the city's civil rights movement.
"Anthony Resigns Rights Post," *Newark Evening News*, July 14, 1963, 12.

26. Investigation, September 9, 1947, Investigative Files Office Report, box 1,
Urban Colored Population Commission Records, New Jersey Department
of State, Trenton; Lydia Davis Barrett, interview by the author, Montclair,
NJ, April 2005; and *Hearings*, 11, 18.

27. Curvin, interview, 2004. Curvin's Youth Council friends included Wil-
liam Payne and Stanley Aronowitz. Payne, also active in the Newark
Coordinating Committee, later won a seat in the New Jersey State Senate.
Aronowitz became a leader of Students for a Democratic Society and a
radical sociologist. On earlier civil rights protest, see Kevin Mumford,
Newark: A History of Race, Rights, and Riots (New York: New York University
Press, 2007), 45–47.

28. "CORE Leaders Call for Store Boycott," *Newark Sunday News*, September 9,
1962, 16.

29. "2 Protests by CORE: White Castle Diners in Newark, Orange Are Picketed," *Newark Evening News*, July 22, 1963, 5.

30. Ibid.; Curvin, interview, 2004; Robert Curvin, interview by the author,
South Orange, NJ, August 8, 2007; "Police Picketed by Newark CORE,"
New York Times, August 4, 1963, 56; and "Police Brutality and Bias
Charged at Newark Rally," *New York Times*, September 9, 1962, 73.

31. On African American support of Addonizio during his mayoral campaigns, see Luther Carter, "Negroes Demand and Get Voice in Medical
School Plans," *Science*, n.s., 160, no. 3825 (April 19, 1968): 291. A flyer
circulated in the early 1960s called for a "courageous and militant NAACP
Branch in Newark." Identifying four NAACP officials who worked for the
city, the flyer's author claimed that the Addonizio administration had
bought the organization's quiescence for the price of their combined salaries. Undated flier, container 3, DSA Papers. Similar claims were debated in
the *New Jersey Afro-American*; see Lee Johnson, "Inside Newark," *New Jersey
Afro-American*, May 9, 1964.

32. Douglas Eldridge, "Rights Board Finds Bias at School Job," *Newark Evening
News*, July 10, 1963, 14.

33. Curvin, interview, 2007.

34. Curvin, "Persistent Minority."

35. "Carlton B. Norris, City NAACP Head," *Newark Sunday News*, September 8,
1963, C4, sec. 2.

36. Ibid. On municipal officials' interference with NAACP leadership elections, see Curvin, "Persistent Minority," 47–49.

37. Toni-Michelle C. Travis, "The Unfinished Agenda," *PS* (American Political Science Association) 19 (Summer 1986): 610–17.

38. Curvin, "Persistent Minority," 47–49.

39. John L. Dotson, "Some Go to Work," *Newark Evening News*, July 8, 1963, 1.

40. Curvin, interview, 2007.

41. Eldridge, "Rights Board Finds Bias," 14.

42. Harry Burke, "School Officials Meet with Contractors, Stop Work," *Newark Evening News*, July 5, 1963, 1; Harry Burke, "Barringer Pot Boils: Union May Refuse All School Jobs," *Newark Evening News*, July 7, 1963, 1; and John L. Dotson Jr., "Union Men Balk," *Newark Evening News*, July 9, 1963, 1.

43. Burke, "Barringer Pot Boils," 1.

44. Eldridge, "Rights Board Finds Bias," 14.

45. Ibid.

46. "Bias Panel Adds CORE," *Newark Evening News*, July 16, 1963, 1; and Douglas Eldridge, "Truce Called: Barringer Dispute Up to Negotiators," *Newark Evening News*, August 15, 1963, 8.

47. Harry Burke, "Building Trades Reject Demands," *Newark Evening News*, July 24, 1963, 1.

48. Ibid.

49. Bob Shabazian, "Pickets to Return to Barringer Site," *Newark Evening News*, July 25, 1963, 1.

50. "2nd Showdown Due on Barringer Jobs," *Newark Evening News*, July 28, 1963, 6.

51. *U.S. v. United Association of Journeymen*, 1973 U.S. Dist. Lexis 14881.

52. *Hearings*, 59. In Vehling's IBEW Local 52, one-half of the apprentices were the sons of union members, while relatives made up a large portion of the other half. On craft union members' conviction that the employment of relatives and friends constituted a "property right of the working class," see Jill Quadagno, "Social Movements and State Transformation: Labor Unions and Racial Conflict in the War on Poverty," *American Sociological Review* 57, no. 5 (October 1992): 624.

53. "Job Goes On despite Barringer Pickets," *Newark Evening News*, July 29, 1963, 1, 5.

54. "2nd Showdown Due"; and "President of State NAACP to Seek Rights Unity Here," *Newark Evening News*, August 5, 1963, 5.

55. "2nd Showdown Due."

56. US Department of Labor, Bureau of Apprenticeships and Training, "Manpower Requirements and Training Needs in Construction Occupations, 1960–70," December 1959, 3, Reports, 1959, Subject Files of Secretary James P. Mitchell, 1953–1960, NC-58, entry 36, box 334, RG 174 General Records of the Department of Labor (hereafter DOL). In 1959 the construction industry employed 3.8 million people, 3 million of whom were categorized as skilled.

57. Ibid., 4.
58. Ibid.
59. Memorandum to Secretary James P. Mitchell from Millard Cass regarding Proposal of Training through Government's Contracting Authority, April 6, 1960, Boards folder, Subject Files of Secretary James P. Mitchell, 1953–1960, NC-58, entry 36, box 334, RG 174, DOL.
60. Ibid.
61. Ibid.
62. Ibid.
63. Memorandum to Secretary and Undersecretary from the Director of the Bureau of Apprenticeships and Training regarding "How BAT's and Training Promotion Strengthens Apprenticeships," September 1, 1960, Boards folder, Subject Files of Secretary James P. Mitchell, 1953–1960, NC-58, entry 36, box 334, RG 174, DOL.
64. Memorandum to Undersecretary O'Connell from Newell Brown regarding NAACP Report, March 16, 1960, National Industry Promotion, 1960, Subject Files of Secretary James P. Mitchell, 1953–1960, NC-58, entry 36, box 334, RG 174, DOL.
65. Ibid.
66. N. Snyder, "Nondiscrimination in Apprenticeship and Training, the Regulations and Their Effect," National Industry Promotion, January 1–February 16, 1967, Records of Secretary of Labor W. Willard Wirtz, 1962–1969, box 456, AT2–1, RG 174, DOL.
67. Alfred W. Blumrosen, *Black Employment and the Law* (New Brunswick, NJ: Rutgers University Press, 1971), 232–33; and *Hearings*, 59.
68. John L. Dotson, "Job Picketing Will Resume at Barringer," *Newark Evening News*, August 13, 1963, 10.
69. Harry Burke, "Building Unions Refuse Job Data Asked by Pfaus," *Newark Evening News*, August 9, 1963, 7; "Pledge to End Job Bias," *Newark Evening News*, August 9, 1963, 7; and Harry Burke, "Chief Asks Joint Rights Unit," *Newark Evening News*, September 17, 1963, 18.
70. Douglas Eldridge, "Truce Called: Barringer Dispute Up to Negotiators," *Newark Evening News*, August 15, 1963, 8.
71. Douglas Eldridge, "Negro Groups Seen Gaining in Projects to Get Jobs," *Newark Evening News*, August 18, 1963, 12.
72. Ibid.
73. Francis Warren, interview by the author, Philadelphia, PA, March 21, 2006.
74. Ibid.
75. Guian McKee, *The Problem of Jobs: Liberalism, Race and Deindustrialization in Philadelphia* (Chicago: University of Chicago Press, 2008), 120.
76. Douglas Eldridge, "Attack on Job Bias Shows Some Gains," *Newark Evening News*, September 17, 1963, 1; and "Job Rights Group Bids Others Join,"

Newark Evening News, September 20, 1963, 2. Twenty-two businesses had identified 125 vacancies, for which 41 black workers were hired.

77. On equal employment policies before affirmative action, see Stacy Kinlock Sewell, "'The Best Man for the Job': Corporate Responsibility and Racial Integration in the Workplace, 1945–1960," *Historian* 65, no. 5 (2003): 1125–46.

78. Plans for Progress Blue Program biographies, Plans for Progress folder, box 8, entry 4, Office of Chairman, Stephen Shulman (1966–1968), Records of the Equal Employment Opportunity Commission (EEOC), National Archives and Records Administration, College Park, MD (hereafter NARA). State officials identified the BICC as a model for other cities. "Committee Report on Building Trades, Printing Trades, and Other 'Closed Shop' Industries," Employment Committee, Bi-partisan Conference on Civil Rights, Apprenticeship Training folder 3, box 4, Thompson Papers.

79. Curvin, interview, 2007. At the time, CORE was negotiating with Pabst, Charles Bessler Company, Public Service, RCA, Tung Sol, and Western Electric. Notes of meeting with New Jersey Bell Telephone, February 12, 1964; "Agreement reached with A&P," December 15, 1963 (sets goal of hiring two hundred black and Puerto Rican clerks from Newark in 1964); and "CORE Employment Committee Projects and Personnel," September 1, 1963. All from private papers of Robert Curvin (hereafter Curvin Papers).

80. CORE activists reported that Bell Telephone executives seemed to expect CORE to fulfill the employment agency functions of the Urban League. Notes of meeting with New Jersey Bell Telephone, February 12, 1964, Curvin Papers.

81. Ibid.

82. "Addonizio Voices Hope for Pact on Negro Jobs," *Newark Evening News*, August 27, 1963, 12; and "Board Acts on Job Bias," *Newark Evening News*, August 28, 1963, 8.

83. Douglas Eldridge, "Rights Unit Study Essex Job Pact," *Newark Evening News*, September 1, 1963, 7.

84. The exact number of minority workers employed as a result of the Barringer protest is difficult to ascertain. Of the forty-two job seekers the Newark Coordinating Committee referred, only one, an electrician, was actually employed through the unions. "Addonizio Voices Hope." The Newark Board of Education had immediately responded to the protest by requiring unions to dispatch integrated crews to all school jobs (including Barringer), but this policy yielded only five African American hires—three painters, one carpenter, and one laborer. "5 Negroes Hired for School Jobs," *Newark Evening News*, August 9, 1963, 1.

85. Bruce Bahrenburg, "Elizabeth Plan, Hughes Tells Job Bias Pact," *Newark Evening News*, September 19, 1963, 1–2.

86. Ibid.

87. Ernest Thompson and Mindy Thompson, *Homeboy Came to Orange: A Story of People's Power* (Newark, NJ: Bridgebuilder Press, 1976), 158.

88. Rebecca Doggett, interview by the author, Newark, NJ, April 7, 2005.

89. "A Report on the Current Status of the Negotiations between the Greater Newark Coordinating Council and Rutgers University and Newark College of Engineering," folder 3, Apprentice Training, box 4, Thompson Papers.

90. Thompson and Thompson, *Homeboy Came to Orange*, 159.

91. In May 1964 Rutgers University announced that contractors must submit information on the composition of their workforce before construction could begin. "Contractors Asked to Give Racial Forecast for Project," *New York Times*, May 5, 1964, 37.

92. Thompson and Thompson, *Homeboy Came to Orange*, 159.

93. "Rutgers to Crack Down on Unions," *New Jersey Afro-American*, February 6, 1965.

94. "Hail Jersey Gov's Racial Bias Search," *Amsterdam News*, February 6, 1965, 24.

95. "Rights Groups Plan for New Rutgers Job Demonstrations," *Newark Evening News*, October 7, 1965; Thompson and Thompson, *Homeboy Came to Orange*, 165; and Ernest Thompson to NAACP Executive Board, October 1965, folder 9, box 4, Thompson Papers.

96. *Hearings*, 382–416; and Cohen, *Consumers' Republic*, 241–51.

97. Doggett, interview; notes of meeting with New Jersey Bell Telephone, February 12, 1964, Curvin Papers; and undated Newark Coordinating Committee "white paper" on Rutgers Law School and Newark College of Engineering campaigns, Curvin Papers.

98. "Rights Groups Plan for New Rutgers Job Demonstrations."

99. "Danzig Tells Rights Groups, Keep Up Bid for Building Jobs," *Newark Evening News*, October 15, 1965.

100. Thompson and Thompson, *Homeboy Came to Orange*, 165.

101. The overlap between the Newark Coordinating Committee's labor activism and black political challenges can be seen in "Report of Committee for Negro Progress," May 17, 1966, folder 6, box 4, Thompson Papers.

102. Bayard Rustin, "From Protest to Politics: The Future of the Civil Right Movement," *Commentary*, February 1, 1965, http://www.commentarymagazine.com/article/from-protest-to-politics-the-future-of-the-civil-rights-movement/ (accessed April 2, 2014).

103. Ibid., pt. I.

104. Ibid., pt. III.

105. Ibid.

CHAPTER 2

1.   Annelise Orleck and Liza Gayle Hazirjian, *The War on Poverty: A New Grassroots History, 1964–1980* (Athens: University of Georgia Press, 2011), 11.

2. Leila Meier Rice, "In the Trenches of the War on Poverty: The Local Implementation of the Community Action Program, 1964–1969" (PhD diss., Vanderbilt University, 1997), 13. Rice distinguishes between two prevalent models of community action: the mayoral co-optation category, into which the vast majority of cities fit, and the insurgent control model category, which claimed far fewer, including Newark.

3. Michael L. Gillette, *Launching the War on Poverty: An Oral History*, 2nd ed. (New York: Oxford University Press, 2010), 249. Scholars have highlighted the attacks on community action programs for allegedly fomenting unrest during the 1967 uprising, but my chapter demonstrates that the groundwork for dismantling—or at least containing—Newark's War on Poverty was established well before then. See Rice, "In the Trenches of the War on Poverty"; Michael Parenti, "Power and Pluralism: A View from the Bottom," *Journal of Politics* 32, no. 3 (August 1970): 501–30; Jill Quadagno, *The Color of Welfare: How Racism Undermined the War on Poverty* (New York: Oxford University Press, 1994); Jennifer Frost, *An Interracial Movement of the Poor: Community Organizing and the New Left in the 1960s* (New York: New York University Press, 2001); and *America's War on Poverty: City of Promise*, directed by Susan Bellows, executive producer Harry Hampton (PBS Video, Blackside Inc., 1995).

4. Scholars of Newark's War on Poverty have relied heavily on Office of Economic Opportunity records. This chapter draws on those records too but also incorporates sources that have not received much scholarly attention, including Cyril DeGrasse Tyson, *Two Years before the Riot! Newark, New Jersey, and the United Community Corporation, 1964–1966* (New York: Jay Street Publishers, 2000). This is a massive compendium of newspaper articles, correspondence, and memos generated by the UCC during Tyson's brief tenure as its first executive director. Tyson intersperses documents reproduced in their entirety with his own recollections and interpretations of the early struggle for the UCC. I also used the papers of Douglas Eldridge, a reporter for the *Newark Evening News* who covered the UCC. His papers became available at the Newark Public Library while I was researching this book. They contain meeting notes, organizational fliers and publications, transcripts, and drafts of the city council investigation of the UCC.

5. Junius Williams, interview by the author, Newark, NJ, November 30, 2004.

6. Tyson, *Two Years before the Riot!*, 256, 490–91. Community economic development politics of the 1970s reflected Tyson's critique. See Stewart E. Perry, "National Policy and the Community Development Corporation," *Law and Contemporary Problems* 36, no. 2 (Spring 1971): 301.

7. Donald Malafronte quoted in *America's War on Poverty: City of Promise*.

8. Susan Youngblood Ashmore, *Carry It On: The War on Poverty and the Civil Rights Movement in Alabama, 1964–1972* (Athens: University of Georgia Press, 2008), 21.

9.   Early histories of the War on Poverty portrayed it as a flawed, even peril-
     ously counterproductive, experiment. Commentators from across the
     political spectrum also contrasted the legislation's lofty promises with its
     modest accomplishments and prolific failures. See Daniel Patrick Moyni-
     han, *Maximum Feasible Misunderstanding: Community Action in the War
     on Poverty* (New York: Free Press, 1969). Later analyses delved into the
     ironies and inconsistencies of the War on Poverty from the vantage point
     of Reagan's America and the decline of midcentury liberalism. See Peter
     Maris and Marin Rein, *Dilemmas of Social Reform: Poverty and Community
     Action in the United States* (Chicago: University of Chicago Press, 1982); and
     Allen J. Matusow, *The Unraveling of America: A History of Liberalism in the
     1960s* (1982; Athens: University of Georgia Press, 2009). Other scholarship
     emerged amid calls for welfare reform and depicted the fate of the War on
     Poverty within a well-established pattern of backlash against direct aid to
     the poor. Popular right-leaning criticism of the War on Poverty surged af-
     ter the 1992 Los Angeles riot refocused national attention on poverty and
     underemployment in a presidential election year. Critics blamed the his-
     toric legislation for abetting the "feminization of poverty," contributing to
     urban crime rates, and embracing a systemic explanation for poverty and
     delinquency that excused moral laxity. For more on these dynamics, see
     Quadagno, *Color of Welfare*; Michael Brown, *Race, Money, and the American
     Welfare State* (Ithaca, NY: Cornell University Press, 1999); Michael Katz,
     The Undeserving Poor: From the War on Poverty to the War on Welfare (New
     York: Pantheon Books, 1989); and Michael B. Katz, ed., *The "Underclass"
     Debate: Views from History* (Princeton, NJ: Princeton University Press,
     1992). Recent scholarship diverges from national synthesis and pays more
     attention to local variation. What Robert Bauman calls a "long history"
     interpretation of the War on Poverty positions community action agencies
     as a bridge among multiple social movements and a foundation for some
     institutions that endured beyond the 1960s. Robert Bauman, *Race and the
     War on Poverty from Watts to East L.A.* (Norman: University of Oklahoma
     Press, 2008). In addition, see Orleck and Hazirjian, *War on Poverty*; Ash-
     more, *Carry It On*; Kent B. Germany, *New Orleans after the Promises: Poverty,
     Citizenship, and the Search for the Great Society* (Athens: University of Geor-
     gia Press, 2007); Steven Gregory, *Black Corona: Race and Politics of Place in
     an Urban Community* (Princeton, NJ: Princeton University Press, 1998);
     Matthew J. Countryman, *Up South: Civil Rights and Black Power in Phila-
     delphia* (Philadelphia: University of Pennsylvania Press, 2007), 258–327;
     Frost, *Interracial Movement of the Poor*; Annelise Orleck, *Storming Caesar's
     Palace: How Black Mothers Fought Their Own War on Poverty* (Boston: Beacon
     Press, 2005); and Wendell Pritchett, *Brownsville, Brooklyn: Blacks, Jews,
     and the Changing Face of the Ghetto* (Chicago: University of Chicago Press,
     2002).

10. Joseph A. Califano Jr., *The Triumph and Tragedy of Lyndon Johnson* (New York: Simon and Schuster, 1991), 86–92; and Michael Harrington, *The Other America* (New York: Macmillan, 1962).

11. Alice O'Connor untangles the social theories undergirding maximum feasible participation, including the notion of "community competence" advanced by sociologist Leonard S. Cottrell in studies of troubled families. Cottrell argued that participation itself constituted a kind of therapy, mitigating social disorganization and equipping families with problem-solving skills. Alice O'Connor, *Poverty Knowledge: Social Science, Social Policy, and the Poor in Twentieth-Century U.S. History* (Princeton, NJ: Princeton University Press, 2001), 126–27.

12. Moynihan, *Maximum Feasible Misunderstanding*, 87; and Ashmore, *Carry It On*, 18–20.

13. Califano, *Triumph and Tragedy of Lyndon Johnson*, 75.

14. Matusow, *Unraveling of America*, 239–40. Dozens of constituents' letters written to Johnson castigated him for his emphasis on job training. They argued that the only real solution to poverty was employment and counseled him to revive public works. Few writers perceived value in community action or considered the new social services created by the legislation, perhaps its most significant—and sustainable—jobs program, as work. Letters file, General Records Relating to Public Reaction to OEO Programs, 1967–1971, Inspection Division, Office of Economic Opportunity and Legal Services, RG 381, National Archives and Records Administration (hereafter NARA).

15. Califano, *Triumph and Tragedy of Lyndon Johnson*, 11.

16. Irving Bernstein, *Guns or Butter: The Presidency of Lyndon Johnson* (Oxford: Oxford University Press, 1996), 95–97, 542.

17. Ashmore, *Carry It On*, 26.

18. *America's War on Poverty: City of Promise.*

19. Alice O'Connor (*Poverty Knowledge*, 125) traces community action back to the Chicago School and practices of the early twentieth-century settlement house.

20. Layli Phillips, "Recontextualizing Kenneth B. Clark: An Afrocentric Perspective on the Paradoxical Legacy of a Model Psychologist-Activist," *History of Psychology* 3, no. 2 (2000): 142–67; and Ben Keppel, *The Work of Democracy: Ralph Bunche, Kenneth B. Clark, Lorraine Hansberry, and the Cultural Politics of Race* (Cambridge, MA: Harvard University Press, 2015), 97–132.

21. Cyril DeGrasse Tyson, *Power and Politics in Central Harlem, 1962–1964: The HARYOU Experience* (New York: Jay Street Publishers, 2004), xii, 208, 326.

22. Ibid., xii; and Phillips, "Recontextualizing Kenneth B. Clark," 161.

23. See Richard A. Cloward and Lloyd E. Ohlin, *Delinquency and Opportunity: A Theory of Delinquent Gangs* (New York: Free Press, 1960).

24. Mitchell Sviridoff, ed., *Inventing Community Renewal: The Trials and Errors That Shaped the Modern Community Development Corporation* (New York: New School University, Milano Graduate School, Community Development Research Center, 2004), 117–18.

25. Ibid.

26. This theory departed significantly from prevailing assumptions about delinquency. Victoria Wolcott shows that authorities categorized fights among black and white teenagers in Buffalo, New York, as delinquency to either minimize youth violence as mere immaturity or to pathologize black youth. Both explanations obscured the role of residential segregation and discrimination in fueling conflict. Victoria Wolcott, *Race, Riots, and Roller Coasters: The Struggle over Segregated Recreation in America* (Philadelphia: University of Pennsylvania Press, 2012), 125–57.

27. Tyson, *Power and Politics*, x, 353; and "Youth in the Ghetto and the Blueprint for Change," *Harlem Youth Report* 5 (1964).

28. Sviridoff, *Inventing Community Renewal*, 117. Mobilization for Youth's rent strikes and school boycotts led to complaints that it fomented diversionary rebellion against some of the institutions—schools and social service agencies—best situated to help impoverished youth. Keppel, *Work of Democracy*, 133–76.

29. Kimberly Johnson, "Community Development Organizations, Participation, and Accountability: The Harlem Urban Development Corporation and the Bedford-Stuyvesant Restoration Corporation," *Annals: Journal of the American Academy of Political and Social Science* 594 (July 2004): 109–24.

30. Sviridoff, *Inventing Community Renewal*, 118–19; and Charles V. Hamilton, *Adam Clayton Powell, Jr.: The Political Biography of an American Dilemma* (New York: Atheneum, 1991), 426–27.

31. Tyson, *Two Years before the Riot!*, 30–37.

32. This statistic was based on the new poverty level, devised in 1964. On its development, see Katz, *Undeserving Poor*, 115; and O'Connor, *Poverty Knowledge*, 166–95. The actual proportion of poor residents in the state approached 14–17 percent, if it accounted for those who earned an annual income of only slightly more than $3,000 for a family of four. J. Hooper, "12% Called Poor: N.J. Figure Based on LBJ Criteria," *Newark Sunday News*, January 12, 1964.

33. Rice, "In the Trenches of the War on Poverty," 183; Robert Curvin, "The Persistent Minority: The Black Political Experience in Newark" (PhD diss., Princeton University, 1975), 3; and Hooper, "12% Called Poor."

34. Bernstein, *Guns or Butter*, 97.

35. Tyson, *Two Years before the Riot!*, 17–19, 24–25.

36. Rice, "In the Trenches of the War on Poverty," 185; and Robert Curvin, interview by the author, Newark, NJ, September 16, 2004.

37. Rice, "In the Trenches of the War on Poverty," 187.

38. Matusow, *Unraveling of America*, 255.

39. Quadagno, *Color of Welfare*, 53.

40. Rice, "In the Trenches of the War on Poverty," 135.

41. Quadagno, *Color of Welfare*, 53–56; and Orleck and Hazirjian, *War on Poverty*, 17.

42. Moynihan, *Maximum Feasible Misunderstanding*, 87.

43. United Community Corporation Executive Committee meeting minutes, May 17, 1965, folder 16, Douglas Eldridge Papers, Newark Public Library (hereafter Eldridge Papers); Elaine Helbein, "Head Starters Start Happily," *Newark Evening News*, July 11, 1967, 7; and Rice, "In the Trenches of the War on Poverty," 191.

44. Rice, "In the Trenches of the War on Poverty," 193.

45. Correspondence, Angel Torres, Samuel Arroyo, Hilda Hidalgo, and Luis Morales of the Council of Puerto Rican Organizations to the UCC Board, May 14, 1965, folder 16, Eldridge Papers.

46. Douglas Eldridge, "Self-Help Co-op Cuts Costs," *Newark Evening News*, July 5, 1967, 22.

47. Tyson, *Two Years before the Riot!*, 125–34, 146–47; and Rice, "In the Trenches of the War on Poverty," 187–88.

48. "What Constitutes Representation of the Poor?," *New Jersey Community Action Newsletter* (September–October 1965), Legal Services, Inspection Division, Office of Economic Opportunity, RG 381, NARA; and United Community Corporation, memo to Board of Trustees from Education Task Force, March 17, 1966, Eldridge Papers.

49. On the SDS, see Frost, *Interracial Movement of the Poor*; David Gerwin, "The End of Coalition: The Failure of Community Organizing in Newark in the 1960s" (PhD diss., Columbia University, 1998); and Rice, "In the Trenches of the War on Poverty," 185.

50. On the goals of those involved, see Gerwin, "End of Coalition," 34–82.

51. Komozi Woodard, interview by the author, Yonkers, NY, June 9, 2004; Williams, interview; and Frost, *Interracial Movement of the Poor*, 12–20.

52. Gerwin, "End of Coalition," 27.

53. On the role of the UAW in the founding of the SDS, see Peter B. Levy, *New Left and Labor in the 1960s* (Urbana: University of Illinois Press, 1994).

54. Rice, "In the Trenches of the War on Poverty," 192–94.

55. Gerwin, "End of Coalition," 117; and Pritchett, *Brownsville, Brooklyn*, 194. ERAP advanced this comparison on the basis of the local organizing that the Mississippi Freedom Democratic Party had accomplished in the state prior to its defeat at the Democratic National Convention in August 1964. For more on the Mississippi Freedom Democratic Party, see John Dittmer, *Local People: The Struggle for Civil Rights in Mississippi* (Urbana: University of Illinois Press, 1995), 242–302.

56. Gerwin, "End of Coalition," 75–78.

57. Ibid., 129.

58. Tyson, *Two Years before the Riot!*, 335–36; and Gerwin, "End of Coalition," 154–55.
59. Rice, "In the Trenches of the War on Poverty," 188.
60. Gerwin, "End of Coalition," 164.
61. Ibid., 165.
62. Ibid., 166–67.
63. Tyson, *Two Years before the Riot!*, 383.
64. Ibid., 388, 391, 529.
65. Douglas Eldridge, "Weequahic Area Board," *Newark Evening News*, December 16, 1965.
66. Ibid.; Douglas Eldridge, "City Bars Funds, Demands Anti-poverty Group's Data," *Newark Evening News*, October 7, 1965; and United Community Corporation Executive Committee meeting notes, December 15, 1965, Eldridge Papers.
67. United Community Corporation Executive Committee meeting notes, December 15, 1965, Eldridge Papers; Gerwin, "End of Coalition," 65–75; Lizabeth Cohen, *A Consumers' Republic: The Politics of Mass Consumption in Postwar America* (New York: Alfred A. Knopf, 2003), 220.
68. Tyson, *Two Years before the Riot!*, 392.
69. Moynihan, *Maximum Feasible Misunderstanding*, 150.
70. *America's War on Poverty: City of Promise.*
71. Dittmer, *Local People: The Struggle for Civil Rights in Mississippi*, chaps. 2–3; and Charles Payne, *I've Got the Light of Freedom: The Organizing Tradition and the Mississippi Freedom Struggle* (Berkeley: University of California Press, 1995), 19–69.
72. Marjorie Hunter, "Patronage 'Fiesta' in Poverty Attack Charged by Powell," *New York Times*, April 12, 1965.
73. Tyson, *Two Years before the Riot!*, 104.
74. Douglas Eldridge, "City Bars Funds," 1; Bob Shabazian, "UCC Giving Data to City," *Newark Evening News*, October 8, 1965, 1; and Tyson, *Two Years before the Riot!*, 304–5.
75. Hamilton, *Adam Clayton Powell, Jr.*, 369–406, 452–55.
76. Nick Kostopulos to William Haddad and Robert Clampitt, memorandum concerning New Jersey Office of Economic Opportunity, CAP, New Jersey, General—Newark, Essex County folder, Inspection Reports 1964–67, Inspection Division, Office of Economic Opportunity and Legal Services, RG 381, NARA; and Warren Weaver, "New Jersey G.O.P. Told to Act with Care," *New York Times*, February 7, 1965.
77. Tyson, *Two Years before the Riot!*, 338.
78. "Poverty Unit Probe Gains Turner, Joins Criticism of Hiring of Out of Towners," *Newark Evening News*, October 10, 1965, 43.
79. "Baptist Editor Hits City Poverty Plan," *New Jersey Afro-American*, December 12, 1964.

80. Nick Kostopulos to William Haddad and Robert Clampitt (see n. 76 above). Letters from the public to the OEO supported Kostopulos's warnings about salaries. See Letters file, General Records Relating to Public Reaction to OEO Programs, 1967–1971, Inspection Division, Office of Economic Opportunity and Legal Services, RG 381, NARA.

81. In its first year of operation, the UCC required matching funds equal to 10 percent of its budget, around $200,000. Lawrence O. Houston Jr. of New Jersey Office of Economic Opportunity to Richard W. Boone, Director of Program Policy at Office of Economic Opportunity, April 26, 1965, "New Jersey" folder, Inspection Reports 1964–67, Inspection Division, Office of Economic Opportunity and Legal Services, RG 381, NARA; and Tyson, *Two Years before the Riot!*, 342, 569.

82. Tyson, *Two Years before the Riot!*, 305–36, 348–49.

83. "Statement of United Community Corporation," undated, folder 11, Eldridge Papers, 37–38. In *Roe v. Kervick*, 42 N.J. 191 (1964), the court rejected a claim that the New Jersey Constitution prohibited the contribution of state funds to area redevelopment agencies. *Simon v. O'Toole*, 108 N.J. 32 (1932), offered an earlier precedent in support of the UCC: Newark had subsidized housing developed by Prudential Insurance Company on the grounds that it would ameliorate overcrowding.

84. Ashmore, *Carry It On*, 8.

85. Newark City Council, "The Report of the Council Committee to Study the Anti-poverty Program for the City of Newark, New Jersey," December 1965, Eldridge Papers, 8. As Andrew Morris argued, New Deal policymakers initially "repudiated the subsidy of private institutions, seeing them as a conservative effort to forestall the development of a public welfare system." Private agencies focused on professionalization and specialized services after the New Deal, but by the early 1960s, competition for funding, new theories of addressing poverty, and extensive public criticism of social service agencies prompted a reconsideration of their relationship to government. Andrew Morris, "The Voluntary Sector's War on Poverty," *Journal of Policy History* 14, no. 4 (2004): 279–85.

86. Newark City Council, "Report of the Council Committee to Study the Anti-poverty Program."

87. "Statement of United Community Corporation," 28–31.

88. Newark City Council, "Report of the Council Committee to Study the Anti-poverty Program," 1–2.

89. Tyson, *Two Years before the Riot!*, 338–49.

90. Newark City Council, "Report of the Council Committee to Study the Anti-poverty Program," 2.

91. Ibid., 9.

92. Ibid., 3.

93. Douglas Eldridge, "New Jersey One of Biggest Poverty War Areas," *Newark Sunday News*, December 5, 1965, 1.

94. Douglas Eldridge, "Jersey's Poverty Programs Praised by Federal Officials," *Newark Evening News*, November 9, 1965; and Rice, "In the Trenches in the War on Poverty," 188–90. The OEO also praised job training programs, the Blazer Youth Council, Career Oriented Preparation for Employment (COPE), a summer recreation program run with the Police Athletic League, Legal Services clinics that served nearly two thousand, and the Preschool Council's Headstart program.

95. "Shriver Defends OEO," *New York Times*, November 5, 1965; and Joseph A. Loftus, "Democrats Alter Plan on Poverty," *New York Times*, August 28, 1966, 1.

96. Fred Powledge, "Newark Aides Seek Antipoverty Role," *New York Times*, November 1, 1965, 1.

97. Newsletter, September–October 1965, Office of John C. Bullitt, Inspection Division, Office of Economic Opportunity and Legal Services, RG 381, NARA.

98. Califano, *Triumph and Tragedy of Lyndon Johnson*, 69.

99. Robert Dallek, *Flawed Giant, Lyndon Johnson and His Times, 1961–1973* (New York: Oxford University Press, 1998), 330–31.

100. Califano, *Triumph and Tragedy of Lyndon Johnson*, 78–80.

101. Orleck and Hazirjian, *War on Poverty*, 15.

102. Tyson, *Two Years before the Riot!*, 353.

103. [Rabbi] Jonathan J. Prinz, letter to the editor, "Warring on Poverty," *New York Times*, November 14, 1965, E11.

104. Powledge, "Newark Aides Seek Antipoverty Role," 1.

105. Tyson, *Two Years before the Riot!*, 359.

106. "Summary Report of the Investigative Task Force of the Ad Hoc Subcommittee on the War on Poverty Program," 1966, Shriver/Powell letters file, Inspection Division, Office of Economic Opportunity and Legal Services, RG 381, NARA.

107. Walter H. Waggoner, "Newark Stirred over Poverty Aid," *New York Times*, December 12, 1965, 81.

108. "Statement of United Community Corporation," 3–5.

109. Ibid., 28–29; "Poverty Probe Set," *Newark Evening News*, October 27, 1965, 18.

110. Waggoner, "Newark Stirred"; and Walter H. Waggoner, "Newark Dispute on Poor Resumes," *New York Times*, December 24, 1965, 42.

111. Wilbur Cohen, "Discussion," in *The Presidency and the Congress*, ed. William S. Livingston, Lawrence Dodd, and Richard Schott (Austin: University of Texas Press, 1979), 300–301.

112. Tyson, *Two Years before the Riot!*, 623–33, 637–38, 645. "The tactic of charging and investigating local antipoverty agencies for fraud would be used again and again to defund successful grassroots antipoverty programs" (Orleck and Hazirjian, *War on Poverty*, 16).

113. Rice, "In the Trenches in the War on Poverty," 187–92.

114. Quadagno, *Color of Welfare*, 66–67. Subsequent investigation of OEO programs revealed that established city agencies—not new community

action programs—more commonly violated the spirit of the antipoverty program by hiring city workers instead of the unemployed for extra summer positions.

115. Tyson, *Two Years before the Riot!*, 621.
116. Powledge, "Newark Officials Ask Role in Antipoverty Program."
117. Tyson, *Two Years before the Riot!*, 517.
118. "UCC Meeting," *Newark Evening News*, October, 26, 1965.
119. "Statement of United Community Corporation," 41; and Tyson, *Two Years before the Riot!*, 527.
120. Tyson, *Two Years before the Riot!*, 524; and Rice, "In the Trenches in the War on Poverty," 203.
121. Governor's Select Commission on Civil Disorder, *Report for Action* (Trenton: State of New Jersey, 1968), 90.
122. Quadagno, *Color of Welfare*, 48–52; and Moynihan, *Maximum Feasible Misunderstanding*, 156.
123. Governor's Select Commission on Civil Disorder, *Report for Action*, 88.
124. Ibid., 46.
125. Ibid., 92.
126. *America's War on Poverty: City of Promise.*
127. Gregory, *Black Corona*, 139–78.
128. Matusow, *Unraveling of America*, 232.
129. Louis O. Kelso and Patricia Hetter, "Equality of Economic Opportunity through Capital Ownership," in *Black Business Enterprise: Historical and Contemporary Perspectives*, ed. Ronald W. Bailey (New York: Basic Books, 1971), 233.
130. Matusow, *Unraveling of America*, 256; and Barbara Cruikshank, *The Will to Empower: Democratic Citizens and Other Subjects* (Ithaca, NY: Cornell University Press, 1999), 82–86.
131. Governor's Select Commission on Civil Disorder, *Report for Action*, 92.
132. The first quotation is from Jack Walker, and the second is from Mary Smith, in *America's War on Poverty: City of Promise.*
133. Governor's Select Commission on Civil Disorder, *Report for Action*, 89.
134. Orleck and Hazirjian, *War on Poverty*, 12.
135. Curvin, "Persistent Minority," 59.
136. "Organizations Win in Newark Wards," *Newark Evening News*, April 22, 1964.
137. Parenti, "Power and Pluralism," 514. For Parenti, Newark voters' failed challenge to entrenched Democratic Party candidates and the impediments to meaningful black representation exposed the inadequacy of pluralism as a prevailing explanation of political conflict in US cities.
138. Ibid., 513–16.
139. Rice argues that Wolfe lacked Tyson's skill at balancing a "middle-class orientation" with a palpable commitment to maximum feasible participation of the poor ("In the Trenches in the War on Poverty," 204–5).

140. Germany, *New Orleans after the Promises*, 8–9.
141. Morris, "Voluntary Sector's War on Poverty," 275.
142. Ibid., 299.
143. Cruikshank, *Will to Empower*, 68, 71.
144. Rhonda Y. Williams argues that the contest over community action in Baltimore produced "wariness and weariness," prompting "some poor people to abandon or avoid government-generated antipoverty programs." Rhonda Y. Williams, "'To Challenge the Status Quo by Any Means': Community Action and Representational Politics in 1960s Baltimore," in Orleck and Hazirjian, *War on Poverty*, 77.

CHAPTER 3

1. Press release, May 25, 1958, MSS 562, box 3, folder 27, Wisconsin State Historical Society, Madison; and Ashley A. Foard and Hübert Fefferman, "Federal Urban Renewal Legislation," 120–23, and Harold Kaplan, "Urban Renewal in Newark," 242–46, both in *Urban Renewal: The Record and the Controversy*, ed. James Q. Wilson (Cambridge, MA: MIT Press, 1966).
2. Leo P. Carlin, "Program for America's City," National ACTION Conference, May 4, 1959, MSS 562, box 3, folder 28, Wisconsin State Historical Society, Madison.
3. Press release, May 25, 1958.
4. Carlin, "Program for America's City."
5. Stanley B. Winters, "Turbulent Decade: Newark since the Riots," in *From Riot to Recovery: Newark after Ten Years*, ed. Stanley B. Winters (Lanham, MD: University Press of America, 1979), 1.
6. Junius Williams, interview by the author, Newark, NJ, September 14, 2006.
7. Michael Lipsky and David J. Olson, *Commission Politics: The Processing of Racial Crisis in America* (New Brunswick, NJ: Transaction Books, 1977), 19–20.
8. Early studies grounded in firsthand accounts identify the Newark uprising's immediate causes, debate the decisions made by authorities, and parse activists' involvement. Recent scholarship informed by cultural studies broadens the interpretative frame: Lizabeth Cohen has argued that the uprising was in part a consumer riot, both a revolt against and attempt to join the ranks of middle-class consumers whose patronage of malls in largely segregated suburbs had contributed to the decline of Newark's business districts. Lizabeth Cohen, *A Consumers' Republic: The Politics of Mass Consumption in Postwar America* (New York: Alfred A. Knopf, 2003), 356–79. Kevin Mumford has examined the gendered dimensions of looting and the disparaging depictions of black femininity reinforced in media narratives. Kevin Mumford, *Newark: A History of Race, Rights, and Riots* (New York: New York University Press, 2007), 125–69.

9. Bayard Rustin, "From Protest to Politics: The Future of the Civil Right Movement," *Commentary*, February 1, 1965, http://www .commentarymagazine.com/article/from-protest-to-politics-the-future-of -the-civil-rights-movement/ (accessed April 2, 2014).

10. "Survey Cuts Value of Property in City," *Newark Evening News*, February 9, 1958.

11. "Newark Taxes Top Other Jersey Cities," *Newark Evening News*, February 15, 1958; and "10 West Essex Towns Weigh Tax Strike against County," *Newark Evening News*, February 18, 1958.

12. Carlin was elected following a reform of Newark's municipal government that produced a mayor and city council structure. See John E. Bebout and Ronald J. Grele, *Where Cities Meet: The Urbanization of New Jersey* (Princeton, NJ: D. Van Nostrand, 1964), 69; and John T. Cunningham, *Newark* (Newark: New Jersey Historical Society, 1988), 306–7. On the reform's impact on black and Left political prospects, see Robert Curvin, *Inside Newark: Decline, Rebellion, and the Search for Transformation* (New Brunswick, NJ: Rutgers University Press, 2014), 49–58. For examples of what Carlin hoped to accomplish with the Newark Economic Development Committee, see Guian McKee, *The Problem of Jobs: Liberalism, Race, and Deindustrialization in Philadelphia* (Chicago: University of Chicago Press, 2008), 81–82.

13. Elihu Rubin, *Insuring the City: The Prudential Center and the Postwar Urban Landscape* (New Haven, CT: Yale University Press, 2012), 40–41; "Westinghouse Keeps Faith in Newark, Will Stay," *Newark Evening News*, March 18, 1958; Richard O. Schafer, "City's Civic Leaders Jubilant over Port Build Up Plan," *Newark Evening News*, April 3, 1958; Charles Sullivan, "Start Plans for a New Barringer," *Newark Evening News*, May 9, 1958; and Cunningham, *Newark*, 309.

14. Carlin, "Program for America's City."

15. Jon Teaford, *The Rough Road to Renaissance: Urban Revitalization in America, 1940–1985* (Baltimore: Johns Hopkins University Press, 1990), 27–67.

16. Howard Gillette Jr., "Review Essay: Urban Renewal Revisited," *Journal of Urban History* 33 (September 2007): 342–50.

17. City officials insisted that urban renewal would foster more harmonious race relations as the city's demographics changed. Mayor's Commission on Group Relations, *Newark: A City in Transition*, vol. 1, *The Characteristics of a Population* (Newark, 1959), Charles F. Cummings New Jersey Information Center, Newark Public Library (hereafter NPL). On urban renewal's relation to suburbanization and racial discrimination, see Howard Gillette Jr., *Between Justice and Beauty: Race, Planning and the Failure of Urban Policy in Washington, D.C.* (Baltimore: Johns Hopkins University Press, 1995); Arnold R. Hirsch, *Making the Second Ghetto: Race and Housing in Chicago, 1940–1960* (Cambridge: Cambridge University Press, 1983); Mandi Isaacs Jackson, *Model City Blues: Urban Space and Organized Resistance in New*

Haven (Philadelphia: Temple University Press, 2008); Kenneth Jackson, *Crabgrass Frontier: The Suburbanization of the United States* (New York: Oxford University Press, 1987); and John T. McGreevy, *Parish Boundaries: The Catholic Encounter with Race in the Twentieth-Century Urban North* (Chicago: University of Chicago Press, 1996), 111–32.

18. Charles Zerner, "Big Newark Slum to Be Housing Site," *New York Times,* June 14, 1952, 17.
19. Michael Immerso, *Newark's Little Italy: The Vanished First Ward* (New Brunswick, NJ: Rutgers University Press, 1997), 152.
20. Ibid., 140.
21. Transcript of *Caucus: NJ,* "Newark's Little Italy: The Vanished First Ward," http://www.caucusnj.org/caucusnj/special_series/little_italy.asp.
22. Immerso, *Newark's Little Italy,* 94, 153.
23. Nathan Wright Jr., *Ready to Riot* (New York: Holt, Rinehart, and Winston, 1968), 10–22.
24. Jane Jacobs, *The Death and Life of Great American Cities* (New York: Vintage, 1992), 29–142.
25. While urban renewal devastated Saint Lucy's, it recovered and outlived the Columbus Homes, which closed in 1990. Mary Ann Castronovo Fusco, "How a Church Brings Life to Newark's Little Italy," *New York Times,* October 10, 1999, NJ6.
26. Newark Redevelopment Agency, "Newark Urban Renewal Areas," October 1963, Charles F. Cummings New Jersey Information Center, NPL.
27. Kaplan, "Urban Renewal in Newark," 242–46; and Wendell Pritchett, *Robert Clifton Weaver and the American City: The Life and Times of an Urban Reformer* (Chicago: University of Chicago Press, 2008), 83.
28. Kaplan, "Urban Renewal in Newark," 236–37.
29. Ibid., 67.
30. Ibid., 69–70. For more on the Home Owners' Loan Corporation, see Jackson, *Crabgrass Frontier,* 201–12; and Amy E. Hillier, "Redlining and the Home Owners' Loan Corporation," *Journal of Urban History* 29 (May 2003): 394–20.
31. Adele Oltman, "'A Diabolical Scheme': Urban Renewal and the Civil Rights Movement in Newark in the Early 1960s" (paper presented at "The Long Hot Summers in Retrospect: Urban Unrest in 1960s New Jersey" conference, New Jersey Historical Society, Newark, November 13, 2004), 9.
32. Wright, *Ready to Riot,* 21.
33. Ibid., 49. Wright retained some conservative loyalties to the Republican Party even as he advocated for black economic power. He supported subsidies for black home buyers because he believed renters would "add to social costs from a lack of both civic investment and community pride." Homeownership, he argued, encouraged "a longer range view of both local and national interest." Like councilman Lee Bernstein and Louis Danzig, Wright opposed the addition of inexpensive rentals. He argued

that they "effectively subsidize renter-related irresponsibility and parasitism" (50–51).

34. Ibid., 47; David Gerwin, "The End of Coalition: The Failure of Community Organizing in Newark in the 1960s" (PhD diss., Columbia University, 1998), 65.

35. Gerwin, "End of Coalition," 63.

36. Ibid., 73.

37. Ibid., 75.

38. Ibid., 77–78.

39. Leonard J. Duhl and Mary Jo Steetle, "Newark: Community or Chaos; A Case Study of the Medical College Controversy," undated, Newark, NJ, folder, box 380, Subject Correspondence files (1942–1969), Housing and Urban Development (HUD), National Archives and Records Administration, College Park, MD (hereafter NARA), 13.

40. Kaplan, "Urban Renewal in Newark," 255–57. My interviews with Robert Curvin, Francis Warren, and Junius Williams all attest to the widespread belief that Danzig heavily influenced successive administrations and was one of the most powerful officials in New Jersey politics.

41. Walter H. Waggoner, "Newark Pursues Fight for College," *New York Times*, September 18, 1966, 73; and Duhl and Steetle, "Newark: Community or Chaos," 6–7. Martland Hospital's ratio of two nurses to thirty-nine patients wildly violated the 1:6–8 ratio prescribed by the state.

42. Duhl and Steetle, "Newark: Community or Chaos," 8.

43. Governor's Select Commission on Civil Disorder, *Report for Action* (Trenton: State of New Jersey, 1968), 97–98; Hearings on the Medical College Site, February 13, 1968, 130; Hearings on the Medical College Site, February 17, 1968, 5–6; all in University of Medicine and Dentistry of New Jersey Archive, Newark.

44. Duhl and Steetle, "Newark: Community or Chaos," 1.

45. Ibid., 15.

46. Jackson, *Model City Blues*; Luther Adams, *Way Up North in Louisville: African American Migration in the Urban South, 1930–1970* (Chapel Hill: University of North Carolina Press, 2010), 149–70; and James Q. Wilson, "Planning and Politics: Citizen Participation and Urban Renewal," in Wilson, *Urban Renewal*, 407–10.

47. Governor's Select Commission on Civil Disorder, *Report for Action*, 61.

48. Bob Shabazian, "New Hearings Needed for Medical College," *Newark Evening News*, February 1, 1968, 13.

49. Duhl and Steetle, "Newark: Community or Chaos," 12–13. By 1967 Newark had received $325 million in federal funds and operated the fifth-largest urban renewal program in the United States. The NHA received $350,000 in 1962 to devise a plan to integrate residents' concerns into its agenda, but Executive Director Louis Danzig never delivered it.

50. Hearings, February 13, 1968, 32.

51. Ibid., 158–59.

52. Governor's Select Commission on Civil Disorder, *Report for Action*, 7–8.

53. Ibid., 12–14. The site selection committee for the hospital preferred a suburban location, but trustees of the Medical College, many with ties to state and local officials, pressured the committee to reconsider Newark. According to Donald Malafronte, aide to Mayor Addonizio, municipal officials believed that the Medical College officials were ambivalent about locating in Newark and consequently made excessive land demands that they did not anticipate the city to meet. Determined to win the college, municipal officials decided to exceed the selection committee's expectations by offering 185 acres, including the plot they had already identified in addition to "the worst slum area" that surrounded it.

54. Governor's Select Commission on Civil Disorder, *Report for Action*, 12–4; and John DeSimone, interview by Adele Oltman, Clark, NJ, December 11, 2003.

55. Governor's Select Commission on Civil Disorder, *Report for Action*, 12–14.

56. Mayor's Commission on Group Relations, *Newark: A City in Transition*, vol. 1, 36–37. This report recommended a campaign to improve relations between police and black residents. See also *Human Relations News from the Mayor's Commission on Group Relations* 1 (August 1956), NPL. In the late 1950s an investigative series for the *Newark Evening News* exposed inadequate training, low morale, and poor management of the department. See "No incentive for Newark Cops to Do a Good Job," *Newark Evening News*, January 21, 1958, 1; and "City Probing Police Force," *Newark Evening News*, February 4, 1958, 1. Nearly a decade later, the police force remained underpaid, undertrained, and understaffed (Governor's Select Commission on Civil Disorder, *Report for Action*, 31).

57. Governor's Select Commission on Civil Disorder, *Report for Action*, 31; and Tom Hayden, *Rebellion in Newark: Official Violence and Ghetto Response* (New York: Vintage Books, 1967), 15.

58. Governor's Select Commission on Civil Disorder, *Report for Action*, 11–12; "Anthony Resigns Rights Post," *Newark Evening News*, July 14, 1963, 12; memo, Ad-Hoc Committee for Improving the Operations of the Newark Commission on Human Rights to Mayor Hugh J. Addonizio, March 5, 1963, Daniel S. Anthony Papers, container 10, NPL. The Mayor's Commission on Group Relations changed its name to the Newark Commission on Human Rights around 1962.

59. Other highly publicized deaths of black men at the hands of the Newark police reinforced distrust, including the beating death of Barnard Rich, who police initially claimed had committed suicide in custody, and Walter Mathis, seventeen, shot during a traffic stop. Wright, *Ready to Riot*, 76–77.

60. Governor's Select Commission on Civil Disorder, *Report for Action*, 107–8.

61. Amiri Baraka, *The Autobiography of LeRoi Jones* (Chicago: Lawrence Hill Books, 1997), 366.

62. Untitled photo of Robert Curvin, http://www.ncas.rutgers.edu/institute
-ethnicity-culture-and-modern-experience/memory-and-newark-july-1967
(accessed January 21, 2014).

63. Governor's Select Commission on Civil Disorder, *Report for Action*.

64. Addonizio's proposed "Blue Ribbon Commission" never happened. Lipsky
and Olson, *Commission Politics*, 243.

65. Wright, *Ready to Riot*, 2.

66. Hayden, *Rebellion in Newark*, 26.

67. Baraka, *Autobiography of LeRoi Jones*, 375.

68. Hayden, *Rebellion in Newark*, 33.

69. Ibid., 32.

70. Ibid., 37–38.

71. Ibid., 47; and Governor's Select Commission on Civil Disorder, *Report for
Action*, 117–18.

72. Hayden, *Rebellion in Newark*, 65.

73. Ibid., 33.

74. Governor's Select Commission on Civil Disorder, *Report for Action*, 120–22,
143–44.

75. Ibid., 138–39. Only three of the fatalities—a drug overdose, a heart attack,
and a collision—were not shootings.

76. Two riots took place during the week of July 11. The looting and clashes
with police that followed Smith's arrest constituted the first; the second,
instigated by the arrival of the National Guard, accelerated the destruction of businesses by authorities under the guise of a search for snipers.

77. Bud Lee, cover photograph, *Life*, July 28, 1967.

78. Robert Dallek, *Flawed Giant: Lyndon Johnson and His Times, 1961–1973*
(New York: Oxford University Press, 1998), 413; and Joseph Califano Jr.,
The Tragedy and Triumph of Lyndon Johnson (New York: Simon and Schuster,
1991), 209.

79. Governor's Select Commission on Civil Disorder, *Report for Action*, 130–32.

80. Califano, *Tragedy and Triumph of Lyndon Johnson*, 210–11.

81. Jill Quadagno *The Color of Welfare: How Racism Undermined the War on
Poverty* (New York: Oxford University Press, 1994), 52.

82. Califano, *Tragedy and Triumph of Lyndon Johnson*, 210–13; and Lipsky and
Olson, *Commission Politics*, 108.

83. "Art of the Impossible," *City*, April 1969, 18–19.

84. Mitchell Sviridoff, ed., *Inventing Community Renewal: The Trials and Errors
That Shaped the Modern Community Development Corporation* (New York:
New School University, Milano Graduate School, Community Develop-
ment Research Center, 2004), 23.

85. Transcript of Urbanism Conference, 3, October 27, 1967, box 18, Paul N.
Ylvisaker Papers, 1939–1992, Harvard University Archives, Cambridge, MA.

86. Duhl and Steetle, "Newark: Community or Chaos," 50.

87. Transcript of Urbanism Conference, 17.

88. Ibid., 8.
89. Ibid., 7.
90. Ibid., 9.
91. Sol Stern, "When the Black G.I. Comes Back from Vietnam," *New York Times*, March 24, 1968, SM27.
92. Transcript of Urbanism Conference, 55.
93. Ibid., 31–32.
94. "Brown's Camden Visit Gets Mixed Reaction," *Chicago Daily Defender*, August 31, 1967, 14; and "Violence Follows Brown Speech in Camden, New Jersey," *Chicago Daily Defender*, September 2, 1967, 26.
95. Transcript of Urbanism Conference, 33.
96. Howard Gillette, *Camden after the Fall: Decline and Renewal in a Post-industrial City* (Philadelphia: University of Pennsylvania Press, 2005), 75–77, 86–88.
97. Transcript of interview with Ronald Sullivan of the *New York Times*, "New Jersey Report," *John Scott Program*, Channel 9, September 3, 1967, folder WOR, box 21, HUGFP 142, Paul N. Ylvisaker Papers, 1939–1992, Harvard University Archives, Cambridge, MA.
98. Barbara Cruikshank, *The Will to Empower: Democratic Citizens and Other Subjects* (Ithaca, NY: Cornell University Press, 1999), 69.
99. Baraka, *Autobiography of LeRoi Jones*; Cunningham, *Newark*; Hayden, *Rebellion in Newark*; Ron Perambo, *No Cause for Indictment: An Autopsy of Newark* (New York: Holt, Rinehart, and Winston, 1971); and Shabazian, "New Hearings Needed for Medical College," 13.
100. "U.S. Court Says Jersey Unions Must Drop All Racial Barriers," *New Jersey Afro-American*, January 30, 1971; aide-mémoire for the Undersecretary from Joseph Freitas Jr., December 29, 1967, Subject Correspondence files (1942–1969), Newark, NJ, folder, box 380, HUD, NARA; and Duhl and Steetle, "Newark: Community or Chaos," 1.
101. Dallek, *Flawed Giant*, 322.
102. Alice O'Connor, "Swimming against the Tide: A Brief History of Federal Policy in Poor Communities," in *Urban Problems and Community Development*, ed. Ronald F. Ferguson and William T. Dickens (Washington, DC: Brookings Institution Press, 1999), 104.
103. Dallek, *Flawed Giant*, 318.
104. McKee, *Problem of Jobs*, 256.
105. O'Connor, "Swimming against the Tide," 104; and Pritchett, *Robert Clifton Weaver*, 298.
106. O'Connor, "Swimming against the Tide," 96–97; Raymond A. Mohl, "Shifting Patterns of Urban Policy," in *Urban Policy in Twentieth Century America*, ed. Raymond A. Mohl and Arnold R. Hirsch (New Brunswick, NJ: Rutgers University Press, 1993), 16–17; and Christopher Klemek, *The Transatlantic Collapse of Urban Renewal from New York to Berlin* (Chicago: University of Chicago Press, 2011), 129–70.

107. Robert Halpern, *Rebuilding the Inner City* (New York: Columbia University Press, 1995), 118.

108. Quadagno, *Color of Welfare*, 103.

109. Memo for Newark Medical College File, January 27, 1968, RG 207, stack 130, row 2, compartment 24, shelf 4, entry 55, Subject Correspondence files (1942–1969), box 380, NARA; and Duhl and Steetle, "Newark: Community or Chaos," 22.

110. "Report: NJCMD Past, Present, and Future," June 26, 1970, folder 8a, box 25, Record Group B-3-H, Special Collections, University of Medicine and Dentistry of New Jersey Archive.

111. Duhl and Steetle, "Newark: Community or Chaos," 28–30.

112. Hearings, February 13, 1968, 27–28, 48–52. Harry Wheeler and Junius Williams, who had been selected as a negotiating team by those affected by the Medical College, sparred with Reverend Perry, who was from the neighborhood and who questioned their ability to represent the community. Alfred F. Brown, an African American aide to the NHA's Danzig, asked how the negotiating committee would respond to community members who disagreed with them. Williams replied that those disagreements would be resolved in separate meetings, not in negotiating sessions with hospital and government officials. Louise Epperson chastised both Brown and Perry for criticizing the negotiating committee at a critical moment, especially because they had failed to support community opposition efforts in the past.

113. Ibid., 4–8.

114. Ibid., 9.

115. Duhl and Steetle, "Newark: Community or Chaos," 32–33; and Robert R. Cadmus to Robert Weaver, December 12, 1967, Subject Correspondence files (1942–1969), box 266, entry 55, shelf 2, compartment 22, row 2, stack 130, RG 207, NARA.

116. Sviridoff, Inventing Community Renewal, 29.

117. Hearings, February 13, 1968, 27–28, 48–52.

118. Ibid., 20.

119. "Interaction with the Inner City—an Interview with Robert R. Cadmus, MD, President of the New Jersey College of Medicine and Dentistry," *Hospitals: Journal of the American Hospital Association* 42 (September 1, 1968).

120. Duhl and Steetle, "Newark: Community or Chaos," 55; and Williams, interview.

121. Duhl and Steetle, "Newark: Community or Chaos," 34.

122. On Williams's work with the Newark Area Planning Association and the Newark black power movement, see Junius Williams, *Unfinished Agenda: Urban Politics in the Era of Black Power* (New York: North Atlantic Books, 2014), 163–90, 211–72.

123. Duhl and Steetle, "Newark: Community or Chaos," 55.

124. Ibid., 36.

125. Hearings, February 13, 1968, 21.

126. Hearings, February 17, 1968, 11.
127. The following memos confirm Williams's claim that the city failed to respond adequately to questions about the schedule for construction and the number of families requiring relocation. Robert Weaver to Robert Cadmus, December 26, 1967; Don Hummel, Assistant Secretary for Renewal and Housing Assistance, to James G. Banks, Office of Community Development, December 18, 1967; and Robert E. McCabe to Don Hummel, December 18, 1967; all in Subject Correspondence files (1942–1969), box 266, entry 55, shelf 2, compartment 22, row 2, stack 130, RG 207, NARA.
128. Hearings, February 13, 1968, 95.
129. Ibid., 88–89.
130. Duhl and Steetle, "Newark: Community or Chaos," 27–28.
131. Hearings, February 17, 1968, 27, 32–33. Cadmus had in fact contributed a US Public Health Service memo that recommended 150 acres as optimal for a modern research hospital and a minimum of 50.
132. Kaplan, "Urban Renewal in Newark," 254.
133. Ibid., 250–51, 246.
134. Ibid., 257.
135. Sharper's comments referred to the fact that many of the plots of city-owned land that community negotiators hoped to use for replacement housing had already been claimed by a private developer based in Long Island, NY: Jack Parker Associates. Hearings, February 13, 1968, 167–68.
136. Hearings, February 17, 1968, 31–32.
137. Duhl and Steetle, "Newark: Community or Chaos," 28.
138. Hearings, February 19, 1968; and Duhl and Steetle, "Newark: Community or Chaos," 36.
139. Duhl and Steetle, "Newark: Community or Chaos," 50–51.
140. For more on urban renewal in Newark, see Gerwin, "End of Coalition"; Immerso, *Newark's Little Italy*; Oltman, "'Diabolical Scheme'"; and David Levitus, "Planning, Slum Clearance, and the Road to Crisis in Newark," *Newark Metro*, September 2005, http://www.newarkmetro.rutgers.edu/reports/display.php?id=173 (accessed November 1, 2007).
141. Duhl and Steetle, "Newark: Community or Chaos," 45–46, 49.
142. Ibid.
143. Ibid., 50–51.
144. Ibid., 42–44.
145. Ibid., 47.
146. Ibid., 47–48.
147. Ibid., 49.
148. After the Barringer High School demonstrations, activists targeted construction projects at Rutgers Law School and Essex County Community College, among others. "Rights Groups Plan for New Rutgers Job Demonstrations," *Newark Evening News*, October 7, 1965; and Rebecca Doggett, interview by the author, Newark, NJ, October 9, 2007.

149. Duhl and Steetle, "Newark: Community or Chaos," 51.
150. *America's War on Poverty: City of Promise*, directed by Susan Bellows, executive producer Harry Hampton (PBS Video, Blackside Inc., 1995).
151. Luther Carter, "Newark: Negroes Demand and Get Voice in Medical College Plans," *Science* 160, no. 3825 (April 19, 1968): 292; and *America's War on Poverty.*
152. "U.S. Court Says Jersey Unions Must Drop All Racial Barriers," *New Jersey Afro-American*, January 30, 1971, 1.
153. Hearings, February 17, 1968, 11.
154. "Report of the Meeting of the Business and Industrial Coordinating Council," August 1969, Newark "Q" file (Q Files), NPL.
155. Gustav Heningburg, interview by the author, Newark, NJ, December 6, 2006.
156. "Hughes Threatens Suit to Put Blacks in College Site Job," *New York Times*, January 19, 1969. Hughes had been an important advocate for the original Medical College Agreement, but Heningburg and other affirmative action advocates noticed his retreat from confrontation with contractors and unions. Hughes told activists to leave matters to the legal system, but officials offered little reassurance. At a meeting of the Business and Industrial Coordinating Council, for example, James Blair of the New Jersey Division on Civil Rights acknowledged to George Fontaine of the Joint Apprenticeship Training Program that minority journeymen were excluded from major construction projects across the city, but he insisted that "there is no known law to stop unions from discriminating." "Report of the Meeting of the Business and Industrial Coordinating Council," July 1969, Newark "Q" file, NPL.
157. "Hearings Asked on Bias in Building Trades Jobs," *Newark Sunday News*, March 1, 1970.
158. Joyce v. McCrane, Bricklayers, et al., 1970 U.S. Dist. Lexis 9004.
159. "U.S. Court Says Jersey Unions Must Drop All Racial Barriers," *New Jersey Afro-American*, January 30, 1971.

CHAPTER 4

1. Douglas Eldridge, "Heningburg Urges Businessmen to Have Faith in City's People," *Newark Evening News*, January 13, 1970.
2. A growing body of recent scholarship analyzes the range of views and strategies black power encompassed, a range often ignored or distorted by early accounts. More scholars have also moved beyond the most familiar organizations, such as the Black Panthers or the Student Nonviolent Coordinating Committee, to examine the institution building that took place within local contexts. On the roots and influence of black power, and some of its varieties, see Jeffrey Ogbar, *Black Power: Radical Politics and African-American Identity* (Baltimore: Johns Hopkins University Press,

2004). On the intersection of cultural and political strategies within nationalism, see Amiri Baraka, *The Autobiography of LeRoi Jones* (Chicago: Lawrence Hill Books, 1997); Scot Brown, *Fighting for US: Maulana Karenga, the US Organization, and Black Cultural Nationalism* (New York: New York University, 2003); and Komozi Woodard, *A Nation within a Nation: Amiri Baraka (LeRoi Jones) and Black Power Politics* (Chapel Hill: University of North Carolina Press, 1999). Recent scholarship has sought to recover and contextualize black power within the longer scope of black activism. For debates over periodization, see Sundiata Keita Cha-Jua and Clarence Lang, "The 'Long Movement' as Vampire: Temporal and Spatial Fallacies in Recent Black Freedom Studies," *Journal of African American History* 92, no. 2 (Spring 2007): 265–88.

3. "Heningburg Heads Urban Coalition," *Chicago Daily Defender*, May 18, 1968.

4. Ibid.; Gustav Heningburg, interview by the author, Newark, NJ, December 6, 2006; and box 32, folder 9, Urban League (1956–57), A92–19, Harold L. Oram Papers and Records of the Oram Group Inc., 1939–1992, Philanthropy Collections, Ruth Lilly Special Collections and Archives, Indiana University–Purdue University Indianapolis Library.

5. Baraka, *Autobiography of LeRoi Jones*; and Walter H. Waggoner, "Negro Businessman Asks End of Companies' 'Plantationship,'" *New York Times*, April 7, 1968.

6. In 1969 Mayor Hugh J. Addonizio was indicted—and later convicted—of conspiracy and extortion, along with several council members. His campaign for reelection in 1970 unfolded alongside a federal investigation. John T. Cunningham, *Newark* (Newark: New Jersey Historical Society, 1988), 335–37.

7. Gustav Heningburg, interview by the author, Newark, NJ, July 13, 2004.

8. Heningburg was employed by both Oram Group Inc. and the NAACP Legal Defense and Education Fund at the time. "Heningburg Heads Urban Coalition," 28.

9. "The Morning after Newark's Nightmare," *Business Week*, July 22, 1967.

10. Kenneth Gibson lost to Addonizio in 1966, prior to his 1970 victory.

11. In 1968 the Business and Industrial Coordinating Council compiled a list of 150 Newark organizations that advanced black economic and political opportunity, including ward-level political groups, antipoverty agencies, tenants groups, unions, business associations, civil rights organizations, and community action programs. BICC, Greater Newark Community Organizations list, July 1968, Newark "Q" file, Charles F. Cummings New Jersey Information Center, Newark Public Library (hereafter NPL).

12. "Morning after Newark's Nightmare."

13. Ibid.

14. Heningburg, interview, July 2004.

15. "Emergency Convocation: The Urban Coalition," August 24, 1967, folder 1, box 482, series 200, R.G. 1.2, Rockefeller Foundation Archives, Rockefeller Archive Center, Sleepy Hollow, NY (hereafter RAC).

16. "The Urban Coalition Report," December 1968, folder 1, box 482, series 200, R.G. 1.2, RAC.

17. In "Emergency Convocation," Lindsay employs an interesting reversal of the phrase "other America." Michael Harrington's 1962 investigation of poverty in rural Appalachia, entitled *The Other America* (New York: Macmillan, 1962), was credited with mobilizing popular support for the War on Poverty. "The other America" became shorthand for those who remained disenfranchised, impoverished, and alienated in the midst of postwar affluence. Harrington's title also reflected the muckraking tradition that includes Jacob Riis's *How the Other Half Lives* (1890). Lindsay inverted the reference in his speech: his "other America" refers to the beneficiaries of US prosperity, namely, Lindsay and the other attendees at the Emergency Convocation.

18. GNUC, *Annual Report*, New Jersey Reference, Charles F. Cummings New Jersey Information Center, NPL.

19. Stacy Kinlock Sewell, "'The Best Man for the Job': Corporate Responsibility and Racial Integration in the Workplace, 1945–1960," *Historian* 5 (2003): 1125–46. Carl Kaysen defines the "soulful corporation" in "The Social Significance of the Modern Corporation," *American Economic Review* 47, no. 2 (1957): 311–19.

20. These aesthetics are evident in many issues of *City Magazine*, especially October 1967. See also "Agenda for Positive Action: State Program in Housing and Community Development," folder 2, box 482, series 200, R.G. 1.2, RAC.

21. "Emergency Convocation."

22. "Urban Coalition Action Report," April 1968, folder 1, box 482, series 200, R.G. 1.2, RAC.

23. Ibid.; and William V. Shannon, "Will There Be an Urban Coalition?," *New York Times*, August 6, 1967. Hubert Humphrey echoed the call of Whitney Young of the Urban League for a "domestic Marshall Plan" in a speech delivered after the Detroit and Newark riots.

24. "A Guaranteed Job for Everyone Is Proposed by the Urban Coalition," *New York Times*, January 31, 1968.

25. "Emergency Convocation."

26. Ibid.

27. Ibid.

28. Ibid. For more examples, see *City Magazine*, especially October 1967. See also "Agenda for Positive Action."

29. Urban Coalition Action Council, "National Action Conference on Equal Housing Opportunities," January 18, 1968, 6–8, folder 1, box 482, series 200, R.G. 1.2, RAC. See also Charles V. Hamilton and Stokely Carmichael,

Black Power: The Politics of Liberation in America (New York: Vintage Books, 1967), 44–49; and Malcolm X, *The Autobiography of Malcolm X* (New York: Ballantine Books, 1999), 281.

30. "National Action Conference on Equal Housing Opportunities."
31. In a speech to an Urban League convention, Young defined black power in terms of choice: "to live in harmony with whites, to live among themselves amid decent surroundings—even to exclude whites if they wish" (Ogbar, *Black Power*, 151). Young also participated in the Congress of African People. With its emphasis on "working coalitions between black nationalist and civil rights organizations," Woodard argues, the congress was "a major departure from the traditional competition" among black organizations (*Nation within a Nation*, 95, 162–65).
32. Irving Spiegel, "Gardner Calls for Negro Role in Urban Solutions," *New York Times*, May 6, 1968.
33. "Gardner Urges Moderates to Curb Racial Extremism," *New York Times*, May 27, 1968.
34. "Black Phoenix," *New York Times*, July 22, 1967.
35. Woodard, *Nation within a Nation*, 88 (see 84–87 for more on "revolution or reform").
36. Amiri Baraka, "The Practice of the New Nationalism," in *Kawaida Studies: The New Nationalism* (Chicago: Third World Press, 1972), excerpted in Clement Price, *Freedom Not Far Distant* (Newark: New Jersey Historical Society, 1980), 286–87; and Maulana Karenga, "US," in *Encyclopedia of Black Studies*, ed. Molefi Kete Asanti and Mambo Ama Mazamba (Newcastle on Tyne: SAGE Publications, 2004), 460.
37. Heningburg, interview, 2004.
38. Ibid.
39. See chapter 2.
40. Robert C. Ruth, "Black Leadership Hit on Heningburg Issue," *Newark Evening News*, December 7, 1968; and "Blamed for Split Urban Coalition Group Hit," *Newark Evening News*, December 8, 1968.
41. Heningburg, interview, 2006.
42. United Community Corporation Executive Committee meeting minutes, March 16, 1968, Douglas Eldridge Papers, NPL.
43. Ruth, "Black Leadership Hit on Heningburg Issue"; "Blamed for Split Urban Coalition Group Hit"; and Douglas Eldridge, "Urban Coalition Expands Board, 4 Critics Included," *Newark Evening News*, February 12, 1969 (available in Heningburg Papers, Charles F. Cummings New Jersey Information Room, NPL).
44. United Community Corporation Executive Committee meeting minutes, March 16, 1968, Douglas Eldridge Papers, NPL; and Heningburg, interview, 2004.
45. Heningburg, interview, 2004.

46. Proof of the endurance of this relationship can be seen in how Ministers for Addonizio persisted in its support of the mayor in his 1970 campaign against Kenneth Gibson, after he and several councilmen had been indicted. Komozi Woodard, interview by the author, Yonkers, NY, June 9, 2004; and Robert Curvin, interview by the author, Newark, NJ, September 16, 2004.

47. George Hallam, "Love Festival Draws 35,000," *Newark Evening News*, October 6, 1969 (available in Heningburg Papers, Charles F. Cummings New Jersey Information Room, NPL).

48. Heningburg, interview, 2004.

49. Kitty Taylor, "NJ Happenings," *New Jersey Afro-American*, October 11, 1969.

50. Heningburg, interview, 2004; and Guy Sterling, *The Famous, the Familiar, and the Forgotten: 350 Notable Newarkers* (Newark: GSNewark, 2014), 10.

51. Heningburg, interview, 2004.

52. Ibid.

53. "A 'Brickbat' and a 'Bouquet' for Newark Urban Coalition," *New Jersey Afro-American*, December 6, 1969.

54. Ibid.

55. Woodard, *Nation within a Nation*, 142; "Convention Aims to 'Narrow Down' Black Candidates," *New Jersey Afro-American*, November 1, 1969; and "Huge Success: 3-Day Meeting Claims Unity," *New Jersey Afro-American*, November 22, 1969.

56. "Curvin Defends Convention Again," *New Jersey Afro-American*, December 13, 1969.

57. "A 'Brickbat' and a 'Bouquet.'"

58. "Salvation Army Cites Heningburg," *New Jersey Afro-American*, May 24, 1969.

59. Don Prial, "Black Middle Class Urged to Take Reins," *Newark Evening News*, January 5, 1970.

60. Douglas Eldridge, "Heningburg Urges Businessmen to Have Faith in City's People," *Newark Evening News*, January 13, 1970.

61. Richard J. H. Johnston, "Group in Newark Seeks Bias Study," *New York Times*, January 21, 1970.

62. Heningburg, interview, 2004.

63. Secretary of Labor George Shultz targeted eighteen cities for the Philadelphia Plan but prioritized six: Atlanta, Boston, Detroit, Los Angeles, Newark, and Seattle. "Shultz Warns 18 Cities to End Bias in Building Jobs," *New York Times*, February 10, 1970.

64. Harry Burke, "U.S. Unit Probes Hiring Bias Here," *Newark Evening News*, February 9, 1970, 1; and James M. Naughton, "U.S. Will Extend Minority Job Aid," *New York Times*, September 30, 1969, 1. Federal hiring goals were derived from the predicted growth in the construction industry for a given municipality.

65. Naughton, "U.S. Will Extend Minority Job Aid," 1; and John David Skrentny, *The Ironies of Affirmative Action: Politics, Culture, and Justice in America* (Chicago: University of Chicago Press, 1996), 193–95.

66. See Jefferson Cowie, *Stayin' Alive: The 1970s and the Last Days of the Working Class* (New York: New Press, 2010), 230–44.

67. "Construction Ban Lifted by Nixon," *Newark Evening News*, March 17, 1970.

68. "Plan Would Make Building Unions Take New Members," *Newark Evening News*, February 11, 1970.

69. Skrentny (*Ironies of Affirmative Action*, 203) refers to meetings held in December 1969 at which administration officials discussed the potential of the Philadelphia Plan to diminish construction unions' power and provoke a "war" with organized labor. Hugh Davis Graham, *The Civil Rights Era: Origins and Development of National Policy, 1960–1972* (New York: Oxford University Press, 1990), 339–40; and Dean J. Kotlowski, *Nixon's Civil Rights: Politics, Principle, and Policy* (Oxford: Cambridge University Press, 2001), 106–7.

70. Johnston, "Group in Newark Seeks Bias Study"; and "Newark Presbytery Favors Construction Bias Inquiry," *Newark Evening News*, January 28, 1970.

71. Hy Kuperstein, "Trade Unions Mostly White," *Newark Evening News*, March 18, 1970.

72. Hy Kuperstein, "Bias in Hiring Denied by Ironworkers Union," *Newark Evening News,* March 19, 1970.

73. Kuperstein, "Bias in Hiring Denied by Ironworkers Union." Newark was hardly alone; see Brian Purnell, "Revolution Has Come to Brooklyn: Construction Trades Protests and the Negro Revolt of 1963," in *Black Power at Work: Community Control, Affirmative Action, and the Construction Industry,* ed. David Goldberg and Trevor Griffey (Ithaca, NY: Cornell University Press, 2010), 25–27.

74. Greater Newark Chamber of Commerce Taskforce, "Survey of Jobs and Unemployment," III2, table 1, Charles F. Cummings New Jersey Information Center, NPL. Based on survey and census data, authors estimate that Newark lost a net 24,000 jobs between 1958 and 1971, with nearly two-thirds of the loss occurring between 1968 and 1971.

75. Kuperstein, "Bias in Hiring Denied by Ironworkers Union."

76. "Imposed Hiring Plan Nears for Newark Building Trades," *New Jersey Afro-American,* March 7, 1972.

77. "U.S. Says Newark Area Slights Minority Workers," *New York Times*, June 3, 1970; and Harry Burke, "U.S. Unit Probes Hiring Bias Here," *Newark Evening News*, February 9, 1970.

78. "Shultz Warns 18 Cities to End Bias in Building Jobs"; and Burke, "U.S. Unit Probes Hiring Bias Here."

79. "US Labor Department Sets Job Bias Hearing in Newark," *Newark Evening News*, March 5, 1970.

80. Heningburg, interview, 2004.

81. Newark owned the land on which the Port Authority built the airport. Under a fifty-year lease arranged in 1947, the Port Authority paid Newark $100,000 per year for its use. But as the airport grew in importance, critics decried the arrangement as a "giveaway." In 1966 several lawsuits challenging the tax-exempt status of some airport facilities prompted the Port Authority to renegotiate. Under the new lease, annual rent paid to Newark increased to $1 million and the city also received a portion of airport revenues. Ben Shiriak, memorandum, "The City of Newark and the Port of New York Authority," 1972, 8–11, Counsel Files, 1970–1973, Port Authority (General), William T. Cahill, Governors, New Jersey State Archives, Trenton.
82. Heningburg, interview, 2004.
83. Ibid. Heningburg was not prosecuted for the action. Donald MacNaughton, the chairman of Prudential Insurance Company and a GNUC board member, chastised him because Heningburg's protest had interfered with the schedule of Eastern Airlines, in which MacNaughton's company was heavily invested.
84. Ibid.
85. Shiriak, "City of Newark and the Port of New York Authority."
86. Speculation is unavoidable here since the relevant portion of the Port Authority's archives was destroyed in the World Trade Center attacks.
87. Heningburg, interview, 2004.
88. Robert Lindsey, "Integration May End Newark Airport Building Stoppage," *New York Times*, February 27, 1972. Lindsey mentions pressure for federal intervention exerted by Cahill and Tobin.
89. "Williams Routs Gross," *Newark Evening News*, November 4, 1970; Joseph F. Sullivan, "Williams, Gross in Finale," *Newark Evening News*, November 2, 1970; and Heningburg, interview, 2004.
90. Robert Lindsey, "Newark Bias Fight Halts Airport Work," *New York Times*, October 30, 1971. Three hundred workers were employed on the terminal project, of whom 22 percent were minority. Among the skilled workers, who made up a little more than half of the workforce, the minority representation was 12 percent.
91. "Agreements to Guarantee Hiring of Minorities Signed in Newark," *New York Times*, January 23, 1972; and Annual Report 1971, Counsel Files, 1970–1973, Port Authority (General), William T. Cahill, Governors, New Jersey State Archives, Trenton. Provisions extended immediately to La Guardia and JFK Airports, but Rutgers University, the municipal government of Newark, the Ideal Toy Company, and others also agreed to the Newark Plan.
92. Robert Lindsey, "Newark Job Pact to Aid Minorities," *New York Times*, February 26, 1972.
93. "TWA New $22 Million Terminal to Assure Minority Building Jobs," *New Jersey Afro-American*, March 4, 1972; and "Imposed Hiring Plan Nears for Newark Building Trades."

94. "A Breakthrough in Minority Hiring," *Business Week*, April 8, 1972, 74–75.

95. Herbert Koshetz, "Minority Employment: Progress Is Slow," *New York Times*, May 14, 1972.

96. "Imposed Hiring Plan Nears for Newark Building Trades."

97. "Newark's Black Leaders Are Hopeful of Achieving Construction Job Goals," *New York Times*, October 17, 1972.

98. Koshetz, "Minority Employment."

99. "Newark's Black Leaders."

100. Ania Savage, "Newark Sees Airport Helping Economy," *New York Times*, July 9, 1972, 64.

101. "Blacks Hail Trainee Plan on Newark Airport Job," *New York Times*, August 20, 1972.

102. Ibid.

103. "Airport Project Bias Claimed in Newark," *New York Times*, August 25, 1972; Bob Queen, "Five Minority Ironworkers Paid $1,000 Weekly to Do Nothing at Airport," *New Jersey Afro-American*, September 2, 1972; and Koshetz, "Minority Employment."

104. Author's interview with Marty Schwartz, Newark, NJ, May 4, 2005.

105. Ibid.

106. Ania Savage, "Construction Union at Airport Starts Training Blacks," *New York Times*, October 1, 1972.

107. Sandra King, "Dispute on Minority Jobs Ended at Newark Airport," *Star-Ledger*, September 13, 1972; and Savage, "Construction Union at Airport." Under the consent decree, ironworkers offered two programs for minority recruitment: one for young men who had completed tenth grade and passed a state-administered physical and aptitude test; and one for older workers in good health who could read and write. The Newark Plan, in contrast, had the most accommodating criteria, considering all minority men who were "able and willing to work."

108. Savage, "Construction Union at Airport"; and "Newark Black Leaders Are Hopeful of Achieving Construction Job Goals," *New York Times*, October 17, 1972. By the end of October, 162 trainees were at work on over a dozen construction projects.

109. Paul Delaney, "Nixon Held Likely to Drop Program of Minority Jobs," *New York Times*, September 4, 1972; Kotlowski, *Nixon's Civil Rights*, 112–13; and Stacy Kinlock Sewell, "'Left on the Bench': The New York Construction Trades and Racial Integration, 1960–1972," *New York History* 83, no. 2 (2002): 203–34. As president of the New York City Building Trades Council, Peter Brennan presented himself as a moderate advocate of civil rights while quietly eviscerating affirmative action programs. Nixon appointed him secretary of labor in 1972, signaling his own retreat from the Philadelphia Plan.

110. "N.A.A.C.P. Sees End of Jobs Rights Plan," *New York Times*, September 8, 1972.

111. In the autumn of 1973, Mayor Gibson incorporated the Newark Plan requirements into all city contracts valued over $25,000. Rudy Johnson, "Gibson Proposing Minority-Hiring Plan," *New York Times*, November 4, 1973; and "$480 Million Project Brings Minority Hiring Training," *New Jersey Afro-American*, April 12–16, 1977.

112. Trevor Griffey, "'The Blacks Should Not Be Administering the Philadelphia Plan': Nixon, the Hard Hats, and 'Voluntary Affirmative Action,'" in Goldberg and Griffey, *Black Power at Work*, 134. On national policy debates, see Kotlowski, *Nixon's Civil Rights*; and Skrentny, *Ironies of Affirmative Action*.

113. Thomas J. Sugrue, "Affirmative Action from Below: Civil Rights, the Building Trades, and the Politics of Racial Equality in the Urban North, 1945–1969," *Journal of American History* 91 (June 2004): 145–73. Sugrue challenges the "top-down" analysis that characterizes historiography of affirmative action and urges scholars to explore the "distant backdrop" to which grassroots movements have been relegated.

114. Laura Warren Hill, "Fighting for the Soul of Black Capitalism: Struggles for Black Economic Development in Postrebellion Rochester," in *The Business of Black Power: Community Development, Capitalism, and Corporate Responsibility in Postwar America*, ed. Laura Warren Hill and Julia Rabig (Rochester, NY: University of Rochester Press, 2012), 46–47.

115. "Minority Firms Awarded Terminal 'B' Contract," *New Jersey Afro-American*, September 22, 1973; and "Bus Company Wins Airport Contract," *New Jersey Afro-American*, July 13, 1974.

116. Heningburg, interview, 2004.

117. "Newark NAACP Unveils Black Economic Venture," *New Jersey Afro-American*, March 1, 1969.

118. The ICBO predated the GNUC and was launched locally in 1965 by the New Jersey Regional American Jewish Congress and the Urban League of Essex County.

119. "Interracial Council Will Spur Black Businessmen," *New Jersey Afro-American*, March 15, 1969; and Chester L. Coleman, "Agency Helps Minority Businesses," *Newark Evening News*, January 13, 1970. In 1969, 183 individuals completed ICBO courses.

120. Douglas Eldridge, "Black Capitalists Encouraged by Profits and Pride," *Newark Evening News*, January 25, 1970.

121. Douglas Eldridge, "Williams Resigns from Urban Coalition Post," *Newark Sunday News*, April 5, 1970.

122. Baraka, *Autobiography of LeRoi Jones*, 421–23; and David Barrett, interview by the author, Columbia, MD, January 29, 2005. Barrett, a founding member of the Committee for a Unified Newark, spent childhood summers in Virginia in the care of his uncle, Hugo A. Owens, a dentist who served the black community of Portsmouth, Virginia. The fact that his business was not dependent on white clientele permitted Owens to take greater risks in his advocacy of civil rights. As president of the Portsmouth NAACP, he

launched a successful campaign to integrate the public library. The cultivation of an independent black business enabled him to effectively gain
and leverage political power. James T. Rule and Muriel J. Bebeau, "Hugo A.
Owens: Dentist, Civil Rights Leader, Politician," *Quintessence International*
31 (November 10, 2000): 753–863.

123. Woodard, *Nation within a Nation*, chap. 5. Their thwarted attempts to
realize such economic development goals in collaboration with local officials (the subject of chapter 5) led to the cultural nationalists' wholesale
denunciation of capitalism.

124. *The Black Power Movement*, pt. 1, *Amiri Baraka: From Black Arts to Black
Radicalism*, ed. John H. Bracey Jr., Sharon Harley, and Komozi Woodard
(Bethesda, MD: University Publications of America, 2000), microfilm, reel 2.

125. See Laura Warren Hill and Julia Rabig, "Towards a History of the Business
of Black Power," in Hill and Rabig, *Business of Black Power*, 25–33.

126. Kotlowski, *Nixon's Civil Rights*, 134–36.

127. Juliet E. K. Walker, The History of Black Business in America: Capitalism,
Race, Entrepreneurship (New York: Twayne, 1998), 270–75.

128. Dick Roberts, *The Fraud of Black Capitalism* (New York: Pathfinder Press,
1970); Robert L. Allen, *Black Awakening in Capitalist America* (Garden City,
NY: Doubleday, 1969); and Earl Ofari Hutchinson, *The Myth of Black Capitalism* (New York: Monthly Review Press, 1970).

129. Woodard, Nation within a Nation, 219–24; and Baraka, *Autobiography of
LeRoi Jones*, 427.

130. T. Keith Glennan to Dana S. Creel, May 20, 1968, folder 1, box 462, series
200, R.G. 1.2, RAC; National Urban Coalition press release, September 28,
1970, folder 3209, box 332, series 18.1, R.G. 1.2, RAC; and John Herbers,
"Urban Coalitions Split by Revolts," *New York Times*, October 5, 1969.

131. Sydney H. Schanberg, "Urban Coalition Moves on Slums," *New York Times*,
October 10, 1967.

132. John Price Jones Inc., "A Fund-Raising Plan for the National Urban Coalition's 1972 Administrative Budget," 2–3; and "Schedule of Corporate Analysis and Assignments," appendix A; both in George A. Brakeley Jr. Files,
1928–1995, MSS 013, box 14, Ruth Lilly Special Collections and Archives,
Indiana University–Purdue University Indianapolis Library.

133. "Schedule of Corporate Analysis and Assignments."

134. Ibid. The Great Atlantic and Pacific Tea Company, a New Orleans–based
company, had many complaints brought against it for segregated facilities. Commission Decision Files (Document Control Systems, 1966–1996),
boxes 1–5 of 46, RG 403, National Archives and Records Administration,
College Park, MD.

135. John Price Jones, "Fund-Raising Plan for the National Urban Coalition's
1972 Administrative Budget."

136. "Schedule of Corporate Analysis and Assignments"; and John Herbers,
"Urban Coalition Council Urges a Cut in the Defense Budget to Meet
'Problems of Nation,'" *New York Times*, June 26, 1969.

137. Urban Coalition, Third Annual Report, 1971, folder 3211, box 334, series 18.1, R.G. 1.2, RAC; and Walter H. Waggoner, "A 'White NAACP' Set Up in Newark," *New York Times*, May 4, 1973.

138. Report to the Ford Foundation, National Center for Urban Ethnic Affairs, p. 5, PA 710-0071, reel 4403, section V, Ford Foundation Archives, New York; and Perry L. Weed, *The White Ethnic Movement and Ethnic Politics* (New York: Praeger, 1973), 17. See also Michael Novak, *The Rise of the Unmeltable Ethnics* (New York: Macmillan, 1972).

139. National Urban Coalition, "Progress Report: 1972," Commonwealth Funds, 18.1, box 334, folder 3211, shelf 7, room 204, unit 11, RAC.

140. Fred J. Cooke, "Mayor Kenneth Gibson Says—," *New York Times*, July 25, 1971.

141. "Urban Coalition in Newark Says It Is Facing Extinction," *New York Times*, November 23, 1971.

142. Cooke, "Mayor Kenneth Gibson Says—."

143. Cunningham, *Newark*, 330.

144. Harry B. Webber, "1,000 Turn Out for Heningburg Testimonial," *New Jersey Afro-American*, October 19, 1974.

145. See Robert E. Weems Jr., *Business in Black and White: American Presidents and Black Entrepreneurs in the Twentieth Century* (New York: New York University Press, 2009).

CHAPTER 5

1. Rudy Johnson, "Stella Wright Project Is Closing," *New York Times*, April 1, 1974, 66.

2. "Tenants' History of a Project from a 'Heaven' to 'Hell Hole,'" *New York Times*, July 18, 1974.

3. Newark Housing Authority, A Study of the Social Effects of Public Housing in Newark, N.J. (Newark, NJ, 1944), 16–17.

4. Reginald Roberts, "Rap Group Called Naughty for Filming in Newark," *Star-Ledger*, February 21, 1992; and Naughty by Nature, "Everything's Gonna Be Alright (Ghetto Bastard)," Tommy Boy Records, 1991, compact disc.

5. "Blasts from the Past: Stella Wright Homes," http://www.implosionworld.com/15structures5.htm (accessed August 1, 2014).

6. On tenants' role in shaping public housing, see Rhonda Y. Williams, *The Politics of Public Housing: Black Women's Struggle against Urban Inequality* (New York: Oxford University Press, 2004).

7. Laura Maslow-Armand, "The Newark Tenant Rent Strike: Public Housing Policy and Black Municipal Government," *Patterns of Prejudice* 20, no. 4 (1986): 25–26.

8. See John Baranski, "Something to Help Themselves: Tenant Organizing in San Francisco's Public Housing, 1965–1975," *Journal of Urban History* 33, no. 2 (2007): 418–42.

9. On the broad sweep of tenant protest, see Ronald Lawson, "The Rent Strike in New York City, 1904–1980," *Journal of Urban History* 10, no. 3 (1984): 235–58; and Michael Lipsky, *Protest in City Politics: Rent Strikes, Housing, and the Power of the Poor* (Chicago: Rand McNally, 1970).

10. Williams, *Politics of Public Housing*, 8–10, 155–91. Williams's study also counters ahistorical claims that public housing was an "unmitigated failure" (8).

11. D. Bradford Hunt, *Blueprint for Disaster: The Unraveling of Chicago Public Housing* (Chicago: University of Chicago Press, 2009), 7.

12. Glen Fowler, "Tenant Activists Gaining Momentum in the Nation," *New York Times*, October 26, 1969, R1.

13. Williams, *Politics of Public Housing*, 41–45.

14. Hunt, *Blueprint for Disaster*, 3.

15. *The Pruitt-Igoe Myth*, directed by Chad Freidrichs (New York: First Run Features, 2011), DVD.

16. See chapter 3; and Harold Kaplan, "Urban Renewal in Newark," in *Urban Renewal: The Record and the Controversy*, ed. James Q. Wilson (Cambridge, MA: MIT Press, 1966), 242–46. In the 1940s the Newark Housing Authority proved more receptive to integration than its peer agencies in other cities. Wendell Pritchett, *Robert Clifton Weaver and the American City: The Life and Times of an Urban Reformer* (Chicago: University of Chicago Press, 2008), 83–84.

17. Governor's Select Commission on Civil Disorder, *Report for Action* (Trenton: State of New Jersey, 1968), 55.

18. "Comprehensive Consolidated Management Review Report of the Newark Housing Authority," HUD Newark area office, 1971, Office of Assistant Secretary for Housing Management Dunnells, 1969–1973, RG 207, National Archives and Records Administration, College Park, MD (hereafter OASHM Dunnells); Raymond A. Mohl, "Shifting Patterns of American Urban Policy since 1900," in *Urban Policy in Twentieth-Century America*, ed. Arnold R. Hirsch and Raymond A. Mohl (New Brunswick, NJ: Rutgers University Press, 1993), 15–17; and Maslow-Armand, "Newark Tenant Rent Strike," 22.

19. "Crime Plea Heeded: Housing Projects to Get Police," *Newark Evening News*, May 7, 1964.

20. "Will Hire 42 Special Police for Housing Project Patrol," *Newark Evening News*, July 10, 1964; and Maslow-Armand, "Newark Tenant Rent Strike," 18.

21. Williams, *Politics of Public Housing*, 48–51, 125–26. According to Williams, African American women in Baltimore public housing abided by codes of working-class respectability in parenting, work, leisure, and civic life: "As members of a striving class," she writes, "one's style of life was as important, if not at times more important, than wealth" (48).

22. Hunt, *Blueprint for Disaster*, 173.

23. "City to Strengthen Housing Protection," *Newark Evening News*, May 21, 1964; and "Will Hire 42 Special Police." In December 1963 the Supreme

Court ruled that the city was responsible for the protection of the nearly forty thousand residents in public housing (nearly 13 percent of the city). "Start This Week, City Police Given Housing Patrols," *Newark Evening News*, March 3, 1963.

24. "Crime Plea Heeded."
25. Governor's Select Commission on Civil Disorder, *Report for Action*, 85. Aid to Families with Dependent Children constituted the largest portion of welfare expenditures in Essex County, costs borne by federal, state, and county governments.
26. Some of these changes are evident in a comparison of the "Fifth Annual Report of the Tenant Relations Division, 1958–59" and the "Annual Report of the Tenant Relations Committee, 1963," both published by the NHA. New Jersey Documents, Newark Housing Authority, Newark Public Library (hereafter NPL). The latter report indicates an increase in juvenile delinquency, "undesirable conduct," and household discord. Tenant disputes with the housing authority climbed. The report corroborates tenants' anecdotal accounts, but it is unclear from limited data if problems increased or if officials were more attuned to them.
27. Hunt, *Blueprint for Disaster*, 184–85. Employment levels and income of Chicago's public housing tenants dropped precipitously after 1967, while the proportion of recipients of Aid to Families with Dependent Children swiftly rose.
28. See David Gerwin, "The End of Coalition: The Failure of Community Organizing in Newark in the 1960s" (PhD diss., Columbia University, 1998).
29. "Negro Groups Seen Gaining in Projects to Get Jobs," *Newark Evening News*, August 18, 1963.
30. Joyce Smith Carter, interview by the author, Newark, NJ, February 27, 2007. The Stella Wright rent strike was the boldest campaign against substandard housing in Newark but hardly the only one. See *State Clearing House Report* 20 (July 1970), folder 3, Department of Community Affairs, Counsel's Office Subject file, 1970–1973, Governor Cahill Papers, New Jersey State Archives, Trenton.
31. "Tenants Ask Voice," *Newark Evening News*, May 4, 1969; and "Housing Delegates Set Goals," *Newark Evening News*, May 5, 1969.
32. "Housing Project Remedy Proposed," *Newark Evening News*, October 7, 1969.
33. See chapter 2.
34. Owen T. Wilkerson, "Newark Tenants Ask Rent Control," *Newark Evening News*, November 13, 1969.
35. Baranski, "Something to Help Themselves," 419–24.
36. Clarence Lang, *Grassroots at the Gateway: Class Politics and Black Freedom Struggle in St. Louis, 1936–75* (Ann Arbor: University of Michigan Press, 2009), 213.
37. Ibid., 187.

38. Ibid., 215.

39. William A. Diaz, *Tenant Management: An Historical and Analytical Overview* (Washington, DC: Manpower Demonstration Research Corp., March 1979), 99–102.

40. Joan Cook, "Leader in Rent Strike at Stella Wright Houses Named Head of Newark Tenants' Organization," *New York Times*, January 14, 1974.

41. Fr. Tom Carey to Fr. Leo Mahon, June 1, 1968, San Miguelito Mission: Manuscripts, 2/3, Notre Dame Archive, University of Notre Dame, South Bend, IN; and Todd Hartch, "Leo Mahon and Ivan Illich: Folk Religion and Catechesis in Latin America," *International Bulletin of Missionary Research* 36, no. 4 (2012): 185–88; and http://obits.nj.com/obituaries/starledger/obituary.aspx?pid=153862859 (accessed July 12, 2014).

42. Joseph F. Sullivan, "Is Newark Rent Strike Near End?," *New York Times*, February 13, 1972, 72.

43. Premilla Nadasen, *Welfare Warriors: The Welfare Rights Movement in the United States* (New York: Routledge, 2005), 19–20.

44. See Ronald Lawson and Mark Naison, eds., *The Tenant Movement in New York City, 1904–1984* (New Brunswick, NJ: Rutgers University Press, 1986); and Williams, *Politics of Public Housing*, 175–76.

45. On the interplay of national, state, and local welfare rights activism, see Annelise Orleck, *Storming Caesar's Palace: How Black Mothers Fought Their Own War on Poverty* (Boston: Beacon Press, 2005), 98–167. On similar dynamics between local and national tenant organizations, see Williams, *Politics of Public Housing*, 180–83.

46. Douglas Eldridge, "Rent Strike Impact at Projects Disputed," *Newark Evening News*, April 2, 1970.

47. "Rent Strike Endorsed by 6 Candidates," *Newark Evening News*, April 6, 1970.

48. "Tenants Picket," *Newark Evening News*, May 1, 1970. Toby Henry insisted that 60 percent of the families in Stella Wright (about eight hundred) had withheld rent since April, while NHA officials insisted that the impact of the strike was much smaller. "Says Rent Strike Strong at Homes," *Newark Evening News*, May 5, 1970.

49. Eldridge, "Rent Strike Impact at Projects Disputed."

50. "Newark Tenants Win Eviction Process Stay," *Newark Evening News*, May 15, 1970.

51. "Two Active Tenants Groups May Combine for Strength," *Newark Evening News*, August 10, 1970.

52. Harris David, "The Settlement of the Newark Public Housing Rent Strike: The Tenants Take Control," *Clearinghouse Review* 10, no. 103 (June 1976): 103. Although the number of participants in the rent strike varied by time and building, nearly 11,000 of the over 35,000 residents of public housing withheld rent at the strike's peak in 1973.

53. "Group Moves to Expand Rent Strike in City," *Newark Evening News*, November 2, 1970; Lawson, "Rent Strike in New York City," 248–53. Lawson's

analysis of state laws and tenant strategies in New York is relevant here. The legality of using escrow funds in housing disputes was established by 1930 and became more commonly used in rent strikes in the 1960s, when lawyers in the tenant movement argued that they could strengthen tenants' leverage, persuade judges that the tenants were prepared to pay back rent upon the resolution of their demands, and encourage more tenants to join the strike.

54. "Joint Inspections Due at Projects," *Newark Evening News*, September 22, 1970.
55. Hunt, *Blueprint for Disaster*, 15–16.
56. Mohl, "Shifting Patterns of American Urban Policy," 9.
57. Maslow-Armand, "Newark Tenant Rent Strike," 85.
58. Rachel G. Bratt, *Rebuilding a Low-Income Housing Policy* (Philadelphia, PA: Temple University Press, 1989), 58.
59. Hunt, *Blueprint for Disaster*, 16, 19–20.
60. Ibid., 26–27; and John Herbers, "Operating Costs Found Too High for Tenant Income in Public Housing Crisis," *New York Times*, June 25, 1970, 25.
61. Bratt, *Rebuilding a Low-Income Housing Policy*, 58.
62. Baranski, "Something to Help Themselves," 419.
63. Bratt, *Rebuilding a Low-Income Housing Policy*, 97.
64. Hunt, *Blueprint for Disaster*, 8.
65. Steven R. Weisman, "U.S. Warns Newark to Cut Housing Waste or Lose Aid," *New York Times*, January 29, 1971.
66. "Comprehensive Consolidated Management Review Report."
67. Ibid.; and "Newark Tenant Group Refuses to Disclose Data on Rent Fund," *New York Times*, February 15, 1972. Tenants made similar complaints about Chicago's high-rises. Hunt, *Blueprint for Disaster*, 221–29.
68. "Comprehensive Consolidated Management Review Report."
69. Ibid.
70. Ibid. Without $3 million in operating subsidies, the NHA would have accumulated a deficit of $3.8 million in 1971.
71. Ibid.
72. Ibid.
73. Norman V. Watson to George Romney, April 2, 1971, OASHM Dunnells.
74. Francis Warren, interview by the author, Philadelphia, PA, March 21, 2006; and Junius Williams, interview by the author, Newark, NJ, September 14, 2006.
75. Watson to Romney.
76. "Final Draft of the Security Proposal of the Stella Wright Tenants Association," April 7, 1971, OASHM Dunnells.
77. "CETA Primer," *Journal of Housing* 10 (1975): 515–17.
78. Stella Wright Tenants Association, "Proposal for Minimal Depopulation of Stella Wright Homes," April 22, 1971, box 9, entry 94, compartment 13, row 3, stack area 130, OASHM Dunnells.

79. Ibid. The tenants' proposal prefigured the Section 8 program emerging in policy circles. Pritchett, *Robert Clifton Weaver*, 337–40. On criticism of high-rise housing for large families with young children and the federal response, see Hunt, *Blueprint for Disaster*, 131–33, 148–50.

80. G. Richard Dunnells to Richard C. Van Dusen, July 31, 1971, OASHM Dunnells.

81. Ibid. HUD officials aimed to enhance their leverage with the city. Dunnells suggested that "the Department explore . . . the question of what quid pro quos might be extracted from Gibson." "Gibson Irons Out Dispute on US Housing Funds," *Star-Ledger*, August 22, 1971. See also Joseph D. Sivolella to Kenneth Gibson, December 15, 1971, OASHM Dunnells.

82. "Confidential Working Draft," OASHM Dunnells. HUD officials dismissed tenants' proposal for depopulation as "totally infeasible" given housing demand, yet not long afterward, they proposed shutting down Stella Wright altogether.

83. William L. Brach to James Sweeney, September 8, 1971, OASHM Dunnells.

84. Norman V. Watson to S. William Green, February 24, 1972, OASHM Dunnells.

85. Chester L. Coleman, "Cash Sought," *Newark Evening News*, February 7, 1971; and Joseph F. Sullivan, "Is Newark Rent Strike Near End?, *New York Times*, February 13, 1972.

86. Sam Glasser, "NHA Tenants Balk on Court Order," *Newark Evening News*, February 15, 1972.

87. "Newark Tenant Group Refuses to Disclose Data on Rent Fund," *New York Times*, February 15, 1972, 30.

88. "Is Newark Rent Strike Near End?"; and "Agency Fails to Get Rent Strike Funds," *New York Times*, November 18, 1972.

89. "Rent Strike Seen as 'Inhibiting Aid,'" *New York Times*, February 22, 1972.

90. Williams, *Politics of Public Housing*, 173–74.

91. Hunt, *Blueprint for Disaster*, 218.

92. J. Michael Callan to James Sweeney, October 28, 1971, OASHM Dunnells.

93. "Tenant Association in Newark Faces Contempt Charges," *New York Times*, February 24, 1972.

94. C. Richard Dunnells to Bill Gifford, June 29, 1972, OASHM Dunnells.

95. Norman V. Watson to Fr. James Finnegan, May 2, 1972, and Dunnells to Gifford, both in OASHM Dunnells; and *In the matter of Peter Bridge*, 1972 N.J. Super. Lexis 430.

96. Joseph F. Sullivan, "Rent-Strike Plagued Stella Wright to Be Shut by Newark Housing Authority," *New York Times*, February 6, 1974. On teacher strikes, see Steve Golin, *The Newark Teacher Strikes: Hopes on the Line* (New Brunswick, NJ: Rutgers University Press, 2002).

97. Joseph F. Sullivan, "Motives of Rent Strikers Are Deplored by Gibson," *New York Times*, June 8, 1974.

98. Maslow-Armand, "Newark Tenant Rent Strike," 21.

99. Komozi Woodard, interview by the author, Yonkers, NY, June 9, 2004.

100. The teacher strikes involved beatings and numerous arrests. Golin, *Newark Teacher Strikes*, 154–66.

101. "Newark Tenant Group Refuses."

102. It was Herbert's own court order that had idled the funds for the past six months by prohibiting new deposits or withdrawals.

103. Joseph Sullivan, "Newark Rent Strike Chiefs Facing Court," *New York Times*, December 17, 1972; and "Judge Says Rent Strike Chiefs Seek to Be Martyrs," *New York Times*, December 19, 1972.

104. In the matter of Michael Callan, Harris David, and Gerald Clark, 1973 N.J. Super. Lexis 693.

105. "Judge Says Rent Strike Chiefs Seek to Be Martyrs," *New York Times*; and "2 Rent Strikers Get 45-Day Terms," *New York Times*, January 4, 1973.

106. In the matter of Michael Callan, Harris David, and Gerald Clark, 1973 N.J. Super. Lexis 693.

107. Joan Cook, "Fresh Federal Aid and Tenant Gains Bring a New Era for Jersey Project," *New York Times*, July 28, 1975. The Ford Foundation and HUD financed the tenant management program, with oversight from HUD.

108. Governor's Select Commission on Civil Disorder, *Report for Action*, 56.

109. "Newark Tenant Group Refuses."

110. "Rent Strike Over, Newark Asserts," *New York Times*, January 26, 1973.

111. Fred Ferretti, "Judge Urges Razing for All Buildings in Newark Project," *New York Times*, April 4, 1973.

112. "Tenants Revive Strike in Newark," *New York Times*, July 2, 1973.

113. *McCray v. Beatty*, 1974 U.S. Dist. Lexis 7571.

114. *Newark Housing Authority v. Aiken*, N.J. Dist. Ct., Essex County, November 29, 1973.

115. Joan Cook, "Judge Slashes Rent by 80 Percent in Strike at Newark Project," *New York Times*, November 28, 1973.

116. Ibid.

117. "Newark's Housing Worst, 30-City Survey Concludes," *New York Times*, November 12, 1973, 70.

118. Joan Cook, "HUD Scores Newark Rent Reduction," *New York Times*, November 29, 1973.

119. Quoted in David, "Settlement of the Newark Public Housing Rent Strike."

120. *McCray v. Beatty*, 1974 U.S. Dist. Lexis 7571.

121. Sullivan, "Rent-Strike Plagued Stella Wright to Be Shut by Newark Housing Authority." Though Henry meant it as a humorous aside, his comment highlights an often-neglected thread of 1970s history: the creation of what the counterculture might call "intentional communities" grounded in intensive participatory decision making was hardly the sole province of rural communards.

122. "Newark Archdiocese Urges Gibson Act to Avert Stella Wright Shutdown," *New York Times*, February 7, 1974.

123. Sullivan, "Rent-Strike Plagued Stella Wright to Be Shut by Newark Housing Authority."

124. *McCray v. Beatty*, 1974 U.S. Dist. Lexis 7571.

125. Johnson, "Stella Wright Project Is Closing."

126. Joseph F. Sullivan, "Court Delays Stella Wright Shutdown 30 Days for a Hearing for the Tenants," *New York Times*, April 3, 1974; and "Rent Cut at Newark Project; Court Is Critical of Conditions," *New York Times*, April 11, 1974. A former US attorney, Lacey made his reputation attacking corruption among public officials, including former Newark mayor Hugh Addonizio. Anthony F. Shannon, "Still in Midst of Battle," *Star-Ledger*, September 20, 1992.

127. Average rents were $50–$60 a month, but the full cost of maintaining an average unit amounted to $106, with a combination of public subsidies covering the difference. "Rent Cut at Newark Project"; and *McCray v. Beatty*.

128. "Rent Cut at Newark Project."

129. *McCray v. Beatty*; and Joan Cook, "Fresh Federal Aid and Tenant Gains Bring a New Era for Jersey Project," *New York Times*, July 18, 1974.

130. On tenant movements successfully exploiting discord among government elites, see Andrew Wood and James A. Baer, "Strength in Numbers: Urban Rent Strikes and Political Participation in the Americas," *Journal of Urban History* 32, no. 6 (2006): 871–73.

131. *McCray v. Beatty*. Heningburg's "quiet competence, the respect he enjoys in this community, and his concern," wrote Lacey, "made him an invaluable catalyst in the settlement discussion."

132. Ibid.

133. "Newark Redevelopment and Housing Authority, 1974 Annual Report," Division of State and Regional Planning, New Jersey State Archives.

134. David, "Settlement of the Newark Public Housing Rent Strike," 108.

135. Richard D. Baron, "St. Louis Tenant Management Corporations Bringing Major Transformation of Public Housing," *Journal of Housing* 6, no. 74 (1974): 267.

136. Ibid., 268; and Diaz, *Tenant Management*, vii–xxxvii, 130, 153, 177. Starting in 1976, Manpower Demonstration Research Corporation (MDRC) funded tenant management demonstration projects in Jersey City, NJ; Louisville, KY; New Haven, CT; New Orleans, LA; Rochester, NY; and Oklahoma City, OK, while others unaffiliated with MDRC operated in Washington, DC; Koolau Village, HI; and Boston, MA.

137. Diaz, *Tenant Management*, 130–48.

138. David, "Settlement of the Newark Public Housing Rent Strike," 108.

139. Johnson, "Tenants at Stella Wright."

140. Rudy Johnson, "Newark's Tenant Managers," *New York Times*, October 17, 1976.

141. David, "Settlement of the Newark Public Housing Rent Strike," 109.

142. See Diaz, *Tenant Management*; and Maslow-Armand, "Newark Tenant Rent Strike," 18.
143. David, "Settlement of the Newark Public Housing Rent Strike," 110.
144. Reginald Roberts, "Tenants Authority Meet on Powers," *Star-Ledger*, May 19, 1995.
145. Maslow-Armand, "Newark Tenant Rent Strike," 20.
146. Ira Katznelson, *City Trenches: Urban Politics and the Patterning of Class in the United States* (Chicago: University of Chicago Press, 1981), 19.
147. Ibid., 6.
148. Ibid., 120–21.
149. Frances Fox Piven and Richard Cloward, as quoted in ibid., 188.
150. Towanda Underdue, "Newest NHA Official Sizing Up Work Ahead," *Star-Ledger*, June 15, 1992; and Reginald Roberts, "Newark Tenants Claim Pressure by Officials," *Star-Ledger*, July 20, 1990.
151. Reginald Roberts, "Stella Wright Homes Last to Come Down," *Star-Ledger*, April 26, 2002.
152. Harris David, of Legal Services of New Jersey, who had advised striking tenants two decades earlier, represented the coalition. *Newark Coalition for Low Income Housing et al. v. Newark Redevelopment and Housing Authority*, 524 F. Supp. 2d 559; 2007 U.S. Dist. Lexis 92553.
153. Jennifer Del Medico, "City Razes Three of Seven Stella Wright High Rises," *Star-Ledger*, April 28, 2002; and Christine V. Baird, "Last Newark High-Rise Project Is Demolished," *Star-Ledger*, May 12, 2002.
154. *Newark Coalition for Low Income Housing et al. v. Newark Redevelopment and Housing Authority*.

CHAPTER 6

1. Avis C. Vidal, *Rebuilding Communities: A National Study of Urban Community Development Corporations* (New York: Community Development Research Center, Graduate School of Management and Urban Policy, New School for Social Research, 1992), 8–10; and Alexander Von Hoffman, *House by House, Block by Block: The Rebirth of America's Urban Neighborhoods* (Oxford: Oxford University Press, 2003), 15–16.
2. Harry Boyte, *Backyard Revolution: Understanding the New Citizen Movement* (Philadelphia, PA: Temple University Press, 1980), 5–12.
3. Suleiman Osman, "The Decade of the Neighborhood," in *Rightward Bound: Making America Conservative in the 1970s*, ed. Bruce J. Schulman and Julian E. Zelizer (Cambridge, MA: Harvard University Press, 2008), 110.
4. Alice O'Connor, "Swimming against the Tide: A Brief History of Federal Policy in Poor Communities," in *Urban Problems and Community Development*, ed. Ronald F. Ferguson and William T. Dickens (Washington, DC: Brookings Institution Press, 1999), 113–14.

5. Rebecca Doggett, interview by the author, Newark, NJ, October 9, 2007; and Newark Coordinating Committee to Vincent J. Murphy, President of New Jersey AFL-CIO, September 11, 1964, folder 3 (Employment Committee, Bi-partisan Conference on Civil Rights, Apprenticeship Training), box 4, Ernest Thompson Papers, Rutgers University Special Collections, New Brunswick, NJ (hereafter Thompson Papers).

6. Ernest Thompson and Mindy Thompson, *Homeboy Came to Orange: A Story of People's Power* (Newark, NJ: Bridgebuilder Press, 1976), 37–53.

7. "Work Draft of the Proposal to Further Implement a Tri-city Community Organization for Development, Utilizing a Wide Range of Indigenous and Integrated Resources in Newark, Paterson, and Jersey City," n.d., folder 10, box 4, Thompson Papers.

8. David Barrett, interview by the author, Columbia, MD, January 29, 2005.

9. Lydia Davis Barrett, interview by the author, Montclair, NJ, April 2005.

10. Ibid.

11. David Barrett, interview.

12. Lydia Barrett, interview.

13. Pat Foley, interview by the author, Newark, NJ, December 12, 2006.

14. Ibid.

15. Ibid.

16. The Committee for a Unified Newark became the Congress of African People around the time that Newark activists broke with the US Organization (Maulana Ron Karenga's Los Angeles–based group) and that Newark nationalists asserted their own agenda. Devin Fergus, *Liberalism, Black Power, and the Making of American Politics, 1965–1980* (Athens: University of Georgia Press, 2009), 190–91. On the manifold activities of the Committee for a Unified Newark and its successor Congress of African People, see Komozi Woodard, *A Nation within a Nation: Amiri Baraka (LeRoi Jones) and Black Power Politics* (Chapel Hill: University of North Carolina Press, 1999). My goal is to place black nationalists' community development and housing efforts—carried out by a separately incorporated organization called Kawaida Inc.—in conversation with the other first-generation CDCs operating in the city. I refer to the group as CAP/Kawaida Inc. to emphasize this element.

17. Cyril Degrasse Tyson, *Two Years before the Riot! Newark, New Jersey, and the United Community Corporation, 1964–1966* (New York: Jay Street Publishers, 2000), 256, 490–91. Others involved in early community development efforts shared Tyson's criticism. See Stewart Perry, "National Policy and the Community Development Corporation," *Law and Contemporary Problems* 36, no. 2 (Spring 1971): 297–308.

18. Isolated partnerships among government agencies, philanthropists, and civic groups had produced mixed-income housing in Newark before, but their numbers and complexity grew in the late 1960s. Bob Shabazian, "City Ready to Aid Negroes with Redevelopment Plan," *Newark Evening*

News, February 3, 1966; Bob Shabazian, "Blame FHA in Squeeze," *Newark Evening News*, July 22, 1966; "New Newark Goal Is Set by Hughes," *Newark Evening News*, September 21, 1967; and Bob Shabazian, "Brick Towers Project to Get Mortgage," *Newark Evening News*, January 5, 1968.

19. Nathan Wright Jr., *Ready to Riot* (New York: Holt, Rinehart, and Winston, 1968), 47; and Nathan Wright Jr., Diocese of Newark, to William K. Fox, Chairman of Tri-City Citizens Union for Progress, n.d., MS 1180, AC 3251, box 4, folder 3, Thompson Papers.

20. Hearings on the Medical College Site, February 13, 1968, 20, University of Medicine and Dentistry of New Jersey Archive, Newark.

21. William Linder, "An Urban Community Development Model" (PhD diss., Fordham University, 1988), 209.

22. On other first-generation community development organizations, including Ironbound Community Corporation, Unified Vailsburg Service Organization, and La Casa de Don Pedro, see Julia Rabig, "What's the Matter with Newark?," *Shelterforce, Journal of the National Housing Institute*, Fall 2008.

23. The back-to-the-land movement became an iconic representation of 1960s counterculture. Steven Conn, "Back to the Garden: Communes, the Environment, and Antiurban Pastoralism at the End of the Sixties," *Journal of Urban History* 36 (November 2010): 831–48. But interest in intentional communities was also reflected in the often socially conservative neighborhood movement. The urban neighborhood became, Osman argues, "a site of imagined ethnogenesis" that promised escape from the veneer of assimilation ("Decade of the Neighborhood," 118).

24. See Robert Halpern, *Rebuilding the Inner City: A History of Neighborhood Initiatives to Address Poverty in the United States* (New York: Columbia University Press, 1995), 221–33; O'Connor, "Swimming against the Tide," 106–14; Vidal, *Rebuilding Communities*, 8–14; and Von Hoffman, *House by House*, 2–16.

25. Perry, "National Policy and the Community Development Corporation," 298. D. Bradford Hunt notes that legislators considered offering subsidies to nonprofits and civic organizations for the construction of affordable housing under the Housing Act of 1937. While the provision was sidelined, this debate foreshadowed the role CDCs would play. D. Bradford Hunt, *Blueprint for Disaster: The Unraveling of Chicago Public Housing* (Chicago: University of Chicago Press, 2009), 26, 30.

26. William H. Simon, *The Community Economic Development Movement: Law, Business, and the New Social Policy* (Durham, NC: Duke University Press, 2001), 3–5.

27. John Kain with Joseph P. Persky, "Alternatives to the Gilded Ghetto," *Public Interest* 14 (Winter 1969): 74–75. On internal colonialism, see Charles Pinderhughes, "21st Century Chains: The Continued Relevance of Internal Colonialism Theory" (PhD diss., Boston College, 2009), 16–39.

28. Andrea Gill, "'Gilding the Ghetto' and Debates over Chicago's Gautreaux Program," 201–2; and Nishani Frazier, "A McDonald's That Reflects the Soul of a People: Hough Area Development Corporation and Community Development in Cleveland," 69–70; both in *The Business of Black Power: Community Development, Capitalism, and Corporate Responsibility in Postwar America*, ed. Laura Warren Hill and Julia Rabig (Rochester, NY: University of Rochester Press, 2012).

29. Robert L. Allen, *Black Awakening in Capitalist America* (New York: Anchor Books, 1970), 221; and William K. Tabb, *The Political Economy of the Black Ghetto* (New York: W. W. Norton, 1970), 51–55.

30. Guian McKee, *The Problem of Jobs: Liberalism, Race, and Deindustrialization in Philadelphia* (Chicago: University of Chicago Press, 2008), 208.

31. V. P. Franklin, "'The Lion of Zion': Leon H. Sullivan and the Pursuit of Social and Economic Justice," *Journal of African American History* 94, no. 1 (Winter 2011): 39–41.

32. Robert Bauman, *Race and the War on Poverty from Watts to East L.A.* (Norman: University of Oklahoma Press, 2008), 96.

33. Ibid., 97–103; and Ramón A. Gutiérrez, "Internal Colonialism: An American Theory of Race," *Du Bois Review* 1, no. 2 (September 2004): 281–95.

34. Brian Purnell, "'What We Need Is Brick and Mortar': Race, Gender, and the Early Leadership of the Bedford-Stuyvesant Restoration Corporation," in Hill and Rabig, *Business of Black Power*, 226–33.

35. Mitchell Sviridoff, ed., *Inventing Community Renewal: The Trials and Errors That Shaped the Modern Community Development Corporation* (New York: New School University, Milano Graduate School, Community Development Research Center, 2004), 61.

36. McKee, *Problem of Jobs*, 110; and Sviridoff, *Inventing Community Renewal*, 62, 75.

37. Purnell, "'What We Need Is Brick and Mortar,'" 226–33.

38. Nishani Frazier, "A McDonald's That Reflects the Soul of a People: Hough Area Development Corporation and Community Development in Cleveland," in Hill and Rabig, *Business of Black Power*, 76–83.

39. Ibid.; Purnell, "'What We Need Is Brick and Mortar,'" 226–33.

40. Purnell, "'What We Need Is Brick and Mortar,'" 231–33.

41. Bauman, *Race and the War on Poverty*, 107; and Annelise Orleck, *Storming Caesar's Palace: How Black Mothers Fought Their Own War on Poverty* (Boston: Beacon Press, 2005), 260–61.

42. David J. Erickson, *The Housing Policy Revolution: Networks and Neighborhoods* (Washington, DC: Urban Institute Press, 2009), 4.

43. Laura Warren Hill, "Fighting for the Soul of Black Capitalism: Struggles for Black Economic Development in Postrebellion Rochester," in Hill and Rabig, *Business of Black Power*, 45–67.

44. Perry, "National Policy and the Community Development Corporation," 297–98, 301.

45. "Work Draft," 13–16, folder 10, box 4, Thompson Papers. On the evolving theories of poverty in the 1960s, see Michael B. Katz, *The Undeserving Poor: From the War on Poverty to the War on Welfare* (New York: Pantheon, 1990); and Alice O'Connor, *Poverty Knowledge: Social Science, Social Policy, and the Poor in Twentieth-Century U.S. History* (Princeton, NJ: Princeton University Press, 2001).

46. Bruce J. Schulman, *The Seventies: The Great Shift in American Culture, Society, and Politics* (New York: Da Capo Press, 2001), 26; and David J. Erickson, "Community Capitalism: How Housing Advocates, the Private Sector, and Government Forged New Low-Income Housing Policy, 1968–1996," *Journal of Policy History* 18, no. 2 (2006): 167–204.

47. O'Connor, "Swimming against the Tide," 111–13.

48. On Wright's involvement, see William K. Fox, "Report on Tri-City Citizen's Union for Progress, Inc.," October 1968, folder 10, box 4, Thompson Papers.

49. Constitution of Tri-City Citizens Union for Progress, folder 10, box 4, Thompson Papers.

50. Memo, William K. Fox, Chairman, to judicatory executives and the appropriate boards serving the Tri-City, April 1, 1967, Newark, NJ, folder, Source Materials, Newark-Portland, Records of Case Studies and Task Forces, National Commission on Neighborhoods, RG 220, Carter Presidential Library, Atlanta, GA (hereafter Carter Library).

51. Minutes, Tri-City meeting, October 9, 1967, Newark, NJ, folder, Source Materials, Newark-Portland, Records of Case Studies and Task Forces, RG 220, Carter Library.

52. The AME New Jersey Conference, General Convention of Baptists, New Jersey Baptist Convention, Episcopal Diocese, Methodist Northern Conference, and the Reformed Church of America provided tens of thousands of dollars in initial grants to Tri-City. Memo, William K. Fox to judicatory executives; and Constitution of Tri-City Citizens Union for Progress.

53. Thompson and Thompson, *Homeboy Came to Orange*, 167. The area selected was bounded by South Tenth Street on the east, by South Orange Avenue on the north, and by Springfield Avenue on the south. Minutes, Tri-City Special Meeting at Mt. Zion Baptist Church, September 25, 1967, Newark, NJ, folder, Source Materials, Newark-Portland, Records of Case Studies and Task Forces, RG 220, Carter Library.

54. Minutes, September 25, 1967.

55. "Background and Organization," 1979; and Robert W. Burchell, James W. Hughes, and George Sternlieb, "Housing Costs and Housing Restraints, Newark, NJ" (Center for Urban Social Science Research, Rutgers University, New Brunswick, NJ, 1970); both in Newark, NJ, folder, Source Materials, Newark-Portland, National Commission on Neighborhoods, Records of Case Studies and Task Forces, RG 220, Carter Library.

56. "Background and Organization." West Side Park comprised four census tracts: 26, 27, 34, and 35. The neighborhood had a slightly higher rate

of poverty than the rest of Newark and a higher percentage of female-headed homes than the Newark city average of 27 percent. West Side Park residents' median income fell below the city median of $7,735.00. Over 20 percent of West Side Park residents survived on incomes below the poverty line; the city average was 18 percent.

57. This founding group of black professionals included a teacher, a social worker, a physician, a business owner, and a funeral home director. Walter Berry and his son, an attorney, were the sole white contributors. "Black Capitalism and a 'Social Approach' to Rehab in a Major Ghetto," *Builders' Choice: The Whirlpool Magazine for the Building Industry*, Summer 1969, Newark, NJ, folder, Source Materials, Newark-Portland, Records of Case Studies and Task Forces, RG 220, Carter Library; and Teare and Buck Attorneys to Earnest Thompson, January 2, 1969, box 4, folder 10, Thompson Papers.

58. Ibid.; and "Background and Organization."

59. "Background and Organization"; and Burchell, Hughes, and Sternlieb, "Housing Costs and Housing Restraints," 88.

60. "Black Capitalism and a 'Social Approach.'"

61. Burchell, Hughes, and Sternlieb, "Housing Costs and Housing Restraints," 68–69.

62. "Black Capitalism and a 'Social Approach.'" Whirlpool supplied appliances for the housing development Amity I. Burchell, Hughes, and Sternlieb, "Housing Costs and Housing Restraints," 67.

63. "Black Capitalism and a 'Social Approach'"; and Kwame Turé (Stokely Carmichael) and Charles V. Hamilton, *Black Power: The Politics of Liberation* (1967; repr., New York: Vintage, 1992), 40–46.

64. Burchell, Hughes, and Sternlieb, "Housing Costs and Housing Restraints," 98.

65. Doggett, interview; and Thompson and Thompson, *Homeboy Came to Orange*, 171–73.

66. Real estate companies' interest in early community-based development efforts was advanced as a kind of "corrective capitalism." O'Connor, "Swimming against the Tide," 80–81; N. Pierce and C. Steinbach, *Corrective Capitalism: The Rise of America's CDCs* (New York: Ford Foundation, 1978); and Charles J. Orlebeke, "The Evolution of Low-Income Housing Policy, 1949–1999," *Housing Policy Debate* 11, no. 2 (2000): 489–520. Builders and developers benefited from provisions of Section 236 of the Housing Act of 1968, which offered federally subsidized mortgages to developers serving low- and middle-income markets. Paul George Lewis, "Housing and American Privatism: The Origins and Evolution of Subsidized Home-Ownership Policy," *Journal of Policy History* 5, no. 1 (1993): 28–51.

67. Doggett, interview; and "Background and Organization," 10.

68. Head Start hired Rebecca for a position in Puerto Rico running a program similar to the Newark Preschool Council she had helped organize with federal funding from the War on Poverty.

69. "Background and Organization," 11.

70. Orlebeke, "Evolution of Low-Income Housing Policy," 489–520.

71. Chris Bonastia, "Hedging His Bets: Why Nixon Killed HUD's Desegregation Efforts," *Social Science History* 28, no. 1 (Spring 2004): 19–52.

72. Barbara Collins Turner, "Case Study Report on the Tri-City Citizen's Union for Progress," July 1978, Records of Case Studies and Task Forces, Misc. Projects and Issues File, San Antonio through Atlanta, RG 220, Carter Library.

73. Turner, "Case Study Report," 12. Tri-City sold Amity Village in 1978.

74. "Background and Organization," 12.

75. Annual Report of the Florence and John Schumann Foundation 1976, Newark-Portland, Tri-City folder, Records of Case Studies and Task Forces, RG 220, Carter Library.

76. Ibid.

77. Rebecca Doggett's experience working for Head Start in Newark and Puerto Rico influenced the People's Center. Edward F. Zigler and Sandra Bishop-Josef, "The Cognitive Child versus the Whole Child: Lessons from Forty Years of Head Start," in *Play = Learning: How Play Motivates and Enhances Children's Cognitive and Social-Emotional Growth*, ed. Dorothy G. Singer, Roberta Michnick Golinkoff, and Kathy Hirsh-Pasek (Oxford: Oxford University Press, 2006), 15–35.

78. Maso P. Ryan, President, and Rebecca Andrade, Exec. Director, "Redeem the Cities! 1974 Summary Report and 1975 First Quarter Report," Tri-City folder, Newark-Portland, Records of Case Studies and Task Forces, RG 220, Carter Library.

79. "Background and Organization," 13.

80. Ryan and Andrade, "Redeem the Cities!"

81. Newark Commission on Human Rights, "Public Hearing: Report on Conditions in the Hispanic Community" (Newark, NJ: City Clerk's Office, 1976), 16.

82. Newark Commission on Human Rights, "Public Hearing," 17.

83. Ibid., 21.

84. Turner, "Case Study Report," 42.

85. "Background and Organization," 14.

86. Memo, William K. Fox to judicatory executives."

87. Turner, "Case Study Report," 33.

88. Ibid., 25.

89. "Black Capitalism and a 'Social Approach'"; and Burchell, Hughes, and Sternlieb, "Housing Costs and Housing Restraints," 66.

90. Burchell, Hughes, and Sternlieb, "Housing Costs and Housing Restraints," 9. Despite close scrutiny and favorable attention from Carter's urban policymakers, Tri-City received little federal support. Project Rehab supplied some funding for Amity projects 2B, 4, 5, and 6, which were later turned over to a conventional developer, the NADC. "Background and Organization," 8, 9.

91. "Background and Organization," 18. Tri-City was a member of the Emergency Committee to Save Childcare, a coalition of providers with state and city contracts that received matching grants of 25 percent from the city.
92. Memo, William K. Fox to judicatory executives; and Toni Caldwell, chief operating officer, Tri-City, interview by the author, East Orange, NJ, June 10, 2008.

CHAPTER 7

1. For more on the historiography and the economic dimensions of the black power movement, see Laura Warren Hill and Julia Rabig, "Toward a History of the Business of Black Power," in *The Business of Black Power: Community Development, Capitalism, and Corporate Responsibility in Postwar America*, ed. Laura Warren Hill and Julia Rabig (Rochester, NY: University of Rochester Press, 2012), 15–44.
2. Amiri Baraka, *Selected Poetry of Amiri Baraka / LeRoi Jones* (New York: William Morrow, 1979).
3. Cynthia Young, "Havana Up in Harlem," in *Soul Power: Culture, Radicalism and the Making of a Third World Left* (Durham, NC: Duke University Press, 2006), 18–53.
4. Amiri Baraka, *The Autobiography of LeRoi Jones* (Chicago: Lawrence Hill Books, 1997), 246.
5. Ibid., 273.
6. Ibid., 179–274. The complex relationship between radical art and political action in Baraka's work is taken up in Nita M. Kumar, "The Logic of Retribution in Amiri Baraka's 'Dutchman,'" *African American Review* 37, no. 2 (Summer–Autumn 2003): 273–75.
7. Gene Jarrett, *Deans and Truants: Race and Realism in African American Literature* (Philadelphia: University of Pennsylvania Press, 2011), 1–15, 14–15, 169–72; and Komozi Woodard, *A Nation within a Nation: Amiri Baraka (LeRoi Jones) and Black Power Politics* (Chapel Hill: University of North Carolina Press, 1999), 89, 162.
8. Woodard, *Nation within a Nation*, 227. On *ujamaa*, see Bonnie Ibhawoh and J. I. Dibua, "Deconstructing Ujamaa: The Legacy of Julius Nyerere in the Quest for Social and Economic Development in Tanzania," *African Journal of Political Science* 8, no. 1 (2003): 59–83. In Chicago, Sokoni Karanja sought to adapt Nyerere's socialist vision to black institutions, including the Centers for New Horizons. Alexander Von Hoffman, *House by House, Block by Block: The Rebirth of America's Urban Neighborhoods* (Oxford: Oxford University Press, 2003), 117–18.
9. Woodard, *Nation within a Nation*, 168–71, 220. On the relationship among these organizations and their functions, see Imamu Amiri Baraka, "Strategies and Tactics of a Pan African Nationalist Party," Committee for a Uni-

fied Newark, 1971, 16–17, in *The Black Power Movement*, pt. 1, *Amiri Baraka: From Black Arts to Black Radicalism*, ed. John H. Bracey Jr., Sharon Harley, and Komozi Woodard (Bethesda, MD: University Publications of America, 2000), microfilm, reel 2, series 5. Organizations such as the CFUN, later CAP, Baraka explains, should cultivate "strong organized cadres" of nationalists that would bring like-minded organizations into alliance and eventually run candidates for office. Lydia Davis Barrett, interview by the author, Montclair, NJ, April 2005; David Barrett, interview by the author, Columbia, MD, January 29, 2005; and Robert Allen, *Black Awakening in Capitalist America* (Trenton, NJ: Africa World Press, 1992), 141, 157–71.

10. Scot Brown, *Fighting for US: Maulana Karenga, the US Organization, and Black Cultural Nationalism* (New York: New York University, 2003), 33–38, 102, 138–44, 147.

11. Woodard, *Nation within a Nation*, 226.

12. Keith Mayes, "'A Holiday of Our Own': Kwanzaa, Cultural Nationalism, and the Promotion of a Black Power Holiday, 1966–1985," in *The Black Power Movement: Rethinking the Civil Rights–Black Power Era*, ed. Peniel Joseph (New York: Routledge, 2006), 239–41. Baraka enthusiastically advanced Kawaida in Newark until 1971, when he and Karenga had a falling out and their philosophies diverged. Baraka, *Autobiography of LeRoi Jones*, 402–7.

13. Woodard, *Nation within a Nation*, 227.

14. National Black Assembly Law and Justice Committee, Kawaida Towers Inquiry, April 16, 1973, in Bracey, Harley, and Woodard, *Black Power Movement*, pt. 1, reel 2, series 5. See testimony by architect Majenzi Kuumba (Earl Crooms) and attorneys Raymond Brown and Vernon Clash.

15. "Newark Project Gets Under Way," *New York Times*, October 13, 1972, 84.

16. National Black Assembly Law and Justice Committee, Kawaida Towers Inquiry, testimony of architect Majenzi Kuumba (Earl Crooms) and drawing of Kawaida Towers.

17. Woodard, *Nation within a Nation*, 229; and Baraka, *Autobiography of LeRoi Jones*, 429.

18. Editorial, *Italian Tribune News*, August 27, 1971, 2.

19. "Imperiale Takes Issue over Agency's Status," *Italian Tribune News*, August 27, 1971, 1.

20. Michael Immerso, *Newark's Little Italy: The Vanished First Ward* (New Brunswick, NJ: Rutgers University Press, 1997), 140–41.

21. Other institutions involved with white ethnic revival were the Center for the Study of American Pluralism, led by Reverend Andrew M. Greeley, and the National Project on Ethnic America, led by Irving Levine and affiliated with the American Jewish Committee. Lewis Feldstein, "Now That We Are Beautiful, Where Do We Go?," February 1974, 26, Report 002899, Ford Foundation Archives, New York.

22. The Ford Foundation's expenditures on civil rights and integration projects generated outsized controversy and prompted tax reform legisla-

tion in 1969 to curb philanthropic support for political organizations. Representative Wright Patman, a Republican, argued that philanthropies violated the basis for their tax-exempt status when they funded programs too partisan to promote the public good. See Waldemar A. Nelson, *The Big Foundations* (New York: Columbia University Press, 1972), 9–20. Karen Ferguson, in *Top Down: The Ford Foundation, Black Power, and the Reinvention of Racial Liberalism* (Philadelphia: University of Pennsylvania Press, 2013), 3–5, 210–54, shows that the Ford Foundation, which sought to "manage racial conflict and inequality during the civil rights era and beyond" (3), also attempted to extract from a multifaceted mass movement an elite black power leadership along lines similar to the National Urban Coalition.

23. Kwame Turé (Stokely Carmichael) and Charles V. Hamilton, *Black Power: The Politics of Liberation* (1967; repr., New York: Vintage, 1992), 58–84.

24. Stephen Adubato to Geno Baroni, April 26, 1972, Newark 1971 folder, CBRN 42/1, Notre Dame Archive, South Bend, IN.

25. National Black Assembly Law and Justice Committee, Kawaida Towers Inquiry, testimony by Kaimu M'tetezi (David Barrett).

26. "Imperiale Takes Issue over Agency's Status," 1.

27. Woodard, *Nation within a Nation*, 230.

28. David Halbfinger, "Anthony Imperiale, 68, Dies; Polarizing Force in Newark," *New York Times*, December 28, 1999, B9.

29. David R. Colburn and George Pozzetta, "Race, Ethnicity, and the Evolution of Political Legitimacy," in *The Sixties: From Memory to History*, ed. David Farber (Chapel Hill: University of North Carolina Press, 1994), 131; and Woodard, *Nation within a Nation*, 231.

30. "Legislator in Protest at Baraka's Building," *Chicago Daily Defender*, November 22, 1972, 5.

31. "Blue-Flu Halts Work on Building Project," *Chicago Daily Defender*, November 29, 1972, 26.

32. Joseph F. Sullivan, "Newark Housing Stirs Hot Debate," *New York Times*, November 11, 1972, 37; "Cops Get Blacks to Job," *Chicago Daily Defender*, December 5, 1972, 20; and Woodard, *Nation within a Nation*, 235.

33. National Black Assembly Law and Justice Committee, Kawaida Towers Inquiry.

34. Woodard, *Nation within a Nation*, 235.

35. Ibid., 239.

36. Joseph F. Sullivan, "Kawaida Project Is Backed by a Steelworkers Local," *New York Times*; and "N.J. Clergy Backs Housing Project," *Chicago Defender*, July 21, 1973.

37. Temple of Kawaida, press release, March 9, 1973, in Bracey, Harley, and Woodard, *Black Power Movement*, pt. 1, reel 2, series 5.

38. National Black Assembly Law and Justice Committee, Kawaida Towers Inquiry.

39. Sullivan, "Kawaida Project Is Backed by a Steelworkers Local"; and "N.J. Clergy Backs Housing Project."

40. North Ward Clergy, "Kawaida-Community Liaison Proposal," March 1973, in Bracey, Harley, and Woodard, *Black Power Movement*, pt. 1, reel 2, series 5.

41. *Cervase v. Kawaida Towers, Inc.*, 124 N.J. Super. 547 (1973).

42. Baraka, *Autobiography of LeRoi Jones*, 412–14. Baraka was also positioned as a mediator among various Left and nationalist factions (428). For more on the Gary conventions, see Henry Hampton, Judith Vecchione, Steve Fayer, Orlando Bagwell, Callie Crossley, James A. DeVinney, Madison Davis Lacy, et al., *Eyes on the Prize* (PBS Video, Blackside Inc., 2006), DVD; and Woodard, *Nation within a Nation*, 184–90, 203–15.

43. Lydia Barrett, interview.

44. Linda Holmes, "Kawaida: It's More than a Dispute," *Information: A Paper for the People of Newark* 1, no. 4 (March 1973): 8; and *Information* 2, no. 3 (December 1973): 12–13, Gustav Heningburg Papers, Charles F. Cummings New Jersey Information Center, Newark Public Library, Newark, NJ.

45. Woodard, Nation within a Nation, 252.

46. See War Stories section of Amiri Baraka, *Tales of the Out and the Gone* (New York: Akashic Press, 2007), 17–130.

47. Baraka, David Barrett, and other cultural nationalists joined a cross section of Newark's black leaders to create the Minority Economic Development Industrial and Cultural Enterprises (MEDIC), which vetted business proposals and channeled federal loans and technical assistance to local minority-owned businesses, including several in Baraka's orbit. MEDIC newsletters, 1971, folder 3, box 4 of 7, series IV, Gustav Heningburg Papers, Charles F. Cummings New Jersey Information Center, Newark Public Library, Newark, NJ.

48. Kimberly Springer, "Black Feminists Respond to Black Power Masculinism," in Joseph, *Black Power Movement*, 104–18. On the origins of the debate over the structure and status of the black family, see E. Franklin Frazier, *The Negro Family in the United States* (Chicago: University of Chicago Press, 1939). Daniel Patrick Moynihan, assistant secretary of labor under President Johnson, built upon many of Frazier's arguments in *The Negro Family: The Case for National Action* (Washington, DC: Office of Policy Planning and Research, US Department of Labor, 1965). On the political influences—intended and otherwise—of Moynihan's report and feminist criticism of its assumptions, see Lisa Levenstein, *A Movement without Marches: African American Women and the Politics of Poverty in Postwar Philadelphia* (Chapel Hill: University of North Carolina Press, 2009), Kindle e-book, loc. 2535–57; Annelise Orleck, *Storming Caesar's Palace: How Black Mothers Fought Their Own War on Poverty* (Boston: Beacon Press, 2005), 230–34; Deborah Gray White, *Too Heavy a Load: Black Women in Defense of Themselves* (New York: W. W. Norton, 1999), 212–34; and "The

Moynihan Report Revisited: Lessons and Reflections after Four Decades," special issue, *Annals: Journal of the American Academy of Political and Social Science* 621, no. 1 (January 2009).

49. Anna Julia Cooper, *A Voice from the South by a Black Woman from the South* (Xenia, OH: Aldine Printing House, 1892), 60.

50. Brown, *Fighting for US*, 120–23.

51. Ibid., 152–57; and Kimberly Springer, "Black Feminists Respond to Black Power Masculinism," in Joseph, *Black Power Movement*, 105–18.

52. Daniel Matlin, "'Lift Up Yr Self!' Reinterpreting Amiri Baraka (LeRoi Jones), Black Power, and the Uplift Tradition," *Journal of American History* 93, no. 1 (2006): 91–116.

53. Lydia Barrett, interview.

54. Baraka, *Autobiography of LeRoi Jones*, 424, 436–40; and Lydia Barrett, interview.

55. Lydia Barrett, interview.

56. Ibid.

57. Woodard, *Nation within a Nation*, 233.

58. Lydia Barrett, interview.

59. Baraka, Autobiography of LeRoi Jones, 436–40.

60. W. E. B. Du Bois, *The Souls of Black Folk* (1903; repr., New York: Modern Library, 2003), 3–7; and William Styron, *Confessions of Nat Turner* (New York: Random House, 1967). Black intellectuals' criticism of Styron's first-person novelization of Turner's rebellion appears in John Henrik Clarke, ed., *William Styron's Nat Turner: Ten Black Writers Respond* (Boston: Beacon Press, 1968).

61. David Barrett, interview.

62. Nikki Giovanni, "Black Poems, Poseurs, and Power" (1969), in *Call and Response: Key Debates in African American Studies*, ed. Henry Louis Gates and Jennifer Burton (New York: W. W. Norton, 2008), 711–15.

63. Beverly A. Williams, "Mayor Hatcher Calls UN 'Men of the People,'" *New Jersey Afro-American*, October 13, 1973. Barrett is pictured along with two other CFUN Unity Party candidates—Alfonso Roman (candidate for Essex County freeholder) and Frank Hutchins (fellow candidate for the New Jersey General Assembly)—and Mayor Richard G. Hatcher of Gary, IN, at an awards breakfast, illustrating CFUN's attempts to tie local campaigns to the broader sweep of minority electoral victories. On CFUN's political strategies, see David Hugo Barrett, "Inside Out: A Memoir of Black Power in Newark, 1967–1974," unpublished manuscript.

64. Baraka, *Autobiography of LeRoi Jones*, 424.

65. Lydia Barrett, interview.

66. Ibid. Baraka (*Autobiography of LeRoi Jones*, 428) acknowledged the "new tensions and explosions inside our various organizations" and wondered whether they could have been mitigated.

67. Lydia Barrett served as executive director of the Urban League of Essex County from 1992 to 1998 and, more recently, helped found and direct the Montclair Fund for Women. David Barrett, after working for years in the information technology sector, now teaches algebra at an alternative public school in Howard County, MD. He serves on the board of the Alpha Foundation of Howard County, MD, which targets educational inequality by providing scholarships and educational mentoring to prepare black high school students for college.

CHAPTER 8

1. Notes for flyer, Operation Understanding meeting, February 25, 1968, personal collection of Pat Foley, Woodcliff Lake, NJ.
2. Alan Ehrenhalt, "New Life in Newark," *Governing Magazine*, July 2007.
3. Mary Ward, *Mission for Justice: The History of the First African-American Catholic Church in Newark, NJ* (Knoxville: University of Tennessee Press, 2002), 25, 30.
4. Ibid., 25–35, 50–55. The founders pursued a strategy similar to that of Polish and Italian immigrants. John T. McGreevy, *Parish Boundaries: The Catholic Experience with Race in the Twentieth Century Urban North* (Chicago: University of Chicago Press, 1998), 29–53.
5. Cecelia Faulks, interview by the author, Newark, NJ, November 14, 2006.
6. Ward, *Mission for Justice*, 52, 55, 63.
7. Joyce Smith Carter, interview by the author, Newark, NJ, February 27, 2007. Carter did not recall the exact date of this concert, but Sun Ra was a fixture of the Black Arts Movement. He performed and recorded in Newark in the 1960s, collaborating with Amiri Baraka on *A Black Mass*. Amiri Baraka and Sun Ra & His Myth Science Arkestra, *A Black Mass*, Jihad Records, 1968, vinyl recording.
8. Carter, interview.
9. Ward, *Mission for Justice*, 88–92.
10. Richard J. Bord and Joseph E. Faulkner, *The Catholic Charismatics: The Anatomy of a Modern Religious Movement* (University Park: Pennsylvania State University Press, 1983), 61.
11. Galatians 2:20.
12. Political activism was a common outgrowth of Cursillo involvement, but it was not intrinsic. "The Spirituality of the Cursillo Movement," summary of a talk by Rev. John Randall, a spiritual director of the R. I. Cursillo Movement, 1968 (personal collection of Pat Foley).
13. Charles Payne, "Ella Baker and Models of Social Change," *Signs: Journal of Women in Culture and Society* 14 (Summer 1989): 885–900.
14. Bord and Faulkner, *Catholic Charismatics*, 61.
15. Pat Foley, interview by the author, Newark, NJ, December 12, 2006.

16. The Christian Family Movement encouraged small groups of families to discuss the application of Catholic teachings to parenting and married life. Jeffrey M. Burns, *Disturbing the Peace: A History of the Christian Family Movement, 1949–1974* (South Bend, IN: University of Notre Dame Press, 1999); and notes for flyer, Operation Understanding meeting, personal collection of Pat Foley.

17. David and Pat Foley, City-Suburban Liaison Committee, Christian Community Movement, n.d., personal collection of Pat Foley.

18. Ward, Mission for Justice, 104.

19. Other participants are named in William Linder, "An Urban Community Development Model" (PhD diss., Fordham University, 1988), 124; and Ward, *Mission for Justice*, 106.

20. Bob Guskind, interview by the author, Newark, NJ, July 11, 2006; and Neal Peirce and Robert Guskind, *Against the Tide: The NCC, 1968–1969* (Newark, NJ: New Community Corporation, 1993), pt. 4. While it is difficult to assess the effectiveness of Operation Understanding, one tally indicates that its discussions were attended by nearly two thousand people in 1968. *Understanding* 1, no. 3 (June 25, 1968).

21. Foley, interview.

22. Photographs of "Ghetto Tours," folder 8, box 1, Biographical Information, ser. 1, Gustav Heningburg Papers, Charles F. Cummings New Jersey Information Center, Newark Public Library, Newark, NJ (hereafter NPL).

23. Komozi Woodard, interview by the author, Yonkers, NY, June 9, 2004.

24. Douglas Eldridge, "Last Ghetto Tour Grim but Hopeful," *Newark Evening News*, August 18, 1968.

25. *Understanding* 1, no. 2 (April 24, 1968), personal collection of Pat Foley.

26. *Understanding* 1, no. 2 (April 24, 1968); David Foley to Richard Hughes, February 25, 1968, personal collection of Pat Foley; and Governor's Select Commission on Civil Disorder, *Report for Action* (Trenton: State of New Jersey, 1968).

27. *Understanding* 1, no. 3 (June 25, 1968), personal collection of Pat Foley.

28. Foley refers in this article to a series of crucial New Jersey State Supreme Court decisions. In 1975 the court decided on a case brought by the NAACP against the suburban township of Mount Laurel. The court found Mount Laurel's minimum lot size requirements for single-family homes exclusionary; only the wealthy could afford five acres. The decision struck down a zoning requirement common throughout the state. A second decision in 1982, *Mount Laurel II*, established low-income housing requirements for New Jersey communities. Barbara G. Salmore and Stephen A. Salmore, *New Jersey Politics and Government: Suburban Politics Comes of Age*, 2nd ed. (Lincoln: University of Nebraska Press, 1998), 198. The issues of taxation and residential inequality at the heart of the *Mount Laurel* decisions intertwined with perennial challenges to state education funding. In 1973 the court decided in *Robinson v. Cahill* that the state's failure to

adequately fund public schools amounted to a constitutional violation. Under mandate from the court, the state legislature implemented a long-debated income tax in 1976. Salmore and Salmore, *New Jersey Politics and Government*, 8, 191, 197. Subsequent decisions in *Abbott v. Burke* heralded more specific remedies, including equalized funding between impoverished urban and wealthy suburban districts. *Abbott v. Burke*, 119 N.J. 287, 575 A.2d 359 (N.J. 1990). These decisions—made in attenuated fashion, subject to backsliding and loopholes in their implementation—did not ultimately benefit Newark residents as Foley anticipated. Salmore and Salmore, *New Jersey Politics and Government*, 197–98. See also Harold Gillette Jr., *Camden after the Fall: Decline and Renewal in a Post-industrial City* (Philadelphia: University of Pennsylvania Press, 2005), 171–85.

29. *Doing Today Those Things*, 1969, booklet produced by the NCC and the New Community Foundation, 8–9 Newark Quasi file, NPL. Bounded by Jones Street on the east, Bergen Street on the west, South Orange Avenue on the north, and Fifteenth Avenue on the south, the plot lay within the jurisdiction of Newark's Model Cities program and abutted the New Jersey College of Medicine and Dentistry to the north. Approximately five thousand residents lived within the NCC target area. Douglas Eldridge, "Church Unit, Negroes Set Slum Area Attack," *Newark Evening News*, February 29, 1968.

30. *Doing Today Those Things*. Community development activists employed "cycles of poverty" and other rhetoric consistent with the "culture of poverty" analysis most controversially advanced by Senator Daniel Patrick Moynihan in *The Negro Family: The Case for National Action* (Washington, DC: Office of Policy Planning and Research, US Department of Labor, 1965) even as they disavowed many of the report's implications. See Michael B. Katz, ed., *The Underclass Debate: Views from History* (Princeton, NJ: Princeton University Press, 1992).

31. *Doing Today Those Things*.

32. Ibid.

33. "Out of the Ghetto," *Newark Evening News*, March 1, 1968.

34. *Doing Today Those Things*; and "Suburbanites Tour Ghetto to Kick Off Fund Campaign," *Newark Evening News*, May 11, 1969.

35. "Archdioceses Hears Housing Loan Plan," *Newark Evening News*, September 21, 1968.

36. Ward, *Mission for Justice*, 145, appendix 3; and "Newark Archdiocese to Introduce New Mass," *Newark Evening News*, March 21, 1970, 12.

37. Ward, *Mission for Justice*, 145, 150.

38. Robert S. Lecky and H. Elliott Wright, eds., *Religion, Racism, and Reparations* (New York: Sheed and Ward, 1969), 114–26.

39. Clarence Lang, *Grassroots at the Gateway: Class Politics and Black Freedom Struggle in St. Louis, 1936–1975* (Ann Arbor: University of Michigan Press, 2009), 210.

40. "Map Rebuilding Job," *Newark Evening News*, April 27, 1969.
41. "Group Launches Drive for $1 Million Newark Housing Fund," *Newark Evening News*, May 1, 1969.
42. Linder, "Urban Community Development Model," 124.
43. *Doing Today Those Things*.
44. Ibid.
45. Douglas Eldridge, "Newark Group Gets State Housing Aid," *Newark Evening News*, August 19, 1970.
46. "Livingston Drive to Aid City Ward," *Newark Evening News*, February 22, 1970.
47. Linder, "Urban Community Development Model," 124.
48. Faulks, interview.
49. See http://www.habitat67.com (accessed April 28, 2007).
50. Peirce and Guskind, *Against the Tide*, pt. 10.
51. Linder, "Urban Community Development Model," 48.
52. Annelise Orleck, *Storming Caesar's Palace: How Black Mothers Fought Their Own War on Poverty* (Boston: Beacon Press, 2005), 115–17.
53. Peirce and Guskind, *Against the Tide*, pt. 5. For more on stigmatization of public housing during the 1970s and 1980s, see Lisa Levenstein, *A Movement without Marches: African American Women and the Politics of Poverty in Postwar Philadelphia* (Chapel Hill: University of North Carolina Press, 2009), Kindle e-book, loc. 1258–1614; and Rhonda Y. Williams, *The Politics of Public Housing: Black Women's Struggle against Urban Inequality* (Oxford: Oxford University Press, 2004), 101–4, 110–14. See also Michael B. Katz, *The Undeserving Poor: From the War on Poverty to the War on Welfare* (New York: Pantheon, 1990).
54. Foley, interview.
55. Ward, *Mission for Justice*, 118. Smith was an early board member of the United Community Corporation and led the Central West Services League.
56. Peirce and Guskind, *Against the Tide*, pt. 12.
57. Ibid., pt. 8.
58. Foley, interview; and Pilar Perez, "Nursery Strapped for Funds," *Star-Ledger*, March 30, 1975.
59. "Comprehensive Consolidated Management Review Report of the Newark Housing Authority," HUD Newark area office, 1971, Office of Assistant Secretary for Housing Management Dunnells, 1969–1973, RG 207, National Archives and Records Administration, College Park, MD (hereafter NARA).
60. Linder, "Urban Community Development Model," 158.
61. Ibid.
62. Perez, "Nursery Strapped for Funds."
63. Joseph F. Sullivan, "Nursery Fights Inflation's Pinch and Seeks Aid," *New York Times*, April 6, 1975.

64. Kathleen D. McCarthy, ed., *Lady Bountiful Revisited: Women, Philanthropy, and Power* (New Brunswick, NJ: Rutgers University Press, 1990).

65. Mary Garrahan, "When Help Is Needed, 'Some Things Have to Go,'" *Advocate*, July 11, 1968.

66. Premilla Nadasen, *Welfare Warriors: The Welfare Rights Movement in the United States* (New York: Routledge, 2005), 165–68; and Orleck, *Storming Caesar's Palace*, 98–130.

67. Linder, "Urban Community Development Model," 1–20.

68. Ibid., 118.

69. Ibid., 110. Proponents of these models occasionally insisted that they would yield a more effective delivery of social services, but they rarely employed the free-market metaphors that became a hallmark of welfare reform less than two decades later.

70. Ibid., 119.

71. Avis C. Vidal, *Rebuilding Communities: A National Study of Urban Community Development Corporations* (New York: Community Development Research Center, Graduate School of Management and Urban Policy, New School for Social Research, 1992), 1–105, 107–8.

72. Linder, "Urban Community Development Model," 115.

73. Ibid., 48; and Ralf Dahrendorf, *Class and Class Conflict in Industrial Society* (Palo Alto, CA: Stanford University Press, 1959).

74. Linder, "Urban Community Development Model," 158; and Suleiman Osman, "The Decade of the Neighborhood," in *Rightward Bound: Making America Conservative in the 1970s*, ed. Bruce J. Schulman and Julian E. Zelizer (Cambridge, MA: Harvard University Press, 2008), 114.

75. David Harvey, *A Brief History of Neoliberalism* (Cambridge: Oxford University Press, 2005), 45–47.

76. Raymond A. Mohl, "Shifting Patterns of Urban Policy since 1900," in *Urban Policy in Twentieth-Century America*, ed. Arnold R. Hirsch and Raymond A. Mohl (New Brunswick, NJ: Rutgers University Press, 1993), 20.

77. "Report on Issues Discussed at Planned Variations Coordinators' Meeting," February 14 and 15, 1972, Planned Variations Conferences Folder, container 7, Office of Assistant Secretary for Community Development, Floyd H. Hyde, entry 93, shelf 02–03, compartment 13, row 3, stack 130, RG 207, NARA.

78. *Cities Are People: How Dare We Not Save Them?* (Ralph Hall Productions, Hollywood, CA, 1972), narration and dialogue in Film Folder, container 5, Office of Assistant Secretary for Community Development, Floyd H. Hyde, entry 93, shelf 02–03, compartment 13, row 3, stack 130, RG 207, NARA.

79. Edward J. Berkowitz, *Something Happened: A Political and Cultural Overview of the Seventies* (New York: Columbia University Press, 2006), 224–26; Jefferson Cowie, *Stayin' Alive: The 1970s and the Last Days of the Working Class* (New York: New Press, 2010), 227–28, 300; and Bruce J. Schulman, *The*

Seventies: The Great Shift in American Culture, Society and Politics (New York: Da Capo, 2001), 193–217.

80. *Cities Are People: How Dare We Not Save Them?*

81. Ibid. See chapter 2 for conflict between the Newark City Council and various War on Poverty organizations.

82. Joint Statement, National League of Cities and United States Conference of Mayors, "America's Urban Challenge: A Required National Response," June 1972, US Conference of Mayors folder, container 2, Office of Assistant Secretary for Community Development, Floyd H. Hyde, entry 93, shelf 02–03, compartment 13, row 3, stack 130, RG 207, NARA.

83. "Planned Variations: A Step toward the New Federalism," September 7, 1971, Planned Variations folder, container 7, Office of Assistant Secretary for Community Development, Floyd H. Hyde, entry 93, shelf 02–03, compartment 13, row 3, stack 130, RG 207, NARA.

84. Neil Kraus and Todd Swanstrom, "Minority Mayors and the Hollow Prize Problem," *PS: Political Science and Politics* 34, no. 1 (March 2001): 103–4.

85. Kimberly Johnson, "Community Development Organizations, Participation and Accountability: The Harlem Urban Development Corporation and the Bedford-Stuyvesant Restoration Corporation," in "Race and Community Development," special issue, *Annals: Journal of the American Academy of Political and Social Science* 594 (July 2004): 111.

86. Memo from Ross Boyle to Executive Staff, "Community Development Goals," August 30, 1971, Community Development Objectives folder, container 2, Office of Assistant Secretary for Community Development, Floyd H. Hyde, entry 93, shelf 02–03, compartment 13, row 3, stack 130, RG 207, NARA.

87. Wendell Pritchett, *Robert Clifton Weaver and the American City: The Life and Times of an Urban Reformer* (Chicago: University of Chicago Press, 2008), 338.

88. Michael J. Rich, *Federal Policymaking and the Poor: National Goals, Local Choices, and Distributional Outcomes* (Princeton, NJ: Princeton University Press, 1993), 11.

89. Joseph Feinberg, "Remarks on Housing and Community Development Delivered before the State Planning Task Force," November 5, 1975, "Misc. Records of State Planning Taskforce" folder, box 01, Series Joseph Feinberg, Division of Housing and Development, Department of Community Affairs, Misc. Records, LOC B-06–09–01, New Jersey State Archives, Trenton.

90. Linder, "Urban Community Development Model," 185.

91. Foley, interview.

92. Vidal, Rebuilding Communities, 108.

93. Peirce and Guskind, *Against the Tide*, pt. 8.

94. Sara E. Stoutland, "Community Development Corporations: Mission, Strategy, and Accomplishments," in *Urban Problems and Community Development*, ed. Ronald F. Ferguson and William T. Dickens (Washington, DC: Brookings Institution Press, 1999), 197, 230.

95. Foley, interview; and Guskind, interview.

96. Barbara Stewart, "Bill Linder and His City of Hope," *New York Times*, February 18, 1996; and Alan Ehrenhalt, "New Life in Newark," *Governing Magazine*, July 2007.

97. Guskind, interview.

98. Ibid.; Jeffrey C. Mays, "Newark Nonprofit Alleges Backlash," *Star-Ledger*, August 18, 2002, 23.

99. Linder, "Urban Community Development Model," 99, 4, 209.

100. Komozi Woodard, *A Nation within a Nation: Amiri Baraka (LeRoi Jones) and Black Power Politics* (Chapel Hill: University of North Carolina Press, 1999), 222.

101. Harry Boyte, *Backyard Revolution: Understanding the New Citizen Movement* (Philadelphia, PA: Temple University Press, 1980), 8.

102. Osman, "Decade of the Neighborhood," 111, 115.

103. Tom Comerford, Queen of Angels, to Leo Mahon, San Miguelito, March 28, 1969, and Tom Comerford to Leo Mahon, April 22, 1969, CSNN2–5, Notre Dame Archive, University of Notre Dame, South Bend, IN.

104. Anne Enke, *Finding the Movement: Sexuality, Contested Space, and Feminist Activism* (Durham, NC: Duke University Press, 2007), 5.

105. Governor's Select Commission on Civil Disorder, *Report for Action*, 87, 167–78; and National Advisory Commission on Civil Disorders, *Report of the National Advisory Commission on Civil Disorders* (1968; repr., Dallas, TX: Schlager Group, 2008).

106. Joseph P. Shapiro, "'They Are Not Our Issues,'" *U.S. News and World Report*, May 18, 1992, 26; Nicholas Lemann, "The Myth of Community Development," *New York Times Magazine*, January 9, 1994, 27; and Alice O'Connor, "Swimming against the Tide: A Brief History of Federal Policy in Poor Communities," in Ferguson and Dickens, *Urban Problems and Community Development*, 113–14.

CONCLUSION

1. "Heningburg Airs Black Views Racial Hope Lies in Youth," *The Miller* 29, no. 3 (November 26, 1969).

2. Douglas Eldridge, "Heningburg Urges Businessmen to Have Faith in City's People," *Newark Evening News*, January 13, 1970.

3. Harry B. Webber, "1,000 Turn Out for Heningburg Testimonial," *New Jersey Afro-American*, October 19, 1974.

4. Barbara G. Salmore and Stephen A. Salmore, *New Jersey Politics and Government: Suburban Politics Comes of Age*, 2nd ed. (Lincoln: University of Nebraska Press, 1993), 56.

5. Neil Kraus and Todd Swanstrom, "Minority Mayors and the Hollow Prize Problem," *PS: Political Science and Politics* 34, no. 1 (March 2001): 102–4.

6. Philip W. Smith, "Gibson Urges Caution on Citizen Group Roles," *Star-Ledger*, February 1, 1978.

7. See Mike Sheridan, "Newark's Rebirth," *People Express*, March 1986, for an example of business boosterism regarding construction of the Gateway Complex of office towers. Not all Newark residents stood to benefit from this development, which featured tunnels and skyways that permitted workers to move between the city's main rail station and their offices without walking Newark's streets. Downtown small-business owners who had previously served the city's white-collar commuting workforce argued that they faced "possible extinction" because of this "self-containment." "Newark: An Attitudinal Study," 11–12, Image Campaign 1, box 5, Newark Collaboration Group, Newark Public Library (hereafter NPL).

8. "Next Century Newark," *New York Times*, September 20, 1986, 26.

9. Keyes Martin Public Relations, "A Communications Plan to Develop an Identity and Positive Image for the City of Newark," September 25, 1986, Image Campaign 1, box 5, Newark Collaboration Group, NPL.

10. Decision Research results of phone poll, Image Campaign 2, box 6, Newark Collaboration Group, 1984–88, NPL.

11. Memo to NCG executive committee members, Rapporteur Reports on Public Forums, October 9, 1986, City Life Public Forums folder, Strategic Plan, box 2, Newark Collaboration Group, 1984–88, NPL.

12. Ibid.

13. Richard Cammarieri, interview by the author, Newark, NJ, December 20, 2007.

14. Roland Anglin, interview by the author, New Brunswick, NJ, May 28, 2008.

15. Nicholas Lemann, "The Myth of Community Development," *New York Times Magazine*, January 9, 1994, 27; and Avis C. Vidal, *Rebuilding Communities: A National Study of Urban Community Development Corporations* (New York: Community Development Research Center, Graduate School of Management and Urban Policy, New School for Social Research, 1992), 5–10.

16. Kathe Newman, "Newark, Decline and Avoidance, Renaissance and Desire: From Disinvestment to Reinvestment," *Annals of the American Political Science Association* 594, no. 1 (2004): 38.

17. Cecelia Faulks, interview by the author, Newark, NJ, November 14, 2006; and Cammarieri, interview.

18. James Briggs Murray, Community Development Oral History Project, Schomburg Center for Research in Black Culture, New York, NY.

19. Vidal, *Rebuilding Communities*, 15. The Enterprise Foundation was another support network.

20. Howard Gillette, *Camden after the Fall: Decline and Renewal in a Postindustrial City* (Philadelphia; University of Pennsylvania Press, 2005), discusses the interplay between neighborhood and municipal efforts to reconstruct the similarly distressed city of Camden, NJ. He underscores the opportunities lost without strong regional planning and attention to policies that benefit suburban growth.

21. Jennifer Wolch, *The Shadow State: Government and the Voluntary Sector in Transition* (New York: Foundation Center, 1990).

22. Ibid., xvi.

23. Robert W. Lake and Kathe Newman, "Differential Citizenship in the Shadow State," *GeoJournal* 58, no. 2/3 (2002): 110, 113, 116, 117.

24. Allan Mallach, Diane Sterner, and Amanda Frazier, *Cities in Transition: New Jersey's Urban Paradox* (Trenton: Housing and Community Development Network of New Jersey, 2006).

Index

INDEX

Aronowitz, Stanley, 51, 256n27
Ashby, Harold, 23
Associated Community Teams (ACT), 47, 55
AT&T, 128

Babyland daycare center, 140 *fig.*, 141 *fig.*, 153, 223–24, 230
back-to-the-land movement, 299n23
backyard revolution, 173
Bakara, Amina, 206, 208–10
Bakara, Amiri, 79–80, 100–102, 107–8, 112, 125, 138 *fig.*, 158, 176, 179–80, 187, 214, 305n12, 308n66; antipathy for the New Left, 203, 307n42; and feminism, 205–6; as a fixer, 195–99, 202, 207–11, 305n9; his New Ark, 8, 198, 203, 233–34; poetry, 196, 309n7; shift of focus toward labor, 210, 307n47
Baker, Ella, 215
Baroni, Geno, 200–201
Barrett, David, 5–6, 174–77, 180, 201, 208–11, 287n122, 307n47, 308n63, 309n67
Barrett, Lydia Davis, 174–77, 180, 206–11, 309n67
Barringer High School protest (1963), 23–26, 28–30, 32, 34–37, 60, 94, 259n84, 278n148
Bass, Joe, 5, 82, 135 *fig.*
Bateman, Elma, 219
Bauman, Robert, 182, 262n9
Beatty, Pearl, 156
Bedford-Stuyvesant Restoration Corporation, 182–84
Benson, Jeffrey, 122
Bernstein, Lee, 53–56, 60–61, 63, 272n33
Berry, Walter, 187, 302n57
black activism, 37, 94, 101, 108, 124, 184, 280n2; women's, 144, 148, 157
Black and Puerto Rican Construction Coalition, 114–15, 117–21, 123, 168
Black and Puerto Rican Political Convention, 112, 149, 158
Black Arts Movement, 130, 196, 309n7
Black Arts Repertory Theater, 196, 198
black business, 124–26, 288n122
black capitalism, 6, 14, 124–27, 131, 181, 188
black churches, in opposition to the GNUC, 111
black civic organizations, 12

black clergy, 29
Black Clergy Caucus, 217
black cultural nationalism, 14–15, 125–26, 176–79, 197–99, 205, 233, 288n123
black cultural revolution, 15
black economic power, 46, 100, 107, 126, 272n33
black electoral victories, 4, 101, 112, 238
black empowerment, 106
black extremism, 106–7
black families, and gender roles, 205
black femininity, 270n8
black freedom movement, 2, 4–6, 13, 15, 18, 85, 126, 182, 184, 210, 228, 234, 243, 252n65; institutionalization of, 7; white backlash, 202
black homeownership, 75–76, 272n33
black institution building, 126
"Black Manifesto," 219
black migration from the South, 26, 146, 225. *See also* Great Migration
black militancy (militant black power), 84–85, 94, 106–7, 113, 204, 206
black nationalism, 100, 107–8, 113, 196, 204, 206, 208–11, 214, 236
Black Panthers, 6, 102, 109–10, 201, 279n2
Black People's Unity Movement, 85
black political capital, 29, 269n137
black political power, 1, 12, 24, 71, 85, 100, 107, 168; and urban crisis, 3
black power, 3, 15, 18, 37, 84, 99–102, 106–8, 165, 167, 170, 195, 200–201, 220, 230, 249n18, 253n69, 279n2, 282n31; activism, 12, 101, 112–13, 126, 144, 198; and corporate power, 124; grassroots politics, 130–31; and neighborhood politics, 179; scholarship on, 210
black power movement, 4, 177, 197; in Newark, NJ, 2, 6, 89
black rioters, 82–83
black social capital, 34
black women, 144, 148, 157, 183–84, 205–6, 213, 221, 235
Black Women's United Front, 176
blacks, in alliance with Puerto Ricans, 112, 146, 191, 194
black-white urban-suburban solidarity, 212, 216
Blair, James, 279n156
Blake, Eustace L., 29–30

320

Heiskell, Andrew, 103, 105
Heller, Walter H., 44
Heningburg, Gustav, 1–3, 7, 13–14, 19,
    95–96, 99, 137 *fig.*, 143, 209, 217, 237,
    241, 279n156; airport runway protest,
    1–3, 118–19, 285n83; background,
    100–102, 280n8; and the Black and
    Puerto Rican Construction Coalition,
    114–21, 123, 168; and black capitalism,
    124–26; as head of the Greater Newark
    Urban Coalition, 102–3, 107–11, 129–
    31; positioning himself as a middle-
    man, 111–13, 130; role in Newark rent
    strike, 158, 163, 165, 169, 296n131
Henry, Toby, 137 *fig.*, 148, 150, 156, 159–
    63, 292n48, 295n121
Herbert, Ward J., 149, 156, 159, 295n102
Hidalgo, Hilda, 60
Hill, Laura Warren, 124
Hirsch, Susan E., 251n32
Hodgson, J. D., 120–21
hollow prize metaphor, 5, 238
homeownership, 128, 178, 186, 218, 236,
    240
Home Owners' Loan Corporation, 75
HOPE VI program, 169
Hopkins, Ike, 192
Hough Area Development Corporation,
    183
House Education and Labor Committee,
    55, 60
housing, 7, 11–15, 18, 40, 72–74, 87, 93,
    178–80, 186–87, 219–20, 236, 299n25;
    affordable, 155, 178, 186, 189, 212,
    221, 229, 233, 244, 251n40, 299n25;
    cooperatively owned, 186–89, 192, 194,
    240; linked to political organizing,
    192; low-income, 181, 230–31, 233;
    mixed-income, 170, 298n18; as a right,
    143; subsidized, 14, 145, 162, 169, 190,
    229. *See also* public housing
housing activism. *See* tenant (housing)
    activism
Housing Act of 1937, 145, 150, 165
Housing Act of 1949, 72, 144–45, 151
Housing Act of 1954, 69–70, 77
Housing Act of 1968, 173, 302n66
Housing and Community Development
    Act of 1974, 169, 173, 229, 294n79
Housing and Urban Development Act of
    1970, 179–80

housing authorities, 149, 151–52, 157. *See
    also by specific city*
Housing, Education, and Welfare Depart-
    ment (NYC), 46
housing policy, federal, 128, 229
housing projects. *See* public housing
housing rehabilitation, 187, 191–92, 229,
    236
Hughes, Richard J., 39, 55, 80–83, 87–88,
    95, 107, 279n156
Humphrey, Hubert, 281n23
Hunt, D. Bradford, 144–46, 150, 299n25
Hutchings, Phil, 51
Hutchins, Frank, 308n63

Imperiale, Anthony, 201–3
inclusion, of marginalized groups, 32, 49,
    59, 88–89, 191
income eligibility, for area boards, 52
inequality, 6, 11, 16–17, 19, 24, 26, 43, 83,
    91, 129, 226, 238; economic, 32, 124;
    residential, 218, 310n28
inflation, 16, 115
integration, 45–46, 107, 131, 198, 234,
    305n22; of businesses and corpora-
    tions, 35–36, 125–27; of construction
    trades and their unions, 33, 39, 96, 114,
    117, 122, 202–3; of housing, 74; of pub-
    lic space, 40. *See also* school desegrega-
    tion (integration)
intentional communities, 295n121,
    299n23
interracial collaboration, 16, 26, 48, 51,
    113, 131, 158, 175, 179, 200–203, 216–
    19, 230
Interracial Council for Business Opportu-
    nity (ICBO), 124–25, 287n118, 287n119
ironworkers, and Ironworkers Local 11, 38–
    39, 115–16, 121–22, 286n107

James, Sharpe, 143, 232
Jarrett, Gene, 197
Javits, Jacob, 183
Jefferson, Kim, 63
Jim Crow, 5, 12, 38
jobs, 44–45, 64–65, 105, 178, 238
job training, 15, 44, 60, 64, 102, 117,
    142, 178, 182–83, 242, 263n14,
    268n94. *See also* trainees, on con-
    struction jobs
Johnson, Kimberly, 228

 HISTORICAL STUDIES OF URBAN AMERICA
Edited by Lilia Fernández, Timothy J. Gilfoyle, Becky M. Nicolaides, and
Amanda I. Seligman, James R. Grossman, editor emeritus.